always up to date

The law changes, but Nolo is always on top of it! We offer several ways to make sure you and your Nolo products are always up to date:

Nolo's Legal Updater

We'll send you an email whenever a new edition of your book is published! Sign up at **www.nolo.com/legalupdater**.

Updates @ Nolo.com

Check **www.nolo.com/update** to find recent changes in the law that affect the current edition of your book.

Nolo Customer Service

To make sure that this edition of the book is the most recent one, call us at **800-728-3555** and ask one of our friendly customer service representatives. Or find out at **www.nolo.com**.

please note

We believe accurate and current legal information should help you solve many of your own legal problems on a cost-efficient basis. But this text is not a substitute for personalized advice from a knowledgeable lawyer. If you want the help of a trained professional, consult an attorney licensed to practice in your state.

NOLO

2nd edition

Negotiate the Best Lease For Your Business

by Attorneys Janet Portman and Fred S. Steingold

Second Edition	JULY 2005
Editor	MARCIA STEWART
Illustrations	LINDA ALLISON
Cover Design	TONI IHARA
Book Design	TERRI HEARSH
Production	SARAH HINMAN
Proofreading	EMILY K. WOLMAN
Index	THÉRÈSE SHERE
Printing	CONSOLIDATED PRINTERS, INC.

Steingold, Fred.
   Negotiate the best lease for your business / by Fred S. Steingold and Janet Portman. --
2nd ed.
     p. cm.
   Rev. ed. of: Leasing space for your small business/ by Janet Portman and Fred S.
Steingold. 1st ed. 2001.
   Includes index.
   ISBN 1-4133-0216-5
   1. Commercial Leases. 2. Office leases. 3. Small Business--Management. I. Portman,
Janet II. Portman, Janet. Leasing space for your small business. III. Title.

HD1393.25P67 2005
658.15'242--dc22

200540536

For information on bulk purchases or corporate premium sales, please contact the Special Sales
Department. For academic sales or textbook adoptions, ask for Academic Sales. Call 800-955-4775 or
write to Nolo, 950 Parker Street, Berkeley, CA 94710.

Acknowledgments

We couldn't have written this book without the assistance and support of many people.

We'd like to thank Jake Warner, Nolo's founder and executive publisher, for his conviction that we could write this book—and patience while we did it. To the extent that readers find the text clear and to the point, credit goes to our meticulous editor, Marcia Stewart, who can spot a mushy sentence a mile away and fix it in a trice. Others at Nolo who helped include:

Stan Jacobsen, who provided valuable research assistance

Tamara Traeder, who offered useful editorial advice

Terri Hearsh, who designed the book and threw in a little editing, gratis, and

Mike Mansel, of Argo Insurance Group in Pleasanton, California, who is technically not a Noloid but whose generous help on insurance issues over the years makes him part of the family.

Thanks go also to the Practicing Law Institute, whose programs and materials on commercial leasing were invaluable.

Table of Contents

Introduction

Part I: Finding and Evaluating Space and Developing a Negotiation Strategy

1 What Kind of Space Do You Need?

6 Your Negotiation Strategy

Part II: Common Lease Terms

7 Lease Basics

8 The Length of Your Lease

9 Rent

17 Foreclosures, Condemnations, Guarantors, and Other Clauses

Index

Introduction: Using This Book to Negotiate Your Commercial Lease

Your business has been a success and you are ready to move into a better place. You have decided to streamline your operations and rent a more efficient space. Your home business is bursting out of the garage and definitely needs its own location. *Negotiate the Best Lease for Your Business* is a useful guide that can help both the person considering a commercial lease for the first time, as well as the person who has been down this path before and would like to negotiate a more favorable lease for his or her business. It's helpful for all types of businesses—from retail stores in strip malls to one-person consulting firms downtown to small manufacturing firms.

A. How Leases Are Made and What They Look Like

The lease that you and your landlord sign defines your legal relationship. It's a contract in which:

- you agree to pay rent and abide by other conditions (such as using the space for a consulting business only or not displaying outside signs unless the landlord first approves them), and
- your landlord agrees to let your business occupy the space for a set amount of time, perhaps with a number of listed amenities such as on-site parking and weekly janitorial service.

Along with your insurance policy and your loan documents, your lease will be one of the most important legal documents in your filing cabinet.

Typically, you'll be working with a lease form that's been written by the landlord or the landlord's lawyer—and you can bet that neither one of them will be looking out for your best legal or business interests. You need this book to even the playing field, so that the landlord's proposed lease is just the starting point from which you'll negotiate changes.

1. There Are No "Standard" Leases

Contrary to what a landlord may have you believe, there is no such thing as a "standard" lease. (That's why this book does not include a lease agreement.) Unlike other aspects of business, there are surprisingly few legal constraints on what tenants and landlords agree to do. Even if the landlord starts with a form that's widely used in your community, printed and distributed by a big real estate management firm, or accepted by other tenants who lease from this landlord, it can always be modified. The only constraints on your landlord's ability to negotiate come from preexisting promises to other tenants in the building, and obligations to lenders or insurers.

Commercial leases can and should reflect the give-and-take between the landlord and tenant—one size simply doesn't fit all. No matter how official-looking the document that comes out of the landlord's or broker's briefcase, keep in mind that it's negotiable.

Just how negotiable depends on decidedly nonlegal issues such as how tight the market is for your desired space, how badly the landlord wants to rent the space to you, and how badly you want it. Within the range of negotiability, however, your knowledge of what you want out of your lease space, and your understanding of the meaning and interrelatedness of lease clauses will determine the success of the lease negotiation.

2. How Leases Are Organized

Leases are usually organized by numbered paragraphs or clauses. Often, the Arabic or Roman number is followed by a title (such as "II. Term"), but the title may not alert you to what the clause covers (consider "III: Subordination"). To compound matters, lawyers often dress the body of these clauses in dense legal verbiage or burden them with mile-long sentences. The chart below, "Common Major Lease Clauses," may help you match a clause title to its subject matter, and it steers you to the appropriate place in this book where we discuss the clause, explain how it will affect your business, and suggest negotiating strategies for modifying it.

B. How This Book Can Help You Negotiate a Favorable Lease

This book is divided into two major sections. Part I helps you think through the type of space most appropriate for your business. All businesses have some common concerns regarding rental space, such as cost, responsibility for improvements, air quality, and safety, but different types of business have differing priorities—the retail store manager is concerned about parking, foot traffic, and personality of the neighborhood; the startup business owner may be thinking primarily about cost and the manufacturing business operator will be thinking about loading docks and access to highways. Part I will help you develop not only your list of "must have" characteristics for your particular commercial space, but also a negotiating strategy to achieve them at the best terms possible. While this book may not be appropriate for someone developing a highly complex chemical facility, it will help most business owners and managers think about the general needs of their businesses, and the specific space characteristics that will serve those needs.

If you already know exactly want you want in your space and in your lease, go directly to Part II, Common Lease Terms (Chapters 7 through 17). "Common Major Lease Clauses," shown at the end of this introduction, will give you a quick roadmap to the dozens of specific clauses covered in the second part of the book. Chapters 7 through 17 address specific lease provisions, their legal meaning, how they will affect your business, and how to change a particular clause to get what you want out of your lease. The types of lease terms covered in these chapters include rent, security deposits, improvements and alterations, maintenance, parking, renewal options, and other provisions common to most leases, such as restrictions on use of the premises and the landlord's right to terminate the lease.

Reading this book will help you understand the dense, incomprehensible language of most commercial leases, what dangerous terms you should avoid, what tenant-friendly terms to press for, and what clauses you can live with. You'll find all the information and strategies you need to negotiate with an experienced landlord. This practical guide also suggests ways that you can work cost-effectively with an experienced real estate lawyer, broker, and other professionals as you negotiate your lease.

Guide to Icons Used in This Book

 Reference or further reading: This icon lets you know where you can read more about the particular issue or topic discussed in the text.

This icon means that you may be able to skip some material that doesn't apply to your situation.

 This icon alerts you to a practical tip or good idea.

This is a caution to slow down and consider potential problems you may encounter.

Common Major Lease Clauses

Clause name	What it's about	Where it's discussed
Parties or Lessor and Lessee or Landlord and Tenant	The names of the landlord and tenant	Ch. 7, Sec. B
Premises	A description of the space you're renting	Ch. 7
Rent	Explains how the rent is calculated	Chs. 4 & 9
Term	When the lease begins and how long it will run	Ch. 8
Deposit	The security deposit demanded by the landlord	Ch. 10
Hold Over	What happens if you don't move out as planned at the end of your lease	Ch. 8, Sec. D
Use	Restrictions and requirements on how you use your rented space	Ch. 7, Sec. D
Utilities	Explains how utilities are metered and how costs are apportioned	Ch. 12, Sec. B
Taxes	Describes which taxes you will have to pay for, and how much	Ch. 9, Sec. B
Insurance & Indemnity	Covers which insurance policies you must take out or pay for	Ch. 9, Sec. C; Ch. 15
Security	Covers the building security and who pays for it	Ch. 13, Sec. E
Parking	Describes available parking and how it's paid for	Ch. 13, Sec. A
Maintenance	Covers the common area maintenance (CAM) costs you have to pay for	Ch. 12
Alterations & Repairs	Explains which alterations you may make and whether you need permission; delegates repair duties	Ch. 11

Common Major Lease Clauses (continued)		
Clause name	**What it's about**	**Where it's discussed**
Assignment & Subletting	Describes the conditions under which you can turn space over to another tenant	Ch. 14, Sec. F
Options	Covers your rights to extend, expand, or contract the amount of space you rent or the lease term. May also cover your right to buy the property	Ch. 14, Secs. B–E
Defaults & Remedies	Explains what happens if you or the landlord fails to live up to the lease	Ch. 16
Destruction	Covers what will happen if all or part of the building is destroyed	Ch. 14, Sec. G
Condemnation	Describes what happens to your lease if the building is condemned by a government entity	Ch. 17, Sec. C
Subordination, Nondisturbance, & Attornment	Financing clauses covering what happens if your landlord's lender forecloses on a loan that's secured by the building	Ch. 17, Sec. A
Estoppel	Explains your duty to provide a signed statement that you and the landlord are complying with the lease terms	Ch. 17, Sec. B
Attorney Fees	Your agreement as to who pays the winner's fees and costs if a disagreement ends in litigation	Ch. 16, Sec. E
Guaranty	Your promise that you will provide someone who will guarantee your financial duties under the lease. The guarantor must also sign the lease	Ch. 17, Sec.G
Dispute Resolution	The mechanism for settling disputes, short of resorting to a lawsuit	Ch. 16, Sec. D

Part I:

Finding and Evaluating Space and Developing a Negotiation Strategy

Chapter 1

What Kind of Space Do You Need?

Read This Chapter If ...

This chapter is for those of you who are considering a move, evaluating a likely rental, or thinking about subletting. It's especially useful in the following situations:

- You're a newcomer to the game of commercial leasing, and need basic information such as how landlords measure space.
- You'd like some tips on how to evaluate space, particularly whether it fits your needs.
- You're interested in expansion or purchase rights in your lease.
- You'd like guidance on how to systematically arrive at your rental priorities, which can form the basis for your lease negotiation strategy.

You can skip this chapter if you're an old hand at commercial leasing and understand space measurement, or you've already picked out your rental and need information on negotiating the lease.

Your business needs should shape your search for commercial space. Rent will be an obvious consideration, as will the building's location, and the size of the space. But for most small businesses, finding the right space involves considering more than price, location, and size. Parking, the ease of making improve-

ments, the types of nearby complementary and competing businesses, and numerous other factors, such as the building's image and potential for expansion, may affect your choice of a rental space.

Depending on your requirements, the number of rentals that will satisfy them will, naturally, shrink.

EXAMPLE: John's company, Hi Fives, manufactures sports equipment. He'll need space with a loading dock and floors strong enough to support his equipment. The image of the neighborhood isn't much of a factor, nor is the makeup of nearby businesses.

EXAMPLE: Mary's business, a children's clothing store, will do best if it's near other retail establishments, preferably those that parents are likely to frequent. She's on the lookout for welcoming, ground-level space, with lots of windows and light.

Forces beyond your control may further limit your choices. The availability of commercial space will depend in large part on current market conditions. Sometimes the vacancy rate is high, meaning you'll have a good selection of rental spaces and relatively low rents. Other times the vacancy rate is low, meaning you'll have fewer choices and higher rents. But regardless of your requirements or market conditions, you can almost always locate suitable space if you're willing to invest some time and effort into the process.

Whether you're a small start-up or a long-term established business—a fledgling Internet enterprise or a bookstore passed down from your grandfather—you should begin each search by carefully thinking through your needs. This chapter shows you how to analyze what's most important in a rental—before you hit the pavement or engage a broker to help you find the right spot. A clear understanding of what you do (and don't) want for your business will save precious time and money, commodities that you undoubtedly want to plow into the business itself.

A. Do You Need to Move Now?

Before you plunge headlong into the search for suitable commercial space, think carefully about whether you really need to find space now. It may make more sense to run your business from your home. Or, if you're already renting space but looking to move, you might consider ways to improve your current lease situation, and avoid the expense and inconvenience of relocating.

1. Working From Home

If you're just starting out in a business that doesn't require significant space or ready access to the public, maybe you can keep expenses low by working out of your house or apartment. You may have space in your basement or garage or spare bedroom that you can use for your business. Or, it may be possible to devote a corner of the dining or living room to business purposes, while using the rest of the room as part of your residence. Attractive office furniture is widely available that blends nicely with regular household furnishings.

Home-based businesses are quite feasible these days because technology lets you keep in touch with the world through faxes and email. And delivery companies such as UPS and Federal Express compete with the U.S. Postal Service for moving packages and hard copies of documents speedily and reliably to virtually every imaginable location. Credit cards can facilitate the purchase or sale of goods and services from or to a home-based business.

But while your house or apartment may work just fine if you have a small office-type business or are working as a consultant, it normally won't meet your space needs if you're in a retail or wholesale business that requires customers or clients to come to you. Similarly, service businesses—such as restaurants and repair services—require commercial space.

If a home business seems right for you, make sure there are no legal restrictions to your working at home. In particular, here's what to check:

- **Local zoning ordinances.** These may restrict the type and amount of traffic, bar outside signs, prohibit or limit the number of employees, and set a limit on the percentage of the floor space that can be devoted to the business. Contact the office of your city attorney, city manager, or mayor for information on zoning ordinances that may affect your business.

- **Deed restrictions in condominiums and planned unit developments.** These often prohibit commercial activities, including home businesses. Review your covenants, conditions, and restrictions (CC & Rs) for details.

- **Apartment leases or rental agreements.** These sometimes specify that the premises may be used for residential purposes only, or restrict use to specified businesses, such as family daycare.

Even if there are no restrictions, a home business may not work for you personally.

You might not want customers or business associates intruding into your family's space, and you may be concerned that you'll have a hard time putting business aside if it's as close as the next room. Many home business entrepreneurs have a hard time resisting the attractions (and distractions) of the kitchen, television, and household chores. And if you have small children, working at home may be especially difficult.

Businesses that are run from home may also need to comply with federal and state laws regarding access for disabled persons. (See Chapter 12, Section D, for more on this issue.)

If you run a home business, you may need special insurance. Your homeowner's policy may not apply if you use the premises—your home—for commercial purposes. This means that even if you merely have a computer and a file cabinet that you use to run your home-based business, your policy may not cover business property that is destroyed in a fire or other disaster at your home. Even worse, once you begin using the home as a place of business, your homeowner's insurance may not protect you if someone, even a nonbusiness visitor, is injured at the home. Be sure to raise these concerns with your insurance agent or broker, who may suggest that you purchase a commercial policy or a special business rider to your homeowner's policy. (Chapter 9, Section C, explains business insurance issues for non–home-business outfits in detail.)

Resources on Home Businesses

This book focuses primarily on leasing commercial space. Of course, doing business at home is still a viable option for many small businesses. Fortunately, there's a lot of valuable guidance out there if you decide that home is where the business is—and will be for the foreseeable future.

The Legal Guide for Starting & Running a Small Business, by Fred Steingold (Nolo), provides helpful information about the legal issues involved in operating a home-based business, including how to comply with zoning ordinances and private land use restrictions, and getting the right kind of insurance.

Tax Deductions for Home Businesses, by Stephen Fishman (Nolo), gives home business owners the information they need to take advantage of the many tax deductions available especially for them.

The "business & human resources" section of Nolo's website at www.nolo.com has many articles useful to home business owners, covering starting your business, business structure, and related topics.

A good starting point on the Web is www.bizoffice.com, which provides numerous links to other sites for home-based businesses.

2. Staying in Your Current Rental

Perhaps your business already occupies commercial space but you feel, for one reason or another, that it's time to move. Maybe you've outgrown your current digs and need more spacious quarters; or you've had your fill of your nickel-and-diming landlord. But first, look closely at whether it is at all possible to stay put. Moving can be costly and inconvenient. For one thing, you'll need to pack up your furniture and equipment—and maybe your stock of goods, too, if you have a retail or wholesale business. Then there's the cost of hiring a moving company or at least renting a truck to make the move. Depending on your business, you'll need to change your stationery, brochures, and advertising; and you may have to buy new furniture and equipment. What's more, you may lose valuable employees who cannot (or don't want to) make the transition to a new area. Your day-to-day operations will be interrupted and you may lose customers or clients who can't find your new location or feel it's inconvenient.

While moving doesn't present insurmountable obstacles, maybe you can avoid a move entirely by working with your landlord to solve problems with your current rental. Landlords will often do what it takes to keep a tenant from leaving, because it can be expensive to carry empty space and then revamp it for another occupant.

So make a list of the problems that make you want to move and see if they can be overcome. Here are a few examples:

- **Too pricey.** If the space is too expensive or you need less room because of downsizing your business, the landlord may be willing to let you bring in a sublet or reconfigure the space.
- **The wrong interior look.** Sometimes, space can be vastly improved by simple improvements such as adding or removing interior walls or installing better lighting.
- **Insufficient space.** If you don't have enough space, maybe the landlord will let you take over an adjoining space (if it's empty) or allow you to move to a larger space within the building—alternatives that are likely to be cheaper and less disruptive than moving to a completely new location.
- **Building security or services.** If you're concerned about intruders or shabbiness, ask the landlord to provide better security and maintenance.

At least explore these possibilities. You have nothing to lose by asking your landlord.

Before you charge off to your landlord's office, however, take a minute to consider whether your list of gripes represents truly important issues for your business. One way to measure their importance is to compare your dissatisfactions with what you would look for in a new rental. In Section B, below, we suggest ways to organize and rank your rental priorities. If you go through that exercise and find that the items on the top of the list are precisely those that are missing from your current location, you know it's time to act.

3. Buying Instead of Renting

You may want to take a moment to consider whether now is the time to buy instead of rent. Don't immediately assume that you can't afford it—your monthly rent won't necessarily be that much less than a mortgage payment. Here are some advantages of owning commercial property:

- Instead of pouring money down the drain, you're making an investment (if you can afford a down payment, your monthly payments may be similar to a rent payment).
- Ownership increases your ability to get a loan. The Small Business Administration (SBA) likes making loans secured by real estate.
- If the property appreciates, that will give you additional capital for the business in the future (through refinancing).
- As an owner, you have more control over the space and improvements.
- If you shut down, you can lease or sell the property.

Before you completely dismiss the idea, talk with your financial advisors to see if it makes sense to consider owning commercial space, and do a little research on the types and costs of available properties.

Check Your Current Lease Before You Leap

If you're currently renting space and plan to move elsewhere, check your lease first. Here's what to look for:

- **The exact termination date.** Try to begin your search for new space well enough in advance so that you won't feel rushed. If the termination date is too far off, however, you may be forced to begin your new lease before the old one is over. It's a delicate balance—you don't want to be responsible for a period of double rents, nor do you want a gap between lease periods. If you're a very desirable tenant in a tenant's market, you might be able to get a new landlord to cover your rent at your former location.

- **The possibility of a buyout.** If you need to move before the current lease expires, look to see if you can leave early by paying a "buyout amount." This is money that the landlord accepts in exchange for letting you out of your lease early.

- **Staying longer.** If your new space isn't ready on time—a common problem—

it would be smart to find out if you can continue to occupy your current space after the stated termination date. You might be able to negotiate a short-term extension of your current lease. If the landlord won't give you an extension, check to see whether your lease imposes onerous "hold-over" provisions. Landlords typically charge big rents to tenants who don't leave on time. Holdover provisions are explained further in Chapter 8, Section D.

- **Options and sublets.** An option clause in your current lease could significantly affect your decision and ability to move. Your lease may give you the option to renew, and perhaps pick up additional space as well. If you nevertheless want to move, it may be wise to investigate whether you can exercise the option—but instead of using it yourself, sublet the space at a profit and move your operation to a new location. See Chapter 14 for detailed explanations of options and subletting.

B. Setting Your Priorities

If you're convinced that it really is time to move, you'll need to think carefully about what you need, would like, and won't abide. To help you, we've developed a list of features that concern most businesses. Don't be constrained by our list—if other points are important, by all means add them. Your goal is to end up with a concise statement—expressed in words (downtown area) or numbers (maximum $3,000 rent) of what you must have, would like, and absolutely cannot accept.

As you go through the issues discussed below, prepare a Rental Priorities Worksheet like the one shown at the end of this chapter. You may need to refer to other chapters as you go—for example, if you need the ability to expand, check out Chapter 14, Section C, which explains how tenants secure expansion rights in the lease. Write your conclusions under one of the following headings:

- Essentials—essential issues or features you're looking for in a rental space, such as a maximum rent, a specific location, or minimum square footage.
- Compromise—features that you'd like but that aren't crucial to your decision of whether to rent a particular space, such as proximity to specific types of businesses or neighborhoods.
- Unacceptable—features that you absolutely want to avoid, such as lack of public transportation or the inability to expand into contiguous space. We also call these your "no-ways."

Our sample Rental Priorities Worksheet has been filled out to reflect how a particular business (in this case, a consignment shop) ranked its requirements for new commercial space.

Once you have a "master" worksheet, make copies and take one with you every time you visit a potential space. At that point you'll fill in the rent, address, and other information on a particular property, and note how it measures up to your priorities. Chapter 3, Section A, explains how to use your Rental Priorities Worksheet when finding and visiting potential rental space.

Bring your partners and key employees into the loop. Review your rental priorities together and make sure you agree on the basics. Consult with your staff, too—for example, if your business has specific computer needs, you'll want input from technical employees as to what you must look for, access-wise, in a new location. You don't want to invest enormous energy in seeking that perfect business site, only to learn that one of your business partners or key employees requires windows that open or space that's near public transportation. Similarly, if you feel strongly that your business should offer on-site parking to customers, you'll want to make sure that important players in the business share this desire and are willing to pay for it.

The better you know your business, the easier it will be to describe your ideal rental. Of course, it will be easier to list the "must haves" and the "not necessaries" if your business is up and running, smoothly and profitably, than if you are just starting out and haven't tested the market or the viability of your product or approach. That said, however, even fledgling enterprises will benefit from preparing a Rental Priorities Worksheet, which will force you, at the very least, to think ahead about the surroundings and amenities that will help your business prosper.

As you prepare your list of rental features, ranking each according to its importance to your business, remember that your hard work will translate directly into a more efficient rental search. Assuming your self-assessment is realistic (not too many of you should plan to move into Trump Towers) and focuses on major issues (like size and rent), you'll be able to quickly and accurately zero in on those rentals that are real possibilities, saving time and energy for the job that needs you most—running your business.

C. Rent, Deposits, and Improvements

The first issues to consider are the most obvious and, for many of you, the most important. Figure out the maximum rent your business can afford to pay per month. And if the landlord asks you to put down a security deposit before you move in, think about whether your reserves can handle a particularly big hit in the first month. Finally, consider how much money you can afford to spend to alter the space to fit your needs and tastes.

1. Rent

When you lease commercial space, the monthly rent bill is likely to be more complicated than the monthly rent for an apartment or house. That's because many landlords charge you not only for square footage, but also for other regular expenses, such as real estate taxes, utilities, and insurance. If you rent in a multitenant building, you're likely to be asked to pay your share of common area maintenance, too. If you rent the entire building, you may be asked to foot the entire bill for these costs. How to determine the exact cost of a rental space is explained in detail in Chapter 4. For now, understand that your rent figure may need to be big enough to cover multiple, recurring expenses.

Put a realistic cap on the amount you're prepared to pay. A fancy location may feed your ego—but paying for it can drive you out of business. The simple truth is that most small businesses can't afford Fifth Avenue. If you are certain that location will bring fame and fortune, you can always move up (see Chapter 14 for advice on crafting a lease that gives you maximum mobility). It is much harder, let alone disheartening, to start off in deluxe digs and have to retreat to humble quarters.

2. Deposits

Many commercial landlords require tenants to pay one or two months' rent up front as a security deposit, which the landlord will dip into if the tenant fails to pay the rent or other sums required by the lease (such as insurance or maintenance costs). Bear in mind that the amount of the deposit for commercial rentals is not regulated by law, but is instead a matter of negotiation. Landlords tend to demand high deposits from new or otherwise unproven businesses—which are often the least able to produce, and tie up, a large chunk of cash.

If you expect that you'll be asked for a high deposit, include in your worksheet the maximum you can pay up front. Security deposits (including alternatives to cash deposits, such as a letter of credit, and ways to get the deposit returned during the tenancy) are explained in depth in Chapter 10.

3. Other Improvements and Expenses

Security deposits aren't the only up-front costs that tenants may face during the first few months of operation in a new location. Unless you are fortunate enough to find space that is configured and finished just as you would like it, you'll want to modify the space to fit your needs and tastes. These modifications are known as your "improvements."

There are several ways that landlords and tenants can allocate the cost of improvements (Chapter 11 describes each in detail). You might find a landlord willing to foot the entire bill (which is the next best thing to finding space that's perfect already). But for now, don't count on it. Instead, think about the demands of your business and how they translate into space requirements. Will a generic office space do quite nicely? If so, you don't have to plan on spending much to fix it up. Or do you have a business with special needs, such as a veterinarian's office that needs special lights, plumbing fixtures, alternate power sources, and ventilation? If this describes your situation, you'll need to put some resources into readying the space, even if you find a rental that is appropriate in every other respect. For purposes of your Rental Priorities Worksheet, figure out what it would cost to make usable but bare-bones space ready for your business and add that dollar amount to your list.

D. Location

The physical location of your business is likely to be important to you, your employees, your customers or clients, or your suppliers. The more people and groups you need to please, the smaller the number of possible rentals that will fit the bill. This section explores some of the considerations regarding location.

1. Neighborhood and Neighbors

Being in the right part of town and even on the right street can be an important factor in the success of a small business. If you have an upscale restaurant, for example, you may want to lease space in the entertainment district or be part of restaurant row. Or you may prefer to locate in an area of new suburban housing where you'll be the only eatery for miles around. Your priorities worksheet should indicate the degree of importance you assign to location—and spell out your ideal location in as much detail as possible. If your business places a low priority on location, consider yourself lucky, for you have fewer limitations on the number of rental spaces that will be acceptable to you.

EXAMPLE: Jake runs a roommate-finding business—people looking for shared rentals register with Jake's service and wait to be connected with an appropriate match. Jake would like to open a branch in a certain university town, as close to the campus as possible. Jake won't bother looking at rentals in the town's financial or upscale shopping districts, nor will he be interested in the suburban shopping malls. Because the number of potential rentals is rather small, Jake's search may take a while, but he won't waste time looking at geographically inappropriate places.

It can be just as important to be near (or far away from) certain neighbors as to be in a particular neighborhood. If peace and quiet are important, you won't want to be in a building with an aerobics studio upstairs. On the other hand, there may be certain neighbors whom you'd like to have around. A physician, for example, would like to offer his patients the convenience of a medical lab next door; and a car repair shop will benefit from the nearby presence of a welder. Again, the more you can focus on important features of your rental, the more you will narrow your search and the more efficient you'll become.

Downtown or the 'Burbs?

It used to be that there was only one place to locate your business—in the downtown, business section of town. But with the development of suburbs came the opportunities for setting up shop in a mall in basically residential areas. There are significant differences between downtown and suburbia. Downtown, the rental space is likely to be vertical (you may need more than one floor), whereas space in a mall (which is often one-story) is usually horizontal. In many cities, rents tend to be higher downtown, in part because land may be more expensive there. Also, labor and material costs may be higher downtown, and security, parking, trash removal, and lighting can be more expensive. If you plan to be open on weekends, you'll want to avoid a downtown area that's deserted between Friday evening and Monday morning.

2. Commuting Time

We'll assume that there aren't too many folks who would voluntarily choose a long commute. But a moderate or long commute may be more onerous for some than others. If spending an hour each morning and night getting to and from work is unacceptable, give a high priority on your worksheet to a short commute. On the other hand, you may regard a moderate commute, especially by train or bus, as a good time to read the paper or attend to correspondence. You might also be willing to put up with a commute in exchange for doing business in a reasonably priced location or one more convenient for your customers or clients. In either case, you'd probably assign a lower priority to having a reasonable commute to and from your business.

Besides considering your personal preferences, don't forget how location will affect your employees' commutes. Play it safe and assume that most, if not all, will want shorter rather than longer travel times. If you depend on a large number of modestly compensated workers, there should be moderately priced housing within a reasonable commuting distance. If employees have to commit a large portion of their time and earnings traveling long distances to affordable housing, you'll likely lose them to more convenient job opportunities. And consider the other end of the spectrum, too—well-paid employees must be within reasonable striking distance of the neighborhoods where they'll want to live.

3. Access to Public Transportation

The value of being close to public transportation is closely related to the issue of commute time. If there are ample and attractive trains, buses, and subways, the acceptable commuting radius for employees will expand.

If you're a retail establishment, however, the issue of public transportation may assume an added importance. A business that depends on foot traffic will benefit from close proximity to a bustling transit point or center. And if your business is convenient to a major bus or transit line, customers are more likely to choose it over a comparable establishment that's less conveniently located.

4. Expressways, Freeways, and Throughways

If employees and customers are likely to come from out of town or from a wide geographic area, you may place a high priority on being located near an expressway. Telling people to "Get off at Exit 10 and go two blocks north—we're on the corner" can make access really convenient.

E. Length of the Lease and When It Begins

It may be important for you to secure a space that will be yours for a long time to come—or you might want the flexibility of a shorter lease. Do you need to find a place right away? Or do you have the luxury of shopping around until you see the perfect spot? You need to assign a value—a priority—to the length of the lease and when it's available. This section provided an overview of key issues regarding the term of a lease. For a more extensive discussion, see Chapter 8.

1. Length of the Lease

The "term" of your lease means its chronological life. Your lease could be as short as month to month, or run for one, five, ten or even 15 years. As long as you satisfy the important conditions of the lease (such as paying rent and other costs), you have the right to remain in the space until the lease expires. And unless the other terms of the lease provide otherwise, they, too, are guaranteed for the life of the lease. For example, your landlord cannot ignore the lease's promises to provide on-site parking and janitorial services. You'll need to decide whether to pursue a short-term or long-term lease.

a.   Short-Term Leases

Occasionally, a small business that's just starting out will do better with a lease permitting it to occupy the space for a limited period—either from month to month or for a short fixed term. This might seem attractive if you just want to test the waters, have great uncertainty about the prospects for

your business, or wouldn't mind leaving on short notice.

If you want the most flexibility, look for space that's offered on a month-to-month basis (month-to-month leases are often also called "rental agreements"). A month-to-month rental automatically renews each month unless you or your landlord gives the other the proper amount of written notice to terminate the agreement. Under a month-to-month agreement, the landlord can also raise the rent or change other terms with proper written notice. You can negotiate how much notice is required. If you don't address the issue in your rental agreement, the law in your state will dictate the amount of notice required. In most states, this is 30 days.

Another way to set up a short-term tenancy is to sign a lease for a short but fixed period of time—say, 90 days or six months. This type of lease terminates at the end of the time period you've established. Unlike a month-to-month tenancy, it's not automatically renewed. You and the landlord can, however, negotiate lease language specifying what happens at the end of the fixed period covered by the lease. You could provide, for example, that if you stay in the space beyond the stated period, your tenancy becomes a month-to-month tenancy.

A fixed-term lease—even for a short term—gives you the assurance that the landlord can't boot you out on short notice. It also means, of course, that you're obligated to pay rent throughout the lease term, unless you can negotiate an escape clause that gives you the right to end the lease earlier. (Termination clauses are explained in Chapter 14, Section G.)

The clauses in a month-to-month or short, fixed-term lease—other than those dealing with the length of the tenancy—are much the same as those in any other written lease. So even though you and the landlord can call it quits after a short time, be sure to consult the rest of this book to make sure you understand the implications of your commitment, however brief it may be.

b. Long-Term Leases

Many small businesses and landlords prefer the protection of a lease that lasts a year or more. There are many solid business reasons why both sides look for long-term commitment, such as:

- **Minimizing transaction costs.** As you're about to discover, it takes a lot of time (and money) to find and secure good rental space. Your landlord, too, will spend money on brokers and lawyers. Although businesspeople can amortize these expenses—spread the expense over several years and take tax write-offs for each year—it's still better to minimize the number of times you go through these leasing courtships.
- **Minimizing improvement costs.** Chances are that you'll have to alter the space you'll ultimately lease to fit your business needs. (Improvements are ex-

plained in Chapter 11.) You and the landlord will negotiate who pays for these expenses. Whoever pays won't want to do it again soon.

- **Establishing your business.** For retail tenants who depend on steady, return customers, it's important to stay put. If you're one of these, a long-term lease will allow you to build up a faithful customer base. Even non-retail tenants may lose business if suppliers or partners aren't willing or able to follow you to new quarters.
- **Simplifying the leasing situation.** There's a lot to be said for long-term familiarity. Once you and the landlord get used to each other and establish workable relations, you'll be able to direct attention and energy to your business. If you frequently start over with a new landlord, you'll have to go through the break-in period all over again.
- **Locking in a good deal.** If the space is desirable, you may want to make sure that you'll have it for some years to come. Ideally, you'll want to set a rent that will stay steady as rates around you rise with the market. Be forewarned that landlords have a way of making sure that they, too, reap the benefits of increased value—it's called "rent escalation," explained in Chapter 9, and it allows them to raise the rent as the value of the property goes up. But even if the lease provides for increased rents as the years pass

by, you may still come out ahead compared to starting anew in a different location.

Of course, there are drawbacks to signing a multiyear lease. The most obvious is that you will, indeed, be legally obligated to lease this space for a considerable length of time. But keep in mind that even a long-term lease can be quite flexible if it lets both you and the landlord make adjustments depending on the success of your business or the overhead costs of the landlord. Likewise, you can turn a short lease into a long one by the use of an option to renew. In Chapter 14, we'll guide you through the lease clauses that provide for the growth or contraction of your lease term.

You'll get more in the way of improvements with a long-term lease. If you go for a short-term lease, the landlord probably won't do much to fix up the space—maybe just clean the carpet and slap on a coat of fresh paint. Any other improvements will probably have to be done at your expense. With a longer lease, the landlord is much more likely to pay for substantial improvements, or at least pick up a good chunk of the tab.

2. Move-In Date

You may need to set up shop as soon as possible. If your start-up is ready to roll or your current lease is up, an immediate move-in date will be high priority, although

you may have to contend with delays caused by improvement work. But before you turn down a great place because it isn't instantly available, you might see if there are any alternatives to fill the gap. For example, you might be able to work out of your home or sublet temporary quarters for a few months; or perhaps you can negotiate with your current landlord for a short extension. The downside to frequent moves, however, is that changing your address too often can confuse and alarm customers.

F. Size and Physical Features

Almost every tenant is concerned about the size of the rental. You'll want enough space but not too much, which would be needlessly expensive. And you'll want the space to be well laid-out, comfortable, and welcoming to employees, clients, and customers.

1. Size of Space

The amount of space you need may be very clear to you, or it may be an unknown. An existing business that's moving because its present rental is too small knows with some certainty how much space it will need; a new enterprise is less sure.

As you head into your rental search, it's important to be as precise as possible regarding your minimum and maximum space requirements. Professionals known as "space planners" can help determine how much square footage you need and how to use it. (Chapter 3, Section B, discusses how space planners can help.) When you combine your present space needs with your plans for the future (expansion on the horizon?) and the term, or length, of the lease you want, you'll know what to look for.

Chapter 4 explains in detail how landlords measure square feet. For now, understand that the various ways can result in significant differences in the amount of real, usable space. If your space needs are critical and you need at least a certain square footage, specify in your list that the footage must exclude the thickness of interior and exterior walls, elevator shafts, and other structural aspects of the building.

Don't leave your estimate of needed space without considering the possibility that your business might need *less* space in the future, even as it prospers. Is outsourcing on the horizon for you? Think about the space-saving results of relying on computer files instead of paper files (no need for a file room now), or using online services instead of local resources (do you need a space for storing books, magazines, and manuals if they're available online?), or using an off-site company to take the place of your on-site servers (no need for a server room). Will your need for support staff diminish as employees become adept at their own word processing or other computer tasks? With the advent of flex time and home telecommuting, many businesses find that they need less space than they originally planned.

⚠️ **It's expensive to rent space that you don't use.** Resist the temptation to rent more space than you need, even if it's a great deal, unless you are quite certain that you will soon grow into it. Getting rid of unneeded space (subleasing and assessing) is expensive.

2. Interior Needs

The configuration of a rented space is as important as its overall size. For example, you may need lots of storage space, private offices, cubicles, and a few small meeting rooms; or you may be fine with one open area that you'll break up with furniture or portable partitions. Ceiling height may be an issue if you have unusual equipment, and the number and capacity of electrical outlets or plumbing facilities may be important. You may want to provide kitchen facilities for employees, a lunchroom or lounge, or even a shower for those who want to bike to work or exercise at noon. Some of these features can be customized to fit your needs; others (such as ceiling height) cannot.

Think of your move to new quarters as an opportunity to streamline the way work is done and eliminate awkward systems or configurations. Start by consulting your employees for their ideas. Everyone in your business is bound to have an idea of how things could work better if the operation were arranged a little differently. For instance, it might make sense to place certain employees near others with whom they frequently interact. To do so, you might need to place walls, fixtures, or equipment in a particular order. You might be able to evaluate these suggestions on your own and reduce them to concrete designs to implement them, or you may want to consult a space planner (discussed in Chapter 3, Section B).

EXAMPLE: Begone Tours, a travel agency, began looking for larger quarters when their new tour line—wilderness treks in Midwestern states—became wildly popular. Begone's owners gathered the staff to discuss their ideas for new space. Several people suggested moving the marketing department closer to the sales force and providing for a central, out-of-the-way storage area for files, brochures, and video equipment. Realizing that Begone's website would play an increasingly important part in the business, the owners planned to look for space that would accommodate a larger technical force who would need a quiet, undisturbed area of their own.

3. Soundproofing

Good sound insulation between rooms within your space and in the walls separating your space from that of adjacent tenants may be very important—especially in an office setting. If soundproofing is essential for your business, indicate this on your worksheet. Sometimes you can cheaply fix a sound problem by playing background music or buying a white-noise machine to mask the sound. These are not ideal solutions, but they may be a way to salvage a space that in other respects has all the right stuff.

4. Operating Windows

Fresh air may be free but it's not always available in today's buildings. Many landlords feel that real windows—ones that open and close—will compromise the efficiency of the building's heating, ventilating, and air-conditioning system, known in the trade as HVAC. (And if the heater is blasting while the windows are wide open, you, too, will bear some of the cost, since tenants typically pay for a portion of the HVAC costs, as explained in Chapter 12, Section B.) Still, there are buildings around that do contain operating windows, so if you highly value fresh air on demand, note this on your worksheet.

5. Control of Heating and Cooling

In some buildings, you have to take whatever the HVAC system happens to be pumping out. In others, you may have one or more thermostats within the space you lease. If being in charge of heat and air-conditioning controls is important, highlight it on your worksheet.

Individual control of your work climate will be high priority if you or employees work on weekends or nights, when building-wide ventilation and heating controls are typically turned off. In addition, if there are widely differing activities going on in the building—a gym on the first floor and a group of therapists on the top floor—think about whether a one-climate-fits-all approach is likely to meet everyone's needs. If your area of the country experiences particularly hot summers and cold winters, pay some attention to the exposure of your potential space—a western exposure, for example, is going to get much warmer in the summer than a similar space in the building that faces north. If you're worried about shivering while others sweat, or vice versa, place "climate control" high on your list.

6. Storage Space

Some buildings have extra storage space for tenants in a basement or other out-of-the-way area. If you need space for items that you use only occasionally, access to a separate storage area may be a priority. This can reduce clutter and free up your rental space for important uses (archived files or spare parts, for example).

7. Private Restrooms

Many buildings offer restrooms that are shared by several tenants. If you prefer to have restrooms within your leased space for the exclusive use of employees and customers, give this item a high-priority rating.

8. Technological Capacities

If your business depends heavily on computers and access to the Internet, you'll need to be sure that any space you're considering can accommodate your needs. Consider issues such as:

- **Riser capacity.** Computer cables typically run throughout the building in conduits called "risers." When the riser is full, you can't add more cables. If there are other techno-heavy tenants in the building, there may be competition for riser space. Especially if you plan on significant growth, sufficient riser size (and a guaranteed portion of it) will be a high priority for you.

- **Floor strength.** Computer equipment, especially servers, can be very heavy. In addition, if you intend to have an "open" work environment with few walls, understand that this will result in more people per square foot than in a traditional, with-walls office. You may need to look for floors that are reinforced.

- **Internet service providers (ISPs).** Check to make sure that the building owners or management will accept more than one ISP. Some buildings have exclusive contracts with one ISP, which is no longer legal in light of a Federal Trade Commission's ruling ("FCC Final Forced Access Rule and Notice of Further Proposed Rulemaking," Docket Numbers 99-217, 96-98, and 8857). Still, the news may not have filtered down to your landlord. When there is only one ISP, you're likely to see expensive hookup and monthly charges.

G. Other Tenants and Services in and Near the Building

It may be important to your business to be in a building with certain types of tenants—for example, businesses that are complementary to yours or provide a needed service. Lawyers, for example, may want to locate in a building where many of the other tenants are also lawyers, accountants, title companies, or copy services. Health-care professionals may want to be near a hospital, pharmacy, or other related health services, such as an x-ray lab. Or you may want to find a building that houses a health club, coffee shop, or a fast copy service that you, your employees, or customers will find handy. Note these preferences on your worksheet.

On the other hand, you may want to avoid buildings that contain certain types of businesses, such as those that compete with yours. Note that, as well, in your worksheet. You may want to avoid others, either because of the nature of the clientele or because of parking issues. For example, if you operate a children's dance studio, you probably won't want a bar as a next door neighbor. On the other hand, if you have a bakery, a bar won't interfere with your business since the hours of operation are distinctly different.

Your neighbors down the street may be just as important to you as those down the hall. For instance, a research-and-development company may prefer to locate near a university for easy access to technical libraries. A real estate broker may find it convenient to be near banks, title companies, and insurance agencies. A mail-order business may find it helpful to be close to a post office or overnight shipping facility. Whatever your special requirements, if they're important enough, list them on your worksheet.

H. Parking

For many businesses, it's essential to have ample parking—whether a designated lot on the building site, on the street, or in a nearby parking lot or garage. Parking may be a high priority for several reasons. If public transit is inadequate, people will need to drive to your business. If your business involves selling or servicing large items such as stereo equipment, customers will need nearby parking.

If parking is a requirement for you, remember that your landlord may impose an additional charge for on-site parking. (Alternatively, you might want to rent space in a nearby lot.) Also, be aware that you won't be guaranteed a specific number of spaces or spaces at a designated location unless the lease says so. Chapter 13, Section A, explains negotiating for parking.

I. Building Security

If crime is a known problem in the neighborhood and customers or employees are assaulted or robbed, you may be found partially responsible if you have not taken reasonable steps to prevent criminal incidents or at least warn of them. Your landlord, too, may ultimately bear some responsibility, but the portion of a jury award or settlement figure that you end up paying is hardly the point. You never want to be in a position of worrying about customers' and employees' safety, and you never want to be drawn into a lawsuit, even one that you win, if you can at all avoid it.

Security is a bigger issue for some businesses than for others. Enterprises that are open late, handle large amounts of cash, deal in easily fenced merchandise, attract large numbers of vulnerable customers, or are poorly staffed will have more to worry about than others. If your business is likely to be attractive to a burglar or assailant, you'll want both a safe area and a well-secured building. These two requirements should be high on your list of priorities.

- **The neighborhood.** Your local police department is a good source of information on the safety of various areas in your town or city. If certain neighborhoods are charming, convenient, and cheap, but come with alarming crime statistics, you'll want to look elsewhere.

- **The building.** Your business may need internal security as much as it needs to be in a safe environment. Flimsy locks on doors or windows are invitations to the wrong folks—even if the neighborhood is safe, you don't want to be the first on your block to host a mugging or a burglary. Reasonable security steps may include adequate outside and inside lighting, strong locks, limited entry, alarm systems, and even security guards.

J. Image and Maintenance

The way a building looks—and how it's maintained—will be important to some and practically irrelevant to others. In general, the more your business serves the public, the more important is the building's appearance. If no one ever sees or visits your business, it may not matter much, except to you and your employees.

1. Image

A building's image and the neighborhood's prestige are intangible and may or may not be important to you. A high-tech business may want to locate in a sleek, modern building in an office park. A children's store may prefer something warmer or more homelike. An expedition outfitter may be looking for a rugged, rambling building that suggests the atmosphere of the great out-doors. A nonprofit environmental organiza-tion with lots of volunteers may find that an upscale neighborhood or building works against their fundraising efforts. Your "look" is definitely a matter of taste and a fair amount of guesswork. If image is important, treat it as a high priority and be as specific as possible about the "right" type of neighborhood or building for your business.

2. Maintenance

Some landlords skimp on routine mainte-nance, which can give property a down-at-the-heels appearance. That's not always a drawback—rent may be lower in a building that's not spiffy—and you may be in a business where appearance doesn't matter too much. But if a well-maintained building is important, as it will be for most tenants who are concerned about image, add that to your worksheet.

3. Nonsmoking Policy

If your business has a nonsmoking policy and is leasing in a multitenant building, un-derstand that the building-wide ventilation and heating systems may still permit smoke from other tenants' spaces to waft into your space. To guard against such pollution, you'll need to satisfy yourself that the air in your space isn't mixed with the air from other spaces in the building—or that the building strictly enforces a nonsmoking policy for everyone. Be aware that state law may restrict smoking, too.

4. Visibility and Signage

If your business needs to be seen—for example, you run a coffee bar that depends in large part on drop-in trade from pedestrians and motorists—make sure that the space you're considering is visible from the sidewalk or street. You'll also need to find out whether local ordinances will permit the kind of signage you want, and whether the landlord will allow it. If your business falls into this category, make visibility and signage a high priority.

5. Special Requirements

Your business may have special needs that can make or break a deal. A plastic surgeon who does procedures in the office may need to be sure the building has a backup power source to provide uninterrupted electricity. A photographer may need adequate plumbing and ventilation for a darkroom. Be sure to note any special needs when you put together your Rental Priorities Worksheet.

K. Expansion or Purchase Potential

If you plan on growing your business or would like to own your building in the near future, you may want to locate space now that has the potential for expansion or purchase. You'll save yourself the hassle and expense of another search and move to new space, and you may be able to lock in favorable expansion or purchase terms now, in your lease.

1. Ability to Expand Space

After the first year or two, you may need more space. Depending on your expectations for growth, you may feel that the ability to take over additional space in the building is a high-priority factor. You'll want to nail down your right to occupy additional parts of the building in a lease clause giving you the right of first refusal when space opens up. Negotiating for this right is covered in Chapter 14, Section D.

2. Potential Purchase

If you're leasing an entire building or are a major tenant in a multitenant building, don't discount the possibility that you may want to own the building someday. If this is your goal, note that on your worksheet.

Rental Priorities Worksheet for "Terri's Threads"

Address: _____

_____

Contact: _____

Phone #: _____ Email: _____

Rent: _____ Deposit: _____

Other Fees:_____

Term: _____ Date Seen: _____ Date Available: _____

Brief description of rental space and building: _____

_____

_____

_____

Essentials

Yes	No	
☐	☐	1. Near residential shopping area, upscale neighborhood, lots of foot traffic.
☐	☐	2. Rent less than $2,000 per month.
☐	☐	3. Minimum 1,000 square feet.
☐	☐	4. Separate employee and customer restrooms.
☐	☐	5. One floor, rectangular, separate storage room(s) in back.
☐	☐	6. Sufficient electrical outlets and capacities to support computers for inventory and accounts.
☐	☐	7. Available by March 1.

Rental Priorities Worksheet for "Terri's Threads" (continued)

Compromise

Yes	No	
☐	☐	1. Parking on street or by arrangement in nearby lot. _____
☐	☐	2. Main interior space divisible into two rooms (one for examining clothing brought in by consignees). _____
☐	☐	3. Ability to locate two sets of dressing rooms along opposite walls. _____
☐	☐	4. Neighboring businesses stay open into early evening at least one day per week. _____
☐	☐	5. Landlord willing to lease for 3-5 years and give option to extend longer.
☐	☐	6. Major transportation lines nearby. _____

Unacceptable

Yes	No	
☐	☐	1. Risky crime area. _____
☐	☐	2. Other consignment shops within a three-mile radius. _____
☐	☐	3. No lease less than three years. _____
☐	☐	4. No personal guarantee for the rent. _____

Notes: _____

_____

_____

_____

_____

There are different ways that you can assure yourself of the chance to buy a building that you're renting. In the lease, you and the landlord can agree that you will have:

- **An option to buy the building at a certain date.** Tenants usually pay for the option when they sign the lease, and sometimes the lease specifies purchase price, too. When the time comes, you can decide whether you want to exercise the option (buy the building).
- **A right of first offer.** The landlord promises that if he decides to sell, he'll approach you first. You'll pay for this option, too.
- **A right of first refusal.** The landlord promises that before he sells it to anyone else, he'll give you a chance to meet the terms of the offer he's considering (if you can meet them, he must sell to you). Again, you pay now for this right.

Purchase options are explained in more detail in Chapter 14. If you think you want an option (and are prepared to pay for it), assign it a value on your worksheet.

L. Preparing Your Rental Priorities Worksheet

Now, let's take a look at a sample Rental Priorities Worksheet. The one just above is by the owners of Terri's Threads, a consignment shop for men's and women's clothing. Terri referred to other places in this book—like the description of how landlords charge for rent, in Chapter 4—before comfortably noting that she could afford no more than $2,000 for rent. (She learned, for example, that if she was going to pay a portion of the building's operating costs, the rent could fluctuate, so she listed the highest amount she could handle, knowing that the real cost might be lower at times.)

Terri will make copies of this worksheet and take one with her every time she visits potential rental space, filling in the location's address and other important information at the top of the form. In the chapters that follow, we'll show how Terri uses this worksheet to evaluate possible rentals.

M. Subleasing Space

Sometimes, the ideal space for your business may be within someone else's tenancy. If you rent space from another tenant, you're subleasing from that tenant (and you're called the subtenant). As a subtenant, you rent directly from the tenant, not the landlord, though you must abide by the lease terms and conditions that the landlord has set up with the tenant. Chapter 14, Section F, explains the legal ins and outs of subleasing in detail (and also covers its close cousin, "assigning").

You may be able to get a great deal as a subtenant. That's because tenants who are willing to share their space usually need to do so—their projected requirements for space didn't pan out as hoped, or their income is insufficient to cover the rent. As long as the tenant's own lease allows it, subleasing is one way to cut the overhead.

There are, however, downsides to being a subtenant. For one, since you're leasing from a tenant, you're dealing with someone who is not in the business of being a landlord and may not know or care about treating a tenant—you—properly and legally. For instance, you may not find your "landlord" reacting as promptly and conscientiously as you might wish when it comes to requests for repairs.

If you are considering renting from another tenant, keep these issues in mind:

- Check to see if the landlord's consent is needed for subletting the space or assigning the lease. If it is, make sure you're not legally bound to take the space until the tenant's landlord has consented in writing.
- Look for clauses in the prime lease (the lease between the landlord and the original tenant) that require the landlord's consent for a use change or alterations of the space. (Use restrictions are explained in Chapter 7, Section D.) Don't sign up unless the landlord gives the needed approvals, in writing.
- Scrutinize the tenant's lease for charges in addition to rent—pass-through charges, for example, for maintenance, taxes, and insurance. Find out if the tenant will be passing on these costs to *you*. (Chapter 9, Section D, explains these additional forms of rent.)
- Get written confirmation from the landlord and tenant that the tenant's lease is in good standing, and that as long as you pay your rent and other required charges, you can continue to occupy your space.
- Include a clause in your lease allowing you to cancel the sublease if the landlord fails to provide building services and repairs. The last thing you want is to be the unhappy recipient of the fallout from a fractious relationship between the landlord and the tenant.

Checklist for Determining Your Space Needs

This chapter will get your space search off to a great start. It should help you:

- determine that you really need to move
- know the maximum rent and deposit you can afford to pay
- identify the ideal location, size, physical features, and services of the property you want
- decide how long a lease you need, and
- prepare a Rental Priorities Worksheet, including features of the rental or lease that you can't abide (absolute no-ways).

Chapter 2

Looking for Space and Using Brokers

This chapter is for readers who haven't found space or will be working with brokers. It's especially useful in the following situations:

- You've decided to hunt on your own and would like some advice on fruitful methods.
- You expect to deal with a landlord's broker, and you want to know what that experience will be like.
- You've decided to hire your own broker and want to learn the process and the pitfalls (it's trickier than you think).
- You and the landlord are sharing a broker (and you want to learn how to protect yourself).

➡ You can skip this chapter if you've already found space and are ready to negotiate, or if neither you nor the landlord is using a broker.

f you've thought carefully about the kind of location and building that will best suit your business, determined the maximum rent you're willing to pay, and set other priorities, you've accomplished quite a lot already. (Chapter 1 guides you through this process.) Now it's time to take your specifications—in the form of your Rental Priorities Worksheet—and check out potential spaces. You can proceed in a

number of different ways, depending on your familiarity with the area, the amount of time you wish to invest in the search, and your contacts with other business people who may be able to steer you towards appropriate property.

Perhaps you'll conduct your search on your own, reading classified ads in newspapers or online, looking for signs or placards in building windows, and soliciting leads from friends and business associates. Or maybe you'll opt for the assistance of a real estate broker. Either way, there are proven steps that will make your search easier. This chapter shows you how to most effectively and efficiently find potential rental space, and explains the various ways you may wish to involve a broker in your search. Chapter 3 goes into detail on how to visit and evaluate prospective spaces and landlords.

A. How to Find Space on Your Own

If the rental market in your area is awash with vacancies, chances are the landlords for those properties have advertised in many places, hoping to reach a wide audience. You won't have much trouble finding out what's available. But if the rental market is tight, landlords can afford to hustle less, knowing that many eager tenants will seek them out. If there are few vacancies for the type of space you need, you'll have to do extra work to find them.

1. Enlist the Help of Personal Contacts

Because some of the best opportunities come via word of mouth, ask friends and other business contacts if they know of available space. Explain your rental space priorities either by phone, in person, or by sending a note. (You can even attach your Rental Priorities Worksheet if you wish.) Start with business owners—particularly those renting space in the part of town that interests you. They may know of enterprises that are moving or folding long before the vacancies are listed in newspaper ads.

There are advantages to being at the head of the pack. Landlords hate to have periods of vacancy, during which they have no rental income. In exchange for your readiness to commit to a rental before it becomes vacant, a landlord might be willing to cut you a better deal on improvements or rent.

Your business advisors—lawyer, accountant, and insurance broker—may also have good leads on space that's about to become available. And if you attend meetings of your chamber of commerce, community service group, or trade organization, spread the word that you're looking for space. It pays to be imaginative. One tenant we know called the area's largest commercial janitorial service, which told him of a couple of businesses that had recently canceled their service contracts in preparation for a move.

2. Do Your Own Space Scouting

The decidedly low-tech method of pounding the pavement still works. Go to the neighborhoods where you might locate and spend some time driving or walking the streets to see what's available. You may see signs in windows or on buildings advertising space that you won't learn of any other way. Some landlords prefer to market their vacancies that way, figuring they can save on advertising costs and broker's commissions.

As you cruise the streets and sidewalks, don't just look for vacant space. A store, studio, office suite, or workshop that's perfect for your business may be occupied by a tenant who is going out of business or moving to another location soon. Take a peek inside building lobbies to see who rents there. If you find a desirable location, ask people in the building if they know of any space opening up soon. You may learn of someone who is about to move on. There's a lot of turnover among small businesses, and you may get lucky.

Exploring a neighborhood at a leisurely pace also gives you the opportunity to closely observe traffic patterns for both vehicles and pedestrians. For example, if your business relies on customers arriving by car, you'll want to see how difficult it is to find parking—important information to know before you get too far into lease negotiations. Be sure to do your investigating during normal business hours.

3. Contact Landlords and Management Companies Directly

In areas that are in high demand, you may need to get more aggressive in your search for available space. Instead of waiting for rentals to come on the market or even hit the grapevine, go right to the landlord and find out what properties are likely to become vacant.

Current tenants in desirable rentals may not want to give you the landlord's name. A tenant may be concerned that, when his lease is up, you may appear and start a bidding war. A simple way to find the owner is to note the address and look up the property in the property tax office in your city. The owner's name and address should be listed.

Next, visit the landlord's office. You may learn of a lease that's about to expire and you may be able to offer terms that will beat the current tenant's deal. Or, perhaps the best you can do is join a waiting list. You never know what will open up.

In addition to contacting landlords directly, consider speaking with management companies in your town or area. These companies perform the day-to-day tasks of running the building on behalf of the land-lord. Often, they are in charge of leasing, too. Because they work for the landlord, they have every incentive to talk to potential tenants. Management companies are listed in the Classified section of the phone book,

and they often have their own signs in the buildings they manage.

4. Check Classified Ads: On Paper and Online

For-rent ads in newspapers are an obvious place to look. Traditionally, the Sunday edition of the local paper contains the most ads for commercial space. The classified ads sections of major newspapers are often available online.

In addition to newspapers, be sure to look online for information on commercial rentals. Many sites have property descriptions that are accompanied by videos or photos, giving you a preview of the space before you even leave your chair.

Almost any major search engine will lead you to sites with information on commercial real estate. For example, we tried Yahoo! and, on the home page's web directory, chose the category "Business." We next went into the subcategories of Classifieds, then Real Estate, then Commercial Properties.

Many sites appeared in the final category, including classified listing services and brokers, giving us the ability to search for listings by type, region, and size. Several allowed us to specify our requirements (such as square footage and maximum rent), then customized the results of our search.

An especially useful site is the one at www.realtylocator.com. After choosing the Commercial Real Estate link, you'll come to a page listing "Directories"—sites that list properties, investment and development groups, and more. Again, many allow customized searches based on geographical area and rental amount. Also, check out www.sior.com, maintained by the Society of Industrial and Office Realtors, with information on experts and properties for lease.

5. Read Trade Publications

Landlords save money when their renovation costs are low. One way they minimize improvement costs is to consistently rent finished space to the same type of business. This means that there will be no or minimal construction work necessary for successive tenants.

> **EXAMPLE:** Years ago, Wellkept Properties installed commercial kitchen facilities at one of its properties. The property was occupied by a succession of restaurants, which varied the décor but not the layout of the food preparation and storage areas. Wellkept can rent the space to

restaurant tenants at favorable rents since it has spent little money on renovations. If tenants want to substantially redesign the seating areas to put their personal touch on the place, the tenants will pay for these improvements themselves.

Trade publications are the natural place for a landlord to advertise finished, business-specific space. For example, a magazine aimed at professional chefs and restaurant owners will often carry ads for improved space previously used by a restaurant. There are magazines aimed at almost every business niche—import car repair shops, garden stores, and coin-operated laundries, to name just a few. To learn whether a publication targets your business area, go to your public library and ask for the following (unfortunately, they're not yet available online):

- **The *Periodical Index*.** Check the Subject Matter headings for your business. For example, a commercial laundry owner would look under Laundry or Sanitation.
- **The Standard Rate and Data Service publication.** This book lists the address and phone number of each trade publication—a terrific aid because most of these industry-specific magazines can't be found at your local newsstand. You'll need to order the latest issue directly from the publisher.

Look for trade publications online, using a search engine such as Yahoo!. To follow-up with our restaurant example, we went to

Yahoo! and chose Business on the home page; then went into the subcategories of Business to Business and Food and Beverage. Sure enough, we found an entry for restaurants, which led us to a page with several links to online publications. Some of them included classified listings.

B. Working With a Real Estate Broker

Many small business owners have easily found space on their own and negotiated the terms of the lease with the landlord. Many others, however, have preferred to get help from a professional real estate broker. You may decide to work with a broker in any of the following situations:

- You've searched long and hard but haven't turned up great space at an affordable price.
- You have limited time available to look for space and would find it convenient to have someone else help narrow the field for you.
- You've had no experience in searching for space or dealing with real estate matters and you feel a bit intimidated by the prospect of doing it all by yourself.
- You're worried that you'll encounter experts working to protect the landlord's best interests—but no one will be looking out for you.

Well, here's good news: It's almost always feasible to hire a real estate professional in the form of a broker who will represent your interests. And there's even better news: Often it will cost you little or nothing to get the benefit of the real estate pro's services. In this section and those that follow, we'll explain:

- what brokers do
- broker licensing
- how to find and choose a broker
- how to work with and pay a broker, and
- how to deal with problems with a broker.

1. Who Can Be a Broker?

To act as a real estate broker, a person needs to get a license. The requirements vary from state to state, but usually involve passing an exam, taking continuing education courses, and adhering to strict rules issued by the state legislature or an administrative commission.

Real estate brokers often employ or contract with (and supervise) state-licensed salespeople. The requirements for becoming a salesperson are less rigorous than those for a broker. In this chapter, we use the term "broker" generically to cover both brokers and salespeople. The term "agent" is also widely used to cover both types of real estate professionals.

Different Roles for Brokers

Since brokers can function in different ways, it pays to know exactly what role a broker is playing in a landlord-tenant transaction. Here are some guidelines:

- **Broker**—The generic term for a licensed intermediary who is working to get a landlord and a tenant to the point of signing a lease.

- **Listing Broker**—A broker who's under contract with a landlord to find a tenant to fill a vacancy. The listing broker's sole legal obligation is to the landlord. A listing broker who finds a tenant and gets a lease signed is paid a commission by the landlord—usually 3% or so of the rent over the life of the lease.

- **Nonlisting Broker**—A broker who's not under contract with a landlord but produces a tenant who eventually signs a lease. Usually the listing broker and the nonlisting broker split the commission. Unless other arrangements are made, the nonlisting broker is an agent of the landlord and—like the listing broker—isn't obligated to look out for the tenant's best interests.

- **Tenant's Broker**— A broker who agrees to represent only the tenant, the best option for a tenant who wants a broker's full attention and undivided loyalty. If the space you end up leasing was listed with a landlord's broker, normally the landlord pays one commission, which is shared by the landlord's broker and the tenant's broker. But if you lease property that hasn't been listed, the landlord may not be willing to pay a commission to your broker. In that event, you must pay the broker. It's best to address the issue of payment in advance in a written contract between you and your broker, as described in Section F, below.

- **Dual Agent**—A neutral broker who tries to work for both the landlord and the tenant in the same transaction. The broker's main duties tend to be mechanical—making sure that the lease details are worked out smoothly. Being fair to both sides can be a challenge. Because of the potential for conflict, some states don't allow brokers to be dual agents.

- **Realtor**—A broker who's a member of the National Association of Realtors. The word "Realtor" has been trademarked by the Association. Brokers do not have to be Realtors.

2. Brokers Who Work for Landlords

In a traditional commercial leasing situation, the landlord lists available space with a broker who then goes out looking for tenants. If a lease gets signed, the landlord pays the broker a commission—typically 3% or so of the rent paid over the life of the lease (excluding any extensions or renewals). The broker with whom the landlord lists the property is called the *listing broker*. If another broker (a *nonlisting broker*) brings in a tenant and a lease gets signed, the two brokers usually split the commission.

Under this traditional way of doing business, the listing broker is the landlord's agent—someone whose primary duty is to look after the landlord's interests. This means that the broker is duty-bound to work out a lease that's as favorable as possible to the landlord. You may find yourself working with a broker under these traditional rules if you respond to an ad for space or call a phone number on a sign in a building window. Similarly, if you go to a broker's office and ask about available properties, you'll be operating under these rules unless you and the broker make other arrangements. Be aware that, legally speaking, even a nonlisting broker is the landlord's agent unless you and that broker work out something different. Obviously, it's crucial for you to know right from the get-go if the broker you're dealing with is obligated to look out for your interests. Laws in most states require brokers to tell you whom they're working for.

Fortunately, these days you're not necessarily stuck with the traditional model in which the broker promotes only the landlord's interests. More and more brokers are willing to align themselves with tenants.

3. Brokers Who Work Exclusively for Tenants

Understandably, you may be uncomfortable dealing on your own with a landlord and the landlord's broker. It's a bit like being involved in a lawsuit where the other side, but not you, is represented by a lawyer—sometimes you can make out okay on your own, but often not. To even things out, you can engage your own broker, who will represent your interests and only your interests.

The best kind of broker to hire is one who consistently works only for tenants. This professional is likely to have the instincts and loyalties that will serve you well, and may be more aggressive and creative than brokers who work with both landlords and tenants. Unfortunately, it may take a while to locate such a broker—and if your business is located in a small community, you may find no one who fits this description. Sections C, D, and F, below, explain the benefits of hiring your own and how to locate and pay a suitable broker.

4. Brokers Who Work for Landlords and Tenants

The next best thing to engaging a dedicated tenant's broker is to find a reputable broker who works for landlords *or* tenants. You'll have an easier time finding a broker like this to work for you. Such arrangements will work just fine when your broker is showing you properties represented by brokers in other offices. Under this scenario, you know that your broker's allegiance will be firmly on your side.

However, the situation gets cloudy if your broker's own office has taken listings for spaces that you want to see. This puts your broker in an awkward position. The broker is duty-bound to find you the best space, regardless of who has the listing, but is also committed to contribute to the success of the office. You may not feel 100% sure about where the broker's loyalties lie. Still, such a relationship can be workable. In Section F, we'll explain how to address this potential conflict in a written contract with your broker.

5. Brokers Who Are Dual Agents

There may another way to handle the situation of your broker showing you space represented by one of the broker's office colleagues, but the solution is not a very satisfying one. The arrangement, allowed in some states, involves asking the broker to step away from his role as an advocate and instead assume a neutral stance. A broker who works like this is known as a *dual agent*. The broker's role is limited to attending to mechanical details and helping to make sure the transaction flows smoothly. For example, a dual agent may check on the zoning classification of the space or shuttle lease proposals back and forth between you and the landlord.

A broker might work as a dual agent when:

- you and the landlord decide you'd like to use one broker between you, or
- your broker shows you space that's been listed with the broker's own office—in this event, your broker and her office associate, who's been engaged by the landlord, both become dual brokers.

The benefits of using a dual broker are limited. You won't really get much, if anything, in the way of useful advice or practical guidance, since the dual agent can't be your advocate. In a nutshell, you can be left high and dry when it comes to knowing whether the deal is advantageous or not. The only sure way to get the benefit of professional real estate services is to sign a contract with a broker who agrees to act solely in your behalf.

EXAMPLE: Tenant Dolores and landlord Andy are using broker George of Tri-County Commercial to put together a lease deal between them. George will be a dual agent. George knows exactly how much Dolores is willing pay for rent and how desperate she is for good space. He also knows how much Andy is willing to accept as rent and how long a lease he'd be willing to grant. Yet, as a neutral agent, George can't use this information on behalf of either party. The best that George can do is to take Dolores's proposed terms to Andy and perhaps offer Dolores a list of qualified inspectors and contractors for her to consult regarding the condition of the property and the cost of improvements. Those benefits are minimal, as far as Dolores is concerned. She's a novice in lease matters and really needs much more help to get a good deal. She wisely decides to hire a broker of her own.

Meanwhile, Andy has decided to stay with George. If George is a broker with professional integrity, he will not share Dolores's secrets with Andy, even though he no longer works for her.

The Multiple Listing Service

It would be very convenient to have a list of all the commercial real estate that's available in your area. After telling your broker what kind of property you need, the broker could simply consult the master list and show you the appropriate properties.

In fact, there is such a system, called the Multiple Listing Service (MLS), which is maintained by brokers in most areas. Brokers who are members of the MLS put their own listings on the system, and can see other properties on the list. Brokers who are not members of the MLS can't post listings there—and usually don't have direct access to the list to see what's available. The MLS system is most active in areas where there is low competition among big, established brokerage houses, who have exclusive listings that they do not share.

The traditional medium for the MLS is a book that is published weekly and distributed to all MLS members. Brokers jealously guard MLS information about commercial space. While it's relatively common for *residential* listings to appear online and be available freely to the general public, that practice hasn't yet spread to commercial space.

If you're talking to prospective brokers who might represent you, find out if they're part of the MLS and, if not, how they plan to overcome this disadvantage. If they don't have an adequate alternative plan for getting you into the leasing market, you may be better off to seek help elsewhere.

C. The Value of Hiring Your Own Broker

Now that you're familiar with how brokers work, you may want to hire your own—one who owes a legal duty only to you. A broker who works exclusively for you has one main assignment—to get you a good deal—*not* to help the landlord quickly fill the space or get top dollar rent. Also, your broker will be free to point out problems with the property or the neighborhood it's in. Beyond that, a good broker can help do the following:

- **Review your Rental Priorities Worksheet (explained in Chapter 1) and help focus your search.** A professional who's familiar with the market should have some idea whether you'll be able to find the space of your dreams. If your list of "Essentials" is totally unrealistic, it's best to know now and do some rethinking.
- **Direct your search.** Using your realistic worksheet, your broker can help you hone in on the spaces most likely to meet your needs. Instead of looking at ten spaces, you might wind up just looking at three.
- **Investigate the details.** A broker who knows what's what and who's who in the world of commercial leasing can help you line up qualified inspectors, contractors, and space planners, as well as check on tax and utility bills if you're going to sign a net lease. (Net leases are explained in Chapter 9.)

- **Analyze lease terms.** An experienced broker can help you evaluate the financial consequences of the landlord's lease terms, and can spot hidden charges that translate into higher rent.
- **Comparison shop.** Assuming the broker knows the whole market, you can find out how the rent at one space you're contemplating stacks up against other spaces in town. It will give you peace of mind to know that you're not overpaying.
- **Learn the key lease terms.** Before taking you on any field trips to see potential space, your broker can find out the key terms of the lease the landlord expects you to sign. The broker can compare these points with your Rental Priorities Worksheet. If there's an absolute incompatibility—you must have a five-year lease but the landlord has already given a neighboring tenant an option on your space that may be exercised in three years—your broker can cross that property off the list and not waste your time.
- **Negotiate the lease.** The broker who's acting as your agent can help in lease negotiations—a terrific boon if, like most people, you don't feel like you're a natural born negotiator.

Are there any disadvantages to hiring your own broker? As explained below in Section F, if you pay your broker on commission, you might have to pay all or a portion of that commission. If your share of the commission is half of 3% of the rent over the life of your lease, you could be looking at a significant amount of money. And because the broker doesn't usually earn any money until a lease is signed, brokers have an interest in closing a deal sooner rather than later. But here, at least, you'll find that market forces will put pressure on brokers to put their client's best interests first. Brokers who develop a reputation for rushing a deal or not bargaining vigorously on a client's behalf will soon find themselves without much business.

Remember, too, that even highly qualified brokers have limitations: They won't have the skills to provide you with sound advice on the physical condition of a building—for that, you'll need to hire an experienced and reputable building contractor.

D. How to Find a Real Estate Broker

Finding your own broker isn't all that different from finding a good doctor, lawyer, or dentist. A hefty application of common sense, professional and personal connections, and some independent research usually yields a good result. The same method works when looking for a broker.

As suggested in Section C, above, you'll be best served if you work with a broker who represents tenants exclusively. A good starting point for your search is to find a

broker who represents buyers—but not sellers—of real estate. These brokers may act as tenants' agents in leasing transactions too, or they may be able to direct you to a kindred spirit who represents tenants only.

Do your best to work with an established broker—one who has been in the business in your geographical area long enough to know how deals are done and how landlords and their brokers work. In addition, experienced and successful brokers will have the financial stability to enable them to firmly put *your* best interests at the front (see the discussion in Section F1, below, on paying a broker so that you minimize the chances of self-dealing). Remember, in most situations a broker gets paid when the deal is done, according to the size of the rent. A broker who isn't hungry will be less tempted to rush negotiations or settle for a more expensive result when patience might produce something better for you.

⚠️ **Avoid a broker who does residential, not commercial, leasing.** Someone who works primarily with houses, condos, and apartments is unlikely to know the ins and outs of the commercial market. Make sure the broker you choose is experienced in helping tenants find office, retail, and other commercial space. But while you shouldn't use a residential specialist to find a business rental, the broker who helped you buy or sell your house may have suggestions for a commercial leasing specialist.

Other commercial tenants in your community may be a fruitful source. Ask them if they have engaged a broker and whom they would recommend. Look for tenants who appear to be running a healthy business (chances are that their good business sense was at work when they chose a broker, too).

You can narrow your field of inquiry by approaching tenants whose businesses are similar to yours, especially if you're in a large city where brokers may have divided the market into niches, with some specializing in office space, others concentrating on restaurants and food stores, and others working mainly with light industry. For example, if you're intending to open an art gallery, you'll want to deal with a broker who's familiar with the commercial space that is appropriate for a gallery. The owner of a currently operating gallery may have found just the broker.

In some cities, brokers may even concentrate on specific neighborhoods. If you want to locate in a particular area, to take advantage of adjoining businesses, traffic patterns, or expected rents, it makes sense to look for brokers who have already done deals in the neighborhood.

Try to get recommendations from several tenants and businesspeople. You may find that the same name or names pop to the top of everyone's list. These are the people to pursue, testing them by the criteria suggested in Section E1, below.

E. How to Choose a Broker

After you have whittled down your list to two or three promising names, you're ready to do a bit more research before you choose a broker. You'll want information both *about* the broker and *from* the broker.

1. Questions to Ask People Who Recommend a Particular Broker

Before singling out one or two brokers with whom you'd like to work, you'll want to ask your contacts the following questions:

1. **What is the broker's reputation for honesty, experience, thoroughness, and accessibility?** The person who has recommended this broker may have the answer. If not, ask other real estate professionals you might know—the agent who sold you your house, for example, or your lender (mortgage lenders work with brokers all the time).

2. **What were the broker's weak points?** In even the best working relationship, there are normally a few bumps along the road. Find out what they were. If these problems are likely to upset you—for example, one prospect won't return calls on Sundays or is always late for appointments—then it's best to know now.

3. **What were the broker's strong points?** There may be one aspect of the space-hunting game that is of para-

mount importance to you, and you'll want to make sure that you find someone who can deliver. For example, if you need space for a specific need such as a gymnastics studio, you'd like a broker with imagination who can think creatively about adapting space to your highly special needs.

4. Would they use the same broker again? This question appears rather obvious, but in fact it's very useful because you'll typically get information that a specific question might not have elicited. For instance, you'll often hear a response that starts "Well, yes, because what I really liked was ..." The rest of the sentence often recounts a personal trait or professional skill, such as attention to detail, which may be important to you.

2. Questions to Ask the Broker

When you're ready to speak with a few brokers who have been recommended by others, make an appointment with each one and come equipped with the following questions.

1. What is the broker's experience with commercial needs like yours? Hopefully, you already know that the broker is familiar with the needs of businesses like yours. But if you're not sure—or even if you think you have a specialist—it's wise to confirm your conclusions. A good starting point is to show the broker your Rental Priorities Worksheet and ask if the broker can help with your kinds of needs. Ask for references from small businesses like yours.

2. What is the size of the real estate office? Sometimes you'll have a choice between a broker in a large real estate office and one in a smaller one. If you're a small business owner with modest space needs, it's possible to get lost in the shuffle if you go with a large firm that primarily deals with big tenants who need space of 10,000 square feet or more. The result may be that you'll get stuck with a less-experienced broker.

3. What are the compensation practices of the broker's office? Most brokers earn their money by straight commissions—they're not salaried. (The various ways to pay your broker are explained in Section F1, below.) Since the commission goes up as the length of the lease, the square footage, and the rent increase, brokers' interests are not exactly aligned with yours. And none of the commission gets paid until the deal is inked, which puts tremendous pressure on brokers to close the deal and move on to the next one. Larger firms, however, may place some brokers on partial salary, reducing their dependence on commissions, which may lessen the pressure to inflate the lease and finalize the lease as soon as possible. This translates into a more long-term approach to your space hunt. For example, a broker on salary might caution you to look further or to renew an existing lease instead of relocating.

Don't be overly impressed by sales skills. Remember that your broker has probably been a salesperson at some time or other (while working as a landlord's broker, for instance). But when a broker works for you, sales skills are less important than hard work, patience, and connections. And don't let your assessment of the broker be driven by the broker's self-promotion—a specialized type of sales pitch.

F. Signing a Contract With Your Broker

If you're satisfied that the skill level, experience, professional situation, and personal style of a broker will suit you, it's time to sign a written contract to cement the relationship. Doing so will protect you from misunderstandings that commonly arise in working relationships that are based on only a handshake, with no written evidence of your agreement.

The broker may produce a preprinted "standard contract," which you'll be asked to sign. If so, proceed with caution. Just as there's no such thing as a standard lease, there's no such thing as a standard broker's contract. It's all negotiable. In this section, we'll look at some issues to consider when you and your broker put together a contract, such as:

- how you will pay your broker
- whether the broker has an "exclusive" or "nonexclusive" arrangement with you
- how your broker will handle any conflicts of interest that may arise, and
- the details of the legwork the broker will do for you.

Hire a broker, not a firm. The last thing you want is to be stuck with a broker's colleague if your broker changes jobs midstream. Be sure to have it in writing: If the broker leaves, you have the option to cancel the contract and go with him.

1. Paying Your Broker

There are no hard-and-fast rules governing how you'll pay your broker. The most common way is to pay the broker a commission based on the value of the lease. This approach is quite problematic for tenants, since it puts the broker's financial interests at odds with yours, as explained in the section describing commissions, below. Fortunately, there are other ways to compensate your broker.

Commission. The broker earns a percentage of the rent over the life of the lease. More precisely, the broker's fee goes up as the tenant's rent, square footage, and lease term increase. But high rent is not in your interests, nor is unnecessary space or a lease term that is too long for your business needs or plans. In short, working on commission introduces a total conflict of interest between you and your broker. Most often the landlord pays the broker, but you'll still be stuck with a high rent, excess space, or a needlessly long lease. The alternative methods of paying brokers avoid this conflict, as you'll see by reading below.

Here's how the commission scheme works in practice. For example, if you're leasing 2,000 square feet at $20 a square foot for three years, the total rent is $120,000 (2,000 x $20 x 3). A 3% commission would amount to $3,600.

If your contract with your broker provides that the broker will be paid only on commission, the broker won't earn anything unless you sign a lease. Sometimes, a broker will ask for an advance against the hoped-for commission (called a retainer), which is deducted from the commission once it's earned. If you don't sign a lease, the broker must return the retainer.

Flat fee. You pay a fixed amount (such as $2,000) for the broker's efforts in looking for space for you, regardless of the success at finding suitable space.

Fee based on success. You pay a fixed amount only if the broker's efforts result in your signing a lease.

Hourly Fee. You pay by the hour for the broker's time.

You and the broker aren't limited to choosing only one payment method. For example, you might agree to pay an hourly fee that will be credited toward a success fee if you ultimately sign a lease.

Which arrangement is best suited for you? Naturally, you'd like energetic assistance with the minimum of expense—and many in the leasing game will tell you that this means choosing some variation on a commission arrangement. There is no simple cure, however, to the conflict problem noted above. Even though you have contracted to pay your broker's commission, many landlords will pick up that expense instead. Here is how it works:

- **The space was listed with a landlord's broker.** If you lease space that's been listed, it's customary for the landlord to split the commission he owes his broker with your broker.
- **The space was unlisted.** If you lease space that was *not* listed with a

broker, the landlord may still pay your broker's commission—primarily to build up goodwill in the real estate community. But if the landlord isn't so inclined, you'll probably be the one to pay the broker. To protect yourself against having to pay an entire commission if the landlord balks, provide in your contract with the broker that the broker will instead accept a lesser, fixed fee from you.

Depending on the fee method you agree on, make sure your contract with your broker covers these additional points:

- **When is the payment due—in installments (if you pay by the hour) or when you've signed a lease?** If the latter, how much time do you have to pay the fee? Naturally, the longer you have to pay the fee, the better, since you'll be incurring moving and leasing expenses at a rapid rate.
- **Do you have to pick up the tab for the broker's expenses, such as travel and advertising?** Obviously, you'd prefer not to.
- **If you pay a retainer or an hourly rate, will you be entitled to a rebate if your broker receives a commission from the landlord?** This understanding is fair, and you'll want to push for it.
- **If you pay a retainer or an hourly rate, will it count toward any commission that you may have to pay?** It should.
- **If the landlord pays a commission, will you still have to pay a success fee?** You shouldn't.

2. Exclusive and Nonexclusive Arrangements

Your contract with your broker needs to resolve more than the matter of who pays the broker. The two of you must decide whether the broker has an *exclusive* relationship with you or a *nonexclusive* one.

Exclusive. The broker earns a fee whether you sign a lease through the efforts of the broker or through anyone else, or even on your own.

> **EXAMPLE:** Tenant Tom signs an exclusive contract with broker Bob. Tom finds space through a newspaper ad and signs a lease. He owes a fee to Bob.

Nonexclusive. You owe the broker a fee only if you sign a lease through the efforts of the broker. The broker does not earn a fee if you find space on your own.

> **EXAMPLE:** Tenant Tom signs a nonexclusive contract with broker Bob. Tom finds space through a sign in a window. He does not owe a fee to Bob.

Most brokers will prefer, naturally enough, to have an exclusive relationship with you. It will commit you to seriously using their expertise and contacts, since you'll have to pay them when you lease any space. Working under a nonexclusive arrangement exposes the broker to the disappointing possibility of working long and hard for you, only to have you secure space on your own. From your prospective, however, you won't want to sign an exclusive contract unless you have high confidence in the broker's ability to deliver a rental, since there's no incentive for you to seek space on your own.

If you are interested in renting space in a particular building or shopping center, you and the broker can agree that you'll owe the broker a fee only if the broker succeeds in delivering space in the property specified in the contract. This arrangement will work well for you if you'd like to be able to do some space-finding on your own, but want an advocate when it comes to certain properties. For example, there may be one or two large, sophisticated landlords who have properties that might suit your needs. You've wisely concluded that you'd like the assistance of a broker when dealing with these owners. On the other hand, you figure you could handle less daunting owners yourself. A contract that limits your broker to pursuing space in the properties owned by sophisticated players frees you to pursue other deals on your own.

> **EXAMPLE:** Tenant Tom signs a specific space contract with broker Bob to secure space in either the regional Riverside Mall or the equally large Country Time Plaza. Tom winds up leasing space from a single-rental landlord on a city street downtown. He does not owe a fee to Bob.

3. Avoiding Conflicts of Interest With Your Broker

Although your broker is duty-bound to find you the best space at the best terms, you can't ignore the fact that the broker or others in the office will represent other tenants along the way—some, perhaps, with space needs similar to yours. And unless you've retained a tenant's broker exclusively, the brokerage may have landlord clients, too—including some who might have space that you will want to see. In either situation, the broker may end up representing two competing parties (two tenant-clients or one tenant-client and one landlord-client). Or, your broker will realize she's representing one party (you) while her associate at the next desk is representing the other (the landlord). Your contract with the broker is the place to address these potential conflicts.

a. Conflicts With Other Tenant-Clients

It's common for experienced real estate brokers to specialize in certain types of space or neighborhoods; that degree of specialization is generally a plus for you. However, the narrower the broker's field, the more likely it will be that the broker will have more than one client who is looking for similar space. Who gets to see the property first? And if both clients are interested, whose interests does the broker push?

For instance, let's say that you're looking for space for a restaurant and the broker has another tenant-client who's looking for similar space. What happens if a terrific restaurant space becomes available? There are two common solutions:

- **The broker bows out.** You can specify in the contract that the broker won't represent either one of you but will find other qualified brokers for each of you.
- **The eager client prevails.** A second solution is to say that the broker will represent the first client who expresses serious interest in the space.

b. Conflicts With Landlord-Clients

If your broker, or anyone in the office, also handles listings for landlords, it's possible that you'll become interested in the property owned by the broker's landlord-client. Your broker cannot effectively represent both of you, since your interests are clearly adverse. Nor can she negotiate against a member of her own office. How should your contract deal with this dilemma? There are two solutions, explained below.

Exclude that particular space. You can specify that space listed by the broker's office is excluded from the range of properties your broker will show you. This will mean that you won't be able to ask your broker to show you these properties or represent you in negotiations with the landlord. But if you really want to pursue a space listed by your broker's office, you

will need the right to terminate the contract so that you can engage another broker. If this is the route you want, be sure that your contract with the broker specifies that you have an option to terminate in this situation if it arises.

Ask the broker to act as a dual agent. The other solution is to ask the broker to act as a dual agent (dual agents are brokers who assume a neutral position in space hunting and lease negotiations, as explained above in Section B4). Here, if the broker's relationship with a landlord-client predates yours, you'll need the landlord-client's consent for the broker to work as a dual agent. A landlord may be willing to give up the benefit of an advocate in exchange for a tepid go-between if you are a desirable tenant who is seriously interested in the space. Conversely, if a landlord approaches your broker (or someone in the office) *after* you have signed a contract with the broker, the landlord will need *your* consent before your broker can be transformed from your advocate into a dual broker.

You can probably see already that neither of the above solutions is very satisfactory. You won't be happy narrowing your range of possibilities if you have to exclude appropriate space. If you terminate your contract and engage a new broker, you'll find yourself negotiating against someone (your ex) who may have a lot of important information about you—your needs, financial situation, and bargaining intentions. And the alternative—reducing your broker to the status of a dual agent—leaves you without a strong advocate. One way to avoid these complications is to look for and hire a broker who works only for tenants, as emphasized several times above.

A trial marriage can mean an easy divorce. See if the broker will agree in the contract that either of you can cancel the contract during the first 15 or 30 days. This will give both of you chance to see if the relationship is working—if it isn't, you can end it easily. Try to include language entitling you to a refund of any fees you pay up front, except for costs actually incurred by the broker, such as those for advertising.

4. Clarify the Details in Writing

Your broker may be willing to perform more services than just showing you space and helping to negotiate a lease. You can expect extra services if you're hiring the broker yourself, as explained in Section C, above. Even if you are not paying the broker directly, you may be able to arrange for some additional services. For example, the broker may be willing to get traffic flow data, utility bill information, or zoning details. Brokers can also arrange for inspections and line up contractors to finish, or "build out," the space. And your broker may promise to show you a minimum number of properties within a specified time, or canvass a specific geographic area. If you and your broker come to understandings like these, don't just rely on the broker's

oral promise. Be sure to list these duties in the contract you sign with the broker.

5. Provide for Searching Without the Broker

At the end of your agreement with the broker, you may find yourself still without a lease. You can, of course, extend the agreement, but you may want instead to terminate the relationship. Problems may arise if you soon thereafter sign a lease for a property that the broker brought to your attention, even if lease negotiations had not started when the broker was still under contract with you.

There's a fair way to handle this situation. Provide that if you sign a lease on your own with a landlord whom the broker brought to you within six months of the end of the brokerage contract, you'll pay full fees. True, this binds you longer than you might wish, but if it also protects the broker from easy abuse from clients who plan an end run.

G. Handling Problems With Your Broker

If you're careful when choosing a broker and spell out your agreement in a contract, you'll reduce the chances of disputes later—but there's no guarantee that all will be smooth sailing. The secret, of course, is spotting problems early. This section lists some common signs of trouble and possible solutions.

1. Signs of Trouble

If you encounter any of the following difficulties, you know that you need to take action:

- **Are your questions being answered?** If important issues are addressed poorly —or not at all—watch out. Eager to close the deal, your broker may be afraid that candor will get in the way. For example, if the broker blows off questions about environmental hazards on or near the property, or if you can't get a straight response to your query regarding the anticipated jump in the landlord's property taxes (you'll probably end up paying for some of it), get pushy.

- **Are there available rentals that the broker is *not* showing you?** A broker who steers you toward certain properties (such as those listed with his office or that promise a higher commission) and away from others may have hidden motives for doing so. It's appropriate to be suspicious. Your broker is supposed to be showing you space that's most suitable for your needs, no matter where it is.

- **Are you being rushed?** Anxious to close the deal and earn the commission, a broker may minimize or gloss over problems with a space or a deal, or

fail to disclose key information. For instance, you may not be told that the anchor tenant in the shopping center you're considering is about to move out. If you're the last to learn about important details like this, be advised: You aren't getting the full, undivided attention of your broker.

- **Is the broker disclosing key information about you?** Your broker may not share important information about you— such as your need to move immediately or your key negotiating points —with the landlord or the landlord's broker. True, this information may speed up the bargaining, but it may also make it harder for you to strike the best possible deal. If you learn that your secrets are being shared, it may be due to the broker's eagerness to close a deal—*any* deal—irrespective of what's best for you.

2. Resolving Problems

If you've kept the lines of communication open with your broker, a face-to-face airing of your grievances may suffice to get things back on the right track. Sometimes, however, depending on the nature of the problem, you need to consider more drastic action, such as:

- **Complaining to the broker's boss, if there is one.** To preserve goodwill, the boss may either take steps to correct the problem or agree to terminate the brokerage contract.

- **Filing a grievance with the local real estate board—or even with the state licensing authorities.** A broker may quickly make peace with you rather than face an embarrassing disciplinary hearing.
- **Agreeing with the broker to arbitrate or mediate your dispute.** The local real estate board may have a procedure in place to handle disagreements.

Contact the state agency that regulates real estate brokers for information on real estate laws and regulations and complaint procedures. Many state agencies have websites. Find yours by looking at your state's home page for the real estate department or commission. To get started, see FirstGov.gov at www.firstgov.gov.

3. Firing Your Broker

If communications have totally stalled or broken down, or your best efforts to improve your broker's performance yield no results, it may be time to end the relationship, as explained below.

There are two common legal grounds for firing a broker. If you can prove them, you're unlikely to be second-guessed by a judge or mediator should your ex-broker file a legal action against you. They are:

- **Breach of contract.** Your written contract should state what your broker's duties are. For example, your contract may say that the broker will show you at least four appropriate spaces within 45 days. If the broker is a slacker and shows you only one space, that's a breach of contract and you probably have the legal right to end the contract.
- **Breach of fiduciary duty.** Even if your contract doesn't specifically say so, you have a right to your broker's undivided loyalty. For example, your broker can't disclose to the landlord or other brokers that you're under extreme pressure to move into new space within 60 days and are prepared to pay top dollar to meet that deadline. Leaking this information without your permission can, of course, undermine your bargaining position—and it's a serious breach of your broker's fiduciary duty. This usually would give you the legal right to fire the broker.

Seek legal advice before you fire your broker. Firing a broker when you don't have a valid legal reason to do so can have serious consequences. For example, if you dismiss your broker improperly but go on to sign a lease on your own or with another broker, you may be liable for the first broker's commission or you may owe other fees under your contract. Since analyzing your ability to fire your broker without repercussions can be daunting, your best bet is to seek advice from an experienced real estate lawyer. A precipitous or unwise decision could come back to haunt you in the form of legal hassles and commission expenses.

Checklist for Finding Space and Working With Brokers

You now have a good idea of how to find suitable space, and you're well-equipped to deal with brokers, be they the landlord's, yours, or one you share with the property owner. You should be in a great position to:

- turn the space-finding options in this chapter into a strategy appropriate for your business
- consider hiring your own broker, especially if the landlord will have one, and particularly if your needs are unique or space is at a premium, and
- find, hire, and work with a broker, even in the complex situation of sharing a broker with the landlord.

■

Chapter 3

Evaluating the Space and the Landlord

Read This Chapter If ...

This chapter is for tenants who have narrowed their search to a particular space, who need to find out more about their prospective landlord, and who suspect that environmental issues might arise. It's especially useful in the following situations:

- You have identified a likely rental and need to determine if it's really appropriate, in terms of size, applicable zoning laws, and its amenability to conform to your design needs.
- You have reason to think that this site has a history with nasty chemicals that could form the basis of an environmental problem for you down the line.
- You will be asked to put down a holding deposit.
- You will be subletting from another tenant.

You can skip this chapter if you're confident that the space you've found is just right and free of any zoning, design, or toxic worries, and you know who your landlord is and how to check up on her financial stability (you can be sure she'll check on yours).

Looking for a space for your business involves a combination of the practical and the emotional:

- "How will my furniture and equipment fit?"
- "Can I afford this place?"
- "Can the space be modified to meet my needs?"
- "Is it available when I need it?"
- "How will my colleagues and I feel about working here?"
- "How will my customers view the space?"
- "Can I stand the daily commute?"

When you compare spaces, you may have to juggle a number of factors, since every rental will have its pluses and minuses. And don't forget the fact that every space has an intangible aspect—the landlord-tenant relationship—that can often spell the difference between a place that works out perfectly and a place that turns out to be just one headache after another. You shouldn't sign a lease until all of your important needs have been addressed.

This chapter guides you through the steps you'll take as you zero in on a suitable rental—from your first visit to more thorough investigation (about the space and the landlord), ending with an eventual decision.

A. Visiting and Evaluating Prospective Space

Since you probably don't have unlimited time available to choose a rental space, you need to make the search process as efficient as possible. This means you'll want to focus on the space that meets your highest priorities. Don't waste time on places that are over-priced, too small, or in second-rate loca-tions. This section explains how to ask the right questions and look in the right places for any space you're seriously considering.

1. Basic Tips for Visiting Rental Spaces

An organized, methodical approach to looking at available spaces will save you lots of time and energy. Here are some key tips to make the search less trying:

Make an appointment. Contact the land-lord, building manager, or broker to arrange for an appointment to visit the property.

Take your time. If you're looking at several commercial spaces on the same day, sched-ule appointments so you're not rushed. For one thing, you want to allow sufficient time to look around, take measurements, and make notes. For another, you want to be on time for your next appointment. Show-ing up late or appearing rushed can make a bad impression on the very landlords and building managers with whom you may soon be negotiating. For space that has real possibilities, definitely return for a second and third look—perhaps bringing along a colleague, spouse, or friend for a second opinion.

Be prepared. Come equipped with a street map, notebook, pen or pencil (or your laptop or handheld computer), pocket calculator, tape measure (to make sure your square footage computations match those of the landlord and to check if your rosewood desk will fit), graph paper, and a camera. Of course, bring your Rental Priori-ties Worksheet (see Chapter 1, Section B, and specific instructions below). It's also a good idea to bring your checkbook, just in case you need to post a good-faith deposit to convince the landlord to hold the space for you until you complete your investigation. (Holding deposits are discussed below in Section F.)

Make a good impression. Especially when space is tight, the landlord may be looking at more than your ability to pay the rent. Everything else being equal, the landlord will prefer a tenant who appears to be businesslike and agreeable, rather than an overly demanding person who will cease-lessly complain about trivial things. For ex-ample, if you spot some fairly minor problems that need fixing—you'd like to replace the fluorescent lighting with incan-descent fixtures—don't mention these items immediately. Save this type of concern for the lease negotiations, after it's clear that the landlord is interested in having you become a tenant.

2. Use Your Rental Priorities Worksheet

If you've done your work in Chapter 1, you'll have before you a list of rental priorities—the Essentials, Compromises, and Unacceptables. We suggested that you enter these on a master Rental Priorities Worksheet, which you should take with you whenever you visit potential space. Follow these steps to use your worksheet:

Step 1: Enter the address, contact person's name, phone number, and email address, plus rent and other key rental terms on the top of the form.

Step 2: As you walk around the space and talk with the landlord, manager or broker, note which Essentials and Compromises are satisfied by this property. If there are aspects that fit your Unacceptables, note those, too.

Step 3: Investigate the lease early on. You want to make sure that you won't be stuck with clauses your business can't live with—for example, a provision requiring a ten-year minimum commitment or one requiring you to keep your business open from 10 a.m. to 9 p.m., Monday through Saturday. (If you've engaged a broker, the broker ought to have given you an idea of the key lease points already.) If the landlord is married to these clauses, you'll want to know that as soon as possible. Be sure to read Chapter 2 for information on brokers, and consult the relevant discussions throughout this book on specific lease clauses.

Step 4: Make notes next to a particular feature that can be changed to meet your needs—for example, "Plumbing is in place for possible private restroom," or "West interior wall may be removable." Commercial landlords are far more likely than residential landlords to allow you to change or customize space to fit your needs. Chapter 11 explains how to negotiate and pay for tenant improvements.

Step 5: Jot down additional features in the section for Notes, such as "Nearby building to be completed in July will add potential customers," or "Prestigious tenants in area will help create the image we're trying to establish."

Below you will find a sample Rental Priorities Worksheet for Terri's Threads, the consignment shop we first met in Chapter 1.

3. Special Issues on Your First Walk-Through

As you walk through the building or office space, filling in your Rental Priorities Worksheet and asking questions, be sure to look around carefully for signs of problems. Make a note of any items of concern but, again, restrain yourself for now from reciting your criticisms to the landlord, manager,

Rental Priorities Worksheet for "Terri's Threads"

Address: ___1234 College Avenue___

Contact: ___Ira Devine___

Phone #: ___555-123-4567___   Email: ___wesellum@coldmail.com___

Rent: ___$2,000___   Deposit: ___One month's rent___

Other Fees: ___Neighborhood Merchants' Association, $100 per month___

Term: ___3 to 5 years___ Date Seen: ___March 3, 20XX___ Date Available: ___April 15, 20XX___

Brief description of rental space and building: _____

___One-story, two-room space in building with three other tenants. Two front entrances,___

___one back door, plateglass windows.___

Essentials:

Yes No

☒ ☐ 1. Near residential shopping area, upscale neighborhood, lots of foot traffic. ___Area is trendy, going upscale, near university and on one major bus route. Underground Metro station one block away.___

☒ ☐ 2. Rent less than $2,000 per month. ___Just makes it, but merchants' association fees and janitorial service will add more.___

☒ ☐ 3. Minimum 1,000 square feet. ___At 1,300 square feet, it's fine.___

☐ ☒ 4. Separate employee and customer restrooms. ___Only one bathroom.___

☒ ☐ 5. One floor, rectangular, separate storage room(s) in back. ___Small storage room in rear.___

☐ ☐ 6. Sufficient electrical outlets and capacities to support computers for inventory and accounts. ___Could be a problem. Need to check with current tenant and electrician re adding outlets, capacity of circuits.___

☒ ☐ 7. Available by March 1. ___Available now, no problem.___

Rental Priorities Worksheet for "Terri's Threads" (continued)

Compromise:

Yes   No

[X]   [ ]   1. Parking on street or by arrangement in nearby lot. _Some street parking._
Grocery store next door; may be able to rent spaces in that lot.

[X]   [ ]   2. Main interior space divisible into two rooms (one for examining clothing brought in by consignees). _Excellent potential for dividing intake from_
sales area.

[X]   [ ]   3. Ability to locate two sets of dressing rooms along opposite walls. _No_
problem; lots of clear wall area where we can put partitions.

[ ]   [ ]   4. Neighboring businesses stay open into early evening at least one day per week. _Quick check of neighborhood shows Thursday as the open night. Need_
to check with merchants' association.

[ ]   [ ]   5. Landlord willing to lease for 3-5 years and give option to extend longer.
3 to 5 seems a possibility. Doubt landlord will go for an option to extend
(neighborhood going upscale, rents may increase a lot).

[X]   [ ]   6. Major transportation lines nearby. _____
Got it.

Unacceptable:

Yes   No

[X]   [ ]   1. Risky crime area. _Appears to be okay. Need to check with local police to get_
crime stats.

[X]   [ ]   2. Other consignment shops within a three-mile radius. _Initial drive-around_
and phone book check reveal none.

[X]   [ ]   3. No lease less than three years. _okay on this._

[ ]   [ ]   4. No personal guarantee for the rent. _Appears not to need a guarantee;_
double-check with broker.

Notes: _This is really great space. Minimal improvements (repaint and ask for carpet),_
although electrical circuitry may be a problem (expensive to expand?). LL knows this area is
getting hot and will probably build in some rent escalation. Push for longest possible lease
or options to extend.

or broker. If you decide to pursue this space, you may want to hire an expert to assess these features, as described in Section B, below. Here are some special things to consider in your first walk-through. Some of these issues may already be noted on your Rental Priorities Worksheet. If not, consider these now.

- **Image.** Look carefully at the impression the building will make on your customers and clients. If it looks shabby to you, it will probably look shabby to others. Appearances do count in many—though not all—businesses. For example, customers won't expect a salvage yard to be spic and span— they'll be delighted if the yard has what they want, no matter what pile it's found under.

- **Damage.** Watch for obvious problems such as loose steps, torn carpet, missing floor tiles, or light fixtures that don't work. Defects that are easily removed, fixed, or covered are less important than those that are expensive to repair or over which you have no control, such as a poor roof.

- **Plumbing.** Check the plumbing by turning on the water faucets and flushing the toilet. Make sure the water pressure and temperature are adequate.

- **Windows.** Make sure that the operable windows (unfortunately, a rarity today) open and close easily. Windows that are accessible from the street, the roof, or adjoining buildings should be

equipped with locks, to prevent burglaries.

- **Security.** Think about how secure the space is in view of the crime history of the neighborhood and the likelihood that your business will be a target. Make sure the doors and locks are in good shape and sturdy enough to deter would-be intruders. Visit a potential site at different times of the day and evening. Is there adequate street and other lighting? Do the drug dealers come out after dark? Is it going to be safe in the evening if you or your employees are working late?

- **Heating and cooling.** Examine the heating, cooling, and ventilation systems. See if there is adequate ductwork to serve all areas, including those that might be enclosed by new walls. Note where the thermostat is located and if there are multiple thermostats for different zones. Determine if you can control the temperature. And make sure that heating, cooling, and ventilation are available outside of normal working hours if this is important to your business.

- **Elevators and common areas.** Walk around the building and check out the elevators, stairways, storage areas, and lobbies. Think about whether disabled people will be able to make their way around without unusual difficulty. You may be obligated to make the space accessible under the Americans With Disabilities Act (discussed in Chapter 12, Section D).

- **Parking.** Investigate the parking situation and, in the case of on-site parking, observe how convenient the space is, whether it's crowded, and whether spaces are set aside for individual tenants.
- **Issues unique to your business.** If you have special requirements—a reception area for a professional's office, for example—check to see whether this feature is already in place or can be added.

Assuming that the space has some possibilities for you, try to evaluate how difficult (and expensive) it would be to fix the problems. Cosmetic changes such as painting the walls are easy and inexpensive. Installing a much wider entry door or reinforcing the floor to accommodate your equipment may be more difficult and costly if it involves structural changes. While tenants and landlords often negotiate substantial improvements in the space (as discussed in Chapter 11), it's normally far better to deal with space that requires relatively little renovation to meet your needs.

Sometimes, problems that look insurmountable can be turned to your advantage by a little imagination. That odd jog in the wall may be the perfect place to house your fax machine or locate your bottled water cooler. Installing a partition may create a private office area for your retail store. At this stage, just content yourself with speculating about some of the possibilities. If negotiations get serious, you can

seek advice from experts such as space planners and contractors as discussed below. Problem space can often be fixed to overcome the problems.

B. Further Investigation of Promising Space

If the special needs of your business are straightforward and few, you may decide, after visiting a prospective site two or three times, that it will do quite nicely. You can then go on to negotiate the lease with the landlord, as we explain in Chapters 5 and 6. But not everyone can proceed so quickly. You may feel that, while the space has several strong points in its favor (rent, location, parking, and image, for example), you ought to investigate some more. It's better to take the time and possibly spend some money now to confirm the suitability of the space than to sign a lease, move in, and then be miserable because of an unresolved problem. Here are some avenues of further investigation worth thinking about.

The bigger your investment, the more you need to investigate. If you are looking at a short-term lease, little rent, or no outlay for improvements, you won't lose too much if the space doesn't work out. But if the rent is significant and the lease term long, and particularly if you expect to spend a lot of money on improvements, it pays to check things out very thoroughly now.

1. Zoning, Building Permits, and Sign Ordinances

Local ordinances can affect your ability to use the space the way you'd like to. For example, a zoning ordinance that allows offices in a certain district may not permit retail uses, and vice versa; or light manufacturing may have a district all its own. The landlord or broker should be familiar with how the property is zoned. Still, it pays to check with a zoning official at City Hall—they're usually part of the planning or building department—to confirm whether the space you're considering is zoned for your business. If the zoning provisions exclude your business, you may decide to try to get an exception (called a variance), but you'll probably need some legal assistance at least at the outset. Like counting your chickens, it's almost always a bad idea to sign a lease before the variance is a reality.

Renovation work such as significant electrical expansions or major plumbing work will require a permit from the building department, and must comply with local building code requirements. Before granting the permit, the building department will review the plans put together by your space planner or contractor to see if they'll pass muster. If your renovations are major and involve substantial construction work, you may have to meet the accessibility requirements of the Americans With Disabilities Act, explained in Chapter 12, Section D.

Signage may also be important to you. Many municipalities have ordinances regulating the size, number, and type of signs that a business can have. If your retail business depends on flashy, eye-catching signs, make sure these will be permitted under any local sign ordinance.

Watch out for possible condemnation. If the space that interests you is threatened by condemnation—a takeover by a government entity for public use—think long and hard about taking a chance. The rent may be low precisely because this cloud hangs over the property. You'll need to pay special attention to the condemnation clause in the lease. See Chapter 17, Section C, for more information on this.

2. Special Business Permits

Depending on the nature of your business, you may need to get a special permit or license before you can open shop. (Don't confuse zoning and permits: Zoning laws regulate where a business can set up shop; permits and licenses control whether they can go into operation.) If you plan to open a restaurant, for example, you'll need to be sure your kitchen gets health department approval and perhaps fire department approval as well. You may also need a liquor license.

Lots of businesses need licenses or permits. The list may include child care centers, gas stations, food stores, dry cleaners, movie houses, and many others. For information on licensing or permit requirements that may affect you, contact the state, county, or city agencies and departments that regulate your business. Be clear on what the requirements are. If you ignore a permit or license requirement, your business can be shut down and you may have to pay a fine as well.

3. Contractor's Inspection and Other Experts' Advice

Your careful visits to a prospective site should give you a good sense of the space's physical condition. Sometimes you need information from someone more experienced in structural matters—for example, a structural engineer or architect, especially if you live in an earthquake or hurricane area. Getting expert advice is wise if you think you'll need substantial renovations—you need to know if the proposed changes are feasible and can be done at reasonable expense. And if your lease will require you to pay some or all of the maintenance and repair costs, you'll want an expert's opinion on what to anticipate. This information will also be invaluable when you negotiate with the landlord over who pays for your improvements (a subject covered in Chapter 11).

If you are renting a large space in an older building for a long term, it can make sense to hire a licensed contractor to thoroughly inspect the space. For a few hundred dol-lars, you can get a written report on the soundness of the roof, walls, and floor; as well as the heating, ventilating, and air-conditioning (HVAC), plumbing, and electrical systems. If necessary, the contractor can bring in inspectors or experts. This information will be critical to you if you have a "net" lease, in which you pay a portion of the landlord's ongoing operating costs. You'll want to know now whether you can expect to be billed for a new roof, air-conditioning system, or other major building system that's on its last legs now. (Net leases are explained in detail in Chapter 9.)

The contractor can also comment on the feasibility of your proposed improvements and the cost—perhaps also suggesting alternatives that will be less expensive.

A reliable personal recommendation is the best way to find an experienced inspector. You can also get referrals from the American Society of Housing Inspectors (ASHI) by checking their website at www.ashi.com.

4. Complex Utility Needs

If you have unique utility needs, such as a requirement for large amounts of electricity, gas, or phone service, hopefully you've already raised your concerns with the land-lord and have received assurances. Or, you've contacted the appropriate service provider and have learned that it will be possible to fill your request. For example, a telemarketing company will need a level of telephone service not required by most businesses. Knowing that, it would be wise to check with the phone company. If they can't expand their service to accommodate you, best to find out now.

5. Space Planners

A space planner is basically an interior designer who's heavy on practicality and light on frills. A good planner can help you adapt a space to your needs. Some space planners are listed as interior designers in the phone book, while others work for architecture firms or stores that sell office furniture and equipment. Space planners not only give advice but may also be able to order furniture and equipment for you at a discount and recommend reputable contractors.

Typically, you explain to the space planner how your business works, including the flow of work, the sharing of equipment, and the amount of customer space needed. The planner then comes up with a floor design that shows how the space can be laid out for maximum efficiency. Either working alone or together with a contractor or architect, the space planner can also design plans and specifications. In addition, the space planner may be able to help you decide on furniture, equipment, and decoration. The planner can, for example, recommend and order floor covering, paint, and wall covering, and even appropriate artwork.

You may get some help with space planning from your landlord. Many landlords have ongoing relationships with a space planner who is familiar with the building. The landlord may be willing to pay the space planner to explore how the space can be adapted for your business. Some landlords provide this service on a no-cost, no-obligation basis, treating the expense simply as a cost of doing business. You're more likely to encounter this service if you lease a large space for a lengthy lease term than a small space for a short while.

Keep in mind that the quality of service provided by space planners whose service is free when you purchase office furniture or equipment may not be as high as an independent professional planner. If your business is unusual, or you have specific requirements that are not easily understood or translated into plans, you may want to hire your own space planner— someone you know can meet your needs. If you hire someone, be sure to check out the planner's qualifications for your business needs by asking for references and even looking at other projects that the planner has designed.

EXAMPLE: Jane and Barry decide to open a child care facility in a suburban shopping mall. They have years of experience and know that the center will run best if play areas, nap rooms, and outside playgrounds are arranged in a certain sequence. They hire their own space planner, who has worked many times in local schools. The planner quickly assesses the pros and cons of the space and advises Jane and Barry on how much it will cost to erect walls, create an additional entrance, and install soundproofing.

C. Environmental Issues to Consider When Evaluating Space

If you're looking at space in a building where hazardous or polluting substances such as solvents or gasoline may have been used, you'll want to ask the landlord what those substances were, when they were used, and how much may be still stored (or simply present) in the building. Depending on what you find, it may be wise to order an environmental inspection before you sign a lease. You don't want to find out in the midst of your lease term that you're sitting on top of a toxic puddle.

➡ **If you're renting office space, chances are you can skip this section on environmental issues.** Office buildings are unlikely to harbor environmental problems for which the government could hold you responsible. Retail tenants are also not likely to have worries. Tenants who will rent industrial space need to pay attention, however.

There may be health concerns of a more immediate nature, too. If the building has deteriorating asbestos or lead paint, or high levels of radon, you need to find out now.

1. Why Pay Attention to Environmental Problems?

Your concern for the environment, your health, and that of customers and employees is certainly motivation enough to check out potential problems. Lest you be tempted to take the issue lightly, however, you should understand that if an environmental pollution problem lands on your doorstep, you have a legal problem of significant proportions. It's in a totally different league, money-wise and headache-wise, than a fight with your landlord over your improvement allowance, a dispute with local authorities over a permit or zoning variance, or a slip-and-trip lawsuit with a customer. Here's why.

- **You may have to pay the entire cost of clean-up even if you were only slightly responsible.** If you're partly at fault for the problem—let's say you use leaky chemical storage tanks that prior tenants have used, too—you can't count limiting your financial responsibility for the consequences. Courtesy of a legal principle known as "joint and several liability," you could end up footing the entire bill for the clean-up cost.
- **Your "compliance with all laws" lease clause may make you responsible.** Your landlord's lease will probably include

What's Covered by the Anticontamination Laws

Many very powerful federal and state laws (and some local laws) target environmental contamination and hazardous substances, including:

- petroleum and petroleum-based products and solvents, natural gas, natural gas liquids, liquefied natural gas, and synthetic gas
- PCBs
- asbestos and asbestos-containing materials
- biological wastes, including sewage, garbage, and waste products from health care facilities or offices
- lead-based paint, and
- other biological or chemical toxins (including those that may be identified in future legislation).

The federal government prohibits, monitors, and regulates environmental contamination via two hefty pieces of legislation:

- The Resource Conservation and Recovery Act of 1976 (42 U.S.C. §§ 6901 and following), often referred to as "RCRA," which deals with contamination leaking from underground storage tanks, and
- The Comprehensive Environmental Response, Compensation, and Liability Act of 1980 (42 U.S.C. §§ 9601-9675), or CERCLA, commonly referred to as the "Superfund," which covers chemical contaminants released from just about everything except underground tanks. Owners and tenants who know of contamination on their property must not only notify the government of its presence, but must then take steps to clean it up.

In addition to these major laws, there are other federal laws that may apply to the property that you are leasing or the operation you intend to run. They include:

- the Clean Air Act (CAA; 42 U.S.C. § 7401 and following), which deals with pollutants released into the air
- the Toxic Substances Control Act (TSCA, 42 U.S.C. § 2601 and following), which tests, regulates, and screens all chemicals produced or imported into the United States that are intended to reach the consumer marketplace
- the Occupational Safety and Health Act (OSHA, 29 U.S.C. § 651 and following), which covers working conditions for you and employees, and
- the Federal Water Pollution Control Act (FWPCA, 33 U.S.C. § 1251 and following), which covers contamination of fresh- and saltwater bodies.

In addition to the federal government, many states (and some localities) have enacted their own statutes and regulations concerning environmental safety in business establishments. Some cover the same ground as their federal counterparts, but many are more stringent and far-reaching. Owners and tenants are held to the most demanding requirements.

The Environmental Protection Agency (EPA) maintains a very useful website at www.epa.gov, which includes links to all federal legislation concerning the environment, plus a small business section that includes frequently asked questions. For information on state and local laws that may apply in your situation, call your state's office of environmental management or use the EPA's listing of state and local offices at www.epa.gov/epapages/statelocal/envrolst.htm.

a clause in which you promise to comply with all laws. This clause is explained in detail in Chapter 12, Section C. For now, understand that this seemingly innocent promise can make you accountable for contamination that surfaces during your tenancy —even if you neither caused nor knew about the problem—such as solvent under your parking lot that leaked from a prior tenant's storage tank. Your landlord may argue that your promise to comply with all laws includes the duty to cleanse the property of toxic substances that are in the ground or structure in violation of federal, state, or local environmental laws.

- **Tough statutes may make you responsible for the clean-up bill, even if you're not at fault.** Government agencies that enforce the contamination and pollution laws may be able to demand clean-up costs directly from you, the current tenant, and simply bypass the former tenant, neighbor, or landlord who may in fact be the cause of the problem. In legalese, you may be "strictly liable" for the mess, which means that you may be ordered to pay even if you didn't intend or even know about the pollution.

As you can see, the government's (and the landlord's) net is often wide and not necessarily fair. Knowing this, you must be vigilant when it comes to even the hint of an environmental problem.

2. Who Should Look Closely at Potential Space

Many tenants won't have to worry at all about environmental contamination. Those who rent space in multilevel office buildings, for example, are unlikely to encounter problems with pollutants in the ground. Well-maintained properties, with insulation and paint in good repair, won't usually pose a health risk to employees and customers.

Some tenants, however, need to be more vigilant when checking out potential space. Tenants in the rental situations listed below commonly experience at least the worry, if not the reality, of environmental pollution and its effects. If you and your business match any of the following scenarios, you need to look closely at the space before committing yourself further.

There are children nearby. If you're renting space in a building near a school, playground, or recreational park, understand that areas where children spend large amounts of time will experience a higher degree of scrutiny (from parents, concerned citizens, and officials) than properties used mainly by adults. Any hint of pollution at or near places frequented by children will normally get a response. If the source is traced to your rented premises, the government will be under pressure to make the owner (and possibly the tenants) deal with the problem quickly and effectively.

You are close to a current or former gas station. The underground storage tanks used by all gas stations have failed with dismaying frequency over the years, allowing gasoline to seep into the ground and contaminate soil and groundwater. If you're renting space on or near the site of a current or former gas station, the chances are higher that there's gasoline in the ground than if you were far removed from these establishments.

Prior tenants or neighbors used toxic materials. Enterprises such as dry cleaners, auto repair shops, and even hardware stores that sell paint thinner in bulk may have been careless in their storage and disposal habits. Biological wastes that weren't handled properly, such as kitchen garbage that's allowed to cause mold, can cause problems, too. You don't want to pay for the consequences.

You'll be using toxic materials. If your business involves any of the substances that are likely to be viewed as potential toxins, you need to be especially careful because even the smallest contribution to a pre-existing problem can expose you to the entire clean-up cost.

You have deep pockets. As noted above in Section 1, sometimes the government can demand clean-up costs from tenants who contributed very little to the contamination problem (joint and several liability), or from tenants who had nothing to do with the problem other than being the unfortunate tenant at the site when the problem was discovered (strict liability). If you are a bit player, the government may not bother with you; on the other hand, if you have the ability to pay, the chances that you will be sent the bill go way up.

Wetlands are nearby. If you're renting space on or near a wetland (a marsh or seasonally wet area, such as a field that naturally floods in winter), you'll be subject to the Federal Water Pollution Control Act, which directs the Environmental Protection Agency (EPA) to monitor water quality in fresh- and saltwater bodies. This means extra scrutiny for the area around your rental, so you'll want to be sure the property is clean before you move in.

Deteriorating asbestos is present. Many buildings are insulated with asbestos fibers, which break down over time and enter the

airstream. Breathing asbestos fibers is a known health hazard. If you're looking at a building with asbestos insulation, find out whether it is intact (if so, it's usually best to leave it in place). But if the insulation has begun to crumble—and especially if you plan improvements that will further disturb it—you may have a problem.

You run a family- or child-oriented business. If the rental you're considering has old paint that's in bad shape, and your business is frequented by children or families (such as a restaurant or day care center), it behooves you to find out whether lead is present (it was added to paint until 1978). Breathing or ingesting the dust from deteriorating lead paint causes health problems, especially in very young children.

You're planning major renovations. If you intend to do extensive remodeling that will involve disturbing the ground (paving for a parking lot or building an addition onto an existing structure, for example), the risk that you'll unearth previously undetected problems and trigger an environmental inquiry goes up.

3. Ask the Landlord About Environmental Problems

Perhaps you've concluded that you ought to do a little environmental sleuthing before pursuing this rental—maybe you fit one or more of the "vulnerable tenant" scenarios described above. The first person to approach in your search for answers is the landlord.

If you don't ask, landlords are not likely to tell—because they may think that they have no legal duty to voluntarily disclose negative environmental information about their property or neighboring land. (Actually, some courts will hold real estate professionals to a duty to disclose, but few professionals know this.) On the other hand, once you raise the issue and ask for specifics, landlords are more apt to tell you what they know. That's because both you and the landlord are legally bound to deal truthfully with one another during your negotiations. If one of you deliberately misleads the other, that's grounds for undoing the whole deal. Most experienced landlords and brokers know the consequences of hiding the facts when a direct answer is called for, and for this reason will usually tell you the truth.

4. How to Check Out the Space for Environmental Problems

Your next step, which is fairly painless and low-tech, is to do some research on the building and the neighborhood.

a. Walk Around and Ask Questions

To begin your inquiry, simply look carefully at the site and talk to other tenants and neighboring businesses. Have government agencies inspected the premises in recent years? Have any repair projects, such as insulation replacement or excavations, suggested potential problems in the structure or soil? If possible, look at the landlord's repair and maintenance records for the building and surrounding grounds, and find out what's behind those names on the invoices. You'll be much more interested in the work done by an engineering firm or environmental consultants than the recommendations of interior designers.

b. Use the Internet

Next, use the Internet to learn if there have been reported environmental problems in the area.

- First, try the EPA's "ZIP code Search," at www.epa.gov/epahome/comm.htm. By typing in a zip code, you can get free profiles on air quality, hazardous waste, surface water quality, and reported chemical releases.
- Second, check out the private site maintained by the Environmental Defense Fund at www.edf.org. Choose the Scorecard link and enter the zip code of the rental space you're considering. In addition to information on air and water quality and known hazardous substances, the site provides links to community websites.

At this point, you may well decide that you face no real risk of encountering an environmental problem. But if you have doubts and still want to pursue a particular space, you'll need to enter the next level of environmental troubleshooting, known as "Phase I" and "Phase II" Reviews.

c. Phase I and II Reviews

A Phase I Review is a more thorough version of the "look and ask" inquiry you did yourself. Usually, prospective tenants hire an environmental consultant to extensively research the history of the site, building, and neighbors. The consultant interviews people who are familiar with the area (perhaps some former tenants or owners), looks at any aerial photos to help determine the past uses of the site, checks government records that would document past users of hazardous wastes at the site, and contacts the EPA to find out whether the site might be considered "sensitive." In short, the researcher acts a bit like a journalist, looking at documents and talking to relevant people.

What should you do if the consultant's Phase I report comes back with worrisome information? How significant is it that the site was once a gas station? What if there is a dry cleaning business next door that was the subject of a clean-up order years ago, or a now-defunct tannery that operated a half-mile away?

Many tenants would be wise to walk away from the deal at this point, especially if they have other, "clean" prospects. But if you think this site is worth pursuing, the next investigative step is to ask for some actual testing of the structure or grounds for evidence of contamination. This type of review is known as a Phase II Review, which will either confirm or refute the disquieting information you learned in Phase I. It's expensive, possibly involving engineers and chemists who may test for actual soil contamination (by taking soil borings), air contamination (by checking air samples), and groundwater problems (by drilling test wells). Can you afford to do this kind of testing? Think of it this way: Since you may end up footing the bill for the cleanup if, indeed, there are real problems that appear during your tenancy, you can't afford not to. In other words, if you can't afford the Phase II testing, you can't afford to lease this space and you ought to look elsewhere.

5. Shield Yourself From Liability for Clean-Up Costs

If you've decided that you have little risk of encountering an environmental problem— either because your own investigation yielded nothing worrisome or because a Phase I or II examination gave the property a clean bill of health—don't put the issue completely out of your mind. You can't totally rule out the possibility that you've missed something or that an accident in the future will place you at risk for paying for clean-up costs.

When you negotiate the lease, you can protect yourself from being legally or financially responsible for contamination that you didn't cause. Chapter 12, Section C, explains in detail how several lease clauses can be worded to your advantage.

D. Learning About the Landlord

Once you've decided that a particular space is worth pursuing, you have one final bit of homework before you approach the bargaining table: Check out the owner of the property. You won't know how strongly you can push for concessions or services— let alone whether you want to do business at this address—unless you have a realistic idea of the financial strength, business reputation, and staying power of the suit in the opposite chair. Nor do you want to enter into a business relationship with people whose finances are stretched so thin that they won't be able to maintain their property or respond to repairs and maintenance chores that fall on their plate. You can be sure that a careful owner will thoroughly investigate *your* business background, credit worthiness, and general reputation. It's completely legitimate for you to do the same. Your need to know a lot about the landlord goes up especially if the landlord will also be doing business in the building (you're going to interact a lot), you're signing a long-term lease, having a well-maintained building is important to your business, or the landlord will be providing basic services (such as janitorial work) that your business needs.

The person or entity who becomes your landlord may be an individual, a partnership, a corporation, or a real estate trust. This section explains the pros and cons of each. It also suggests ways to find out what it's like to do business with the landlord— important information you'll need to know.

1. Types of Owners

In simpler times, tenants in small towns especially could count on there being one individual, or one married couple, as the owner of commercial real estate. Not so any longer. You may encounter owners ranging from individuals to corporations. Each has its attractions and detractions for you, the tenant.

a. Individuals

It's unusual for individuals to own large, complex commercial properties. These holdings are simply too expensive for even very wealthy people. However, individuals often own single properties in suburban or rural areas.

The upside of dealing with a single, local owner is that it's simple. You don't have to make your way through layers of corporate management or penetrate corporate shells to find out who's in charge. When an issue comes up—you want to request heightened security at the building, for example—you'll approach one person who will listen, evaluate, decide, and implement your suggestion. If you're lucky, the owner has both pride and experience in managing the property, and will respond to your reasonable requests. This describes our own experience at Nolo, where we rent from a gentleman who loves his building and treats both it and us with respect and generosity.

On the other hand, if you're dealing with an "accidental" owner (such as someone who has inherited the property), you may be faced with an owner who is neither knowledgeable nor emotionally invested in the well-being and reputation of the building. (Absentee landlords and just plain cheapskates fall into this category, too.) The owner's ability to respond to a sudden expense—a new roof when winter rains have made it clear that the old one won't hold—may be limited by other, more pressing personal demands (like the payments on the owner's own home). In many respects, having to contend with an inept or under-capitalized amateur is the worst position to be in.

b. Real Estate Partnerships

Individuals who have formed legal partnerships own many commercial properties. The partners may be friends, relatives, or business associates. In a legal partnership, each general partner can enter into a contract (such as a lease) on behalf of the partnership, and each individual partner is responsible for the debts and obligations of the partnership.

Another type of partnership is the real estate syndicate—a group of private partners who sell interests in the syndicate to the public. Here is where things can get very complicated (and shaky). The primary funding behind these syndicates may not be solid. To complicate matters, syndicates often are made up of many successive partners—think of a group of nesting dolls —so that it is very difficult to ascertain just who owns what. Arrangements of this type are most common when it comes to office buildings.

From your point of view, having a partnership as your landlord can have worrisome aspects. If the partnership is private—a group of known individuals—you at least know with whom you're dealing. But you must realize that the financial health of the partnership is only as strong as the stability of the individuals. Unless they're accomplished businesspersons, you might be entering the Amateur Hour, headed for the same problems that some individual landlords present. And if the owner is a syndicate with private investors and a series of interlocking subpartners—well, it might take a sleuth to unravel the partnership to the point of being able to gauge the financial well-being of the people who own it.

c. Corporations

Office buildings in particular are often owned by corporations, who use them as corporate headquarters. If there's space left over, it's leased out to other businesses, often ones that are complementary or handy, in a practical sense, to the business of the corporation. For example, a life insurance corporation might find it convenient to lease extra space to accountants, estate-planning lawyers, a restaurant geared for the lunch trade, a dry cleaners, and a day care facility.

If you're able to snare space in such a setup, chances are that you'll enjoy your tenancy. The corporate owner has every incentive to run the building smoothly and with pride, since the appearance of the property contributes to the reputation of the corporation. But since many would-be tenants will covet a spot in this arrangement, the corporation can probably afford to be choosy. During lease negotiations, you may not be able to wring concessions as easily as you would from a hungrier landlord.

d. Institutional Investors

The property that interests you may be the darling of a business entity whose primary line of work has absolutely nothing to do with leasing commercial real estate. Life insurance companies, banks, pension funds, credit companies, and real estate investment trusts (REITs) with money to invest will offer to lend it to commercial property owners. These investors view their chosen properties as valuable cash cows that, managed well, will pay out regular dividends on the investment or payments on the loan. If the investment or loan is large, the lender will insist on having a say in any significant business decision of the owner—and the choice of tenants and the terms and conditions of the lease are prime areas of concern. Although they aren't legal owners in the sense of being named on the property deed, institutional investors can be so crucial to the cash needs of the legal owner that, for all practical purposes, the investor is the one in the driver's seat.

The upside of dealing with institutional investors is that, *if the investors are financially sound,* you usually needn't worry about the financial stability of the legal owners. Sudden expenses won't send them into a tailspin, and they might be more willing and able to accommodate your need for forbearance if you can't pay the rent on time. You'll be dealing with legal owners who, because they have to answer to financial professionals, are likely to do a professional job.

But the fact that your rental will be run with an added layer of oversight will complicate your dealings with the owners. For example, your desire to sublet your current space may be perfectly okay with the owners, but they typically won't be able to sign off on the sublease until the investors have given their permission. Usually good business sense will motivate the investors, but you may find that their criteria are overly exacting.

2. Finding Out Who Owns the Property

Understanding that there are different kinds of "owners," legal and otherwise, is one thing; finding out who owns the building, who will be managing it, and who is authorized to speak for the landlord, is something else. The person you're dealing with—whether it's the landlord, a management representative, or a landlord's broker—should be willing and able to give you clear answers and provide appropriate documents upon request (such as a copy of a deed or letter of authority).

If you can't get clear answers on these issues, all may not be on the up and up. You could spend countless hours in lease negotiations, only to find out that the person you've been dealing with lacks the authority to speak for the real landlord. True, this doesn't happen often, but you can cut the risk to nearly zero by asking questions early on. If you want to confirm information you've been given, visit your local property tax office and look at whose name is recorded as owner of the address you're considering.

⚠ What's here today can be gone tomorrow. The building containing your desired space could be sold, in which case you'd be faced with a whole new landlord overnight—and probably a new management company as well. But knowing about the current landlord can at least give you peace of mind about what's in store for the immediate future.

3. Learning More About the Owner

You'll want to know more about the property's owner than simply their names, although that's a good start. How healthy is the operation? And what's it like to be a tenant in their building? For answers to these questions, you'll need to do a bit of creative investigation.

First, check with the public office where real estate documents are filed (sometimes called the "recorder's" office) to see if there are recorded loans or mortgages on the property. A heavily burdened property may well mean that there will be players behind the scenes. The records in this office can give you additional clues about the character and business practices of the landlord. For example, if the property tax records show that the landlord is delinquent, maybe the landlord will be equally slow in attending to the obligations owed to tenants.

Don't stop at the recorder's office—walk down the hall to the clerk's office for the local trial court. If the court records are searchable, look for the owner's name in the records of defendants and plaintiffs. If these records show that the landlord is frequently in litigation either as a plaintiff or a defendant—well, that's a discouraging sign. Whether the landlord is litigation happy or is routinely getting sued by others, something is amiss. You'd much prefer a landlord who works through problems without the need for lawsuits.

Before you sign a lease, you definitely want to know what it's like on a personal level to deal with this landlord and—if there is one—the building manager and management company. Simply ask other tenants! Learn how they count the pluses and minuses of having their businesses in the building, and listen to what they say about how the landlord responds to requests for maintenance and repairs. Find out how well the HVAC system works and if there have been any problems with security. Also, try to talk to the current tenant of the space you're considering and ask why that tenant is leaving. If it's because the current tenant thinks the landlord is impossible to deal with or the neighborhood is going to the dogs, check further to either confirm or discredit this disquieting information. And if the landlord owns other buildings, the tenants in those buildings can also be a great source of information.

Insurance Companies Call Some Shots, Too

Don't overlook the impact of your landlord's insurance company in the running of your landlord's business. Many business policies require their insureds—your landlord—to impose conditions and restrictions on tenants. For example, during negotiations you may be asked to agree to take out a policy that insures your own business and secondarily names the landlord as an additional insured. If you balk, your landlord may tell you that he simply has no choice in the matter—his insurance company has insisted that you provide this coverage. Understanding which issues are non-negotiable because insurance companies regularly require them will help you gauge the truth of these responses. Insurance matters are explained in more detail in Chapter 15.

4. Renting From a Current Tenant

You may find yourself dealing with a current tenant who wants to sublease some or all of her rented space. It's particularly common for office tenants to lease out unused space. Retailers, too, may want to bring in concessionaires. For example, a grocery store may want to lease space to an espresso bar, or a clothing store may want to have a tailor shop on site.

Landlords typically do not allow their tenants to sublease without their consent. (The ins and outs of subletting are explained in Chapter 14, Section F.) If you decide to pursue a sublet, you'll want to present yourself to the landlord early on, before committing more time and energy to the rental. And you'll need to look at the lease held by the current tenant, since the leasing deal you strike with the tenant must not run afoul of its terms and conditions. For example, if the tenant doesn't have parking privileges or operates under use restrictions, you, too, will be subject to these terms. (Parking and use restrictions are explained in Chapter 13, Section A, and Chapter 7, Section D.)

Assuming you get the nod from the landlord, understand that you will have two landlords: the owner and the original tenant, who probably knows nothing about being a landlord. This could spell trouble for you, for the same reasons explained above in Section 1a when describing "accidental" landlords. On the other hand, if the tenant regularly rents out unused space to others who experience no complications, you might do just fine. If the tenant currently subleases the space, have a conversation with the subtenant about what it's like doing business in this situation.

E. Management Companies

Many landlords—especially those who own a large number of commercial rental units —contract with property management companies to handle lease negotiations. A management company may also take charge of other aspects of the landlord-tenant relationship, such as collecting rent, arranging for repairs, and customizing space for individual tenants. In some communities, a few management companies control a big chunk of the commercial space that's suitable for small businesses.

Sometimes the identity of the building management company is a good clue as to the status (and desirability) of the building or property. Large, well-established companies tend to hook up with stable, relatively trouble-free owners, and will in turn choose low-risk, solid tenants (who will be your neighbors). If a management firm with less luster is in charge of the building in which you're considering space, it can be a sign the building is less desirable. If you begin to see a pattern of attractive properties managed by the same companies, it's reasonable to assume that other properties these companies manage will probably be in the same echelon.

Throughout the lease negotiation process, the management company will be acting for the landlord, in much the same way as a landlord's broker. And after the lease is signed, all of your day-to-day contacts will be with the management company. So it's important to make sure you can work well with the company and that it has a reputation for promptly taking care of tenants' needs. The best source of information on this subject is other tenants in the building you're looking at or in other buildings under the control of the same management company. The landlord may switch management companies someday, but you'd like some assurance going into the deal that you'll be starting off with a company you can work with.

No matter how prestigious the management company, however, you must not forget one important caveat. As with a landlord's broker, a property management company works for the landlord. You can't rely on the company to look out for your best interests. In fact, if a company were to advocate on your behalf and contrary to the landlord's interests, the company would be in violation of its contract with the owner, exposing itself to legal liability.

F. Holding the Space With a Deposit

Some spaces require more research and investigation than others. You might find something that appears to have all the right ingredients, but it will take you another two or three weeks to check it out. In a tight market, the space may not be there by the time you conclude your research if another tenant who's less cautious (or less knowledgeable) comes by and snaps it up.

There may be a way to resolve this problem. A landlord who believes that you're seriously interested and would make an ideal tenant may agree not to lease the space to anyone else until you've completed your investigation—within a reasonable time, of course.

Many landlords will not suspend their own search for a suitable tenant without some hard proof—money on the table—that you're genuinely interested. Here's how to meet that requirement: Offer to post a deposit on the space, which can be held by your broker or the landlord's broker. The deposit holds the space for you pending a favorable resolution of the issues that you're looking into—receiving a reassuring environmental report, for example, or a satisfactory cost estimate for improvements. If you don't get satisfactory answers by a certain date, the landlord returns your deposit. On the other hand, if everything checks out fine, you agree that you'll lease the space and the landlord will apply the deposit towards the rent.

Naturally, you don't want to put down a deposit, spend time completing your investigation, and only then find that you and the landlord can't agree on critical lease terms. To make sure you aren't rushing ahead on a deal that's yet to gel, the best procedure is to actually negotiate the lease first. Then, include a contingency clause in the lease that allows you to cancel within a certain number of days if enumerated issues are not resolved in your favor. For example, the clause might specify that you

may cancel the lease and get your deposit back if the cost of your improvements will be higher than a stated amount.

Landlords may be unwilling to go along with this plan if they think there are other, less persnickety tenants ready to negotiate over the space. To win a landlord over, you might have to agree that the deposit will be nonrefundable. With this arrangement, if you cancel the lease for the stated reasons by the stated date, you can walk away from the lease without legal repercussions, but you will lose your deposit. Although it will hurt to lose the deposit, it may be worth it if the space is terrific, the deposit isn't too large, and you're relatively sure the space will pass muster. Even putting one month's rent at risk can sometimes make economic sense.

EXAMPLE: After searching for six months for space for a ballet studio, Tina thinks she's found the ideal spot. It's in a perfect location, with large walls that will accommodate mirrors, and the rent is within her budget. But Tina is worried about the cost of renovating the space. She and the landlord negotiate and sign a lease that contains a contingency clause allowing Tina to cancel within the next 30 days if her contractor's estimate is beyond her budget for improvements. She posts a deposit equal to one month's rent. Because this is a hot property with many prospective tenants beating on the door, the landlord insists that one-half of the deposit be forfeited if Tina cancels. Otherwise, the deposit will constitute the first month's rent if Tina takes the space. Tina feels that tying up the space is well worth the risk of losing half of the deposit.

Checklist for Evaluating the Space and the Landlord

You've now accomplished a significant bit of homework, and it will pay off soon in your ability to confidently choose this space and wrest advantageous lease terms from the landlord. You should be ready to move on because you've:

- narrowed the spaces you're interested in to only those that meet your rental "Essentials"
- confirmed that the space is really right for you (for example, by checking out zoning)
- hired a space planner, if necessary, to make sure your design intentions will work
- considered whether environmental contamination is a worry and, if it is, taken appropriate steps to eliminate that worry
- researched (as much as you can) the financial situation and business reputation of the property owner, so you can confidently begin to do business with this person and craft your negotiation strategy wisely, and
- understood the mechanics of a holding deposit, should you need to put one down.

Chapter 4

Understanding the True Size and Cost of the Rental

Read This Chapter If ...

This chapter is for tenants whose rent will be figured by the square foot. It explains the odd ways landlords measure space and the two broad ways tenants pay rent—in one steady sum each month, or a base rent plus an ever-varying portion of the landlord's operating costs. And, for shopping center tenants, it explains percentage rent. This chapter is especially useful in the following situations:

- You are renting by the square foot and want to learn (or question) how the landlord measured the space.
- You need to learn the difference between a simple, monthly rent and monthly rent that changes depending on the landlord's operating costs.
- You will be paying "percentage rent" as a tenant in a shopping center.
- You would like some tips in calculating the true rent you'll face over the length of the lease.

You can skip this chapter if you are renting an entire floor or building, where rent is not based on square footage; you understand the difference between a gross lease and a net lease, and can estimate the total cost over the lease term; and you'll not be paying percentage rent (or if you will, you know all about it).

Once you've found space that looks promising and worth pursuing, it's time to figure out the true cost of the rental. Isn't the monthly rent all you need to know? Unfortunately, it's not that simple. For starters, the monthly rent can be a complicated figure, comprising various factors and calculated in downright Byzantine ways. And there are other expenses, which may not be called rent, but nevertheless feel like rent when you pay them on a regular basis. On the positive side, if you're lucky, there may even be some savings—like free rent for the first month or two—that should be taken into account.

There are at least two important reasons why you need to determine the true cost of leasing a given space. First, since no small business is likely to have unlimited funds, you need to make sure that the cost fits your budget. Second, if you're comparing two or three different spaces, you need to know the true cost of each if your comparisons are to mean anything. It may take some effort to reach the answer, but if you approach the task systematically, you'll find it's not too tough.

This chapter covers important issues you'll want to understand before you head into serious, clause-by-clause lease negotiations:

- How has the landlord priced and measured the space (how many square feet will you *really* have available)?
- What other charges will be tacked on to the dollars-per-square-foot amount to make up the monthly rent?

- How can you estimate the true cost of a rental once you factor in the landlord's methods of calculating the square feet?

Other aspects of the deal will be important too, such as the amount of money the landlord is willing to put into your improvements (Chapter 11) and whether you'll be expected to provide some or all of the property maintenance (Chapter 9).

A. How Landlords Measure Square Feet

Commercial space is often advertised and rented on a cost-per-square-foot basis, rather than a descriptive basis (such as "the first floor"). For example, an ad might describe space as "2,000-Square-Foot Office Suite in New Building" or "2,000 Square Feet of Prime Retail Space." However, 2,000 square feet doesn't always mean that you'll pay for and occupy exactly 2,000 square feet. It all depends on two factors:

- how the space you're paying for is measured, and
- whether you'll be paying for a portion of the building's common areas (hallways, lobbies, and the like) in addition to the space you occupy.

This section describes the measuring techniques that can greatly affect the true meaning of the advertised square-foot figure.

1. Are You Renting Thick Walls Besides Usable Space?

Strange as it may seem, many landlords—especially in office buildings—take their measurements from the middle or even the outside of exterior walls. It's a bit like the butcher who charges you for the bone and fat as well as the edible portion of the steak. Obviously, if a landlord uses this method of measurement, you'll wind up paying not only for usable space but also for some or all of the thickness of the walls.

If you're comparing two properties, and one landlord includes wall thickness in the square-foot figure but the other doesn't, you'll need to recompute the size of one of the properties so that it's measured the same way as the other. This is the only way to realistically compare each property's cost. Sometimes you'll find that a space with a higher per-foot price is actually cheaper than a space that charges less per square foot but charges you for the thickness of the walls.

EXAMPLE: Landlord A advertises 1,000 square feet in Building A for $20 a square foot per year. Landlord A doesn't include the walls' thickness, which means that Tom Tenant will get 1,000 feet of usable space for $20,000 per year.

Landlord B advertises 1,000 square feet in Building B at $17.50 a square foot per year. However, Landlord B measures from the outside of the exterior walls and does not subtract the thickness of several interior walls. Tom will be paying $17,500 per year—but is this really a better deal than the one offered by Landlord A?

Before beginning lease negotiations, Tom Tenant takes his tape measure to Building B and, with the help of a space planner, remeasures the space from the insides of the exterior and interior walls. He now has measurements for Building B comparable to the way that Building A was measured. In Building B, he finds that he will have only 800 square feet that he can actually use. At $17,500 per year, this means that Tom would really be paying $21.87 per foot of usable space. On the basis of rent per square foot of usable space, Building A turns out to be a better deal.

2. Paying for Common Areas

In many buildings, there are parts of the structure or grounds that you'll share with other tenants. For example, you and other tenants may share lobbies, hallways, elevator shafts, bathrooms, and parking lots. When you add these spaces up, they can amount to a hefty chunk of the property. Don't assume that the landlord is going to let you use these shared facilities for free.

The landlord may charge individual tenants for a portion of the nonprivate space by using either a *loss factor* or a *load factor*. (Many times the loss factor is also incorrectly referred to as the load factor.) Depending on which method the landlord uses, you may either

- pay for the amount of advertised space, but actually get less square footage (by virtue of the loss factor, explained below in Subsection a), or
- get the full square footage advertised, but pay for more square feet (pursuant to the load factor, discussed in Subsection b).

We'll explain how each method works. Don't be put off by the math—the concept is what matters. If you come away from this discussion understanding that the terms "loss factor" and "load factor" mean that the cost of the rental will go up, you're halfway there.

a. Using a Loss Factor to Reduce Your Square Feet

One way the landlord gets paid for the common area space you're entitled to use but don't pay for directly is to simply reduce your amount of exclusive space—but charge

Computing the Real Cost of a Rental Using a Loss Factor

The table below shows what happens to the true cost of a rental when the landlord uses a loss factor to reduce the amount of space a tenant gets.

Building space for individual tenants' offices	= 10,000 square feet
Nonprivate space (lobbies, hallways, elevators, etc.)	= 2,000 square feet
Total building space	= 12,000 square feet
Loss factor (total building space of 12,000 divided by nonprivate space of 2,000)	= 16.67%

	Advertised Sq. Ft.	Usable Sq. Ft.
Building A	1,000	1,000 x (100% – 16.67%) = 833
Building B (including walls)	1,000	1,000 x (100% – 16.67%) = 833
Building B (excluding walls)	1,000 x (100% – 20%) = 800	833 x (100% – 20%) = 666.4

	Cost Without Loss Factor (Annual Rent ÷ Advertised Area)	Cost With Loss Factor Annual Rent ÷ Usable Sq. Ft.
Building A	$20.00 ($20,000 ÷ 1,000)	$24.00 ($20,000 ÷ 833)
Building B (including walls)	$17.50 ($17,500 ÷ 1,000)	$21.00 ($17,500 ÷ 833)
Building B (excluding walls)	$21.87 ($17,500 ÷ 800)	$26.26 ($17,500 ÷ 666.4)

you for the number of square feet quoted in the ad. Here's how it works. Look back to the example above and assume that both Buildings A and B have 10,000 square feet available to individual tenants plus 2,000 square feet of lobbies, hallways, shared bathrooms, and elevator spaces. The nonprivate space (2,000 square feet) is one-sixth, or 16.67%, of the total building size of 12,000 square feet. The loss factor is 16.67%.

Now, the landlord subtracts 16.67% from 100% (yielding a balance of 83.33%) and multiplies this times the square feet advertised (.833 x 1,000). The result is the square footage that will be exclusively available to Tom, our tenant. To finish our example, Tom will end up with only 833.3 square feet of his own (1,000 x 83.33%) but he'll pay for 1,000 square feet.

The sidebar, Computing the Real Cost of a Rental Using a Loss Factor, shows how the loss factor affects the rent per square foot. You'll see what happens if Landlords A and B figure in the loss factor, which is 16.67% for each building. And when Tom Tenant takes the wall thickness into account in Building B (remember, by using his tape measure he discovered that a full 20% of the advertised space was not usable), the true cost per foot in Building B goes way up.

Take a minute to think about what the numbers in the sidebar tell us. At first, Tom might have thought that Building A was more expensive than Building B, which was advertised at $2.50 per foot less. But the picture changed a lot when Tom considered how much space he would actually use in Building B—only 800 square feet, which made the per-foot cost jump to $21.87. And when the landlords applied a loss factor to compensate them for the unrented common areas, Building A jumped to $24.00 per square foot. But look what happened to Building B—when the loss factor *and* the adjustment for the thickness of the walls was figured in, the true cost per square foot rose to $26.26. Clearly, Tom will do better renting from Landlord A if rent per square foot is the only factor that's

important to him. As we explain later in this chapter, however, other factors will nearly always come into play, including the layout of a particular space and additional charges such as maintenance.

b.   Using a Load Factor to Charge You for More Square Feet

We've just described one way that a landlord may make sure that tenants pay for their share of the common spaces—that is, by reducing the space you get to use exclusively (but charging you for the entire advertised space by including common area space in the rent). Using a load factor is another way. Rather than reducing your amount of usable space, there is an additional charge for the tenant's proportional share of the non-private or common areas.

How do landlords use this type of load factor? Landlords A and B both have 2,000 square feet that they cannot rent out to individual tenants, but they wish to pass on the "rent" for this space to their tenants. They divide this 2,000 square feet by the 10,000 square feet available for private use and find that they must increase each tenant's rent by an additional 20% to cover their proportional share the common area. The sidebar below shows what happens to Tom's rent when this method is used.

Computing the Real Cost of a Rental Using a Load Factor

This table shows what happens to the cost of a rental when the landlord uses the load factor to add to the square feet that the tenant pays for.

Building space for individual tenants' offices	= 10,000 square feet
Non-private space (lobbies, hallways, elevators, etc.)	= 2,000 square feet
Load factor = total nonprivate space/total office space (2,000 ÷ 10,000)	= 20%

	Cost Without Load Factor (Annual Rent ÷ Rented Area)	Cost With Load Factor (Cost Before Load Factor x 1.20%)
Building A	$20.00 ($20,000 ÷ 1,000)	$24 ($20 x 1.20)
Building B (including walls)	$17.50 ($17,500 ÷ 1,000)	$21 ($17.50 x 1.20)
Building B (excluding walls)	$21.88 ($17,500 ÷ 800)	$26.25 ($21.87 x 1.20)

c. The Importance of Discovering the Loss or Load Factor

As you can see from the sidebars above, the use of a loss or load factor has a significant impact on the real cost per square foot of your rented space. Under either method—reducing your exclusive space, as shown in the sidebar Computing the Real Cost of a Rental Using a Loss Factor, or charging you for a portion of the common areas, as shown in the sidebar Computing the Real Cost of a Rental Using a Load Factor—you end up getting less or paying more. You must find out early on whether the landlord will apply a loss or load factor. The method a landlord picks may depend on several factors:

- **Loss method.** If the space is wide open and easily divided into rentable pieces of varying sizes, such as a new office building with no interior walls in place yet, it will be easy for the landlord to advertise one size but, applying the loss factor, actually turn over a smaller space.

- **Load method.** If the space in the building is permanently divided into rentable "chunks," as is true in an older, multitenant retail space, it's likely that the landlord will use the method described in Subsection b, since the square footage for each space can't be reduced without major reconstruction.

⚠️ **If you must have the full square footage as advertised or represented by the broker, make sure that the landlord doesn't apply the loss factor, which decreases your usable space.** For example, if you need a full 1,000 square feet, you don't want to learn that the loss factor will used to charge you for that size but actually deliver less. You'll prefer to have the landlord use the load factor, which will result in your getting the full 1,000 square feet but charging you for more. Raise the issue early on.

Be aware that you may not always be informed of the loss or load factor in your first dealings with the landlord (you may not see it in the ad, for example). But the broker (if there is one involved) will probably know if either factor is operating behind the scenes and should be able to help you compute the true cost of the space.

3. How to Check Square Footage

Now that you understand the different ways that the landlord may measure the building (including walls or not), and that the landlord can ask you to pay for non-private space (by using either the loss or load factor), you're in a position to assess the rental with a critical eye. A floor plan drawn to scale will allow you to check the square footage for yourself, and it's not unreasonable to ask the landlord to supply one. It's also a good idea to double check

the drawing by measuring the space itself, if you can, with a tape measure or yard-stick.

4. Importance of the Layout

The way that a space is laid out—not just its size—will have a lot to do with whether you're getting your money's worth. For example, awkward angles, interrupted work-spaces, or narrow corridors will be less useful than wide-open areas and passage-ways that can accommodate bookshelves, office equipment, dividers, and well-designed work areas. Your rental cost may be less for a $20-per-square-foot space that's efficiently laid out than for an $18-per-square-foot space with an awkward configuration, simply because you'll need less of the $20 per square foot space.

EXAMPLE 2: Tom Tenant is still considering Buildings A and B. He learns that neither landlord is using a loss or load factor. Tom knows that Building A will cost him $20 per square foot (since he's not paying for the walls), and he's getting a full 1,000 square feet. But Building B's true cost is $21.87 per square foot—and, since the 1,000-square-foot figure includes the walls, he's getting only 800 feet of usable space.

Tom's first thought is to conclude that Building A is a better deal—after all, its cost per square foot is lower and

Sample Floor Plan Drawn to Scale

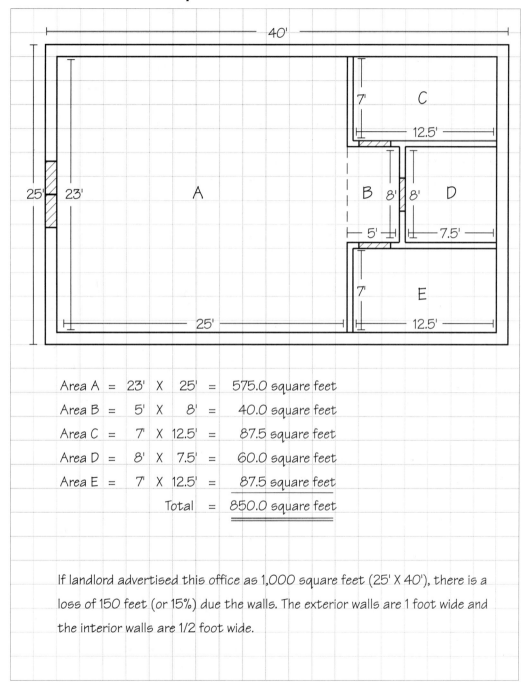

Area A	=	23' X 25'	=	575.0 square feet
Area B	=	5' X 8'	=	40.0 square feet
Area C	=	7' X 12.5'	=	87.5 square feet
Area D	=	8' X 7.5'	=	60.0 square feet
Area E	=	7' X 12.5'	=	87.5 square feet
		Total	=	850.0 square feet

If landlord advertised this office as 1,000 square feet (25' X 40'), there is a loss of 150 feet (or 15%) due the walls. The exterior walls are 1 foot wide and the interior walls are 1/2 foot wide.

he gets a full 1,000 square feet. But the space in Building A is chopped up and not conducive to the way Tom wants to arrange his offices. He'll end up paying for a lot of wasted space if he takes Building A. The space in Building B, on the other hand, is laid out just as Tom would like it. In fact, he won't even need all 800 square feet, and can suggest to the landlord that a portion of it be rented to someone else. In the end, Tom may do better renting less space in Building B, even though the price per square foot is higher than in Building A.

B. Additional Rent: Gross Versus Net Leases

If this is your first foray into the world of commercial leasing, you may be surprised to learn that the rent doesn't necessarily mean what it does when you rent an apartment or house. In a residential situation, rent is normally one fixed amount. You're rarely asked to pay *additional rent*—sums to cover operating expenses such as building insurance, maintenance, or real estate taxes. These costs are, of course, taken into consideration when the landlord sets the rent for an apartment, but they're not added on as separate charges. In a commercial situation, however, you may be asked to pay for some or all of these additional sums.

This section explains the four basic ways that landlords charge for such costs as insurance and property taxes. We start with the most basic method (which corresponds most closely to the typical residential rent) and proceed to the more complicated ones. In Chapter 9, you'll find extensive explanations of the lease clauses that correspond to the method your landlord has chosen. When you're ready to negotiate the lease, you'll need to learn the details as set out in that chapter.

1. Pure Gross Lease

In a pure *gross lease,* you pay only for the use of the square feet that you rent. If, like Tom Tenant, you are renting 1,000 square feet at $20 a square foot, your rent is $20,000 per year. (Remember that this may not be 1,000 square feet of completely usable space, as described in Section A.) The landlord's operating expenses are not added on, although certainly they were considered when the landlord set the price per square foot. Pure gross leases are relatively uncommon—especially when you're dealing with an experienced landlord. If you're offered a gross lease at all, it most likely will be in the context of a one- or two-year lease. On the other hand, you have nothing to lose by proposing a pure gross lease if it would suit your needs.

It's understandable why some landlords are reluctant to propose a pure gross lease. Most commercial tenancies last at least five years—and ten- or 15 year terms are common. During those years, operating costs can rise unpredictably (but the rent is locked in for the duration of the term). The landlord stands to make less profit as the costs of owning and running the property increase. So when gross leases are used, landlords often build in some sort of regular rent increase—such as one tied to the rise in the Consumer Price Index—as a buffer against rising costs. (Chapter 9, Section A, explains how rent escalation works in detail.) But a more effective way for a landlord to cover high operating costs is to put some of them directly on the tenant's plate, as described in the following sections.

2. Gross Lease With Stops

A landlord may be willing to set a fixed rent (a gross lease) if the tenant will be helping out in the event that operating costs rise above a certain level. It works like this: If the landlord's taxes, insurance, and other operating costs exceed a predetermined amount, the tenant begins to pay. In real estate lingo, the point when the tenant starts to contribute is called the *stop level* (because that's where the landlord's share of the costs stops).

The expense that the landlord will be most anxious to cap is the property tax bill (although insurance and common area maintenance costs can be factored in, too). Typically, the landlord and tenant agree that the landlord will pay the taxes for the

first year (called the *base year*). If the taxes go up in succeeding years, the tenant will pay the difference as *additional rent.*

EXAMPLE: Bleak Chic, a trendy clothing store, pays $2,000 a month for its space in a suburban shopping mall. The five-year lease began in 2005, which Bleak and their landlord agreed would be the base year for purposes of property taxes. The tax bill for 2006 is $500 higher than it was in 2005. Having agreed to pay for any property taxes above those assessed in the base year, in 2006 Bleak pays the $500 as additional rent.

Another way to handle increased taxes is for the landlord to agree to absorb a specified amount of property taxes (called a *base amount*), but if the actual tax bill is higher, the tenant pays the added amount.

EXAMPLE: Bleak Chic signs a three-year lease at a second location in 2006. The lease specifies that the landlord will pay property taxes up to a base amount of $4,000 per year. If the tax bill exceeds that, Bleak will pay the difference. Sure enough, in 2007 the taxes are $5,500, so Bleak pays $1,500 in additional rent to cover its tax obligation.

A gross lease with stops puts some of the risks of rising operating costs on the tenant, but if the stop level is high enough (or the base amount big enough), you might never have to chip in. But regardless of where the stop level is placed, the landlord will absorb at least the initial tax amount.

You can imagine that a landlord might want the tenant to absorb the entire cost of taxes, insurance, and maintenance costs—not just the periodic increases in those items. The mechanism for doing this is a *net lease*, described below.

3. Net Lease

The landlord may expect you to pay for the use of the space (the square feet) *and* operating costs (property taxes, mainte-nance, and building insurance). This ar-rangement is known as a *triple net lease* (sometimes just called a net lease), because typically all three of the usual operating costs—taxes, maintenance, and insurance—are passed on to the tenant.

In multitenant properties, each tenant typically pays a proportionate share of operating costs according to the amount of the total rentable space each occupies. For example, a tenant occupying one-tenth of the total rental space would pay one-tenth of these costs. In single-tenant rentals, the tenant sometimes pays the entire cost, or may share it with the landlord. Triple net leases are very common in large properties such as office buildings or big shopping malls, but are widely used in other situations as well.

Since taxes, maintenance, and insurance costs are variable and almost never decrease, it's obvious that a net lease favors the land-

lord. But it may be possible for a tenant to bargain for caps, for the same reason that a landlord with a gross lease will ask for stops—neither side wants to be obligated to an open-ended expense.

4. Net Lease With Caps or Ceilings

If you rent with a net lease, you may be able to insist on a limit to the amount of your increased obligations. For example, you may be able to negotiate an agreement that an increase in taxes beyond a certain point will be borne by the landlord. The same kind of protection can be designed to cover increased insurance premiums and maintenance expenses. If your prospective landlord hands you a net lease, you'll want to press for some protections when you negotiate the lease. Negotiation strategies are explained in Chapter 9.

> **EXAMPLE:** Bleak Chic leaves its outpost in the suburbs when its lease expires. Bleak finds space in a renovated ware-house in The Flats, a light industrial area of town. Bleak's landlord uses a net lease, which obligates Bleak to pay a portion of the landlord's property taxes, property and liability insurance premi-ums, and building maintenance (other tenants in the building pay a propor-tionate share as well). A year after the lease begins, The Flats experiences a renaissance, with coffee bars, book-stores, and restaurants moving in and

doing well. Property taxes go up, but fortunately Bleak foresaw this development and negotiated a cap on the amount of taxes it would be obligated to pay—Bleak will pay only 50% of any increase over its first year obligation.

C. Percentage Rent—Sharing Income With the Landlord

Shopping center landlords often demand a share of a retail tenant's profits in addition to the monthly rent. If you have a retail business and are headed for the mall, you may be asked to pay what's known as *percentage rent.*

➡ **You can skip this section unless you're a retail tenant leasing space in a shopping center or mall.** Not all such tenants will pay percentage rent—typically, only rather large and sophisticated tenants, with hefty sales, fall into this group. If the landlord expects percentage rent from you, you'll find out early in your dealings with the owner or management company.

With a percentage rent lease, you first pay a *minimum rent* under a gross or net lease, as described above in Section B. Then, when your gross sales surpass a specified mark, you begin to pay a certain percent of every additional dollar in sales as additional rent. The percent that's applied is usually an industry standard and isn't subject to much

variation. The *breakpoint* is the amount of gross sales you must reach before the landlord will begin to apply the percentage multiplier and exact a share of your income.

1. Calculating the Breakpoint

There is a standard way to calculate the breakpoint, used by most real estate brokers and professional landlords. This accepted method yields what's known as the *natural breakpoint.* Here's how it's calculated: The landlord computes your yearly minimum sales, then figures out what you would have to make in gross profits if you were paying *only* 7% of sales and had to come up with that same minimum rent amount. That figure is your natural breakpoint. If your gross receipts never get to that point, you never pay percentage rent. But if your gross sales meet and exceed that figure, you begin paying percentage rent on every additional dollar.

> **EXAMPLE:** Moonbucks Coffee leases space in a shopping center and pays $5,000 a month ($60,000 a year) on a gross lease. In addition, Moonbucks is subject to percentage rent of 7%, with a natural breakpoint.
>
> The natural breakpoint is the point where the base rent equals the percentage rent. To calculate it, divide the base rent by the percentage. In this case:
>
> $5,000 ÷ 7% = $71,428

When Moonbucks' sales exceed $71,428, it must pay the landlord 7% of every dollar it brings in as sales.

2. Negotiating the Breakpoint

Many landlords will calculate the natural breakpoint and leave it at that—charging you a minimum rent and collecting percentage rent only after your gross receipts have surpassed the natural breakpoint. But there is no law requiring you to stick to the natural breakpoint when you negotiate the lease. Landlords and tenants can negotiate the breakpoint higher (which means that you won't have to share until you gross more than you would if you were using the breakpoint based on 7%) or lower (in which case you'll begin sharing your income with the landlord sooner than the natural breakpoint).

You may want to take the lead in suggesting a percentage greater than 7%. You may, for example, offer to pay a higher percentage of rent if you think that your income will not be rising rapidly and when it does, it will be sufficient to cover the extra expense (remember, up to that point the income is all yours). You may want to "trade" this concession for an important gain on another issue. For example, agreeing to a higher rate in exchange for a lease renewal option right might be worth it to you.

Conversely, you may want to bargain for a higher minimum rent in exchange for a breakpoint that's above the natural point. Especially if you think your income will rise quickly, you won't want to share it with the landlord until the last possible moment.

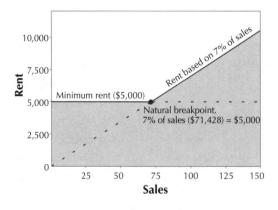

Percentage Rent

D. Computing the True Rental Cost

Once you understand how a prospective landlord measured the space and what kind of rent computation you're being offered (gross or net, with or without variations), you'll be ready to roughly compare the rental costs for two or more places you're considering.

For most small businesses, the best figure to use for budgeting and comparison purposes is the average cost of the lease per month over the life of the lease. Ordinarily, you won't include the security deposit in your calculations because this money will come back to you if you pay your rent on time and meet your other lease obligations. (Chapter 10 discusses security deposits.)

Be aware that in computing lease costs, you may have to estimate some items. If you're being offered a net lease and are paying a portion of the building's property taxes, for example, you can find out what the taxes are for the current year by asking to see the landlord's tax bill (or by checking it yourself in the local property tax office), but you'll have to make an estimate for future years, since taxes can fluctuate. Similarly, asking about the building's maintenance costs and the current property insurance premium will give you an idea of what to expect when you begin chipping in for maintenance and insurance; of course, these amounts can also change.

The following method can help you analyze the true costs of a rental. To make valid comparisons, you have to go through this process and prepare a Rental Cost Worksheet for each space you're considering. Rental Cost Worksheet for Buildings A and B, below, show how Tom Tenant, who is still debating Buildings A and B, compared the cost of renting these properties.

Step One: Determine how many years you'll be occupying the space. Usually, this figure will be a matter of negotiation between you and the landlord, as discussed in Chapter 8. We recommend that you use a figure of 36 months—unless you're signing a shorter lease. Projecting numbers beyond 36 months becomes difficult, even if you firmly believe you'll exercise a lease option to stay on for an additional two, three, or even more years.

Step Two: Determine the basic rent for the space. Here you'll have to do the calculations described in Sections A, B and C.

- **Gross lease.** If rent is quoted solely as a rate per square foot, you and the landlord will need to compute how many square feet you'll be paying for.
- **Net lease.** If you've been given a net lease, you'll need to also have some idea of the maintenance, insurance, and tax costs you'll be facing (although, as explained above, you may have to make do with rough estimates).
- **Percentage rent.** If you're asked to pay percentage rent, you'll need to know where the landlord will set the breakpoint and what the multiplier will be. Then you'll have to estimate your gross receipts and compare that figure with the breakpoint. Figure your percentage rent for the receipts that exceed the breakpoint.

Step Three: Determine the total estimated rent. Once you've estimated the basic rent, under any type of lease, you should figure out the total rent for a three-year (or shorter) period. Remember that even a gross lease may include a built-in rent increase in the second or third year, so you'll need to include this in your computations. That chore is relatively easy if the lease states the new rent amount. It will require some estimating if the lease bases the increases on changes in a cost-of-living index or on increases in the landlord's operating expenses. For example, you might be able to project a cost-of-living increase based on the increases of the previous one or two years. And if the landlord's maintenance expenses have risen gradually over the past few years, you may be able to project expenses based on this trend.

In figuring the rent for three years, deduct any incentives the landlord is offering during the first few months—free or reduced rent, for example, or a moving allowance. (These incentives are explained in Chapter 11, Section E.) Once you've figured the total base rent cost for three years, you'll need to divide that figure by 36 to determine the average monthly cost for rent.

Step Four: Include the cost of utilities. If you're renting in a single-tenant property, you may have to pay directly for utilities (gas, electricity, and water). In a multi-tenant situation, you may be separately metered for utilities and will likewise pay these costs directly to the providers, or you may pay a share of building-wide expenses based on your share of the total space. Question the landlord about the expected cost of supplying the space you're considering. Of course, you'll need to take into account the nature of your own business and how much gas, electricity, and water it consumes. For example, a laundromat with energy-gobbling washers and dryers will use more of these resources than a shoe store.

Step Five: Include other direct costs. If you're going to be the sole tenant in a building, you may have direct costs besides utilities, such as security or neighborhood business association fees. Add these in.

Step Six: Factor in your share of renovation costs. Most of the time, you'll need to fix up your new space to suit your business needs. Some properties will need a lot of work; others will need less. Your improvements can be as extensive as adding walls or removing them, or as simple as new carpet and paint. They may also include special lighting and wiring, including computer wiring, and equipment and furnishings designed specifically for the space. At this point, you probably have some idea of what a particular space will need in order to make it usable for you. (Checking out your space with a planner, which you should have done early in your investigations of this property, is covered in Chapter 3, Section B.)

You and the landlord may negotiate, perhaps long and hard, over who will pay for your improvements. Hopefully, you have an idea now of what the landlord will expect you to contribute. Unless you are reasonably expecting some dramatic concessions when you reach the bargaining table, use this figure for purposes of this worksheet.

Step Seven: Include other costs. There may be additional costs associated with one space that you won't see in another. For example, you may be expected to arrange for your own janitorial service in one location, but have it provided at a building-wide cut rate at another. Parking, too, may be included in the rent at one spot but added on at another. And your business insurance costs may vary depending on the location (insuring your business is covered in Chapter 15). Include these miscellaneous costs of doing business in this category.

Now, total up these additional costs for the three-year period and divide the figure by 36. Add that number to the figure for the average monthly base rent and you'll have a good idea, for budgeting and comparison purposes, of the true cost per month of leasing the space over a three-year period.

EXAMPLE: Tom Tenant decides to give some serious thought to renting Buildings A and B. Both landlords are willing to give him a three-year gross lease without a load factor. Tom knows that Building A will cost him $20 a square foot per year (since he's not paying for the walls), and he's getting a full 1,000 square feet. But Building B's true cost is $21.87 per square foot—and, since the 1,000 square foot figure includes the walls, he's getting only 800 feet of usable space. The real annual rent for A is $20,000, or $60,000 for the life of the lease. The real annual rent for B is $21,870, or $65,610 for the life of the lease.

Next, Tom checks on whether either landlord will grant him any period of free rent (both landlords say no). Landlord A expects Tom to pay his own utility costs (Tom figures they'll be around $200 a month), but Landlord B tells Tom he'll have to pay his share of the building-wide usage (his share is estimated to be $250 a month). Tom knows his renovation costs will be high in Building A (about $10,000 total), since the space is poorly laid out. But the improvement costs in B, which is arranged just right, will be less ($2,000).

Finally, Tom adds in some other direct costs. Landlord A will charge him $1,200 per year for parking; Landlord B had no parking to offer so Tom will have to pay $1,500 a year for parking at a nearby garage. Insurance costs for Tom's business in A's neighborhood are low (about $600 per year), but higher ($900 per year) in B's area, which has a higher crime rate. The costs of cleaning his office suite will run about $2,000 a year in Building A, where Tom can sign on to the building-wide janitorial service, but higher ($3,000 a year) in Building B, where Tom will have to arrange for cleaning on his own.

Tom notes these figures on his Rental Cost Worksheet and compares the results. From a purely financial stand-point, Tom concludes that Building A is a slightly better deal.

Rental Cost Worksheet for Buildings A and B		
	Cost for 3-Year Term	
	Building A	Building B
Rent for entire term	$60,000	$65,610
Utility costs, total	$ 7,200	$ 9,000
Improvements	$10,000	$ 2,000
Parking	$ 3,600	$ 4,500
Insurance	$ 1,800	$ 2,700
Janitorial	$ 6,000	$ 9,000
TOTAL for 36 months	$88,600	$92,510
Average monthly cost	$ 2,461	$ 2,569

There is no such thing as a good "below-market" deal. If you've found space at below-market rates, it's because the space cannot command a market price for *good* space. In other words, something is fishy. Find out before you commit more time and effort to this deal.

Checklist for Determining the Real Cost and Size of a Rental

Good work! You've soldiered on through the arcane methods landlords use to measure square feet, and are now well prepared to accurately understand the three main ways landlords can charge rent and how much this rental will cost. You're ready to prepare your negotiation strategy, once you:

- understand the landlord's measurement system and have applied it to this rental—that is, you know exactly how much space (including common areas) is available

- have determined that the layout works for you (or can be redesigned within a reasonable cost)

- are comfortable with gross and net ways to charge for rent, so that you are ready to negotiate in the system used by your landlord

- understand percentage rent, if you're facing it, and

- have put together the various costs of doing business in this space and know roughly what it will cost you to rent here.

Chapter 5

Setting the Stage to Negotiate

Read This Chapter If ...

This chapter prepares you for your lease negotiation by helping you evaluate and capitalize on the strengths you bring to the negotiating table (and get around the weaknesses). It focuses on key lease terms that will make or break the deal, how to understand a "letter of intent" (a pre-lease proposition from the landlord), and how to find and pay for a lawyer. This chapter is especially useful in the following situations:

- You are new to business or to leasing commercial space and would benefit from some constructive analysis of your business, and advice on identifying and applying to your clout at the leasing game.
- You need help identifying deal breaker clauses.
- You have been handed a letter of intent by your landlord.
- You will be looking for a lawyer to review your lease.

You can skip this chapter if you're an old hand at negotiation and know how your strengths and weaknesses affect the outcome; you know what your deal breakers are and that they're not an issue with this space and its likely lease; your landlord will not use a letter of intent; and you've already found and hired a good lawyer to review your lease or help during the negotiation process.

If you've been shopping for space for a while—considering and rejecting various prospects along the way—you may now be ready to pursue one that fits your budget and requirements as specified on your Rental Priorities Worksheet (described at the end of Chapter 1). Everything's negotiable, as the old saying goes, and the chapters in the rest of this book give you specific tips on negotiating the key clauses that you will encounter in the typical commercial lease. Here, we focus on laying important groundwork for these negotiations and discuss important issues you should resolve before heading for the bargaining table. You must pay some attention to:

- **Your own profile.** What kind of tenant will you and your business appear to be in the eyes of your prospective landlord? The more desirable a tenant you are, the stronger your bargaining power when you negotiate the lease.
- **Deal breakers.** There are a few issues, such as the length of the lease, that you ought to iron out early in the courtship, before you or the landlord have invested significant time and resources in a deal that may ultimately wither.
- **A preliminary commitment.** If there's mutual interest in going forward, you may find it helpful to write down some early understandings in a "letter of intent," which will be revisited when you negotiate the lease. Or, your landlord may send you his own letter, summarizing how the deal is shaping up.

- **How lawyers can help.** No matter how thorough your preparation for the lease negotiations, we suggest consulting with an attorney before signing on the dotted line. If you choose a lawyer with experience, who is willing to work with you without taking over completely, the lawyer's services will be well worth the cost.

⚠ **Pursue one deal at a time.** If you and the landlord are seriously interested in doing business together, neither one should be romancing another partner on the way to the negotiation table. It's reasonable to ask the landlord to refrain from further advertising and to not respond to inquiries from other tenants' brokers while you're in negotiations. Naturally, you too should suspend your search—or at least not be actively negotiating with someone else.

A. How Much Clout Do You Have?

From a landlord's point of view, all prospective tenants are not created equal. Some businesses are financially unstable and may fold during the lease period. Some tenants will be late in paying their rent. Others will be picky, making excessive demands for maintenance and repairs. Still others will operate businesses that aren't compatible with the businesses of other tenants, or will interfere with the image the landlord is trying to create for the building.

If you're in a cold market, where commercial spaces are plentiful, you'll have an obvious advantage. The landlord may be willing to overlook a less-than-stellar financial statement or may even take a chance on you because the alternative—carrying empty space while searching for someone more attractive—is worse. But if you're in a hot market with a low vacancy rate and you're competing with other businesses for the same space, you're more likely to get the space if you can convince the landlord that you'll be an ideal tenant. And you're more likely to win concessions in lease negotiations if the landlord really wants you in the building.

Your Best Foot Forward

You'll be off to a good start with the landlord if you have the following items with
you when you meet for the first time:

- a letter of recommendation or references from your current and prior
  landlords
- a financial statement or bank records
  for your business
- business and personal tax returns from
  the last two taxable years
- your business plan, and
- a copy of your personal credit report.

You may not have to bring these documents out of your briefcase when you meet
with a prospective landlord. But it will help
immeasurably to have them close at hand
if the landlord questions your suitability
(or abilities) and needs reassurance.

1. Your Track Record As a Tenant

The landlord who rents you commercial
space will be taking a chance on your ability
to run a viable business that generates
enough money to cover your monthly
obligations. All but the most naive landlords
will investigate your past performance as a
tenant and a businessperson. The landlord
will probably look into your personal
financial situation, too. Unless you're
clearly a good risk, the lease negotiations
are unlikely to get past first base.

A careful landlord will start with the easiest and most telling question: What kind of
a tenant are you *now?* Your current landlord
will get a call asking about your timeliness
with the rent check, your care of the landlord's
property, your willingness to compromise
when disputes arise, and whether your
requests for maintenance and renovation
have been reasonable. In short, has it been
pleasant to do business with you, or a
nightmare?

The answers to these questions are, at
this point, beyond your control. But you
can make sure that whatever favorable
information your current landlord can impart
will get into the prospective landlord's
hands quickly and in writing. To get a step
ahead of the competition, ask your present
landlord for a letter of recommendation,
detailing your fine qualities as a tenant. A
sample is shown below.

If you're just starting out and have never
rented commercial property, you won't be
able to supply a letter from your current
landlord—so you'll have to think creatively
to come up with a good substitute. References from your bank, business colleagues,
former employers, or even past residential
landlords will all help convince a skeptical
landlord that you're a good bet.

> **EXAMPLE:** Martin worked for several
> years at Dan's Barber Shop, where he
> started as an assistant and then became
> a barber after completing barber school.
> When Dan retired and sold the business
> to his brother, Martin decided to open

Sample Letter of Recommendation From Current Landlord

Old Town Shops
921 Elm St.
Springfield, IL
123-456-789

December 1, 20xx

To Whom It May Concern:

I am writing to recommend Arthur Wouk for the commercial space you have available.

Arthur has been renting 1,200 square feet in our Old Town Shops building since February 1, 20xx, for his antique jewelry store, Deja New. Deja New has grown because Arthur is a hard worker, has good business judgment, has several long-term and dedicated employees, and is always willing to go the extra mile for his customers. Unfortunately, his lease is about to expire, and much as we'd like him to stay, we do not have the additional 800 square feet Arthur needs.

We will be sorry to see Arthur go. He always pays his rent on time, keeps his space in spotless condition, and is reasonable in his maintenance requests. Often, he simply took care of minor problems on his own rather than bother us. The growth of Deja New has had a good effect on other shops in the building, which have profited from the increased number of customers.

I'm confident that you will find Arthur to be a terrific tenant and Deja New a positive influence in your building. If you have any questions, please call me at the number above or email me at Ilsej@coldmail.com.

Sincerely,

Ilse Jones

Ilse Jones, Manager

his own shop. He asked Dan to write him a letter he could show to prospective landlords. Dan's recommendation described Martin's extensive knowledge of the barber shop business and his impeccable record as a trusted and valuable employee. Dan also noted that Martin was a skilled and popular barber and would undoubtedly bring many of his longtime customers with him to his new location. The landlord who read this letter got a good picture of someone who had a reputation for integrity, knew his business, and would "hit the ground running" with a client base—a good sign that the business would prosper from the outset and have no trouble paying its rent.

Some of you, however, may suspect that your past or current landlord will *not* give you a good recommendation. In fact, you may be looking to change locations precisely because of problems with your current landlord. Certainly, you won't volunteer that landlord's name as a contact. But if you're asked, you need to be prepared. Remember the old adage that the best defense is a good offense? Apply it here, tailored to the reason underlying the landlord's lack of enthusiasm. Basically, there are two scenarios (each with endless variations) that your current unhappy tenancy might fit into:

- **The individual (or the situation) was impossible, demanding, unfair, or shifty.** Mentally prepare a description that is accurate but not overblown. Then, explain your position, which

hopefully describes what any reasonable businessperson in your shoes would have done (or not done). In the end, you want your listener to conclude that you made the best of a poor situation and the landlord probably wouldn't recommend *anyone,* let alone you.

EXAMPLE: Susan rented office space from Sal, who owned and operated a medium-sized office building downtown. Almost from the start, Susan began having problems with the landlord. Sal discontinued the security service, which was guaranteed under the lease; refused to fix the plumbing problems in the lobby restrooms; and did nothing about another tenant's habit of leaving trash in the hallways. Susan's requests for a replacement security guard and needed maintenance were unavailing—in fact, Sal grew increasingly hostile and even suggested that Susan was to blame for some of the problems. Anxious to move the moment her lease was up, Susan began looking for other space after two-and-a-half years. Needless to say, she had no intention of listing Sal as a reference.

When Susan spoke with Ed, the owner of an office complex with an attractive vacancy, Susan was prepared. She had mentally rehearsed how she would describe her current tenancy, listing the problems and Sal's lack of cooperation as objectively as possible. She had written statements from other tenants in the building, corroborating the difficult situation created by Sal. Finally, she contacted the landlord who had rented her an office ten years ago. This landlord willingly wrote Susan a letter in which he spoke highly of her as a tenant.

- **You made a mistake or two.** It's always possible that circumstances, igno-rance, or just bad judgment cast a pall over your last tenancy. Try to show how you have moved beyond that point, with some hard evidence if possible. For example, if you were late with a few rent payments be-cause you had trouble meeting your payroll, your business plan should re-flect scaled-back expansion plans, which ought to free up more ready cash. Or, if your former manager had a tendency to stack trash in the com-mon area, explain that you fired the guy and now have a neatnik for a new manager—someone who's me-ticulous about dumping trash the right way.

2. The Health of Your Business

Another way to show that you're a desirable tenant is to give the landlord a positive financial picture of your business. To do so, show the landlord your tax returns or a financial statement from your accountant. (An astute landlord may ask you to sign a waiver that allows him to see these accounts.) If you do turn over financial information,

consider asking the landlord for a letter promising to keep the information confi-dential.

If you have a business plan with realistic goals and specific strategies for meeting them, show it to your prospective landlord. If you don't have a plan, now might be the time to develop one—you'll find it useful in more situations than this. In the meantime, a simple one- or two-page budget may suffice. On the left, list your anticipated sources of income—investors and customers, for example—and the amounts you expect from each within the first year or two of the lease. On the right, itemize your major anticipated expenses. Just the fact that you've carefully thought through the economic issues may be enough to impress the land-lord.

EXAMPLE: Ling had worked for years for a large computer company before opening her new business, 24-Hour Computer Repair. Although impressed with Ling's serious approach to finding office space, landlord Mary was skeptical about Ling's ability to successfully run the new operation. Mary asked Ling for a financial picture of the business in-come and expenses that Ling expected for 24-Hour within the first two years of the lease.

Ling consulted her accountant and her business associates, some of whom had recently worked for small computer service businesses like 24-Hour. They helped her figure her income and expenses like this:

Business Budget

Annual Income

Corporate Accounts	$75,000
Individual Accounts	$50,000
Total Income	$125,000

Annual Expenses

Rent (Gross Lease)	$18,000
Wages and Related Expenses (One Employee)	$35,000
Telephone, Including Yellow Pages Ad	$ 4,800
Equipment and Supplies	$ 5,000
Insurance	$ 1,200
Transportation	$ 6,000
Legal and Accounting	$ 1,500
Total Expense	$71,500
Profit	**$53,500**

Since Ling organized her business as a sole proprietorship, she would earn $53,500 ($125,000 less $71,500) if her estimates proved to be correct. Mary was satisfied that Ling had a viable business plan and agreed to lease her the space.

For help in creating a business plan, see *How to Write a Business Plan*, by Mike McKeever (Nolo). This book will show you how to realistically evaluate your needs, plan for the future, and fit expenses within a budget.

If your business has been rocky for the past few years, be prepared to explain why you believe better times are ahead. Maybe the new location will make a huge difference, or perhaps you're getting a big infusion of cash from an investor or lender that will let you do things right from now on.

What if you're a start-up? You may not have a history as a successful business, but you can still reassure the landlord that you know what you're doing and can be counted on not to fail. Your personal financial status, discussed below, becomes even more important, as does your business plan.

3. Your Personal Finances

Be prepared to divulge the health of your personal finances, for example by showing the landlord your tax returns. You may balk, but the landlord's request is reasonable because, if you're a sole proprietor (a one-person operation) or your business is a partnership, by law you'll be personally responsible for the rent if the business can't cover it. Naturally, the landlord will be curious about your personal finances in case you're called upon to write the rent check.

The situation is much the same if you run your small business as a corporation or limited liability company (LLC). As explained in Chapter 7, Section B, these business forms protect your personal assets *unless* you explicitly agree to put them on the line. Many landlords will indeed insist on personal guarantees from the corporation shareholders or LLC members and, when they do, will want to know how good the guarantees will be. This means that the landlord may want you and the other owners to furnish information about your personal finances. Obviously, a guarantee from an impoverished business owner is no better than a lease commitment from a shaky business.

The personal guarantee will usually be in the lease itself. Usually, a corporate officer or LLC member will sign the lease on behalf of the business. At that point, only the business is on the hook—not the individual owners. But then the owners (the shareholders or LLC members) will sign separately as guarantors, which makes them personally liable for lease payments if the business doesn't pay. Sometimes, these personal guarantees are instead put into a separate document that's signed at the same time as the lease.

Your landlord may also ask for additional guarantors who are not members of your business—a friend, family member, or another businessperson who agrees to stand behind your rent obligations. The lease guarantee clause is explained in detail in Chapter 17, Section G.

Watch out for personal guarantees when signing a lease for a nonprofit group. If you're working with a nonprofit organization such as a 501(c)(3), you may experience some difficulty renting space. Some landlords conclude, however wrongly, that many nonprofits are underfunded and run

by volunteers who will take off when their interest wanes, leaving the organization unstaffed and unable to meet its obligations, including the rent bill. If you encounter this attitude, show the prospective landlord your balance sheets, business plan, and so on—but think long and hard before agreeing to sign the lease as a guarantor. It's one thing to freely give your time, money, and energy to a good cause, but it's another entirely to put your personal assets on the line.

Check your credit report and clean up any problems. Because it's likely that you'll be personally responsible for the rent, the landlord may want a copy of your personal credit report as well as reports for each co-owner of your business. Check your credit report before you start looking for space, so you'll have a chance to correct or clear up any mistakes such as out-of-date or just plain wrong information. Problems with your personal credit won't automatically disqualify you from renting commercial space, but you may have to take additional measures so that the landlord feels comfortable leasing to you. You might, for example, offer to post a larger-than-normal security deposit or to get a credit-worthy person to cosign the lease.

Be aware, too, that credit information is available about businesses as well as individuals. Dun & Bradstreet, for example, keeps tabs on businesses, as do many local credit bureaus. Of course, you want your business credit picture to look as positive as possible.

For information on obtaining your credit file, getting out of debt and rebuilding your credit, see *Credit Repair,* by Robin Leonard (Nolo).

Contacting Credit Bureaus

There are three major credit bureaus in the United States. You can contact any one of them for a copy of your credit report, and can get one free copy per year.

- Experian, 888-397-3742, www.experian.com
- Trans Union, 800-916-8800, www.transunion.com
- Equifax, 800-685-1111, www.equifax.com

---

4. Keep Your Perspective

Get the relationship off on the right foot by concentrating on major issues, such as the type of lease (gross or net), the cost per square foot and the landlord's willingness to pay for improvements you need. Some of these major issues are discussed in Section B, below, with specific details and negotiation tips in other chapters. Of course, all issues—whether major or minor—will have to be addressed sooner or later. But don't press immediately for concessions that should be the subject of give-and-take further down the line. Doing so will signal to the landlord that you lack an essential attribute—proper perspective. That spells "irrational tenant" for some landlords. For example, if you want the landlord to install a few additional electric outlets or replace a window, hold off until you've negotiated more crucial items.

5. What Do You Bring to the Table?

Besides making sure you can meet your financial obligations as a tenant, the landlord will be interested in whether your presence in the building will boost its value and make it a more desirable place for other tenants looking for space. Think of ways your landlord might benefit from having you as a tenant. Of course, you want your business credit picture to look as positive as possible. Point out to the landlord that you might:

- **Attract more customers because your business is compatible with existing tenants.** A café next to a bookstore and a hardware store near a nursery are mutually beneficial combinations.
- **Improve the building's image.** A florist with attractive outdoor displays will enhance any property. A highly regarded nonprofit organization will add a sense of civic responsibility.
- **Leave the building with added value because of the improvements you plan to make.** Your installation of sophisticated lighting and flooring can be used by the next tenant, which will make the space more desirable (and capable of supporting a higher rent) next time it's leased out.
- **Contribute to the building's quiet atmosphere because your business generates little traffic.** The landlord may be looking for a tenant to fill the space but not the parking garage, hallways, or the building's quiet ambiance. If yours is a low-impact business, such as a computer consultant, you might be just the ticket.
- **Provide services needed by other tenants in the building.** The landlord may warm up to the idea of a copy shop in an office building, a pharmacy in a medical building, or a framing shop in a strip mall with a photography shop.

B. Your Landlord's Compliance With the Executive Order on Terrorism

So far we've described the common ways a prospective landlord will check out the health of your business and its track record with former landlords, banks, and lenders. Especially if you are dealing with a large, institutional landlord, you may encounter one more type of "due diligence": Your landlord will investigate you to make sure you aren't a terrorist or affiliated or doing business with a terrorist organization. Don't conclude that the landlord is going to ridiculous extremes, and don't take these questions personally—the landlord is simply complying with Executive Order 13224, which went into effect on September 24, 2001. This section will explain the order's purpose and focus, how landlords investigate tenants in order to comply with the law, and how you may be asked to certify in a lease clause that you are not a terrorist or doing business with one.

1. The Purpose and Reach of Executive Order 13324

Following 9/11, the federal government took steps to prevent terrorists from operating in the United States, and to freeze their assets. The order made it illegal to do business—which includes signing a lease—with any individual or business on a list of terrorist organizations. The U.S. Treasury Department maintains the government's list of "Specially Designated Nationals and Blocked Persons," or "SDNs".

As a result of Executive Order 13224, landlords, brokers, attorneys, and management companies must screen prospective and even current tenants, contractors, and employees against the government's long and growing list of terrorist organizations. Signing a lease or doing business with anyone on the list of SDNs will expose the landlord, broker, and others who must comply with the law to civil and criminal penalties, as well as damaging publicity.

If an organization or entity is on the list of SDNs, it means that the government has frozen all of its reachable assets and no one may begin or continue to deal with it. The list of SDNs is more than 200 pages long, filled with thousands of entries. Many entries include aliases (preceded by the letters "a.k.a."), "doing business as" ("d.b.a.") notes, and individuals' dates of birth. You can view the list on the government website at www.treas.gov/offices/eotffc/ofac/sdn/index.html. The Treasury website also contains articles and forms (for reporting a "match" and a rejected transaction).

2. How Landlords Comply With Executive Order 13224

Landlords and others can check the SDN list for potential tenants and others by simply looking for the name on the list, the way you'd look in a phone book. If the target is an individual or a publicly traded company, this may be the end of the investigation. But if you are a privately owned entity, a careful landlord will also search for the names of all officers and directors, as well as partners, shareholders, and members (for LLCs) having at least a 25% ownership interest in your business.

Checking the list manually can be time-consuming, and large landlords particularly often use software to search electronically for matches to all names, d.b.a.s, and aliases. Websites and companies also offer this service. If your landlord searches the SDN list by buying software, signing on with a website, or outsourcing the search, you may find that you'll be asked to pay for the search, either directly or in the form of administrative fees.

Beware of "false positives." The SDN list contains many common Anglo, Hispanic, and Arabic names, which makes false matches a real possibility. If, unfortunately, your name appears to match an entry on the list, make sure your landlord compares the information you've provided against that on the list—if the information doesn't match, your landlord should proceed with the deal. The government will assist you and the landlord in evaluating and resolving a possible match. Go to the Treasury Department's Office of Foreign Assets Control (OFAC) at www.treas.gov/ofices/eotffc/ofac/faq/one_page.html, or call the hotline at 800-540-6322.

3. Lease Clause Concerning Executive Order 13224

Cautious landlords will not only search for your name on the SDN list, but will also place a clause in your lease in which you certify that you are not a terrorist or working on behalf of a terrorist individual, organization, or anyone on the SDN list. It's likely to be called an "OFAC Compliance" clause, and you have nothing to fear from its inclusion. Just be sure that you aren't, indeed, doing business with anyone on the list of terrorist organizations.

C. Getting Past Deal Breakers

Chapters 7 through 18 explore in detail the many clauses you're likely to find in a commercial lease prepared by the landlord, including security deposit requirements, restrictions on how you use the property, and who will pay for improvements. Before you actually sign a lease and commit yourself to moving to the space, and even before you consider setting down a preliminary outline of the deal in a letter of intent (covered below in Section D), you'll want to review each clause carefully to make sure you understand its legal and practical implications. Depending on your clout as a

prospective tenant, you'll want to negotiate changes where the lease seems unreasonable or inadequate.

But before you get to the point of studying a lease, you'll want to become comfortable with the broad outlines of the deal. If the main features of the lease arrangements aren't to your liking and the landlord appears unwilling or unable to change them, it makes little sense to invest further time and effort in the transaction. By contrast, if you and the landlord see eye to eye on the key terms, or can at least agree to negotiate them, the chances are good that with a bit of give and take, the two of you can work it out.

If you've hired your own broker, some of these issues may have already been raised. One of the advantages of hiring a broker is that, having seen your Rental Priorities Worksheet, the broker knows what your deal breakers are. They're among the items listed in the "Essentials" column (there are other items on your worksheet too, such as "Near a metro line," that are not relevant to your lease negotiations). Hopefully, the broker has done some homework on the space and the landlord and has steered you to an appropriate match.

Obviously, your average monthly expense for the space (discussed in Chapter 4) is very important. If the cost is too high, you'll be faced with a choice of walking away from the deal or burdening your business with an overhead that may limit your ability to grow and may even threaten the viability of the business.

So as soon as the space looks like a serious possibility for your business, raise the following issues at the first meeting with the landlord. If you and the landlord are in synch, it may make sense to put these understandings in a writing, called a "letter of intent," as discussed in Section D.

Nonnegotiable Issues

You and the landlord need to see eye to eye on the following issues before you begin serious negotiations:

- Amount of the rent (or, if it's a net lease, a good approximation). Rent is explained in Chapter 9.
- Size of the space. The ways landlords measure space are explained in Chapter 4, Section A.
- Length of the lease (its term). Lease terms are covered in Chapter 8.
- Options—the landlord's willingness to let you extend the lease or expand into additional space in the future, if that's important to you. Options are explained in Chapter 14.
- Renovations—who pays to fix up your space and make the improvements you want. Paying for renovations is covered in Chapter 11.

If there are other critical, nonnegotiable issues (consult your Rental Priorities Worksheet for the "Unacceptables"), add them to this checklist and raise them as soon as you and the landlord begin talking.

1. The Length of the Lease

You may be looking for a long- or short-term lease. Factors such as the age and stability of your business, your plans for growth, the nature of your work, and the changes you'll expect in the neighborhood will all affect your decision. In Chapter 1, Section E, we explained the differences between short- and long-term leases and asked you to decide, at least preliminarily, what length you would like. In Chapter 8, we'll guide you through the negotiations of the term clause. Now it's time to make sure that the landlord can give you the length of lease that will fit your requirements.

> **EXAMPLE:** Fitness for Life, a gym catering to women, began looking for new quarters when it lost its lease. Since the gym relied heavily on local residents and word of mouth—in short, repeat and steady clients—Fitness wanted a lease that would be long enough to allow the gym to become established. The owner noted "3-year minimum, 5-year desired" on the "Essentials" section of her Rental Priorities Worksheet. When the space checked out okay, the owner made an appointment with the landlord and asked, at that meeting, whether the landlord would rent for the term she wanted.

Unfortunately, the landlord may not be able to give you the length of lease you'd like. The space may be the subject of an option held by another tenant, who may take it some time in the future. For example, in a multitenant property an existing tenant may have an expansion right into "your" space that may be exercised at a specific date. If so, the space will be available to you only until that time. The landlord can't offer you a lease that extends beyond the exercise date of the option-holding tenant.

Even landlords who aren't constrained by preexisting options may still be unwilling to meet your needs. If this happens, look elsewhere.

2. Getting a Short-Term Lease in a Long-Term World

If you're uncomfortable with a lease longer than a year, but the landlord is looking for a tenant to sign up for five years, the deal may not be workable. Is there a reasonable likelihood that the landlord will agree to a shorter term?

The answer will depend on current conditions in the real estate market. Like many other issues in lease negotiations, the landlord's willingness to bend a bit may depend on whether you're the only fish in the water. If the vacancy rate for commercial space is relatively high, obviously the landlord is likely to be more flexible. Vacant space is expensive to carry and the landlord may have to make some compromises to get some rent income flowing in. By contrast, if the rental waters are teeming with would-be tenants, the landlord is more likely to hold fast, figuring that some other

tenant will show up soon who's willing to sign a longer-term lease—and meet the landlord's other demands as well.

If the landlord insists on a lease term that's longer than you'd like, all is not necessarily lost. You may decide to agree to a lease term that's longer than ideal—say, three years rather than one—as long as the lease gives you a way to get out earlier if necessary. To set up this contingency, you and the landlord would agree that you can terminate the lease after a set amount of time (for instance, one year) as long as you pay a predetermined amount, such as a month or two of additional rent. Clauses allowing you to terminate a lease early are explained in Chapter 14, Section G.

You may be able to get out of a long lease by turning over your rental to another tenant—by subleasing or assigning. Most leases allow you to do both, but only with the landlord's consent. If you can find a qualified replacement, this may be your ticket out, since in many states landlords can't unreasonably turn away an acceptable prospect. Chapter 14, Section F, explains subleases and assignments.

3. Is the Space Available?

For some businesses, the move-in date is crucial. For example, if you're already renting space and looking to move, you may have to meet a specific move-out deadline under your current lease. Or, if your business is season-specific (such as tax preparers, who are busiest in the months preceding April 15), you may urgently need to be installed in your commercial space by a certain date to be ready for seasonal demands.

Coordinating your needs with those of the landlord can be difficult. It's easiest when the space is vacant and you and the landlord agree on a firm move-in date that's a month or two away. (Unless the space requires major renovation or is in a new building with no interior improvements in place, this is normally enough time to get everything ready.) But if the space needs major work or you're concerned about whether the current tenant will vacate on time, you may have a problem. Now's the time to deal with it, before getting deep into lease negotiations. If the solutions suggested below aren't feasible, consider looking elsewhere.

Stay where you are a little longer while waiting. Perhaps your current landlord has no one waiting to take over your space and would be willing to allow you to stay on a month-to-month basis. If so, this is an attractive solution, since you can stay for just the amount of time it takes your new space to be available.

If you have a clause in your current lease giving you the right to renew it (an option clause), you may want to consider exercising it. But be careful. Chances are that the option provides for a term that's much longer than the time you need. If so, ask your current landlord to let you exercise the option to renew for a shorter time. If

the landlord refuses and you're obligated for the entire term, you'll have to try sublet when your new quarters become available. But because subletting usually requires the cooperation of the current landlord, this tack may not work. Read the discussion on subletting in Chapter 14, Section F, carefully before considering this route.

Move to an interim location while waiting. Moving twice is certainly expensive and a hassle. But if the space you're waiting for is worth it, this may be your best bet. This solution works best for businesses that don't rely substantially on location, such as a mail-order business, and would not be appropriate for a neighborhood-specific service business, such as a dry cleaners.

4. Options to Expand or Renew Your Lease

When you negotiate a lease, chances are you're not focusing much on what will happen at the *end* of the lease. It's worthwhile, however, to give the matter some attention now—in fact, we hope you considered it when filling in your Rental Priorities Worksheet, as explained in Chapter 1. If your business does well and the location continues to be suitable, you may want to stay another three, five, or even ten years.

In a similar vein, think about whether you'll physically outgrow the space you're considering now. If so, it may be important to have the ability to expand without moving again. Especially if your business is location-sensitive or difficult to set up (involving lots of unique renovation, for example), you may feel that an expansion right is very important.

When the need arises, you may get lucky and find that the landlord will renew your lease or can offer you the extra space. But to guarantee these things, you'll need options to renew and expand. An option—which gives you the right to do or not do some-thing—is usually something you pay for, either directly or in the form of concessions on other lease terms that are important to the landlord. But once you have an option, it's like insurance—the renewal or expansion is there if you need it.

The lease clauses for option rights are explained in detail in Chapter 14. For now, raise the issue to see whether you get a green light. Keep in mind that the landlord may be legally restricted from giving you these option rights. If there's no way that the landlord can give you an option—for example, other tenants in the building may have options on the space you'll be renting once your lease expires—you'll want to know now.

5. Renovations: Who Pays?

If you want to have the space customized to your specifications, you'll have to deter-mine (perhaps with the help of a space planner, architect, or contractor) exactly what needs to be done and what it's likely to cost. In Chapter 11, we explain the many complicated ways that landlords and tenants can split the responsibility and cost of renovations and how to negotiate the best deal. For now, if the expense is significant to you, you'll want to learn if the landlord is amenable to paying for some or all of this work.

If the landlord isn't willing to get involved with making or paying for renovations, you may decide that the other aspects of the deal are so good that you can afford to arrange and pay for the renovations your-self. If so, you'll still need to find out if the landlord will let you make the renovations. The answer may turn on whether the land-lord approves of your plans and feels the work will increase the value of the building. If the space isn't that great and the landlord is adamantly opposed to your plans or your request for assistance, you may want to look elsewhere.

D. Letter of Intent

After you and the landlord have talked over the key terms (deal breakers) outlined in Section C and you find there's mutual interest in your becoming a tenant, the next step is often—but not always—for the landlord to give you a proposed lease to review. The lease will normally contain the terms you and the landlord discussed, plus a number of other legal clauses intended primarily to protect the landlord's interest. Chapters 7 through 18 cover lease clauses in detail and will guide you in negotiating the lease handed to you by the landlord.

Sometimes, however, there's an intermediate stage between the courtship (your mutual interest in doing business) and marriage (signing the lease itself). Think of it as "getting engaged." Like a romantic engagement, this stage reflects your serious commitment to making the deal (the marriage) happen. In real estate lingo, this period of serious commitment is reflected in a written document, called a "letter of intent."

A letter of intent may be written by the landlord or the landlord's lawyer, or by you or your lawyer. The letter summarizes key issues that you've already discussed, such as the deal breakers mentioned above (rent, space, available date, expansion/renewal rights, and renovations), and may mention other aspects of the lease negotiations, such as a timeline for improvement work and moving in. The letter can be legally binding or nonbinding, depending on how it's written and how you and the landlord treat it. In short, the letter of intent may be a mini-lease or a simple road map for future negotiations.

In this section, we'll explain key aspects of letters of intent, including:

- the value—and risks—of writing (or accepting) a letter of intent
- how to respond to a landlord's letter that you're not comfortable with, and
- how to write a clear letter of intent.

1. Value of a Letter of Intent

A letter of intent can play an important psychological role in your developing relationship with a potential landlord. The letter highlights the important issues that have either been resolved or will need to be worked out cooperatively. The letter reflects your belief that a deal is seriously possible, making it more likely that both of you will be comfortable committing additional time and money to make it happen. (For example, you'll feel better about paying a lawyer to review a lease if you know with some certainty that the deal isn't likely to fall apart.) And the letter can perform an important housekeeping function, setting the negotiating steps that will help make the process move more smoothly.

2. Risks of a Letter of Intent

Sometimes, however, using a letter of intent isn't a good idea. For one, if the deal between you and the landlord is quite simple and straightforward, it may be simply a waste of time for you or the landlord to write a letter of intent. You both might be better served by getting right to the lease.

In fact, in the majority of small business lease deals, you're better off doing just that.

But let's suppose that the landlord's lawyer has sent you a letter of intent. What's to worry about other than spending some extra time on preliminaries? Plenty. You need to be very sure that the innocuous-looking letter does not turn into something you're stuck with—a "binding" letter of intent, which may commit you to the rental terms as described in the letter. Unless you take steps, you may be legally stuck with the understandings in the letter, just as you are when signing any lease or contract.

It's rarely a good idea to either receive or write a binding letter of intent. That's because, from a practical point of view, there's little you can do if the landlord disregards the binding nature of the letter and reopens an issue. For example, suppose you receive a letter in which the landlord states that the monthly rent includes a certain number of parking spaces. If the landlord has a change of heart at the negotiation table, you'll have a choice: Either negotiate the issue afresh or sue the landlord in an effort to enforce the letter of intent. Do you really want to get into a legal battle with a landlord over a letter of intent? Of course not. It's better to negotiate the issue now and, if the landlord won't budge and the matter is important to you, walk away from the deal. In Section 3, below, we offer suggestions on how to respond to a letter from a landlord that pushes you to an early commitment. In Section 4, we show you how to write your own letter of intent without making it binding.

The Ties That Bind: How to Recognize a Binding Letter of Intent

What does a binding letter look like? Sometimes, the landlord will clearly label it as such ("Dear Ms. Tenant, Please accept this binding letter of intent..."). More often, however, you have to examine the words and the tone. Here's what to look for:

- **"As we have agreed...."** The landlord states that the two of you have agreed to the terms in the letter. This may create a binding letter (unless you do something about it, as explained below).
- **"Unless I hear from you to the contrary..."** The landlord lists the terms and then invites you to write back if you disagree. If she doesn't hear from you, you may become legally bound.
- **"Yours truly, Mrs. Landlord."** The letter recites the terms of the rental and ends without any of the telltale phrases mentioned above. Even though the landlord hasn't expressly stated that he considers these terms binding, they might become so unless you dispute them by writing your own letter (explained below).

Nonbinding letters, on the other hand, clearly announce themselves as preliminary, rough outlines of lease terms that are yet to be finalized. (See the sample letter of intent, below.) It should reference the need for further negotiations. If you aren't sure whether the letter is binding or not, assume that it is (and take steps to protect yourself, as outlined below in Section 3).

3. Responding to a Letter You Can't Live With

You may receive a letter of intent from your landlord that announces itself as a binding letter—or maybe it just has the tell-tale signs mentioned in the sidebar above. For the reasons explained, you don't want to let a binding letter remain on the table. And even if it's nonbinding, the preliminary understandings may be far too specific and final for your tastes—for example, the letter may spell out a timeline for negotiations that either rushes you or stretches the process too far. For whatever reason, you may reasonably conclude that you can't live with the tone, statements, or plan in the letter. But you'd still like to continue negotiations for this space. What should you do?

You may be tempted to simply ignore the letter. After all, you didn't write it and haven't signed it, so you aren't committed, right? Wrong. Even though *you* may think that the letter is ineffectual, the landlord may assume otherwise. For example, if you don't respond to the landlord's statement that the property will be available on a certain date and not earlier, you may find yourself shut down by an indignant landlord when you try to negotiate the date during lease talks. Far better to clarify the situation by responding in one of the following ways:

1. **Send the landlord a letter that proposes more negotiations before the two of you exchange a letter of intent.** If the landlord's letter has rushed you, apply the brakes. A written request that you prefer to continue informal negotiations before taking the next step should signal that you aren't ready.

2. **Write back with your own letter of intent.** If the landlord's letter recites—or even suggests—binding understandings, it is very important to set the record straight. Be careful, however, that the two of you don't get bogged down in trading conflicting letters. If this begins to happen, it's a sure sign that you don't yet have a meeting of the minds on key points. Instead, back off and reopen the issues that divide you by simply talking about them. You can always reduce them to writing later.

Don't commit yourself to a particular lease form. Your landlord's letter of intent may include a statement that the two of you will use a lease form prepared by the landlord, the landlord's management company, or the landlord's attorney. While this may seem like a benign detail, it can spell trouble ahead if the landlord thinks this means that you won't attempt to change the language of the lease clauses (which have been drafted to favor the landlord, naturally). Once you relinquish your right to bargain, you've given up everything.

4. How to Write Your Own Letter of Intent

Let's assume now that you're the one who writes a letter of intent to your potential landlord. Here's how to do so.

a. Set the Tone

It's usually best to write a letter that simply summarizes key aspects of the hoped-for rental. The issues you may want to cover are listed in Subsection b, below; here, we suggest a workable approach.

Be flexible. The most important part of your letter is a clear statement that you don't intend your letter to be binding. Giving yourself and the landlord room to negotiate is as important as setting some preliminary parameters of your eventual deal.

Give yourself room to negotiate new issues. You don't want a landlord to claim that only those issues raised in your letter of intent should be the subjects of continued negotiations. For example, if you don't mention an improvements allowance in the letter (that's the amount of money the landlord will give you to customize the space to your needs), you want to make sure that you can still negotiate for one before you sign a lease. To ensure that the landlord can't claim that the letter of intent limits the available bargaining points, simply say that future negotiations may cover additional points.

b. What to Include in a Letter of Intent

Your letter will probably cover key deal-breaker terms, such as the move-in date and option possibilities discussed above in Section C, but may be a bit broader, depending on what's most important to

you. Any letter of intent that you write should include the following information:

- the name of the entity that will be the landlord
- the name of the entity that will be the tenant
- a promise to deal exclusively with each other until you sign a lease or one of you walks away—in other words, neither will attempt to strike a deal with someone else while you're negotiating
- a description of the space you'd like to occupy
- the term and move-in date
- the rent and what it will include, such as utilities
- a description of your intended use of the property, and any acceptable restrictions
- renovations and how they will be paid for
- who is responsible for maintenance and repair, and
- any other charges you're obligated to pay.

Of course, you'd want to include any special items that are important to you—signage, for example, or the right to take over adjacent space—which aren't on the above list.

You and the landlord may decide to finalize your leasing arrangement without the use of attorneys (although we suggest otherwise, as explained in Section E, below). The landlord may use the letter as a guide when preparing the lease, turning points in the letter into lease clauses. Because the letter was not binding (hopefully, you didn't let a binding letter get past you), it will be possible to renegotiate these issues. And since a letter usually doesn't cover all the issues in a typical lease, the lease will include new issues, too. Of course, these will also be subject to negotiation, as will any clauses that you might want to add.

c. How the Landlord's Lawyer May Use the Letter of Intent

Many landlords use an attorney to help with the leasing process as it progresses from the letter of intent stage to the prepared lease stage. Typically, the landlord lawyers pull out their "standard lease" from their file cabinets (or call it up on their computers) and compare it to the letter of intent, modifying the lease as necessary to make it consistent with the understandings in the letter. You and the landlord put further negotiations on hold until a draft lease is ready.

The landlord's lease will probably contain other terms that weren't raised in the letter of intent. Many of these terms will be just boiler-plate, lawyerly details—such as a clause specifying that the lease and any amendments represent the entire understanding between the landlord and the tenant. But this isn't always the case. If your letter has left out important points, the landlord's lawyer may put them in (and you can be sure that they're drafted to favor the landlord). The landlord's lawyer isn't necessarily just complicating matters—remember,

the lawyer has been retained to look out for the client's interests, and if the landlord's lawyer spots an issue that needs to be addressed, the lawer is duty-bound to include it. You, of course, are free to object and negotiate.

![!] **See a lawyer before drafting a lease on your own.** Occasionally, a landlord will ask a tenant to draft the lease. Only a small-scale landlord who's new at the game will give up the ability to control the lease. If you encounter one of these unsophisticated souls, get the help of a lawyer so that you can maximize the opportunity to write a favorable lease.

The sample letter of intent, below, shows how you might frame a letter of intent for issues you believe have been settled. You can probably do something similar on your own, but to avoid legal pitfalls, it makes sense to have your lawyer review it.

Sample Letter of Intent

Sports Aplenty LLC
27 Presidents Way
Houston, Texas 55555

July 1, 20xx

Debbie O'Brien, President
Riverside Commerce Associates Inc.
123 Chester Ave.
Fort Worth, TX 55555

Dear Ms. O'Brien:

This is a letter of intent written on behalf of Sports Aplenty LLC ["Sports"]. We believe that the following points represent initial understandings between our company and Riverside Commerce Associates, Inc. ["Riverside"]. Sports and Riverside are free to negotiate on other issues not mentioned here.

1. **Exclusive Dealing:** During the negotiation period, Sports agrees that it will not negotiate for or enter into a letter of intent regarding any other premises, nor will it extend its present lease. Similarly, Riverside agrees not to advertise the premises or negotiate or enter into a letter of intent with any other prospective tenant regarding the premises.

2. **Premises:** Sports proposes to lease from your company the first floor of the Riverside Commerce Plaza, 123 Chester Ave., as shown on the attached building floor plan.

3. **Use:** Sports will use the space for the retail sale of sports equipment and clothing, service and repair of the items we sell, and meeting space for athletic teams that we sponsor. Riverside and Sports will continue to discuss whether Sports will be bound to use the premises for these purposes only.

4. **Term:** The term will be three years, beginning September 1, 20xx, or sooner if the space becomes available sooner.

Sample Letter of Intent (continued)

5. **Options to Renew:** Sports will have two options to renew, each for a period of two years.

6. **Base Rent:** The base rent will be $1,500 per month for the original term of the lease; $1,600 per month for the first option term; and $1,700 per month for the second option term. Sports will not pay additional sums for common area maintenance.

7. **Utilities:** In addition to the base rent, Sports will pay for the cost of natural gas, water, and electricity for the floor. Each of these utilities will be separately metered for the floor. Riverside will pay for the cost, if any, of meter installation.

8. **Improvements:** Before the move-in date, Riverside will provide and pay for the improvements described in the plans and specifications prepared by Lone Star Architectural Group, dated June 1, 20xx.

9. **Maintenance and Repairs:** Riverside will be responsible for maintaining and repairing the ceiling, floor, outer walls, windows, doors, and HVAC system. Sports will be responsible for maintaining everything else within its space, including the fixtures, wall coverings, and flooring.

10. **Taxes:** Riverside Commerce will be responsible for all real estate taxes. Any new taxes, such as a payroll tax, will be paid by Riverside.

11. **Insurance:** Riverside will carry insurance on the building. Sports will insure its own personal property used in the premises and will also carry public liability insurance with $1,000,000 policy limits for injuries to people and $100,000 policy limits for damage to property. Sports will ask its carrier to add Riverside to its policy as an additional insured.

12. **Signage:** Sports will be allowed to install above its front entry the sign shown in the attached sketch. Sports will remove the sign when it moves out and restore the wall to its original condition.

13. **Smoking:** Riverside will enforce a strict nonsmoking policy for all units in the building and all common areas.

14. **Parking:** A marked parking space in front of the store will be provided for the Sports store manager. Sports and Riverside will continue to discuss the possibility of renting additional spaces.

Sample Letter of Intent (continued)

15. **Personal Guarantee:** Joseph Esposito, Sports Aplenty member, and I will personally guarantee payment of the rent for the first 18 months. If you wish, we will provide you with business references and our current financial statement as prepared by our accountant.

If this proposal meets with your approval, please indicate so below and return a copy to me. After we have discussed the unsettled issues and come to an agreement, please prepare a lease for my review.

Yours truly,

Randall Pastor

Randall Pastor
Member/Manager
Sports Aplenty LLC
A Texas Limited Liability Company

Acceptance

Your proposal looks fine to me. After we have finalized negotiations, I will have a lease prepared for you to review.

Riverside Commerce Associates Inc.
A Texas Corporation

By: _____

   Debbie O'Brien
   President

Date: _____, 20xx

E. Finding and Paying for a Lawyer

You may want an experienced real estate lawyer to help you negotiate your lease. This book shows you the lay of the land by explaining the meaning and significance of the clauses in the landlord's lease, but it's no substitute for a legal analysis of the particular lease your landlord has handed to you. While it's true that hiring a lawyer will add expense and perhaps time to your lease negotiations, in the long run it can be worth it. Here are some of the important things a good lawyer can do for you:

- Spot subtle (or even not so subtle) variations on the lease clauses we cover in this book, and explain their meaning to you.
- Warn you of hidden problems (or windfalls) in the lease that aren't obvious to the unprofessional eye.
- Review your Negotiation Strategy Worksheet and offer suggestions (this worksheet is explained in Chapter 6).
- Act as a valuable partner during the sometimes hairy process of hammering out a lease.
- Suggest specific, legally appropriate wording to replace what the landlord has used.
- Help as a buffer between you and the landlord, enabling you to say, "I'm sorry but my lawyer insists on these changes!"

In Chapter 6, we'll explain how to use your lawyer during lease negotiations.

Here, we focus on finding one, and the various ways you can pay your lawyer.

1. Finding and Selecting a Lawyer

Many lawyers in general practice have only limited experience in landlord-tenant legal issues—and even those with some experience may know only about residential tenancies. So if you just pick a name out of the phone book or go to the lawyer who prepared your will, you may wind up with someone who's less than ideal for handling commercial lease issues.

Your best bet is to find a lawyer who regularly represents small businesses. These lawyers are used to working with commercial leases and the problems that come with them. They understand the ins and outs of business tenancies and can often suggest effective strategies that general practitioners don't know about.

It's a good idea to find a lawyer early in the life of your business. Even if you're a committed self-help type who does loads of things on your own, you're likely to need legal services from time to time. Someone who already knows your business plan, personal goals, finances, and everything else about your business will have essential background information when you come in with a legal problem. If an issue requires more specialized expertise than your lawyer possesses—you may need advice on a trademark question, for example—your lawyer can refer you to a specialist.

EXAMPLE: Liz was working as the manager of a kitchen supply store and decided to strike out on her own. Her plan was to create an online catalog operation called PotPort.com. After asking half a dozen small business friends about local lawyers, she found that Bernie—who represented many other small businesses—was just right for her new venture. Liz met with Bernie to explain her plans. Liz asked whether she should form a corporation or an LLC (Bernie recommended an LLC). Bernie helped her with the LLC paperwork but referred Liz to a colleague—an intellectual property specialist—to help her with trademark and domain name issues. A few months later, when Liz found space for her office and warehouse, she came to Bernie to discuss her proposed lease. Bernie was already up to speed about Liz's business and efficiently helped Liz work out a favorable lease.

a. Compile a List of Prospects

Don't expect to locate a good business lawyer by simply looking in the phone book, consulting a law directory, or reading an advertisement. There's not enough information in these sources to help you make a valid judgment. Lawyer referral services operated by bar associations are almost as useless. Usually, these services make little attempt to evaluate a lawyer's skill and experience. They simply list the names of lawyers who have signed on with the service, often accepting the lawyer's self-serving assessment of skills and experience. Fortunately, there are some better sources:

- **People in your community who own or operate excellent businesses.** These people obviously understand quality in other ways, so why not in lawyers? Ask other businesspeople who and how good their lawyer is. Ask about other lawyers they've used and what led them to make a change. If you talk to half a dozen businesspeople, chances are you'll come away with several good leads.

- **People who provide services to the business community.** Speak to your banker, accountant, insurance agent, and real estate broker. These people frequently deal with lawyers who represent business clients and are in a position to make informed judgments.

- **People with businesses like your own.** In some specialized businesses—software design, restaurants, landscape nurseries—it can pay to work with a lawyer who regularly represents clients in that area. Besides being familiar with the way the enterprise operates, this specialist should have experience with the types of legal problems common to the business. For example, a lawyer who has many clients in the restaurant business may have developed expertise in zoning law, liquor licenses, and fire department regulations, as well as the requirements for accommodating people with disabilities. Sometimes specialists charge a little more, but if their unique information is truly valuable, it can be money well spent. Trade associations are often a good place to get referrals to specialists.

- **Other tenants in your new building.** They may have used a lawyer in their dealings with your landlord and have come away feeling they were in good hands. You'll get the benefit of the lawyer's experience with this building and this landlord.

- **The director of your state or local chamber of commerce.** This person may know of several business lawyers who have the kind of experience that you're looking for.

- **A law librarian.** Lawyers in your state who've written books or articles on business law or commercial tenancy law are likely to be practicing lawyers, too. A law librarian can steer you to the best books—if you like what you read, you may want to hire the author.

- **The director of your state's continuing legal education (CLE) program.** A bar association, a law school, or both usually run these programs. Private companies operate them, too. The director can identify lawyers who have lectured or written on business law for other lawyers. Someone who's a "lawyer's lawyer" presumably has the extra depth of knowledge and experience to do a superior job for you—but may charge more.

- **The chairperson of a state or county bar committee for business lawyers.** This person may be able to point out some well-qualified practitioners in your vicinity.

b. Shop Around

After you get the names of several good prospects, shop around. If you announce your intentions in advance, many lawyers will be willing to meet with you briefly at no charge so that you can size them up and make an informed decision.

When you do meet, explain why you're there—you are about to begin negotiations on a commercial lease and want the lawyer to review the landlord's draft and possibly accompany you to negotiation sessions. To help you decide whether to engage this lawyer, you'll need answers to the following questions:

Does the lawyer have experience with business tenancies? While most lawyers who work frequently with small businesses will almost certainly know a great deal about commercial leases and tenancies, there may be some exceptions to the general rule. It pays to inquire specifically about the lawyer's knowledge of commercial leases.

Will the lawyer have time to personally represent you? If not, will the matter be given to an associate? If so, how much supervision, if any, will there be? Obviously, you don't want to engage a highly qualified lawyer, only to find your lease shunted to a brand-new associate who's just learning the ropes.

Lawyer Ratings

Once you have the names of several lawyers, you can learn more about them in the *Martindale-Hubbell Law Directory*, available online at www.martindale.com. You'll also find it at at most law libraries and some local public libraries. This resource contains biographical sketches of most practicing lawyers and information about their experience, specialties, education, and the professional organizations they belong to. Many firms also list their major clients in the directory—an excellent indication of the firm's practice areas. In addition, almost every lawyer listed in the directory, whether or not the lawyer purchased space for a biographical sketch, is rated AV, BV, or CV. These ratings come from confidential opinions that *Martindale-Hubbell* solicits from lawyers and judges.

The first letter is for Legal Ability, which is rated as follows:

A – Very High to Preeminent

B – High to Very High

C – Fair to High

The V stands for Very High General Recommendation, meaning that the rated lawyer adheres to professional standards of conduct and ethics. But it's practically meaningless because lawyers who don't qualify for it aren't rated at all. *Martindale-Hubbell* prudently cautions that the absence of a rating shouldn't be construed as a reflection on the lawyer. Some lawyers ask that their rating not be published, and there may be other reasons for the absence of a rating. For example, a new lawyer may have excellent skills and high ethics, but be too new to the legal community to be known among the local lawyers and judges.

Don't make the rating system your sole criterion for deciding on a potential lawyer. On the other hand, it's reasonable to expect that a lawyer who gets high marks from other business clients and an AV rating from *Martindale-Hubbell* will have experience and expertise.

How will the lawyer charge? Be sure you understand how the lawyer charges for services. (Section 3 discusses various fee arrangements.) Comparison shopping among lawyers will help you avoid over-paying, but only if you're comparing lawyers with similar expertise. A highly experienced small business lawyer may be cheaper in the long run than a general practitioner who charges a lower hourly rate. The experienced small business lawyer should be able to come up with good answers and advice faster than a generalist.

Will the lawyer be accessible? This is a huge issue. Probably the most common complaint against lawyers is that they don't return phone calls, respond to faxes or email messages, and are not available to their clients when needed. If every time you have a question there's a delay of several days before you can talk to your lawyer, you'll lose precious time, not to mention sleep. So be sure to discuss how fast you can expect to have phone calls returned and how you can contact the lawyer in an emergency.

Does the lawyer represent landlords, too? Chances are that a lawyer who represents both commercial landlords and small business tenants has the knowledge to do a good job for you. On the other hand, you may want to steer clear of lawyers who represent landlords almost exclusively. They may be less willing to go to the mat for you if they worry that their reputation in the landlords' community may suffer.

2. Hiring a Lawyer

If you've never hired a lawyer before, you're probably wondering what you can expect when you show up for your first appointment. Well, the experience will vary from office to office—and even among lawyers in the same office. For the truth is, lawyers are quite independent in the way they run their businesses. Unlike physicians, for example, who have insurance companies and the government monitoring virtually every move, lawyers are free from heavy-handed regulation. As a result, many choose to avoid bureaucratic paperwork, which they regard as a time-consuming nuisance.

Old-fashioned as it may seem, the simple handshake is still widely regarded as an acceptable basis for establishing a lawyer-client relationship. But not everyone is so casual—at the other end of the spectrum, where the interaction between you and your lawyer is more formal, you may find yourself handed multiple pieces of paper, such as:

- a client information form, which asks for details on your business, your finances, and who referred you to the lawyer's office
- a brochure describing the law practice and the education and experience of the firm's lawyers, and
- a "retention letter" or a contract, detailing the lawyer's billing practices and describing the extent of the work the lawyer will do for you. In some states, lawyers *must* present you with a retention letter or contract.

If the lawyer you've chosen has dispensed with these formalities, you may not care very much—after all, what does it matter where the lawyer went to law school? But do not let matters proceed until you have raised the issue of fees—and received clear, preferably written responses. Unless you do, you may not know what your lawyer is costing until you receive an unpleasant surprise in the mail.

3.   Common Fee Arrangements

If your lawyer assures you that you'll be well taken care of but tells you very little about the specifics of how you'll pay for the service, ask for some information about fees during your first visit. Like most lawyers who advise small business clients about a lease, your lawyer is likely to use one of the following two fee arrangements.

a.   Paying by the Hour

Paying your lawyer by the hour is the most common method. In most parts of the United States, you can get competent services for your small business for $150 to $250 an hour. Most lawyers bill in six-, ten-, or 15-minute increments. Understand that these are the smallest "chunks" of time that the lawyer will bill for, even if a given task actually took less time. For example, a lawyer who bills in six-minute increments will charge you for the full six minutes even

though a particular phone call lasted only two.

If you are concerned about runaway hourly costs, you can ask the lawyer to agree to a "cap," or an upper billing amount. This means that when the cap has been reached (or is near), the billing will stop (and the lawyer will stop working) until you authorize more work. You might have to do so if you run into an unusual snag that requires many more hours of legal services than either of you anticipated. For example, if a complex environmental issue pops up during negotiations—involving asbestos in your building or an underground storage tank beneath it—your lawyer may reasonably expect payment over and above the cap.

If your lawyer will be delegating some work to a less experienced associate, paralegal, or secretary, the delegated work should be billed at a lower hourly rate. Your fee arrangement should specify the rates for associates and paralegals if they will be in the picture.

b. Paying a Flat Fee

Sometimes a lawyer will quote you a flat fee for a specific job—for example, the lawyer may offer to review your commercial lease for $250. In a flat fee agreement, you pay the same amount regardless of how much time the lawyer spends on the particular job.

When an attorney is highly recommended by others and the flat fee is moderate, this can be a great arrangement for you. But if the assignment is open-ended—for example, it might involve extensive negotiations or a lot of redrafting—a lawyer won't agree to work for a fixed amount. Merely reviewing a lease is one thing—negotiating and drafting is quite another.

To secure a flat fee or cap, dangle the prospect of more work ahead. Explain to the lawyer that yours is a small business with a limited budget. Especially if you're just starting out, mention that you'll have other legal needs in the future if your business succeeds. The possibility of more lucrative work in the future may persuade the lawyer to offer an attractive fee arrangement with you now.

c. Paying the Lawyer's Costs

Lawyers may charge you for more than just the value of their services. Typically, lawyers charge clients for costs that are not included in the lawyer's normal office overhead, such as travel, hiring experts, or other consultants—and some even charge for photocopying! Be sure to find out whether you will be charged for itemized costs and, if so, what they are and how much you'll pay.

d. Get Your Understanding in Writing

Your lawyer should be completely forthcoming with answers to your questions about how you'll be billed, and for what. It's a good idea to ask that these answers be written in a letter or contract (as mentioned above, this is required by law in many states). An old-school lawyer may take your request as a slight breach of etiquette, but don't let that stand in your way.

Checklist for Preparing for Lease Negotiations

Understanding the issues raised in this chapter will pay off in spades when you begin the back-and-forth negotiation process with your landlord. Make sure that you have:

- assembled key business information—such as your financial history, recommendations from prior landlords, business tax returns, and a business plan—that will sell you to the landlord and support your efforts to gain favorable lease clauses
- determined that your deal breakers—such as the length of the lease, move-in date, renovation options, and expansion rights—appear to be satisfied by this lease
- carefully read the landlord's letter of intent, if you got one; have raised questions, if you have them; and are confident that the letter is not a binding contract; and
- lined up a lawyer who is experienced and will work with you through negotiation preparation and lease review.

Chapter 6

Your Negotiation Strategy

Read This Chapter If ...

This chapter will help you craft a solid negotiation strategy, based on everything you've learned about the space, the landlord, the rent, and your own needs. This is how you'll get a lease that's as close as possible to your priorities. Since negotiating is horse-trading, you have to have a plan going in. Everyone should read this chapter unless you expect to accept the landlord's lease "as is."

In theory, all terms of a lease are negotiable. Just how successful you will be, however, depends on market conditions. If desirable properties are close to full occupancy in your city, landlords may not be willing to negotiate with you over rent or other major lease terms. On the other hand, if commercial space has been overbuilt, landlords who are eager to fill empty units will be more likely to bargain.

Even in a tight market, you may discover that you have more negotiating clout than you imagined. A landlord may be anxious to rent the space quickly—and willing to make concessions to make this happen—because:

- the building is new or under construction and the landlord needs cash, fast
- the building is empty, and your tenancy will be an asset, acting as a "draw" to other tenants

- the space is odd or of limited usefulness and not suitable to many tenants, or
- the landlord's lease agreements with other tenants limit the kind of tenant he can rent to—and you fit the bill (arrangements like this are called "exclusive" agreements, explained in Chapter 7, Section C).

While the realities of the market and the nature of the property will influence your bargaining success, they won't entirely dictate it. Your skill as a negotiator (aided, perhaps, by your broker or lawyer) will also influence the outcome. This chapter will show you how to work most efficiently and increase your chances for success. Here are the basic steps:

1. Prepare for negotiations by developing an organized list of lease clauses you do and don't want to see in the final lease—and know which ones you're willing to compromise on. Section A shows you how to prepare a Negotiation Strategy Worksheet.

2. Analyze your Negotiation Strategy Worksheet after comparing it to the landlord's lease to develop an overall strategy, which you can also show to your broker or lawyer for advice. Section B addresses this process.

3. Know what to expect in a negotiation session. Section C explains the experience of lease negotiating.

4. Modify the landlord's lease clauses. Section D explains the mechanics of changing lease language.

When you have finished negotiating and have signed your lease, understand that you shouldn't measure your "success" at negotiating solely by whether you've gotten all (or most of) what you wanted. Seasoned brokers and lawyers will tell you that a truly successful negotiation results in a lease that's not just favorable, but reliable— with few surprises as you live out the length of your tenancy. If you understand how your lease affects the way you conduct your business, you can plan accordingly and hopefully avoid unpleasant consequences.

⚠️ **Read the rest of the book before crafting a negotiation strategy.** Don't proceed unless you understand the legal and practical meaning of the lease clauses in your landlord's lease. Chapters 7 through 18 of this book explain the clauses you're likely to encounter. If you already understand them, fine—it's time to map out your approach to the bargaining table. But if you aren't sure, do your homework now. Unless you understand what each clause means (and how you can press for variations in your favor), you won't be able to negotiate effectively.

A. Your Negotiation Strategy Worksheet

At this point in your pursuit of space and a lease, you should have a good idea of some key aspects of the deal (see Getting Past Deal Breakers, Chapter 5, Section C), and perhaps you've received a letter of intent. Better yet, you may have the landlord's proposed lease in front of you. In addition, you have your own set of priorities (your Rental Priorities Worksheet, discussed in Chapter 1). As you head into negotiations, it will be helpful for you to organize all of this information in a way that makes it clear what you'll bargain hard for, what you are willing to concede, and what you don't care much about.

Does ranking negotiation points according to their desirability sound familiar to you? Hopefully it does, because this exercise is simply the next incarnation of your Rental Priorities Worksheet. We're going to show you how to turn your Rental Worksheet into a Negotiation Strategy Worksheet. To create your new worksheet, take the following steps.

Step 1: Create a Negotiation Strategy Worksheet

Prepare a spreadsheet with four columns, labeled Essential Clauses, Compromise Clauses, Unacceptable Clauses, and OK Clauses. You'll eventually fill these columns with lease clauses that you:

- absolutely must have in the lease (Essential Clauses)
- would *prefer* to have in the lease or would *like* to have changed, if they come from the landlord (Compromise Clauses)
- won't accept (Unacceptable Clauses), and
- are willing to accept as-is (OK Clauses).

The rest of this section explains how to fill in these columns. For now, just create the template. A sample Negotiation Strategy Worksheet is shown below (later, we'll show you how we filled it out for Terri's Threads, the business we first introduced when explaining the Rental Priorities Worksheet in Chapter 1).

Negotiation Strategy Worksheet			
Essential Clauses	Compromise Clauses	Unacceptable Clauses	OK Clauses

Step 2: Review Your Rental Priorities Worksheet for Lease-Related Issues

Take out your Rental Priorities Worksheet and look at the entries in each column— the Essentials, Compromise, and Unacceptable columns. Now, look for entries that have no bearing on your lease negotiations. You'll want to cross these entries off. For example, your wish to be near public transportation, which may be on your Essentials list, is a search issue that is or isn't satisfied by the location you've chosen. The landlord's lease has nothing to do with this priority. By crossing it off the list, you'll avoid confusing an item such as access to public transportation with issues that are related to your lease negotiations.

Step 3: Assign Lease Clause Names to the Remaining Entries on Your Priorities Worksheet

The lease-related entries on your Priorities Worksheet will correspond to some sort of lease clause that deals with that subject. (For now, don't worry about whether this clause is also in the lease given to you by the landlord.) For example, you may have noted in your Essentials column that the lease must be at least three years long. In leasing lingo,

that will be covered by a clause entitled "Term." Write "Term" next to that entry on your Priorities Worksheet. If you aren't sure how to match an entry in your Priorities Worksheet with the clause that concerns it, consult "Common Major Lease Clauses," in the introduction to this book.

EXAMPLE: Terri's Threads developed a Rental Priorities Worksheet to help the owner find suitable space for her clothing consignment business (see Chapter 1, Section L, and Chapter 3, Section A, for an explanation of this process). Now, Terri has found promising space and has received a copy of the landlord's lease. She has taken out her Rental Worksheet and, following Steps 2 and 3 in this section, she crossed out the entries that will not be involved in the lease negotiations; she then assigned a lease clause name to the remaining lease-related entries. Her marked-up Priorities Worksheet is shown below.

Rental Priorities Worksheet for "Terri's Threads"

Address: _____

_____

Contact: _____

Phone #: _____ Email: _____

Rent: _____ Deposit: _____

Other Fees:_____

Term: _____ Date Seen: _____ Date Available: _____

Brief description of rental space and building: _____

_____

_____

_____

Essentials:

Yes	No
☐	☐

☐ ☐ 1. ~~Near residential shopping area, upscale neighborhood, lots of foot traffic.~~

_____

☐ ☐ 2. Rent less than $2,000 per month. _This will be in a clause entitled "Rent." If it's a net lease, other clauses (maintenance, taxes, insurance) will be involved._

☐ ☐ 3. Minimum 1,000 square feet. _"Premises" clause_

☐ ☐ 4. ~~Separate employee & customer restrooms.~~

☐ ☐ 5. ~~One floor, rectangular, separate storage room(s) in back.~~

☐ ☐ 6. Sufficient electrical outlets and capacities to support computers for inventory and accounts. _"Improvements clause" involved here_

☐ ☐ 7. Available by March 1. _"Term clause"_

Rental Priorities Worksheet for "Terri's Threads" (continued)

Compromise:

Yes No

☐ ☐ 1. Parking on street or by arrangement in nearby lot. _"Parking clause"_

☐ ☐ 2. Main interior space divisible into two rooms (one for examining clothing brought in by consignees). _"Improvements clause"_

☐ ☐ 3. Ability to locate two sets of dressing rooms along opposite walls. _____ _"Improvements clause"_

☐ ☐ 4. ~~Neighboring businesses stay open into early evening at least one day per week.~~

☐ ☐ 5. Landlord willing to lease for 3-5 years and give option to extend longer. _"Term clause" and "Option to Renew clause"_

☐ ☐ 6. ~~Major transportation lines nearby.~~

Unacceptable:

Yes No

☐ ☐ 1. Risky crime area. _Check lease for building security/landlord provides._

☐ ☐ 2. ~~Other consignment shops within a three-mile radius.~~

☐ ☐ 3. No lease less than three years. _"Term clause"_

☐ ☐ 4. No personal guarantee for the rent. _"Lease Guarantor clause"_

Notes: _____

Step 4: Read the Landlord's Lease

Get a copy of the landlord's lease and carefully read through it, identifying those clauses that you understand and those that you don't. If you have an electronic file of the lease, write your comments into the clauses and highlight them. If you have only a paper version, copy it and magnify it so that you have lots of room in the margins or between lines to jot down your concerns.

You will probably need to dip into the rest of this book before proceeding. At the very least, read up on the clauses you aren't familiar with. For example, we're willing to bet that you don't understand the concept known as "subordination." If you see a clause with this title in the landlord's lease, read all about it in Chapter 17, Section A. For help in matching the landlord's lease clauses to the appropriate chapter in this book, take a look at "Common Major Lease Clauses," in the introduction to this book.

Step 5: Match Rental Priorities Entries to the Landlord's Lease

Reach for your Rental Priorities Worksheet and put it next to the landlord's lease. Look for clauses in the lease that match your entries on the Priorities Worksheet. When you find a subject-matter match, enter the lease clause number or title on your Nego-

tiation Worksheet in the appropriate column. For now, don't worry about whether the clause actually says what you want it to—you're just looking for the subject matter match.

For example, if one of your "Essentials" is that the space must be available by a certain date, you have already scribbled "Term" next to that entry. Look through the lease for a clause that deals with availability—it's probably captioned "Term," and it may have a paragraph number. When you find it, enter "Clause [number], Term" in the column headed "Essentials." Or, if you noted on the Priorities Worksheet that you cannot personally guarantee your financial lease obligations, look for a clause that's titled "Guarantee" or "Lease Guarantor." If you find it, enter "Clause [number], Guarantee" in the Unacceptable column.

Step 6: Identify the Clauses That You Need to Bargain Over

At this point, you have identified clauses in the landlord's lease that correspond to issues that are on your Priorities Worksheet, and you've placed them in the column that describes how *you* feel about the issue. Fine, the landlord's lease deals with the issue—but is it to your liking? If not, identify those that you'll need to bargain over by putting a check mark against them and adding a little note to yourself describing the modification you'd like.

Let's explain that a bit. To continue with the example in Step 4, you probably saw a clause in the landlord's lease called Term, dealing with the availability of the space. If it specifies the date that you want, great—you can note "OK" next to it, knowing that this one needn't be bargained over. But if the date is not to your liking, put a quick note next to the entry and flag it with a check mark. This will remind you during negotiations that not only is this issue very important to you, but you need to bargain for a change from the initial lease draft. Take a look at Terri's Thread's worksheet, below, to see how she's done it.

landlord is using a stationery-store, canned lease form.

For example, suppose you noted on your Priorities Worksheet that you must have a renewal right. Looking through the landlord's lease, however, you don't find a renewal clause (it's usually labeled as an "option to renew"). But hopefully, the landlord agreed to grant you a renewal right, perhaps saying so in a letter of intent. You must have this commitment in the lease also. So add that lease clause to your Essentials column on the Negotiation Worksheet and put a check mark next to it, to remind yourself that you need to press for its inclusion in the final lease.

Step 7: Enter Your Remaining Lease Clauses From Your Rental Priorities Worksheet

When you finished matching your rental priorities to the landlord's lease (Step 5), you probably discovered that there were some lease-related entries on your Rental Priorities Worksheet that did not have a match in the landlord's lease. They may have been tenant-friendly clauses that a landlord won't give you straight off, such as a promise that the building will be up to code when you take possession (compliance clauses are explained in Chapter 12). Or they may be understandings that the two of you reached in prenegotiation talks that haven't made their way onto the printed lease—a most common occurrence if the

Step 8: Place the Rest of the Landlord's Lease Clauses in the Appropriate Column

At this point, you've picked out the clauses in the landlord's lease that correspond to entries in your Rental Priorities Worksheet, and you've placed each clause in the relevant column of your Negotiation Worksheet. You've also entered the lease-related entries from your Rental Priorities Worksheet that did *not* have a match in the landlord's lease. Now it's time to place the rest of the landlord's clauses in the appropriate columns and to note, again with a check mark and a note to yourself, whether you need to bargain over them.

For example, your landlord may have included a lease clause setting out the way tenants will share and pay for utilities (the utilities clause is explained in Chapter 12, Section B). You may not have thought about this issue when drafting your Rental Priorities Worksheet, but now that you see it on the lease, you need to deal with it. Having read the explanation in this book and, perhaps, discussed it with your broker, you may decide that the clause is fair and acceptable. If so, you'd place it in the "Okay" column. But if you don't like it, or want to vary it slightly, place it in either the Unacceptable or Compromise column, along with a check mark and a quick note on how you'd like the clause to eventually read.

There will probably be lots of clauses to distribute in this way. Some of your entries at this time will be tentative. Even with the help of the explanations in this book, you're bound to have some questions that can be answered only by your broker or lawyer. Be especially careful about dropping clauses into the Essentials and Unacceptable columns. Since these will be the areas where you'll dig in your heels, you want to make sure that the issue is worth the fight (or the concession that you might have to make on another point in order to prevail). You'll also want to make sure that you aren't sending sleeper clauses—ones that are more important than you realize—into the Okay column. When you consult with your lawyer, you should be able to confirm the wisdom of your assignments. (Using your lawyer to review your Negotiation Strategy Worksheet is covered in Section C, below.)

Step 9: Add Additional Clauses to the Negotiation Worksheet

As you know, the landlord's lease is a starting point for negotiations. Not only can you vary its terms—you can add some clauses that you want (such as the ones suggested by the entries on your Rental Priorities Worksheet). And you can be on the lookout for additional clauses the landlord may spring on you during negotiations.

You may also want to add lease clauses that you've learned about from reading this book—clauses that aren't reflected in your Priorities Worksheet and are not in the landlord's lease. For example, suppose you are planning extensive renovations in an old building whose electrical and plumbing systems are undoubtedly not up to code. Having read our discussion in Chapter 12 about code compliance, you now understand that the magnitude of your renovations may trigger expensive compliance duties and high costs. Accordingly, you'll want a "compliance with laws" clause to shift responsibility for the upgrade cost to the landlord. If the lease has no clause entitled "Compliance" and the issue isn't addressed elsewhere in the lease, you'll want to make sure that the issue is raised. To remind yourself to raise this issue, add a clause entitled "Compliance With Laws" to the Essentials column.

EXAMPLE: Let's continue with Terri's Threads. Terri has read the landlord's lease (not shown here) and has looked for clauses that match the subjects on her Rental Priorities Worksheet. She has entered these matches onto her Negotiation Worksheet by writing down the clause number and name of the clause as it appears in the landlord's lease. And she has noted (with a check mark) where further bargaining is needed.

Terri continued to fill in her Negotiation Worksheet by entering clauses from her Rental Priorities Worksheet that did not have a match in the landlord's lease, such as her "Compromise" wish to be able to renew the lease (Step 7). She then distributed the rest of the landlord's lease clauses in the appropriate columns (Step 8). Terri knows she's going to have to consult with her lawyer on the correctness of some of her assignments. Finally, she included some clauses that she read about in this book but which neither she nor the landlord had thought of (they don't appear in her Rental Priorities Worksheet, nor in the landlord's lease), such as a clause specifying that the landlord will warrant that the space is up to code as of the time Terri takes possession (Step 9).

The Negotiation Strategy Worksheet shown below reflects this work. (For purposes of this book, we are showing you a shortened version. A real worksheet would undoubtedly have many more rows, reflecting the many clauses you're likely to encounter in the land-

lord's lease.) Terri will review this with her lawyer when they go over the lease, as explained below in Section C.

B. How to Use Your Negotiation Strategy Worksheet

Let's review where we are. Working with your Rental Priorities Worksheet, the landlord's lease, and this book, you now have a Negotiation Strategy Worksheet that has clustered the lease clauses from each of these sources into one of four possible groups. You have lists of:

- **Essential clauses.** Lease clauses that must be part of the final lease.
- **Compromise clauses.** Lease clauses that you'd like to see included and worded in your favor, but you're willing to compromise, and clauses from the landlord's lease that you'd like to modify if possible.
- **Unacceptable clauses.** Lease clauses that you cannot live with.
- **OK clauses.** Lease clauses in the landlord's lease that are all right as written.

When you listed lease clauses that came out of the landlord's lease, you noted (with a check mark) whether you need to bargain for a variation. And if you want to add a clause to the landlord's lease, you've checked them to remind yourself that these clauses need to be included in the final product.

Now, what should you do with these four columns of information?

- First, analyze each column to see what its entries tell you about your bargaining stance going into the negotiation (Section 1).
- Second, use your understanding to formulate a bargaining plan (Section 2).
- Finally, show your plan to your broker, your lawyer, or both, who can review your placement of each clause and discuss with you the chances of prevailing with your strategy (Section 4).

1. Analyze Your Negotiation Strategy Worksheet

A quick look at each of your four columns should give you an immediate sense of how you're situated, before you take the next step of formulating a bargaining plan. You'll see how the entries in each column point the way to smooth sailing, hard bargaining, or something in between.

a. Essential Clauses

These entries are the clauses you'll insist upon. When you filled out the Negotiation Strategy Worksheet, you put check marks next to the clauses that were either missing from the landlord's lease or present but not in acceptable form. How many check marks are next to the clauses in this column? If there are none, your critical needs have been met already. If there are lots, you know that you have some very important work ahead—you'll need to convince the landlord to change the lease and/or add clauses you want.

b. Compromise Clauses

These clauses are ones that you'd like to add to the final lease, or they have come from the landlord's lease and you'd like to change them a bit. A long list will tell you that you and the landlord have a lot to talk about on issues that are of secondary importance to you. There's lots of room for give-and-take here, which will be handy when you formulate your negotiating strategy.

c. Unacceptable Clauses

The clauses here—ones from the landlord's lease—are ones you can't live with. They're the polar opposite of your Essentials. Obviously, an empty column is best. The more clauses there are, the more convincing (or compromising) you'll have to do.

d. OK Clauses

The clauses in this group are from the landlord's lease, and they are ones that are acceptable as-is (consequently, there shouldn't be any check marks next to them). Also, these clauses aren't of paramount importance to you—ones that are will be matched with an Essentials entry from your Rental Priorities Worksheet and will be

Sample Negotiation Strategy Worksheet for Terri's Threads

Essential Clauses	Compromise Clauses	Unacceptable Clauses	OK Clauses
Rent, Clause 2, gross lease *Too high at $2,400 per month.*	Parking, Clause 9 *Landlord offers three spaces in back lot, need more.*	Personal Guarantee, Clause 18.	Utilities, Clause 11 *All tenants appear to use roughly equal amounts of utilities.*
Square feet, Premises, Clause 1 *OK*	Improvements, Clause 13 *Who pays to erect interior walls/ partitions?*		Maintenance Responsibilities, Clause 16 *Acceptable requirement to clean & repair own space.*
Improvements, Clause 13 *Negotiate for landlord to pay for new circuits since it's a capital improvement.*	Term, Clause 3 *Landlord offers two-year lease. Bargain for three.*		Insurance requirement, Clause 9 *Landlord insists on tenant carrying liability insurance, no problem.*
Term, Clause 3 *OK, available now.*	Option to renew, not part of landlord's lease *Bargain for one.*		

listed (unchecked) in the Essentials column. And because they're not of overriding importance, they are negotiable.

A long list in this column indicates that you have a lot to work with when it comes to offering compromises in order to prevail on another, more important point. That's because the landlord doesn't know that you are satisfied with these clauses—and since she doesn't know this, you may be able to use them as negotiation fodder with little real consequence to you. Subsection 2d, below, explains in more detail how to creatively use this leverage. If there are few entries in this column, you have less negotiation ammunition.

2. Formulate a Strategy

Now it's time to take your analyses of each of the four categories of lease clauses and put them together. How strong is your negotiation position? How can you get what you want?

a. Check the Essentials and Unacceptable Columns

The key to understanding your bargaining position is in these two columns. If the Essentials column is full of unchecked clauses and the Unacceptable column is empty, you're sitting pretty. The only things left to talk about are the Compromise clauses. At the other extreme, if the Essentials column is loaded with checked clauses and the

Unacceptable list is packed, you're in for some heavy sessions.

Most likely, these columns on your Negotiation Strategy Worksheet fall somewhere in between—there are a few checked entries in the Essentials column, and a few unfortunate members of the Unacceptable column. Now then, how do you bargain to remove the checks and empty the Unacceptable list? Subsections b and c show you what to do.

b. Use the Compromise Clauses

These are clauses that you would *like* to add, and clauses from the landlord that you would *like* to modify. How can you use them to secure an Essentials clause or remove an Unacceptable clause? You can argue for an addition or modification from the Compromise list and then, since you aren't wedded to these issues, back off in exchange for the landlord's concession to add or remove a truly important clause.

Tricky? Well yes, but it's nothing new in the world of commercial leasing.

For example, suppose you'd like to have first call on any adjoining space that becomes available—a right that would be included in an extension clause, which would have to be added to the lease. In addition, you'd like to modify the landlord's maintenance clause to include janitorial service for your space. However, you've decided that these two issues are of secondary importance to you, so you've placed them in the Compromise column.

The landlord, however, doesn't know how you really feel about these matters. After pressing hard on both these points, you agree to drop them in exchange for the landlord agreeing to remove the personal guarantee clause, which was number one on your Unacceptable list. True, you are still stuck with an uncertain extension ability and having to do your own cleaning, but it's worth it if you can ditch the guarantor clause.

c. Use the OK Clauses

The clauses in this group are from the landlord's lease, and they're acceptable to you. They are not, however, crucial (otherwise they'd be in the Essentials column). How can you use them? Offer to modify or delete them in favor of the landlord in exchange for getting your way on something more important to you. The next example illustrates how to do this.

EXAMPLE: When Sam made his Rental Priorities Worksheet, he noted on his list of Essentials that he could not pay more than $16 per square foot. Unfortunately, the landlord's lease included a higher rent, but it did give Sam the protection of a maintenance cap, which meant that if maintenance costs rose above the cap figure, the landlord would pay the excess.

As Sam filled in his Negotiation Strategy Worksheet, he placed the landlord's Rent clause in the Essentials column and checked it, indicating that he would have to work very hard to reduce the rent. He placed the maintenance clause in the OK column, unchecked, indicating that the landlord's clause was acceptable. Then he thought about how he could bargain to lower the rent. Inspiration came from the Maintenance clause in the OK list. Sam figured that he might be able to trade the protection of the cap for a lower rent.

During negotiations, Sam asked for a lower rent. The landlord wouldn't budge. Then, Sam offered to forego the cap on the maintenance charges in place of a lower rent, figuring that he would rather gamble on rising maintenance costs than saddle himself with a large rent from the outset. The landlord, on the other hand, was happy to remove the cap, which would mean that the risk of rising maintenance costs would be placed on Sam. This trade worked because, to the landlord, getting a lower rent was preferable to living with the risk of having to pay maintenance costs above a stated figure.

There's another way to use the OK clauses. These are acceptable to you as written, but the landlord doesn't know this. You might want to argue for their modification and then, as a compromise, agree to forego the modification in exchange for the landlord giving you a clause you really want. Again, a bit convoluted, but that's how the game is played.

d.   Set Up Your Trades

A glance at the Essentials and Unacceptable lists gives you a good idea of the hurdles you must overcome to end up with an acceptable lease. And by reviewing your Compromise and OK columns, you know what you've got to work with. Now you need to think of ways to use this negotiation material to nail down your Essential needs and eliminate the Unacceptable clauses.

Keep in mind that your plan at this point is somewhat theoretical. After all, you won't know whether the landlord will be willing to give you what you want in exchange for what you're willing to offer. And you don't want to be so attached to your theories that you fail to take advantage of the dynamics and surprises of the negotiation sessions. Still, it's good to have a rough idea in place, which you'll share with your advisors.

First, think about the compromises, concessions, or extra duties or expenses that would be least painful to you. For example, suppose the landlord's lease includes a clause that places landscaping duties on the owner, which is certainly acceptable to you (you've placed it in the OK column). However, you really want the landlord to help you financially with your improvements by increasing your Tenant Improvement Allowance (improvements are explained in Chapter 11). You might be willing to take on the expense and responsibility of landscaping and regular gardening in exchange for more money for your improvements. If so, this is a place where offering a concession (you'll pay for landscaping) might get you an Essential (financial help at the outset of your lease, when you most need it). Make a list of the concessions or added expenses you're willing to accept in trade for nailing an Essential or dropping an Unacceptable.

Will this method of trading clauses work for you? Yes, if the concession you're offering or the expense you're accepting is important to the landlord. If he sees no value in your offer to take on more responsibility or accept an expense (in trade for something you care more strongly about), he'll say, "No thanks." At that point, the external pressures to rent the space (the market forces) will take over, and the landlord will either give you some of what you want or tell you to look elsewhere.

Second, think of issues that you're willing to argue long and hard over and then, without much disappointment, walk away from—in exchange for something you really want. In a word, are you interested in a bit of bluffing? If so, pick your issues and list them. For example, although you'd like ten parking spaces, you might really be satisfied with the five offered in the lease. Since the landlord doesn't know how you really feel, you can argue vociferously for ten and then, in a spirit of compromise, make do with five in exchange for the use of a storage room, which you wanted all along.

How successful will this approach be? It depends largely on your sophistication as a tenant and the experience of the landlord. Arguing mightily for a concession or perk will get you nowhere (and destroy your credibility) if your position is extreme or unrealistic. Sharing your plan with your advisor, as suggested below, will help you assess the wisdom of your intentions.

3. Factors That Restrict Lease Negotiations

How much latitude will you and the landlord have when it comes to crafting a lease? Most of the time, you're constrained by only two forces—what the law allows and the relative strength of your bargaining positions. Interestingly, the legal constraints are relatively few and far between. You and the landlord are in large measure free to strike your own deal (and must live with the consequences). Compared to a residential lease, which must abide by a wide variety of state, federal, and sometimes local laws, a commercial lease is practically unfettered. We'll alert you to the few places where the law does step in to curtail your deal-making freedom.

a. Restrictions on the Landlord

The landlord's ability to make concessions or offer extras might be subject to some or all of the following practical factors:

- **The terms of other tenant's leases.** The landlord cannot offer you what he has already promised other tenants. For example, you can't demand an option to expand into adjacent space if that space has been leased to another tenant or is the subject of another tenant's expansion clause. Or, if you're in a multitenant retail space, your landlord may have promised other tenants not to bring in certain competing businesses. To honor these promises (and avoid lawsuits by other tenants), the landlord will have to insert a restrictive "use" clause in your lease. (Use clauses are explained in Chapter 7, Section D.)

- **The demands of the landlord's lender.** If your landlord has a mortgage on the property or has used it as collateral for a loan, the lender may have extracted promises that will affect the landlord's leasing decisions. For example, most sophisticated lenders will insist that the landlord carry a minimum amount of insurance on the property. If you'll be paying for all or part of the premiums, you may want to propose a lower amount. The landlord won't be able to negotiate this point if the loan contract requires a specified coverage amount. (Chapter 9 explains how you pay for insurance in a commercial lease; Chapter 15 explains insuring your business in general.)

- **The demands of the landlord's insurer.** Occasionally, the terms of a landlord's insurance policy will affect how the landlord negotiates his leases. For instance, it may exclude coverage for property damage caused by hazardous materials. A careful landlord won't allow these materials on site unless the tenant purchases or pays for additional or extended insurance coverage. During lease negotiations, the landlord will explain that he has to require extended coverage.

b. Restrictions on the Tenant

Like landlords, tenants may have preexisting financial and legal obligations that restrict their ability to bargain without limit. For instance, if you've taken out a loan for your business, your ability to borrow further will be reduced. Your landlord may ask for a security deposit in the form of a letter of credit from your bank—but if your credit is maxed out, you won't be able to deliver (security deposits and letters of credit are explained in Chapter 10). Likewise, if the landlord insists on a lease starting date that

begins before your current lease ends, you won't be able to commit unless you're prepared to pay double rent.

c. Getting Beyond Limitations

Sometimes tenants and landlords can maneuver their way around these external limitations. For example, if you are an especially attractive tenant, a landlord who operates under the watchful eye of his lender may be willing to go back to the lender and argue for a relaxation of the lender's rules. Or, if you're the tenant faced with a period of double rent, you might approach your current landlord and attempt to strike a deal for early termination of your lease.

When you negotiate the lease, be on the lookout for any "my hands are tied" explanations—and question the landlord carefully until you're satisfied that, indeed, he has no options. Be prepared for a similar inquiry when you offer the same explanation.

4. Take Your Worksheet to Your Lawyer or Broker

Our method of analyzing your negotiation position and planning a strategy should give you a good grasp on what you'd like to accomplish and how you're going to do it. But don't march into the negotiation session until you've asked someone with practical and legal experience to review:

- **Your legal and practical conclusions.** Did you correctly understand the meaning and consequences of the clauses in the landlord's lease? Did you accurately match up your Rental Priorities with lease clauses? And did you wisely place them in Priorities columns? For example, you might have mistakenly dropped a clause into the OK group when it ought to belong in the Unacceptable column. Your lawyer can catch errors like this.

- **Your negotiation plan.** Are your intended trades realistic and to your advantage? Are you offering to give away too much or too little? And if you intend to engage in a bit of gamesmanship, is your position credible or too far-out? Your own broker will know the leasing scene and practice in your area, and should be able to advise you on the wisdom of your strategy.

For added practical advice, talk to other successful tenants in leasing situations like yours. These tenants may be able to give you the benefit of their experience. For example, other tenants in the building can clue you in on how difficult their own lease negotiation sessions were, what issues the landlord held firm on, and where he was willing to compromise. You might even ask to look over their leases. Tapping into this resource will be particularly important if you have not hired a broker to represent you.

We suggest that you prepare for your meeting with your lawyer by sending the lawyer a copy of your Rental Priorities Worksheet, your Negotiation Strategy Worksheet, and the landlord's lease, as explained below in Section C. This will give your lawyer an opportunity to review the broad outlines of the deal. Your lawyer may prefer to approach the issues in a different way, but at the very least the worksheet will give both of you a place to begin discussions.

C. How Your Lawyer Can Help With Negotiations

If you're an experienced negotiator, you may be able to do a reasonable job of negotiating your lease by yourself, especially with the help of this book. But even a pro will benefit from at least a little professional help—and if you're relatively inexperienced, you may need a lot more assistance. Your broker, if you have one, will of course be helpful. And, as we recommended in Chapter 5, Section D, a lawyer can round out the team.

This section suggests different ways that you can work with your lawyer. The approach you choose will depend on your budget, your style, and the complexity and length of your lease.

Beware the words, "It will never happen." If you hear this platitude from your lawyer or broker, trying to reassure you on a negotiation issue that concerns you, heed this warning—it's a curse. It will happen. For example, you might think it's unlikely that the building's risers (the conduit that holds communications cables) will fill up, since most of the tenants are retail. Should you press for guaranteed space in the risers? You might wish you had when, two years down the line, most of the retailers have computer terminals that allow shoppers to shop online while at the store—and these retailers have big cable needs.

1. The Minimalist Approach

In our experience, the typical business tenant tries to get by with a minimum of legal assistance, bringing in a lawyer after the lease has been pretty well negotiated and the landlord has prepared a lease to be signed. At this point, many commitments have been made already—some perhaps unwisely. While a lawyer can help by trying to reopen the important issues, it's an inefficient way to proceed.

> **EXAMPLE:** Andrew needed new space for his graphic design office. He answered a newspaper ad for available space and it turned out to be just right. He and Bob, the building manager, talked over the lease terms and Andrew extracted three important concessions. The landlord would pay $2,000 toward the expense of moving Andrew's equipment from his current location and $5,000 toward the cost of renovations; and he would waive the usual security deposit.

A few days later, Bob gave Andrew a 25-page lease that contained the agreed concessions—along with a bunch of other terms that never really came up during the negotiations. Andrew marked up the proposed lease with a yellow highlighter and put notes in the margin about items he didn't understand or would like to change.

Andrew called Lucy, a lawyer who was recommended by one of his business associates, and arranged for her to review the lease within the next four days. Andrew dropped off the lease at Lucy's office and two days later she called him with answers to his questions. She explained the legal gobbledygook, suggested how Andrew could rewrite some clauses to meet his objections, and discussed some of the new issues that needed to be addressed. Lucy offered to prepare a letter to the landlord's lawyer, summarizing changes that Andrew would like to make.

For negotiating purposes, the letter included some requests (such as "Landlord will provide daily janitorial services") that Andrew could easily drop if he needed to. After getting Andrew's approval, Lucy faxed the final draft to the landlord's lawyer. Phone calls ensued—landlord's lawyer to landlord, landlord's lawyer to Lucy, Lucy to Andrew, Lucy back to the landlord's lawyer—and a deal was struck. However, in order to prevail on the added clauses he wanted, Andrew had to make do with a smaller moving allowance and less money for renovations. The landlord's lawyer made the agreed changes. Andrew and the landlord signed the lease.

2. Involve Your Lawyer Early

You might decide that using a lawyer the way Andrew did in the example above is good enough. After all, a lease got signed, although Andrew had to compromise on some early concessions he thought he had nailed down. But Andrew's method isn't the only way to get the job done—and it's not necessarily the best.

Bringing in your lawyer *before* you wrestle with the landlord over concessions and expenses gives you the benefit of professional expertise from the start. If Andrew's lawyer Lucy had been present at the conversation with Bob, for example, she might have asked for a broad outline of the proposed lease and then pressed for an even higher improvements and moving allowance. Lucy would do this knowing that the clauses she intended to add would meet resistance (which she could overcome by agreeing to back down on her improvements and moving demands). Since Andrew didn't even know that he had to bargain for additional clauses when he struck the initial deal with Bob, he lost that chance to gain an advantageous negotiating position.

Especially if you're new at this game, considering a long-term lease, paying top dollar for the space, facing complicated issues, or up against a stubborn or sophisticated landlord, you should consider having your lawyer do more for you. In particular, you can have your lawyer do any or all of the following:

- Sit with you at all bargaining sessions and serve as your spokesperson.
- Draft a letter of intent or rewrite the one the landlord prepares.
- Make sure your legal interests are protected in negotiations over a build-out of new space or major renovation of existing space.

Naturally, you'll be concerned about the added cost of involving your lawyer earlier. To understand the real cost of the lawyer's work, however, you need to consider what's at stake. Let's say you're leasing 3,000 square feet of space at $20 per square foot per year—and you're committing yourself to a five-year tenancy with two options to renew for five years each. Well, if you stay only for the basic five-year term, you'll be paying $300,000 in rent over the course of the lease, plus property taxes, insurance, and maintenance charges if yours is a triple net lease. And over a 15-year period, you'll be closing in on $1 million in rent and related charges! Mind boggling, isn't it?

Now suppose an experienced small business lawyer in your city charges $200 an hour and you use six hours of the lawyer's time to help you negotiate the lease from the get-go. Your cost will be $1,200 (and it's normally tax deductible as a business expense). Even for a cash-strapped business, hiring a lawyer can be a worthwhile investment if it leads to years of peaceful coexistence with your landlord and money-saving terms in the lease.

Only you can determine the extent of legal services that makes sense in your situation. It's partly an economic decision (no business likes to waste money) and partly a decision based on your comfort level. If you're a risk taker, you'll opt for less rather than more legal help. If you tend to be more cautious—especially where big bucks are at stake—you'll choose to have your lawyer do more for you. But whichever route you choose, it's essential to make sure your lawyer understands what you expect the lawyer's role to be.

There is only one dumb question—the one you ask after you've signed the lease. At that point, it's too late to make changes if you don't like the answer. The key to ending up with a lease you can live with—or at least understand—is to know which questions to ask before you sign. There is no better use of your lawyer than to ask questions now.

3. Smooth Sailing With Your Lawyer

Whether you've chosen to use your lawyer minimally or have decided on more extensive legal services, there are several things you can do to help things go smoothly.

Provide copies of important documents. First, give the lawyer a copy of the landlord's lease and any letter of intent you may have received. You might also mark up a second copy of the lease with a highlighter and put notes in the margins so the lawyer can easily spot the clauses that need more work.

Do this before you meet with the lawyer. You can also fax these items, but this can be awkward if the lease is long or the print is small. If the landlord will give you the proposed lease in a digital format—as a file attached to an email, for example—you can send the lease to your lawyer as an email attachment.

Send your Rental Priorities Worksheet and Negotiation Strategy Worksheet. These documents may not be entirely self-explanatory, but don't worry about that now. When you meet, if necessary you can quickly explain

Work Well With Your Lawyer

To help you further in getting the most out of your lawyer, here's a list of do's and don'ts:

DO	DON'T
Make sure your lawyer understands your business. Provide a page or two summary if you're seeing the lawyer for the first time.	Assume your lawyer knows how your business works and what your needs are.
Give your lawyer the letter of intent (if there is one) as well as all correspondence between you and the landlord.	Hang on to the important paperwork and documents until your lawyer asks for them.
Highlight any parts of the landlord's lease that you don't agree with or don't fully understand.	Fax the lease to your lawyer if the print is small or if it may be hard to read after being faxed.
Tell your lawyer what's really important to you—and what's not.	Keep your lawyer guessing about your key concerns and objectives.
Make sure your lawyer will be in town and have time available to get the job done by your deadline.	Assume that your lawyer will be available during your desired time frame.
	Dump the lease on your lawyer's desk at noon and demand that you hear back by 4 o'clock.
Leave phone numbers, fax numbers, and email addresses where your lawyer can easily reach you.	Drop out of sight at a crucial time.
Go out of your way to treat the lawyer's staff with courtesy and respect.	Underestimate the importance of the lawyer's secretary.

how you entered clauses in the Negotiation Strategy Worksheet.

Give your lawyer information about your business and yourself. If you're using this lawyer for the first time, it's a good idea to include a short summary of what your business does and where it's headed. It won't hurt to attach your resume as well, giving the lawyer an idea about your background; and you might want to include your business plan (if you have one, as suggested in Chapter 5) and a balance sheet for your business.

Involve your broker. Make sure your broker (if you have one working for you) is kept in the loop. Bring your broker to the meetings with your lawyer and make sure the broker gets copies of all relevant documents—at least those that pertain to lease issues.

Make sure your lawyer understands the timing of the deal. Sometimes, commercial leasing negotiations are very rushed, tense affairs—particularly when the property at stake is hot and the market is tight. If that's likely to be your situation, tell your lawyer right away. You might say: "I need your feedback by next Monday because the landlord needs a signed lease by next Friday. Is that going to be possible?" A lawyer who knows your time frame can make schedule adjustments to accommodate you—especially if you're a regular client. On the other hand, if you know there's going to be some delay because your lawyer is out of town, you can promptly inform the landlord, explaining that you'll need a few extra days to respond.

Get some face time. We recommend at least some personal contact with your lawyer early on, but don't be too shocked if the lawyer says "Send me the lease. I'll look it over and get back to you." That's less than ideal, because you may become a faceless abstraction. But in today's fast-paced world, legal business is sometimes transacted from afar. Using your lawyer this way is workable, especially if you've had some prior in-person contact.

D. How to Modify the Landlord's Lease

As discussed in this chapter, there are a number of constructive ways to modify the lease presented by the landlord. With the help of your Rental Negotiation Worksheet and perhaps your broker or lawyer, hopefully you now have a lease that includes lease clauses that are important to you—and excludes the ones you can't live with. You probably went through a few compromises along the way, too.

A lawyer who is closely involved in negotiations may make the changes to the landlord's lease that have resulted from your bargaining. But if you are on your own, take care that all of your hard work is accurately reflected in the final document. This section explains how to accomplish this.

1. Modifying the Lease Before It's Signed

After you've negotiated some changes in the landlord's lease, the most important thing is to put the changes in writing. Never rely on oral understandings. In this day of computers and word processing software, the simplest way to make changes is to have the landlord or landlord's lawyer print out a revised version of the lease.

If your modifications are small in number and words, you can instead make these changes on the lease itself by crossing out unacceptable wording and adding new language. You and the landlord should initial each of these changes.

If changes are extensive—particularly if you've added clauses—it may not be necessary for the landlord to include them in an entirely new fresh draft. Instead, you can prepare an addition to the lease, which is one or more pieces of paper that are attached to the lease. In legal parlance, an attachment like this is called an "addendum." Always number your addenda (title them "Addendum 1" and so on), in case you add more later.

The addendum should refer to the main lease, as does our Sample Addendum, below. In addition, the lease itself should refer to the addendum. Why make this second reference? If the addendum is accidentally mislaid and the only document left is the original lease, you'll have no way of proving that the addendum exists unless there is mention of it in the lease.

To reference an addendum, add the following language somewhere on the lease (often, you'll see it on the last page, near the signature lines): "Landlord and Tenant incorporate by reference the attached Addendum [number] dated [date]."

2. Modifying an Existing Lease

Keep in mind that a lease can be modified even after it's been signed. For example, if your landlord agrees six months into your lease to install some partitions for $2,000, you'll want to negotiate an improvements clause, even if it's a relatively simple job. The two of you can do a little mini-negotiating over the clause, just as you would have done had the issue been raised when you signed the lease. When you and the landlord have reached agreement, put your new improvements clause into an addendum and attach it to the lease.

If you add an addendum to an existing lease, it's a good idea to reference the addendum in the lease itself, as explained above in Section 1. Write the reference to the addendum on the last page. Now, however, you both need to sign or initial the reference itself and date each signature. That's because the lease has already been signed and dated, and you can't legally add any language to it unless both of you sign and date the addition—even if it's something as simple as a reference to an addendum.

You can use an addendum to renew your lease, too, if the renewal negotiations do not result in too many variations on the original lease (if you make lots of changes, it's best to start fresh with a new lease). And if you sublet or assign your lease, the landlord's consent and the new tenant's obligations can be detailed in an addendum to the original lease.

3. Conflicts Between the Lease and the Addendum

Sometimes the change that you want to make consists of adding new duties or responsibilities for the landlord or you—for example, you might add a clause during your tenancy that requires the landlord to supply a security service, a task that was not mentioned in the original lease. In this event, the addendum won't be inconsistent with the lease—it will simply add to it.

But you and the landlord may also want to change an *existing* clause in the lease. For instance, you may want to replace a lease clause entirely, or simply add to or edit it. You and the landlord want to make sure that the extent of the addendum's changes is clear. For example, if you intend to change only part of an original clause, you want to make it clear that the rest of the clause remains as it was originally written.

You can specify the impact of your addendum by adding some clarifying language to the new lease clause, as shown in "Writing Addendums," below. You'll also see that we suggest you include language stating that if there is any conflict between the lease and the addendum, the addendum will control. This will ensure that the last word from you and the landlord (the language of the addendum) is really the last word.

Writing Addendums

The kind of change you want to make	What the addendum should say
Add a new clause to the lease on a subject that isn't addressed in the original lease.	Introduce the clause by stating that it adds to the terms and conditions in the original lease and that any conflicts between the original lease and the addendum will be resolved in favor of the addendum.
Delete the entire clause and do not replace it.	Refer to the clause you intend to delete by number and title, and state that it is deleted in its entirety.
Scrap the entire clause and substitute a new one.	Introduce the clause by stating that it takes the place of Clause [number] [title] in the lease.
Add to the original clause but not change it otherwise.	Introduce the clause by stating that it is intended to augment Clause [number] [title] in the lease, but not replace it, and that any conflict between the original clause and the addendum will be resolved in favor of the addendum.
Modify some point in the original clause but not change it otherwise.	Introduce the clause by stating that it is intended to modify Clause [number] [title] in the lease with respect to the subjects covered in the addendum only, and that the rest of the original clause will remain intact. Add that any conflict between the original clause and the addendum will be resolved in favor of the addendum.

EXAMPLE: Terri's Threads has moved into the space she negotiated in Section A. In the final lease, she obtained a Parking clause in which the landlord promised her three spaces in the lot at the back of the building. Two years later, the landlord purchased the adjacent property, which also had a lot in the back. Terri negotiated for the right to lease five places in the new lot. In the Addendum to their lease, Terri insisted on wording that made it clear that the spaces in the new lot were *in addition* to the spaces Terri already rented. This statement will make it clear that Terri now leases eight spaces.

Sample Addendum

Addendum [number]

This is an Addendum to the Lease dated _____ between

_____ (Landlord) and

_____ (Tenant) for

commercial space at _____

_____.

    Landlord and Tenant agree to the following changes and additions to the Lease:

[Insert changes and additions]

    In all other respects, the terms of the original Lease remain in full effect. However, if there is a conflict between this Addendum and the original Lease, the terms of this Addendum will prevail.

Signed: _____ _____
          Landlord   Date

Signed: _____ _____
          Tenant   Date

Checklist for Crafting Your Negotiations Strategy

Let's face it, this chapter was a bear. Will all of your columns and check marks really make a difference in your ability to negotiate a good lease? To the extent you have some wiggle room (that is, to the extent the market is in your favor), the answer is yes, and you'll be glad that you have a plan. Leaving this chapter behind, you now have:

- a marked-up copy of the landlord's lease, which you can show to your broker or lawyer

- a Negotiation Strategy Worksheet that you can use to guide you through negotiations with the landlord, knowing where you will hold fast, where you'll compromise, and where you will cave

- your broker's or attorney's advice on how to proceed, and

- ideas for lease language that better fits your situation.

Part II:

Common Lease Terms

Chapter 7

Lease Basics

I n this chapter and the ones that follow, we'll assume that you've found suitable space and that you and the landlord have agreed on the key features of the lease, such as how much rent you'll pay and how long the lease will run. You may have summarized these understandings in a nonbinding letter of intent (explained in Chapter 5, Section C), or perhaps you simply agreed orally. Either way, now it's time to formally spell out your deal in a binding, written lease. Armed with your Negotiation Strategy Worksheet, you can head into lease negotiations with a plan.

But as you know from having read about the Negotiation Strategy Worksheet in Chapter 6, you can't set up your plan unless you understand the meaning of the landlord's lease clauses. A thorough understanding of common lease clauses will help you avoid hidden, onerous traps. It will also help you bargain for modifications in your favor.

This chapter introduces you to the two clauses that typically appear at the beginning of most leases—the "Parties" clause, naming the landlord and tenant (Section A), and the "Premises" clause, describing the space you're leasing (Section B). It also covers two small but important clauses that sometimes pop up: the "use" clause and the "exclusive" clause, in which the landlord and you agree that you will engage in certain activities (and perhaps not in others) (Section C).

The rest of the chapters in this book explain other important, common clauses. The chart at the end of the introduction to this book provides a road map to these clauses. It shows how we've grouped them and put them into chapters according to common subject matter or where they typically fall in the lease. For example, Chapter 8 explains the "Term" clause, which deals with how long your lease will run and when it will start. The money you'll pay the landlord for the privilege of using the space is covered in the "Rent" and "Security Deposit" clauses, which we cover in Chapters 9 and 10, and so on. The final chapters cover what you'll usually see at the end of most leases—clauses covering how you and the landlord will handle disputes (Chapter 16) and the signature and guarantee clauses at the very end (Chapter 17).

If you run across terms or whole clauses that aren't discussed in this book, get more information before you sign. You may want to see a lawyer. (See Chapter 5, Section D, for tips on how to find and work with a lawyer.)

A. Naming the Landlord and Tenant: Parties to the Lease

Leases generally begin by naming the landlord and the tenant, in a clause entitled "Parties." Or, the clause may be entitled "Lessor and Lessee" (the landlord is the lessor and the tenant is the lessee) or "Landlord and Tenant." Although you might not think so at first, it's important to look at these names carefully. An error in the way you or the landlord is identified can have serious repercussions.

This section explains the legal meaning behind the names you'll find in the Parties clause. Be sure to read it in conjunction with our explanation of the Signature clause in Chapter 17.

1. The Landlord

If you've stayed with us since Chapter 3, in which we advised you to learn a little about the legal owner of the building, you'll appreciate why it's important now to take a careful look at the name of the lessor. Having done your homework, you know that the owner of the property is an individual, partnership, corporation, or LLC. So, who's the landlord?

In the simplest situation, the legal owner will also be the one named as the lessor, or landlord, in the lease. But legal owners are often *not* the ones who negotiate and sign leases. That's because owners can delegate their power to lease their property to individuals or management companies.

If the legal owner is not the person named as the landlord in the lease, make sure that the relationship of the named landlord to the owner is stated in the lease. In addition, be sure you're satisfied that the explanation reflects the true state of affairs. If you have any question as to whether an individual who will sign for the owner does in fact have the claimed authority to act for and bind the owner, ask for written proof, such as a copy of an employment contract or a letter from the owner.

> **EXAMPLE:** Sheila and Dave Green formed a corporation that owns the property that Ted is about to lease. Ted has been dealing with Sam Smith, who said that he manages the Green's properties. Sam is identified as the Landlord in the Parties clause. Ted wisely asked for proof that Sam can act on behalf of the Greens. Sam produced a corporate resolution giving him power to lease property owned by the corporation.

Commercial real estate owners frequently hire property management companies. Some management companies have the authority to bind an owner to a lease, but others have only day-to-day management powers. If a management company is named as the landlord in your lease, it behooves you to ask for proof that the company does indeed have authority to sign a lease. It's not unreasonable to insist on getting a copy of the document that authorizes the company to negotiate and sign leases on behalf of the owner. Without it, you are simply taking the word of the person who prepared the lease.

2. The Tenant

Your business, typically, will be the tenant. When you identify your business as the tenant in a lease—both at the beginning of the lease and at the end where you sign— make sure that you correctly name the business. You must also designate its legal form (partnership or corporation, for instance). The wording is rather simple, as you'll see in "Naming the Tenant in a Commercial Lease," below.

Naming the Tenant in a Commercial Lease

Type of Entity	Identification in the Lease
Sole Proprietorship	John Smith [or] John Smith, doing business as John's Diner
General Partnership	Smith and Jones, a Michigan Partnership
Corporation	Modern Textiles Inc., a Texas Corporation
Limited Liability Company	Games and Such LLC, a California Limited Liability Company

Sometimes a corporation or LLC does business using a name that's different from its official name—for example, an assumed name, fictitious name, or trademarked name. We recommend that you stick to your official name in your lease. For example, let's say your corporation, Ebb Tide Inc., has registered the assumed name of Total Solutions. Your best bet is to identify your business as Ebb Tide Inc., a Florida Corporation, and simply ignore the assumed name. Since there can be only one Florida corporation by that name, you'll avoid any possible confusion about who is the tenant.

3. Different Types of Business Entities

The legal nature of your business entity—a sole proprietorship, partnership, corporation, or LLC—determines whether you'll be personally responsible for paying rent and meeting the other obligations stated in the lease. (If you're not personally responsible, creditors can reach the assets of your business but not your personal assets, such as your home.) The current legal form of your business may be just the type you want. If you've considered the issue and have no need to rethink it, skip this section and go on to read about the clause describing your space (Section C). But if you're just starting out or would like to learn more about the differences between the various legal forms, take a minute to read on.

Most small businesses are established as one of the following:

- Sole Proprietorship—a one-owner business in which the owner is personally liable for all business debts, including the payment of rent and other lease obligations.
- Corporation—a business entity formed by one or more shareholders. Ordinarily, a shareholder isn't personally liable for the corporation's debts.
- Nonprofit Corporation—a business entity formed by two or more directors. Normally, directors are not personally liable for the corporation's debts.
- Limited Liability Company (LLC)—a business entity formed by one or more members. Ordinarily, members aren't personally liable for the LLC's debts.
- General Partnership—a business entity formed by two or more people, all of whom are personally liable for all partnership debts. Again, this includes paying rent and meeting other lease obligations. When two or more people are in business together and haven't formed a limited partnership (see below), corporation, or limited liability company, they're treated as a general partnership by law even if they haven't signed a formal partnership agreement.
- Limited Partnership—a business entity formed by two or more people, at least one of whom must be a general partner. The general partner(s) will be personally liable for the partnership's debts, as explained above. The limited partners do not have this potential liability. However, the limited partners cannot be actively involved in management.

Which business form is best for you? Well, one way to answer this question is to consider the consequences if things go poorly, finance-wise. If you're personally liable for the debts of your business, as you would be if your business were a sole proprietorship or partnership, a landlord—or any other creditor—can reach your personal assets such as your home, car, or savings account to satisfy a court judgment against your business. Obviously, shielding your personal assets from business debts can be a powerful reason to set up your business as a corporation or LLC rather than as a sole proprietorship or partnership.

In reality, however, establishing yourself as a corporation or LLC may not provide the protection you desire. The landlord may be unwilling to rely entirely on the credit of your corporation or LLC—especially if your business is new and doesn't have a financial track record. To provide another source of funds, the landlord may ask you to personally guarantee the lease obligations, and may even ask to have your spouse or other coguarantor sign a lease guarantee. This demand has the effect of destroying the personal financial protection you would normally have as a corporation or LLC. (See Chapter 17 for more on lease guarantees and ways to retain some protection.)

For an in-depth explanation or how to select a legal format for your business, see *The Legal Guide for Starting & Running a Small Business,* by Fred S. Steingold (Nolo), or *LLC or Corporation? How to Choose the Right Form for Your Bussiness,* by Anthony Mancuso (Nolo). Nolo has several titles that will help you set up and run specific forms of business entities, including partnerships, corporations, LLCs, and nonprofits. See order information on the Nolo website at www.nolo.com.

B. Describing the Leased Space

Somewhere near the beginning of your lease, often right after the Parties clause, you'll see a clause that identifies the space that you'll be occupying. This clause is often titled "Premises." If you're leasing an entire building, the clause should simply give the street address (and should describe any outbuildings or lots that come with it). If you're leasing less than an entire building, you and the landlord need to describe the space more precisely.

1. Common Ways to Describe the Premises

"Describing the Premises," below, shows how you can identify various kinds of rented space in a Premises clause. You'll see that some descriptions include the number of square feet. In general, when you're paying rent by the square foot (which is typically the case), you'll want to include the number of feet so that you and the landlord can calculate the rent. On the other hand, if you are paying by the floor or for an entire building, there is no need to include the square footage. (However, if you're paying for maintenance, taxes, and insurance based on the size of your rental, and not all floors are the same size, you'll want to state the footage so that you can calculate the correct portion of the whole that you'll be responsible for.)

If there might be any confusion as to which part of the building you are renting, use a diagram or plan and clearly mark the space (see the sample floor plan in Chapter 4, Section A). You'll want to attach the plan to the lease. Chapter 6, Section D, explains how to add attachments to a printed lease.

In addition to describing the space you'll be occupying exclusively, the lease should also describe the common areas you'll have the right to use along with other tenants. This may include hallways, stairways, elevators, storage space, and conference rooms, as well as parking. Where there's a potential for conflict with other tenants in the building, try to be as specific as possible in spelling out your rights. For example, if your lease gives you the right to use a conference room, you should agree on how often you can use it and the procedure for reserving the room.

Finally, if the landlord restricts your use of certain areas, the lease should specify the areas that are *not* included in the description of the premises.

Be sure you understand how the landlord measured square feet. Landlords have creative—and confusing—methods of measurement. Don't rely on a sketched floor plan, which may not show, for example, that you will also be paying for the thickness of the walls. Chapter 4, Section A, explains square foot measurement techniques.

2. Premises Language to Watch Out For

You might think that a Premises clause is just about as straightforward as a lease clause could be. As long as you understand how the landlord calculated square feet, what could complicate or concern you about a simple description of your space? Well, leave it to ingenious landlords (or their lawyers) to come up with a few. Here are the common wrinkles.

Describing the Premises

Entire building	The building at 320 North Main Street, Ann Arbor, Michigan, including the parking lot.
Entire floor	The entire first floor of the building at 320 North Main Street, Ann Arbor, Michigan. Tenant may also use the kitchen and the storage room next to the kitchen.
Entire wing	The entire west wing (2,500 square feet) of the building at 320 North Main Street, Ann Arbor, Michigan. Tenant may also use the common areas, including the lobby and hallways.
Part of a floor	The west 3,000 square feet of the second floor of the building at 320 North Main Street, Ann Arbor, Michigan, as shown on the drawing in Attachment #2. Tenant may use the conference room on the first floor, which is also available to tenants on that floor, on a first-come, first-served basis.
Suite	Suite 150 (1,000 square feet) in the building at 320 North Main Street, Ann Arbor, Michigan as outlined in blue ink on the drawing in Attachment # 2. Tenant may use all common areas, including the hallways, lobby, elevator, and stairs. Storage areas are not included. Tenant may use Spaces 5, 6, & 7 in the underground parking garage.
Individual office	The corner office in Suite 200 (300 square feet) in the building at 320 North Main Street, Ann Arbor, Michigan as outlined in red ink on the drawing in Attachment # 3. Tenant's clients may wait in the reception area and tenant may use all common areas of the building.

a. Changing the Common Areas

Landlords often write clauses that give them the right to change the common areas at will. For example, in order to create a larger space for another tenant, the landlord might decide to narrow the entryway to your store or chop into the lobby area outside of your office. Changes in the common areas can make your own space less convenient, prestigious, or usable.

If you see language in a premises clause that gives the landlord the right to adjust the common areas at will, try to eliminate it or at least build in a bit of protection—for example, by having the landlord agree in writing not to reduce the access to your space or make your space less visible from the street. Alternately, you might press for an understanding that if a common area reconfiguration works to your disadvantage, the landlord will compensate you monetarily, perhaps by reducing the rent. Be sure to specify that any disputes concerning common area changes will be resolved according to the dispute resolution mechanism in your lease. (The dispute resolution clause is described in Chapter 16, Section D.)

b. Changing Your Space

Believe it or not, some landlords will write a Premises clause that gives them the right to substitute other space—whether in the building or elsewhere—for the space described in the clause.

Most of the time, such a move will be a giant pain in the neck for you. Even if the lease requires the landlord to pay for the cost of a move, it's usually a poor idea to agree to such a deal. Moving to new space involves many costs beyond paying the moving company—redecorating, for example, and printing new stationery and brochures—as well as the possible inconvenience to employees and customers. Even more serious is the possibility that you'll get bumped to a less desirable location.

It's best to resist signing a lease that contains a switcheroo clause. But if you feel you must go along with the lease because other conditions are favorable (let's say the building is in the ideal location for your business), at least try to get the landlord to list in the lease the specific places in the building where you can be moved. You might, for example, limit the new space to the ground floor or within a specified distance from the building's main entrance.

C. The Use Clause and Exclusive Clause

Some landlords want to limit how you'll use the rented space. The limitations can be as broad as what business you'll conduct there, as narrow as what specific services or products you'll offer, or as nebulous as the quality level of your operation. In general, you'll want to avoid strict restrictions on your use of the rented space. Most of the time, you'll count yourself lucky if the lease handed to you by the landlord does not include a use clause.

An exclusive clause is a promise by the landlord that only you and no one else in the mall or building may engage in a particular type of business or carry a certain type of merchandise. Typically, only powerful "anchor" tenants get exclusives. The sections below explain how restrictive and exclusive clauses work together.

1. Different Kinds of Use Clauses

A use clause can be either a restriction on how you do business—telling you what you can't do—or a prescription, telling you what you must do.

a. Restrictive Use Clause

This type of use clause states what you're prohibited from doing. The landlord includes a list of every forbidden use—for example, a prohibition against food sales or consumption or even all retail sales. You're free to do anything that's not on the list. If you look at a restricted use clause and don't see anything that you could imagine doing, it's probably going to be okay with you. But be careful—there may be ways to do business that mesh with what you're doing now that you simply haven't considered. For example, who would have thought that your poster framing business would lend itself nicely to giving classes in the evening to groups of customers who want to learn

how to do it themselves? If your lease prohibits evening operating hours, you won't be able to offer those classes.

You may have to live with a restrictive use clause if the landlord has granted another tenant an "exclusive" clause. In a multitenant building or mall, large and powerful tenants sometimes pry an "exclusive" clause out of the landlord—a promise that the landlord won't rent nearby space to any tenant whose operations would compete with the major tenant (sometimes called an "anchor tenant"). Logically, if one tenant has the lock on a particular use—say, the sale of sports equipment—the other tenants on the property will be restricted from engaging in that use.

b. Getting Your Own Exclusive Clause

Most of the time, you'll encounter a restrictive use clause that restricts you because another, powerful tenant in your mall or building has cornered the market on a particular type of business or merchandise. But what if *you're* that attractive or powerful tenant? There's no reason not to bargain for an exclusive clause for yourself. For instance, you may be the best gourmet coffee business in town, and will want to protect yourself by making sure that no other stores in your strip mall or building will offer coffee and coffee drinks.

Begin by understanding that your landlord won't be able to reserve a business activity to you alone if current tenants' leases don't already restrict them from engaging in that activity. For instance, if the next-door grocery store's lease does not prohibit the store from serving coffee, the store can do so—until that tenant renegotiates its lease. Here is where you may make some inroads—if the landlord can convince the existing tenants that, on balance, their businesses will improve with you in the mix (but you won't move in without an exclusive), the landlord may be able to get them to sign lease addenda, in which they agree not to serve coffee. Only then can the landlord offer you a meaningful exclusive. So, for example, the grocery store may agree to stop selling coffee, figuring that the customers who come to the mall to patronize your business may also decide to do some grocery shopping—which they wouldn't have done otherwise.

If you've succeeded in getting an exclusive, you'll want to pay some attention to what will happen if other tenants violate it. Unless the remedies are easy and quick, the exclusive won't mean much. Ideally, once you have established that one of your neighbors has breached its restrictive use clause (and thereby stepped on your exclusive), you'd like reduced rent, an option to reduce the lease term, and no "cure" period (no time in which the neighbor gets to stop the offending activity without consequences). Most importantly, you'll want an established amount of monetary damages that you don't have to prove—the last thing you want is to go to court to prove how much

business you lost because another tenant moved into your exclusive. The landlord, on the other hand, will want to force you to prove your damages, hoping that if he objects, you won't take the time and trouble to go to court. The landlord will also want an opportunity to convince the violator to stop (a cure period), and will want to offer reduced rent for a short time (at the end of which you get to move out or return to full rent). The extent to which you get your ideal set of remedies will depend, as ever, on your attractiveness as a tenant and the state of the market.

c. Permissive Use Clause

This type of clause enumerates what you can do and, by implication, makes any other activities out-of-bounds. It puts the burden on you to come up with every conceivable use you can think of wanting to engage in at the time you sign the lease. If you later want to do something that's not on the list, too bad. A private post office, for example, might want to be free to offer photocopying, fax transmissions, and the retail sale of greeting cards, but if these activities aren't listed among the permitted uses, they're off limits. Clearly, this type of use clause can be very disadvantageous, since it can box you into a narrow line of business.

A use clause will hamper your ability to sublet or assign. Even if you see nothing wrong with going along with your landlord's use clause as far as *your* business is concerned, remember that any tenant to whom you assign or sublet will also be bound by the clause. (Assigning and subletting are explained in Chapter 14.) Especially if your space is potentially suitable for a wide range of businesses, the use clause will narrow the prospects considerably.

2. Why Landlords Typically Want a Use Clause

Use clauses that dictate the nature of your business are most frequently seen in shopping center leases, where landlords believe that the success of their center depends on a specified tenant "mix" and avoiding overlapping enterprises. Smaller, strip mall landlords are less likely to argue for a use restriction, and landlords offering stand-alone rentals that aren't part of a cluster of rentals ("street deals") rarely include them.

Landlords who lease retail space in multi-tenant properties, including malls, may insist that you sell only "first class" or "high quality" merchandise. The landlord is probably aiming for an upscale ambiance, hoping to attract other fancy tenants by requiring you to maintain a certain standard. But using a completely subjective standard isn't a smart way to go about it. Landlords who want tenants (including you) with good taste and high prices should look for them outright.

3. Use Clauses That Help You

Use limitations can be a two-edged sword. You yourself may actually want protection from competitors or incompatible businesses. For example, if you're a doctor or dentist renting space in a professional building, you understandably may want to protect your professional image by having the landlord agree to rent only to compatible tenants such as a pharmacy, eyeglass store, or home care equipment rental service. If you're a therapist, you may need to ensure that your neighbors' businesses will involve a minimum of commotion (no children's gymnastics classes, thank you). If you're renting space for a camera store that will sell and process film, you may want language in your lease prohibiting the landlord from allowing any other tenant (a drugstore, for example) from selling or processing film. Restrictions that many tenants insist upon include a promise not to rent to check-cashing offices, fast-food restaurants, or video or music stores. It's also common to see powerful tenants obtain the landlord's promise not to rent to government entities (these tenants don't want to have a welfare office, unemployment office, or probation department next door).

It may, however, be unrealistic to expect the landlord to protect your niche. In fact, when it comes to retail businesses, it's questionable whether such protection will actually benefit you. Chances are that the traffic generated by the drugstore mentioned above, for example, will bring customers to your camera store who wouldn't otherwise have come—while picking up their prescriptions, they'll also visit you because they want more sophisticated photography services and equipment than the drugstore offers.

If your lease must include a use clause, try for a permissive clause giving you the broadest rights to use the space, or a restrictive clause that bars only a few, narrow pursuits. For example, you might happily sign off on a permissive clause permitting retail sales as long as it doesn't specify the type of products to be sold. A restrictive use clause in an office lease probably won't be objectionable as long as it prohibits only one or two kinds of subtenants.

4. Use Restrictions Beyond Your Control

Your landlord isn't the only one who can dictate what you do in your business. The government has a say, too—clearly, you can't use your space for illegal uses, which range from the obvious (anyone opening a brothel?) to activities that are off-limits due to a zoning ordinance. For example, if the space you're leasing is zoned for offices, you won't be able to open up a bicycle repair shop unless, against considerable odds, you can get the zoning changed or you qualify for an administrative variance. Your lease need not alert you to any relevant zoning restrictions. Presumably, you've already checked for any zoning ordinances that may affect the space you are about to lease, as suggested in Chapter 3, Section B.

In addition to zoning ordinances, other planning, building, safety, and health ordinances can affect your intended use. An ordinance may require a certain number of off-street parking spaces for some types of businesses, a wheelchair-accessible entrance, or a restroom for customers—common requirements for a restaurant. ■

Chapter 8

The Length of Your Lease

Near the beginning of the lease, you'll see a clause entitled "Term." This clause describes the length of your lease and specifies the starting and ending dates. You may be tempted to cruise right through it—after all, if you want a five-year lease and the Term clause gives you five years, where's the complication? Alas, there's more than one tricky wrinkle and they're apt to be hidden and dangerous.

Nearly all the rights (and responsibilities) you assume when you become your landlord's tenant are affected by the lease's starting and ending dates. For example, you may negotiate to fix the rental space up according to your needs, which will require the right to bring in planners or designers and then start the work. Your lease must give you the ability to get in and schedule work at your convenience. Your responsibilities for paying rent, contributing to the taxes and insurance, and providing for maintenance are clearly tied to the lease starting and ending date. In short, it's imperative that you understand when your many rights and responsibilities *really* begin and end.

This chapter helps you make sense of the dates specified in your Term clause, by:

- explaining in detail the various events, such as the need to buy insurance or shoulder the responsibility for code compliance, that you'll likely encounter at the beginning and end of your lease (Section A)

- alerting you to tricky lease language that has the effect of piling on lease responsibilities without your realizing it (Section B), and

- suggesting how to organize the many important dates in your lease, using a timeline, which will put them in prospective (Section C).

In addition, we'll explain two common issues that are related to the start and finish of your lease:

- what to do if your space isn't ready for you on the date that it's promised (Section A), and

- the consequences to you if you stay beyond, or "hold over," the ending date for your lease (Section D).

A. When Do Your Legal Responsibilities Begin and End?

The beginning date of your lease is obviously important in terms of when you pay rent and when you can open for business. Other starting dates may also concern you—for example, when you can bring in your architect and when you may begin improvement work. The ending date of your lease is often more straightforward than the beginning date. Here's what to look for in the landlord's Term clause.

1. Simple Beginnings

If your experience with leases is limited to renting residential property, you might expect that the starting date of your business lease is a single date, signaling simultaneously your obligation for rent and your right to move in. Well, sometimes it really is just that simple. If you're moving into a space that doesn't have to be fixed up and your rent isn't connected to the volume of your business (that is, you're not paying percentage rent, which is explained in Chapter 4, Section C), there's no reason why the landlord can't hand you the keys and start the rent meter ticking at the same time.

In this situation, look for a straightforward statement in your Term clause saying that your obligation for rent and your right to use the space begin as of a stated date. For example, you may see the term described as "Five years, starting January 15, 2005, and ending January 15, 2010." The clause may specify that rent begins on that date, or the Rent clause (explained in Chapter 9) may cross-reference this date in the Term clause.

⚠ Be sure you understand what "take possession" means. You may think that if the lease allows you to "take possession" on a certain date, you can move in and open up. But some lease clauses will define the term to mean less—that you can begin improvement work and move in, for example, but not begin business. Be sure that the meaning is clear.

2. Complicated Beginnings

The start of many business tenancies is somewhat more complex. There will typically be many beginnings, each tied to one of the many steps you take as you make your way to opening day. For instance, if you or the landlord will be making modifications or improvements to the space before you move in, you'll need to know:

- when your architects or contractors can get into the space to plan your improvements—regardless of whether the current tenant is still there
- when you can take possession of the space—that is, when you have the exclusive right to be in it
- when you can begin the remodeling work
- when you can move in, and
- when you can open for business.

The work you do on your rented space isn't the only source of multiple "beginning" dates. There may be several other lease clauses with starting dates. For instance:

- Your lease may require you to purchase insurance for the property (insurance is explained in Chapter 15). When must the coverage begin?
- You may be obligated to keep the building up to code during your tenancy (code compliance is explained in Chapter 12). When does this responsibility begin?
- You may be obligated to rid the property of toxic contamination or

waste (responsibility for environmental contamination is explained in Chapter 3). When does that duty start?

You probably get the picture. It's important to look carefully at the landlord's Term clause to see what events have been noted —besides your obligation to begin paying rent (most landlords manage to make that clear enough). And it's equally important to see whether important dates mentioned in the Term clause or elsewhere in the lease make sense when compared with the rent-paying date. For example, you wouldn't want to be obligated to begin paying rent just days after you have the right to begin complex renovations. The way to put these dates into perspective is to prepare a time line, as explained in Section C, below.

3. Delayed Beginnings

Despite your best efforts to plan ahead—and even with the cooperation of the landlord— it's possible that your new quarters will not be ready as promised for you to send in your planners, architects, remodelers, inventory, or equipment. Unforeseen events can get in the way, such as:

- **The holdover tenant.** You may be leasing space that is currently occupied by another tenant. Clearly, your ability to move in on time will depend on that tenant's timely departure.
- **The tardy contractor.** If you've leased space in a building under construction, or if your improvements aren't done

yet, you obviously can't move in until they're finished.

- **The stubborn inspector.** Even if the new building is done, you won't be able to move in until local building officials have issued a certificate of occupancy for the building.

One way to handle a not-ready problem that's traceable to the landlord (or the prior tenant) is to negotiate a cutoff date after which you have the right to cancel the lease if the building (or your space) isn't available. If you have decided on substantial remodeling, you'll want this date to be before you begin work. Of course, killing the deal at this point won't be something you'll do lightly, since it will mean that you must begin your search all over again.

An alternative to walking away from space that isn't available as promised (due to the landlord's delay) is to agree now that you'll collect a predetermined amount of monetary damages from the landlord if you have to wait. This sum of money—known as "liquidated damages"—should be a realistic estimate of how much you would lose, per day or per week, if you can't get into the space when you expect to.

The drawback of using a liquidated damages clause is that it's always hard to estimate lost profits—particularly if you're just starting out in business. If you estimate too low, you won't be able to argue for more—you're stuck with the figure in the lease. The upside of having a liquidated damages clause in your lease is that your landlord will have very little "wiggle room" when it comes to paying you for the time you cool your heels—the landlord, too, will be stuck with the negotiated amount. You won't have to sue the landlord to prove your damages (but if the landlord won't pay, you may have to sue to collect).

If you and the landlord reach an agreement about how the two of you will handle a delay, you can put it in the lease clause entitled Term. Or, if you are planning on making improvements to the space you're leasing, you can deal with the issue in the lease clause that covers improvements. (See Chapter 11, Section I, for information on negotiating improvements clauses and allocating the risk of the not-ready space.)

If your losses would be very hard to estimate, forego the liquidated damages agreement. You can always sue the landlord for your actual damages if the space isn't ready and you lose profits while you wait.

4. The End of Your Lease

The ending of your lease term is normally not as complicated as the start can be. That's because, unless you and the landlord have decided otherwise, you won't have to allow for construction time to remove the improvements you installed when you moved in. Normally, the end of your lease is a fairly simple event—you close up, pack up, and off you go.

There are, however, a couple of timing issues that you'll want to understand.

Although the end of the term means the date when you'll stop paying rent, you'll also need to know whether you must be physically out of the premises on the same day. Ideally, you'll get a few extra, rent-free days to remove your belongings. This understanding must be spelled out in the Term clause.

B. The Crafty Use of "As of" [Date]

At the very start of your lease, even before the first clause, you may see this seemingly innocuous phrase: "Landlord and Tenant enter into this lease as of [a date]." The lease will continue on, listing all the clauses and ending with a space for you and the landlord to sign and date the lease. You may not see any other dates in the lease, other than the one that accompanies the signatures. What's the meaning of the date that's specified in the "As of" sentence?

When a lease begins with an "As of" date, all the obligations covered by the lease, unless stated otherwise, take effect *as of that date*. For instance, if the lease obligates you to keep your space in compliance with building codes, or makes you responsible for a portion of the property taxes and insurance, these duties become yours as of the date that follows those two little words. And here's the kicker: Landlords can choose any date they wish for the "As of" date—it may be the date you begin negotiations, sign the lease, start your improvements work, or any date that suits the landlord. In most states, the obligations you undertake in the lease become legally enforceable from the "As of" date onward, even if you physically sign the lease a month later and don't move in for six months!

The consequences of signing a lease with an "As of" date that significantly predates your use of the property can be dire. For example, suppose your lease obligates you to pay for a portion of any code upgrades for your rented space that may be required by amendments to the building code. Ideally, you'd want your lease to specify that you'll be responsible for upgrade requirements that go into effect only *after* your move-in date, or perhaps after you begin work on your improvements. But if the building code is amended after the "As of" date but before the date you move in or even begin work, you may still be on the hook to pay for the upgrades—even though you haven't set foot in the space or turned a penny in profit yet.

It's probably not necessary to spell out the warning here—if the lease contains an "As of" date, get it removed. If the landlord wants you to be responsible for certain contingencies or for specific expenses, the lease can say so directly and the two of you can bargain over them. Using an "As of" date is a sneaky way to commit you to potentially large obligations, and it's no way to begin a business relationship.

C. How to Keep Track of Dates With a Timeline

Do not breeze through the Term clause without making sure you understand what you can—and cannot—do on various dates. The only way to keep track of your rights and responsibilities is to draw a timeline. In addition, plotting the dates will alert you to areas where you may want to bargain for a modification. For instance, if you need time to move in or make modifications but your rent payments begin before you even set foot in the space, you'll be paying rent before you can begin operations. If you can't alter this arrangement, at least you'll know what's in store.

The sample "Timeline for Move to 29 Spring Street," below, shows how one tenant plotted the various dates involved with leasing his new office space. After he was done, this tenant made a list of questions to ask the landlord, including important dates he needed to nail down or change.

Timeline for Move to 29 Spring Street

May 1:   Current tenant's lease expires.

May 1:   Obligation to pay insurance premiums begins. *Try to change this to June 1*

May 10: I get possession of the premises. *See if I can get in earlier without advancing rent date*

June 1: Rent responsibility begins.

Points to raise and clarify:
- When can my space planners come in and take a look around?
- Make sure code compliance clause doesn't commence until May 10, unless I can take possession earlier.
- Check with planner, architect, & contractor to make sure they can complete improvements by June 1.

If the building is under construction, make sure that you won't have to pay rent until it's finished. You may think that this is so obvious it doesn't need to be spelled out in your lease, but some landlords have actually tried to collect rent even before building officials have approved the building for occupancy.

D. Staying After the Term Ends: Holdover Rent

In some leases, the Term clause will address what happens if you don't move at the end of the term (you may also see this issue addressed in a separate clause entitled "Holdover"). The consequences of not moving when the lease is up can be significant, including higher rent or even an unwanted renewed lease. Even though you have every intention of honoring the termination date, it pays to spend time negotiating this clause.

1. The High Costs of Holdover Rent

It's not unusual to see a provision requiring you to pay double or more in rent if you hold over after the lease ends. Do your best to negotiate this figure down to as close to the ending rent as possible. You never know what pressures you'll be facing in three, five, or ten years—common lengths for a commercial lease. You may have no choice but to stay on if your next space is not quite ready when this lease is up. In short, don't count on your present plans and intentions, since forces beyond your control may make it hard to move as intended.

A high holdover rent may also hamper you if you intend to negotiate for a renewal of the current lease. Knowing that you will be facing a punishing holdover rent, your landlord will have a tactical advantage during negotiations, since you'll be under considerable pressure to cave in and quickly strike a deal before the high holdover rent begins.

2. Using Holdover Rent to Limit Your Exposure

After reading the paragraphs above, you might conclude that any holdover rent that exceeds what you'd normally be paying should be avoided. And, in truth, that's often the case. But you might be well-served to agree to a higher holdover figure as long as you get something very valuable in return—a statement that this amount represents all that you will be expected to pay as a consequence of overstaying your welcome.

Here's how it works: Suppose you have stayed on but the landlord has already rented the space to your successor. You can be sure that the new tenant will be unhappy at not being able to move in as planned, and will quite likely look to the landlord for monetary compensation for the delay. For example, the next tenant might have to rent expensive, temporary quarters, or lose valuable business while waiting to open up. The landlord, in turn, will look to you as the true cause of the delay. And if you are in fact the true cause, a lawsuit may force you to reimburse the landlord for any sums that the disappointed tenant has collected from her.

You can limit your financial responsibility by inserting some very important language in the holdover clause. You want it to specify that the holdover rent will *also* count as "liquidated damages" for any monetary loss that your delay has caused the landlord. (Liquidated damages, as explained above in Section A, are monetary damages that are agreed upon in advance.) This will prevent the landlord from suing you for any losses he suffers that result from your not leaving as planned. In other words, even though the holdover rent may be high, you will have the peace of mind of knowing that at least you won't be on the hook for more money if the frustrated new tenant collects from the landlord and the landlord wants to collect from you.

3. Your New Holdover Lease Term

A typical holdover clause will provide that if you don't move as planned, your tenancy will become a month-to-month arrangement, under the same conditions as the original lease. If the lease doesn't raise the issue, the law in most states will apply the same rule.

Watch out for a clause giving the landlord the right to declare the lease renewed for a full term or any term of years. With such a provision, your failure to leave as agreed could result in your starting another long-term lease, which might be very disadvantageous to your business situation.

Some obligations don't end with the lease. Don't assume that all of your responsibilities will end once you move out. Many obligations, such as the responsibility for environmental contamination (discussed in Chapter 3, Section C) will "survive" the ending date of the lease. ■

Chapter 9

Rent

For most small businesses, the amount of the monthly rent obligation is a very important issue. If you prepared a Rental Cost Worksheet as suggested in Chapter 4, you have a rough idea of what to expect for a particular property. Now it's time to look carefully at the landlord's lease clauses to see whether your rent estimates will pan out and to determine any new costs or savings, such as:

- expenses that you didn't anticipate
- savings that may make it possible to shoulder other expenses
- issues that you want to renegotiate, or
- unpleasant surprises that you may not be able to change but can learn to live with.

This chapter explains the many complicated ways that landlords may tote up a monthly bill called "the rent." Keep in mind that here we're explaining only those sums that you'll be obligated to pay the landlord or pay to others on the landlord's behalf. Your own operating expenses, such as your payroll, liability insurance, and phone service, are monthly expenses too, but they're not part of your rent.

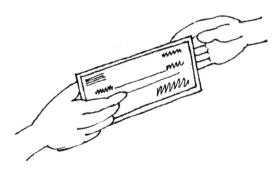

Later chapters in this book cover other rent-related issues, such as the date you start paying rent (Chapter 11, Section I), insuring the rent (Chapter 15, Section C), and termination for nonpayment of rent (Chapter 16, Section A).

Look at the whole deal. The most important rule is to consider the cost of doing business at a particular address, including rent, taxes, insurance, improvement costs, and common area maintenance fees. Decide if your business can afford the total expense of leasing the space—and whether that expense is competitive with the cost of similar space in your community. (Chapter 4, Section D, explains how to calculate the real cost of a rental.) How these costs are spread out among the various components is relatively unimportant. Paying a large amount for insurance or taxes may not be a bad deal if the square-foot rent is substantially below the prevailing market rate.

A. Basic Rent

Every lease will specify a charge for the space itself—a charge that's usually tied to the size of the space you'll be occupying. As we explained in Chapter 4, some landlords choose to charge on a square-footage basis and that's it. There's a flat rate you pay each month and no other calculations need be made before you write the rent check. This arrangement is known as a "gross lease." Other landlords expect that you'll help pay for operating costs—in particular, the real estate taxes, property insurance and building maintenance and operation expenses. This system is known as a "net lease."

If you have a net lease, the amount of the monthly rent check won't be stated precisely in the lease since the charges for the add-on items won't remain constant. You'll need to do further calculations during the life of the lease.

⚠ **Read your lease carefully to determine whether you have a gross or a net lease.** The charges you have to pay aren't always clearly labeled as rent. You may see a rent clause that specifies a rate per square foot but says nothing about your responsibility for taxes, insurance, or maintenance costs—but that may be because these items are covered in separate clauses elsewhere in the lease.

1. Paying for Space in a Gross Lease

If you're sure that you'll be paying a fixed rate for the space and that you'll owe the landlord no additional charges, the rent clause in the landlord's lease ought to be fairly simple. The trickiest issue is how the landlord has measured the space. If it's been measured from the exterior of outside walls with no deduction for the thickness of interior walls, you're paying for a lot of plaster, as explained in Chapter 4, Section A. As suggested there, it's prudent to

measure the space yourself to confirm the landlord's figure, whatever the method that's been used. Clearly, if there's a significant difference you will want to raise the issue during negotiations.

There are other important issues to bear in mind if you have a gross lease. Things may not be as simple as you think. Your landlord might:

- provide for a rent hike during the lease term, or
- make you responsible for certain operating costs in addition to the rent.

Let's look at these possibilities.

a. Rent Escalation

In anticipation of inflation, some landlords want the rent to increase year to year according to some formula. Sometimes the increase is flat and clear, such as an increase of $0.20 per square foot per year.

Another way landlords provide for a yearly rent increase is by tying it to the Consumer Price Index (CPI) for your region. With this approach, the percentage of CPI growth is applied to the base rent—if the CPI goes up 5%, your rent goes up 5% or some portion thereof. A rent increase based on the CPI, however, can turn out to be very expensive for you, for there's no guarantee that the value of the building will increase at the same rate as the CPI. And if the rate of inflation is high, the CPI may be way ahead of your ability to make a profit in your particular business.

Another drawback to using the CPI as the rent escalator is that you'll never know how high the rent can go unless there is a limit or "cap." In fact, a CPI-based rent escalator should have both a ceiling and a floor (known as a "collar"). Why? Let's look at it from your point of view. Suppose you want to take out a loan to cover the expense of a new computer system for your office or a piece of equipment for your shop. Your lender will want to know what your expenses and income are likely to be during the life of the loan (that will give the lender a good idea about whether you'll be able to repay it). Now, if there's no cap on your rent, the lender may worry that your rent could become so expensive that you wouldn't be able to meet your repayment obligations. And if the lender is worried enough, he may deny the loan.

For this reason, you should negotiate for a ceiling to the rent—no higher than you could comfortably afford. Point out to the landlord that the ceiling may never be reached. It *will* mollify your potential lenders, which benefits the landlord as well (you can reasonably argue that a thriving tenant with sufficient capital is one who pays the rent on time). Don't be surprised if the landlord counters with a demand that you agree to a "floor," which will guarantee a minimum rent in case the CPI decreases. Echoing your reasoning, the landlord may argue that without a minimum rent, lenders may worry that the landlord too may not have the income to repay a loan. You may have to settle for a compromise: You get a

cap and the landlord gets a floor, such as an agreement that a decrease in the CPI won't affect the rent until a specified amount of time has passed.

EXAMPLE: Landlord Spiffy Properties LLC and tenant Protobiz Inc. agree that rent increases will be tied to the annual changes in the CPI for their metropolitan area. They also agree that Spiffy will get at least a 2% increase each year and that Protobiz won't have to pay more than a 4% increase. One year the CPI increase is 5%. Protobiz has to pay for only a 4% increase—the cap agreed to in the lease.

b. Gross Lease With Stops

Many landlords are reluctant to offer a pure gross lease—one where, even with a rent escalator, the entire risk of rising operating costs is on the landlord. For example, if the landlord heats the building and the cost of heating oil goes sky high, the tenant will continue to pay the same rent, while the landlord's profit is eaten away by oil bills. To build in some protection, your landlord might offer a gross lease "with stops," which means that when specified operating costs reach a certain level, you begin to pitch in. Typically, the landlord will name a particular year, called the "base year," against which to measure the rise in costs (often, the base year is the first year of your lease). It's a bit like turning a gross lease into a net lease if certain conditions—heightened operating expenses—are met.

If your landlord proposes a gross lease with stops, understand that your rental obligations will no longer be a simple "X square feet times $Y per square foot" every month. As soon as the stop point—an agreed-upon operating cost—is reached, you'll be responsible for a portion of specified expenses—insurance premiums, tax bills, or maintenance costs. During negotiations concerning a gross lease with stops, consider the following points:

- **What operating costs will be considered?** Obviously, the landlord will want to include as many operating expenses as he can, from taxes, insurance, and common area maintenance to building security, capital expenses (such as a new roof), and even legal costs and expenses associated with leasing other parts of the building. Do your best to keep the list short and, above all, clear.

- **Where is the "stop" point?** The landlord will want you to begin contributing to operating costs as soon as they begin to uncomfortably eat into his profit margin. If the landlord is already making a handsome return on the property (which will happen if the market is tight), he has less need to demand a low stop point—but by the same token, you have less bargaining clout to demand a higher point.

- **How are added costs allocated?** If you're in a multitenant situation, will all tenants contribute to the added expense? How will the charges be allocated—according to the amount of space you rent, or according to your use of the particular service? For example, if the building-wide heating bills go way up but only one tenant runs the furnace every weekend, will you be expected to pay the added costs in equal measures, even if you're never open for business on the weekends?

- **Will the stop level remain the same during the life of the lease?** The idea of a stop point is to relieve the landlord from paying for some—but not all—increased operating expenses. As the years pass (and the cost of running the property rises), you'll pay for an increasingly large portion of the landlord's costs unless you can negotiate for a periodic upward adjustment of the stop point. Your ability to press for this will improve if the landlord has built in some form of rent escalation, explained above in Subsection a. Why? Because you can argue that if it's reasonable to increase the rent based on an assumption that operating costs will rise, it's also reasonable to raise the point at which you begin to pay for those costs. To do one without the other allows the landlord, but not you, to adjust expenses based on inflationary increases.

c. "Grossing Up" the Base Year in Multitenant Buildings

If your gross lease in a multitenant building includes a provision allowing the landlord to begin charging you when operating costs rise above a certain level, the landlord will probably include a "gross-up" clause in the lease if the building is not fully occupied during your base year. This clause ensures that you pay your fair share of any increased costs. Here's why this clause is necessary, and how it works.

Suppose you rent one entire floor of a ten-story building, but the rest of the building is vacant. The lease provides that when electricity usage rises above the cost in the first year, you begin to pay 10% of the excess. In the first year, the bill is $100,000, so that becomes the base year. Now, assume that in the second year, all floors are occupied and everyone uses the same amount of electricity, so that the bill for the second year is $1,000,000. Since that's $900,000 above the base year amount, you'll begin paying 10% of $900,000, or $9,000—even though your usage hasn't changed and you should be paying nothing.

The way to remedy this problem is to figure the base year figure as if the building were fully leased, with everyone using the same amount of electricity. To "gross up" the base year figure, then, you'd ask the landlord to make the base-year electricity number $1,000,000 (ten stories of ten tenants, each using $100,000 worth of electricity). Under this scenario, in the second year you'll still pay nothing since the building-wide bill is not over $1,000,000.

Grossing-up is appropriate only for variable costs, such as maintenance, utilities, cleaning, and some repairs. Fixed costs, such as the cost of insurance and property taxes, which don't vary depending on building occupancy, don't require grossing-up.

2. Paying for Space in a Net Lease

A net lease starts out just like a gross lease—it too will include a price per square foot. You'll need to find out how the space was measured and whether the landlord has included a rent escalator, as explained above in Section 1. The negotiation points mentioned there apply in a net lease situation as well.

After you've identified the landlord's lease clause that deals with the square footage calculation, which is known as your *base rent,* your real work begins. Net leases include other periodic expenses—taxes, insurance, and maintenance—which are explained in Sections B through D of this chapter. For each of them, you can negotiate for caps, or ceilings, to the amount you'll be required to pay, as shown in the individual discussions.

There's more than one way to lower the rent. The real cost of the rental includes not just the rent, but your operating costs at this location, including improvement costs. (Chapter 4, Section D, shows you how to compute the real cost.) A landlord who's reluctant to lower the basic rent may be willing to make other adjustments, such as giving you a move-in allowance or a month or two of free rent, which may be even more valuable to you than a lowered square foot price. By doing this, the landlord can truthfully tell other prospective tenants that you're paying a high dollar amount per square foot. (It may sound silly, but some landlords do play this game.) Also, check out what the landlord is willing to do in paying for improvements (often called build-outs) to the space. Lease clauses covering improvements are explained in Chapter 11.

➡️ Sections B through D of this chapter cover items that are considered "additional rent," such as taxes, insurance, and maintenance costs. These normally affect only tenants with net leases. If you have a gross lease, skip ahead to Section E.

B. Taxes As Additional Rent

Property taxes imposed on businesses by state and local governments fall into two general categories:

- personal property taxes, which cover furniture, trade fixtures, equipment, and inventory, and
- real property taxes, which cover the land and building.

Almost always, you alone will be responsible for your business's personal property taxes. This will be true even if the lease says nothing on the subject. Real property (sometimes called "real estate") taxes are often, however, shared by the landlord and tenant.

1. How to Allocate Taxes Between Landlord and Tenant

A common way to place tax responsibility on the tenant is for the landlord to agree to pay all real property taxes for the first year of the lease (sometimes called the "base year"). Then, after the first year, you pick up all or a portion of any increase.

> **EXAMPLE:** Spartan Enterprises leases a small building from Urban Developers for five years. The lease says that in years two through five of the lease, Spartan will pay 50% of any increase in real property taxes beyond the first year amount. Taxes are $3,000 for year one and are paid entirely by Urban. In year two taxes, taxes go up to $3,300. Spartan owes $150 in real property taxes in year two (50% of the $300 increase). Urban pays the remaining $3,150.

A landlord may, however, ask you to pay for more than just the tax increases. You could be asked to pay for all real property taxes, or to split real property taxes 50/50 with the landlord. But the issue of allocation can get pretty complicated, as explained below.

2. Dividing the Taxes Fairly Among All Building Tenants

If you're going to be the landlord's sole renter, it won't be hard to allocate the tax burden between the two of you. Depending on who has the superior bargaining position, either you'll get stuck with the entire bill, a portion of the entire bill (the landlord pays the rest), or all or a portion of any increase. The situation can get a bit trickier, however, if you're going to occupy space in a multitenant building, where many tenants share the tax burden. There are two important issues to bear in mind as you head into lease negotiations:

- Is your portion of the tax bill based on the total rentable space of the property, or on the space that is, in fact, rented?
- Have other tenants' improvements caused the tax bill to grow—and are you indirectly paying for the consequences of these fancy improvements?

Let's look at these two concerns.

a. Rentable Versus Rented Space

If you're going to pay all or a part of the landlord's real property taxes, it's important that the lease clause specify that you'll pay according to your percentage of the property's total rentable space—not the space that happens to be rented when you sign your lease. If you pay according to the total space that happens to be rented at the time, you can end up paying an enormous portion of the tax bill if there are significant vacancies in the building. The example below illustrates the problem.

EXAMPLE: California Sew and Vac has rented 2,000 square feet of the total rentable area of 10,000 square feet in Larry Landlord's building. Sadly for Larry, only half of the total space is actually rented out. Sew and Vac has a net lease that obligates it to pay for a fraction of Larry's property taxes. There are two ways to compute the fraction:

According to the rented space. Larry Landlord would like the calculation to be the result of dividing the amount of space leased by Sew and Vac by the amount of space actually leased in the building, or 2,000 divided by 5,000. Sew and Vac's portion of the taxes would be 40%. The other tenant (or tenants) pay 3,000 divided by 5,000, or 60% of the bill. *The tenants together pay 100% of the tax and Larry pays nothing.*

According to the rentable space. Sew and Vac would like the calculation to be the result of dividing the space it leases by the total rentable area, or 2,000 divided by 10,000. Using this method, Sew and Vac's tax obligation would be 20%. The remaining tenant (or tenants) will pay 30% (3,000 divided by 10,000). *The tenants together pay 50% and Larry Landlord pays 50% of the tax bill.*

You can see why a landlord would prefer to base your tax responsibility on the rented, not rentable, area of the building. Under the first system, the landlord will pass the risk of an empty building onto the tenants—whoever is there will divide the bill among themselves. Under the second system, however, the landlord will pay taxes for the unrented space.

If you see (or expect) significant chunks of vacant space in the building, try hard for a lease clause that bases your share of taxes on the building's rentable space. If it's a hot property with vacancies unlikely and apportionment is based on rented space, you won't have much to worry about.

b. Other Tenants' Improvements

In a multitenant property, you may have neighbors who have put in expensive, value-adding improvements, such as equipment for a restaurant, fancy décor, or extensive computer wiring for an office suite. (Improvements are permanent additions to the landlord's property, as explained in detail in Chapter 11.) You, on the other hand, may end up adding little or nothing to the

value of the property when you move in, asking only for a new carpet, paint, and some special lighting. What's the problem? Your landlord's real estate tax bill is based on the taxable value of the *entire* property, which is computed by factoring in all tenants' improvements. If your tax obligation is based on your pro rata share of the rentable space, without taking into consideration the fact that your neighbors' valuable improvements have upped the tax bill significantly, you'll be paying more than your fair share.

One way to even things out is to bargain for your tax obligations to be based on your pro rata share of the taxable *value* of the entire property, instead of your pro rata share of the entire rentable space. That way, you pay according to the value of your space.

Now, it's unlikely that you can get the tax assessor to separately value individual tenants' spaces in a commercial building. The best way to estimate your fair share of taxable value is to assume that the cost to rebuild the entire property, with each tenant's improvements as they are now, is roughly equivalent to the taxable value of the property (if the tax assessors have been

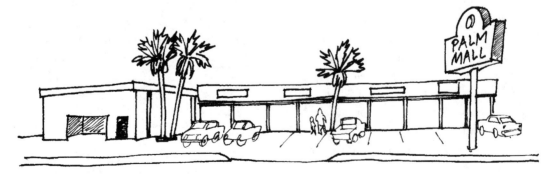

doing their job, these figures should be close). Next, assume that your share of the rebuilding costs (expressed as a percent, by dividing the cost of rebuilding your space by the cost of rebuilding the entire property) will be the same as your share of the taxable value of the property. That's the percentage multiplier that you apply to the tax bill to compute your fair share.

EXAMPLE: A small strip mall in Pacific Cove has three commercial spaces and 10,000 square feet available.

Tenant A leased 2,000 square feet for an auto repair shop, adding a hoist, automatic garage doors, a heavy-duty ventilation system, and extensive electrical wiring, all of which became permanent improvements. Rebuilding this space would cost $150 per square foot.

Tenant B leased 5,000 square feet to use as a distribution center for dry goods. B added nothing to the bare space when he moved in. To rebuild would cost $50 per square foot.

Tenant C leased the remaining 3,000 square feet and added interior walls and some lights for use in its telemarketing business. Rebuilding costs for this space would be $65 per square foot.

The tenants all have net leases, which are all up for renegotiation.

Table 1, below, shows what happens to each tenant's tax obligation if it is figured on the basis of that tenant's portion of the rentable space only. Table 2 shows what happens to each tenant's taxable share when the landlord figures it according to the value of

Table 1. Allocating Taxes According to Rentable Space

Tenant	Rented space (square feet)	Rentable space (square feet)	Ratio (rented space/ rentable space	Tenants' share of the taxes
A	2,000	10,000	20%	20% of the total
B	5,000	10,000	50%	50% of the total
C	3,000	10,000	30%	30% of the total

Table 2. Allocating Taxes According to Replacement Value

Tenant	Replacement cost per foot	Rented space (square feet)	Cost to replace own space	Replacement cost of entire property	Tenants' share of replacement costs	Tenants' share of the taxes
A	$150	2,000	$300,000	**$745,000**	40.3%	40.3%
B	$50	5,000	$250,000	**$745,000**	33.6%	33.6%
C	$65	3,000	$195,000	**$745,000**	26.1%	26.1%

each tenant's rented space. After computing the replacement cost of the property and each tenant's share, the landlord applies that percentage to the tax bill, too.

As you can see from comparing the results of Tables 1 and 2, the tax burdens on A, B, and C will be quite different if the landlord allocates them according to the value each has brought to the property, instead of the size alone of their rentals. Tenant A in particular, who brought in many expensive improvements, will pay twice as much according to the replacement value method. If *you* happen to be Tenant A, no doubt you'll prefer the system shown in Table 1—but it wouldn't be the fairest way of dividing the tax burdens.

When you negotiate with the landlord over how taxes are allocated among tenants, remember that it must be the same for all tenants in the building. The landlord will be constrained by the terms of the leases already in place with other tenants. If, for example, Tenants A and B are already renting under leases that allocate taxes according to the size alone of their spaces, Tenant C won't be able to press for a different system unless C can get the landlord and A and B to rewrite A's and B's leases. Absent some extraordinary clout on your part, it's unlikely you'll be able to accomplish this.

However, there's no reason why the system has to remain the same forever. If you have a lease that's longer than other

tenants in the building, press for a planned switch to a value-based method when all existing tenants are out. Negotiate for a promise from the landlord that all new tenants will be given space-based tax obligations only until all space-based tenants have left. At that point, all of you will convert to a value-based system.

3. How Much Are the Property Taxes?

When you negotiate the lease, ask to see the landlord's property tax bill for the preceding year. If you're asked to pay all or a portion, you'll know the amount—for now. But it's not likely to remain static. The tax amount may rise because:

- **The building is reassessed.** It pays to find out when the tax figure was last adjusted for the property (this information is available from the local tax assessor). If it was recently changed, chances are that you won't see a change in the near future. But if the taxes have remained the same for several years, and especially if property values in the neighborhood have increased or the landlord has improved your building, a tax increase may be in store. Be prepared.

- **The building is sold.** If real estate values increase substantially and the landlord sells the property for a handsome sum, the real estate taxes will probably go up. The fact that the new owner must honor your lease will be cold comfort when you get a monstrous tax bill for your share of the increase.

⚠️ **Is your tax obligation limited to *property* taxes?** Never underestimate the ability of cash-strapped localities to turn to local business as a source of income. Business operating taxes, such as a payroll tax, gross receipt taxes, and even licensing fees, are increasingly popular. You could end up paying some of them if the lease obligates you to pay a portion of the landlord's taxes and does not specify that this means property taxes only.

4. Negotiating Your Tax Obligation

As you review the landlord's lease clause concerning your tax obligations (it may be labeled "Taxes," or it may be buried in the Rent clause), keep the following points in mind for negotiation:

- **Fair allocation among tenants.** If you're in a multitenant building, take a look at the size and value of your neighbors' spaces. If the landlord allocates taxes on the basis of space only and you think this will be unfair, raise the issue. While the landlord may be unable to reconfigure other tenants' tax obligations, he may be willing to consider other ways to compensate you. For example, you might press for a reduction in rent.

- **No new taxes.** Consider pressing for a lease clause that limits your responsibilities to property taxes alone.
- **A cap on your tax liability.** It's great if you can get a binding promise that you'll be excused from paying taxes over a stated amount. This will protect you from additional taxes if a building sale triggers a reassessment.

5. "Proposition 13" Protection for California Tenants

California readers are surely familiar with Proposition 13, the 1978 statewide initiative that limited the increase of both residential and commercial property taxes. Taxes cannot be increased beyond 2%, as measured by 1978 standards, unless the building is sold or substantially rebuilt. Properties that have not changed hands since that time (or for many years) consequently have very low taxes. If you're paying part of the landlord's tax bill, and it's low because the landlord has owned the California building forever and has stayed below the tax assessor's radar, you're sitting pretty—for now. But suppose the landlord sells, and the taxman reassesses? Your contribution will soar.

Political developments, too, could result in a reassessment. Acknowledging that Proposition 13 has hamstrung the state's efforts to adequately provide for public schools, some legislators and citizens (particularly teachers' groups) are pressing for an amendment that will limit Prop 13 to residential properties only. If you are renting in a building that has not been reassessed in some time, either a sale or an amendment to Prop 13 could result in a shockingly high increase in your portion of the tax bill.

Tenants in these situations should try for some "Prop 13 protection." Bargain for a clause that specifies that you won't be hit with Prop 13 increased taxes for three to five years after the reassessment. Be aware, however, that this protection will affect the property's asking price, since prospective buyers will learn that you won't be contributing a full share to the new tax bill. At the very least, however, you might use this as a bargaining chip, adding it to your list of requests and agreeing, eventually, that a modest few will do.

C. Insurance As Additional Rent

Your landlord probably maintains two basic types of insurance coverage:

- a property damage or loss policy, which covers losses from fires or other specific disasters that destroy all or part of the building, and
- a commercial general liability policy, which protects the landlord from claims made by third parties, such as customers who might be injured on the property.

In a typical net lease situation, the landlord asks tenants to pay for all or part of the cost of these policies (in a gross lease, these costs are just figured into the rent amount). Here we discuss the mechanics of how you and the landlord divvy up insurance costs. In Chapter 15, we cover other insurance obligations of concern to landlords and tenants, such as rent insurance and business interruption coverage, which will give you some income if you are unable to operate due to accidents or disasters.

1. How Landlords and Tenants Allocate Insurance Costs

As with other lease clauses, how you and the landlord allocate the cost of insurance depends on your negotiating power and expertise. Hammering out who pays the premiums is no different from negotiating who will pay for improvements.

Don't get sidetracked by thoughts that since the landlord owns the building, the landlord ought to pay to insure it. Instead, recognize that adequately insuring the building will benefit both of you. Now, decide whether you'll use your bargaining power to attempt to modify the extent of your share of the cost or, instead, agree to pay what the landlord has assigned to you and then press for a concession on another lease clause.

2. Property and Casualty Insurance

The most basic type of insurance that you and the landlord need to purchase is called "special form" property and casualty insurance, which together cover damage to the building and some of its contents. This insurance covers the building for fire, smoke damage, explosions, and other disasters or "perils." The policy *won't* cover perils that it specifically excludes, such as damage from floods. If a peril isn't listed as an exclusion, the insurance policy will generally cover it.

Naturally, insurance companies have managed to come up with some pretty important exclusions—in addition to floods, damage from earthquakes, pollution, and civil riots are often excluded. Sometimes, you can purchase separate policies to cover these exclusions—earthquake insurance, for example, is available in areas with known seismic activity. The federal government offers flood insurance for properties on a flood plain. Environmental contamination policies, covering claims arising from asbestos, lead paint, and indoor air problems are increasingly available.

a. What Aspects of the Building Are Covered

Property and casualty insurance will protect the building—roof, interior and exterior walls, stairwells, and parking structures. But what about the items inside the building? Although "contents" are part of the policy name, the policy will by no means cover damage or destruction to everything inside.

Covered. The landlord's own business property, such as maintenance equipment, office supplies, and furnishings, are "contents" covered by the landlord's policy. You'll need to purchase separate insurance to cover your own business property, as explained in Chapter 15, Section A. Improvements to the property that were added to customize the space for your needs will normally be covered because, unless you two have decided otherwise, improvements are by law the landlord's property. (Improvements and trade fixtures are explained in Chapter 11.)

Not covered. In addition to specific exclusions (such as damage from earthquake), damage or destruction to the building's vital systems—heating, ventilation, and so on—are not included in property and casualty insurance. You or the landlord must purchase separate policies for them (see Section 3, below). Your own business property—your trade fixtures, inventory, and other personal property—are also not covered by this policy. Your landlord may insist, in the lease, that you insure these items, as explained in Chapter 15, Section A.

Sometimes landlords and tenants agree that an improvement will not become the landlord's property. For example, if you want to be able to take the improvement with you when you leave, such as an expensive server for your computer network, you will bargain for the right to remove it. In this event, the improvement is *not* covered under the property and casualty policy. Instead, you'll have to insure it as you would a trade fixture.

Finally, many monetary consequences of a fire or other casualty are not included within this coverage. For example, if the building is damaged or destroyed, your lost profits and the landlord's lost rents won't be compensated by the property and casualty policy. If you want coverage for these losses, you'll have to request an endorsement from your broker, which adds this coverage to the policy. Or, you may need separate policies, as explained in Chapter 15.

b.   Single Tenant

If you're renting an entire building, you may see a lease clause requiring you to purchase the property and casualty policy and pay its premiums directly to the insurance company. The clause will normally specify that the policy must be acceptable to the landlord, and may specify minimum policy limits and require a highly rated insurance company. (Insurance company ratings are explained below in Section 7.) The landlord will also want to be named as an "additional insured" on the policy, and will insist that you notify the landlord if you fail to pay a premium or if the policy is canceled. ("Additional insured" is explained below in Section 9.)

Alternatively, the landlord may prefer to purchase the policy and have you contribute to the premiums.

If the landlord already has a property and casualty insurance policy that will be reissued for your tenancy, be sure that the company is aware of the value of your improvements. When the policy was issued, the premiums were based on the value of the building at that time—and the policy limits (the amount of coverage) were set accordingly. Your landlord should contact his broker if your additions add significant value to the building (or pose added risks), so that coverage limits can be increased if necessary. For example, a new outdoor deck for a restaurant or an elevator system is a significant modification that increases the value of the structure. If the building is underinsured, the policy may not cover the extent of any damage.

c.   Keeping the Insurance Alive

You know what happens if insurance premiums aren't paid. The policy cancels within a specified period of time. Then, it may be difficult to reestablish coverage. In the meantime, the landlord's property isn't covered. Running a business without insurance protection is extremely risky.

Because insurance is so important, many leases will give the landlord the right to pay your premiums on your behalf if you're obligated to pay for insurance but you've failed to do so. The reason behind this is simple self-interest. If the lease obligates you to insure the building and you let it go, the landlord will suffer the most from a disaster that isn't covered by insurance. Rather than risk that possibility, the landlord will secure the right to pay the premiums for you and charge you for the cost as additional rent.

Now, suppose you're renting under a gross lease and do not pay directly for insurance premiums. If the landlord fails to make a payment, the policy may be canceled or lapse. If there's a disaster after that, the landlord's own money probably won't be as plentiful or available as a check from the insurance carrier, and your business will suffer as repairs limp along. The solution: Even in a gross lease situation, you want "notification and cure" rights—a promise that you'll be notified by the insurance company (or by the landlord, who will receive reminders and warnings from the carrier) if the premiums aren't paid. Moreover, you also want the right to pay them yourself to keep the policy alive. If you pay for a premium, you should have the right to offset the amount against your rent. (Rent offsets are explained in Chapter 16, Section C.)

d. Multitenant

In most multitenant, net lease situations, landlords purchase the insurance and pass the cost on to the tenants—but how to do this fairly can be a matter of debate (see Section 5 below).

3. Terrorism and the Cost of Insurance

As you're no doubt aware, the cost of insurance premiums depends greatly on the location of the property, the risks inherent in the businesses carried on there, and the track record of the policy holders. Unfortunately, there's another factor in the mix— fallout from the events of September 11, 2001. The huge property losses in New York resulted in higher premiums for all types of insurance as the insurance industry attempted to recover its reserves.

Unfortunately, the ripple effect isn't over yet. After 9/11, carriers stopped writing terrorism insurance, fearing that another attack would bankrupt the industry. In response, Congress passed the 2002 Reinsurance Act, which made the federal government a guarantor of sorts when losses result from terrorist acts made on behalf of foreign entities (the government will pay any losses above a certain level). That Act is set to expire on December 31, 2005. If it is not extended, we'll be back where we were before it—the cost of all insurance will go up as carriers look for funds to cover a potential terrorism disaster. For you, this means that even garden-variety property and casualty insurance costs will again rise—and could even become unavailable. For this reason, super-careful tenants will want lease clauses to obligate them to obtain insurance *to the extent that the coverage is available.*

Will Insurance Fully Compensate Your Losses?

If covered property is destroyed in a disaster or accident, you or the landlord will need to replace it. Whether insurance covers the cost depends on whether the property and casualty policy covers actual cash value or replacement cost.

- **Actual cash value** means that the policy will pay only the fair market value of the destroyed item. But how do you figure the actual cash value? If there is a real market for the item, for example, a slightly used window air conditioner, actual cash value is the going price. But if there is no real market, the actual cash value is the item's replacement cost *minus* depreciation equal to the age of the destroyed item. For instance, a ten-year-old furnace has no market value (who would buy it?). If a new one costs $2,000 and will depreciate at the rate of $50 per year, at the end of ten years that furnace would be worth $1,500. This is the actual cash value,

for insurance purposes, of your furnace today.

- **Replacement cost** means that the policy covers the expense of repairing or replacing the lost property, up to the limit of the coverage you have chosen. To continue with our furnace example, you'd receive $2,000 from the insurance company, as long as the limit of your policy was $2,000 or more, which will cover the entire cost of the new furnace.

Replacement cost coverage is more attractive than actual cash value coverage. Predictably, however, the premiums will be higher. Be sure you understand which kind of insurance you're being asked to buy or pay for. Even though it may be the landlord's property that's involved, you'll be affected if the insurance proceeds are insufficient to cover the loss of something you depend on—like that window air conditioner.

4. Insurance for Building Equipment and Vital Systems

Property insurance covers the building and some of its contents, but not its equipment. Heating, air-conditioning, ventilation, and boilers—the building's vital systems—must be insured under a "boiler and machinery" policy. The policy will pay for repairs if a sudden, unexpected failure or explosion causes damage. It won't pay for replacement that's caused by gradual, normal deterioration. You and the landlord should allocate the responsibility for equipment insurance as you do when considering property and casualty insurance, discussed above.

5. General Liability Insurance

If someone is injured on the landlord's property, you and/or the landlord may be sued. Or, if you or the landlord accidentally damage or destroy someone else's property while it's on the rented premises, the owner may sue you over its loss. With li-

ability insurance, the insurance company will provide the lawyers to represent you and the money to pay a settlement or verdict. This type of insurance, called Commercial General Liability (CGL), is known as "third-party" insurance, since it protects you and the landlord from claims by others. Since lawsuits by third parties can ruin even the best of businesses, it's essential to have an adequate CGL policy protecting you and the landlord.

Most leases prepared by landlords require you to obtain liability insurance and to add the landlord as an additional insured, which means that the insurance company will represent the landlord as well as you if you're both named as defendants in a lawsuit. If money needs to be paid out in a settlement or a judgment, the insurance company will pay that, too. If the landlord already has the general liability coverage, you'll be added as an additional insured and charged for a portion of the landlord's premium.

a. Injuries and Property Damage Covered by CGL Insurance

Commercial General Liability coverage protects you and the landlord from a number of different types of claims. They include:

- physical injuries suffered by people who claim that your carelessness (or that of the landlord) caused their injury, such as a client who trips on a loose carpet in the hallway outside your office, or a customer who's assaulted in your store's restroom

- damage to the property of someone else, again allegedly the result of your or the landlord's carelessness, such as damage your employees cause to a customer's belongings, and

- damages from miscellaneous misdeeds such as defamation, infliction of emotional distress, false imprisonment, and invasion of privacy, such as a client who sues you for carelessly disclosing personal information to third parties.

b. Damages and Losses Not Covered by CGL Policies

It's important to understand that Commercial General Liability policies won't cover damage to or loss to property that you or the landlord own or for which you might be responsible (such as rented equipment). You'll need property and casualty insurance for that, explained above in Section 2.

You and the landlord will also not be covered if the third party's loss is the result of deliberate action or inaction, rather than a mistake or accident. Most of the time, there will be no question that the loss or injury—damage to a piece of rented equipment, injury to a customer—was unintended. But things get trickier when it comes to claims involving personal, nonphysical injuries such as slander and emotional distress. If an insurance company thinks that you or the landlord intended to cause the damage you did, it may balk at covering you.

6. Negotiating a Fair Allocation of Insurance Costs

The simplest way to divide up insurance costs is to allocate them according to the size of each tenant's space—the tenant who rents 25% of the building pays 25% of the insurance costs. This method works fine as long as the tenant mix is composed of similar types of businesses that are more or less equal, risk-wise. Here's why.

When the insurance company set the property, casualty, and liability premiums for your landlord's building, it did so after evaluating the risks of the building as a whole. For example, if the entire structure is filled with office suites, the risk of property damage and liability is relatively low, since there are no dangerous substances in use and large numbers of the public are not coming and going. Conversely, a structure with restaurants and other retail shops is more of a risk, since the chances of damage (such as a grease fire) or a lawsuit (such as a customer's slip-and-fall) are higher. And how should insurance costs be allocated among the tenants? In either situation, it makes sense to share costs according to the size of each tenant's rental, since each tenant is equally responsible for the insurance rate of the building.

Now, what happens if half of a building has accountants' offices but the other half is a restaurant? As far as the insurance company is concerned, the restaurant has increased the risk for the building as a whole, and the premium will be set accordingly. If you happen to be an accountant and your insurance bill is based on the size of your space alone, you'll end up in effect subsidizing the restaurant for the cost of its insurance. On the other hand, if you are the restaurant, you've got it made!

If you've stayed with us since the discussion of property taxes in Section B above, you may recognize this problem as similar to the one encountered there, where one tenant's expensive improvements added taxable value to the property, which all tenants have to pay for in the form of property taxes. The solution there was to allocate taxes according to the size *and* *value* of each tenant's space. The solution for insurance costs is not so simple.

If you find that the property's insurance costs are being driven by operations more risky than yours, ask the landlord's insurance agent or broker to assess your business separately. You may find a cooperative soul who'll give you an idea of what the insurance costs for the building would be without the presence of Risky Business downstairs. With this information, you may be able to press for a reduction of your insurance bill.

The difficulty with this approach, besides finding a broker who'll help you out, is that the landlord has already signed a lease with Risky—and chances are that Risky is sitting pretty with an unfairly low insurance bill each month. The landlord can't shift to Risky what she's taking from you, and she won't be interested in absorbing the difference. The best you can do may be to keep this point in reserve as you negotiate the balance of the lease, pulling it out when you need the moral or fairness advantage while negotiating another point, or simply asking for less rent.

7. Negotiating a Good Commercial General Liability Clause

The landlord's lease may be quite specific on the type and level of CGL insurance you must carry, or it may be quite vague. In addition to understanding what damages and losses are covered, here are some other key points to keep in mind when it comes to CGL policies.

a. Get Primary Coverage

Sometimes, landlords and tenants have multiple insurance policies that may overlap. When a claim is made, the insurance companies argue as to who should step up and handle it. Meanwhile, you get lost in the shuffle. When all is said and done (insurance companies frequently go to court over who should provide coverage), the policy that applies to your loss may not be the best, from your point of view (for example, its limits may be too low to satisfactorily cover the loss).

Your CGL policy will invariably be better than any overlapping policies. If it is written as a "primary" policy, the company that issued it must handle the claim. The lease clause should call for primary coverage.

b. Understand Dollar Limits of the Coverage

Landlords who own multiple properties may have one CGL policy protecting all their properties. Each new tenant joins as an additional insured. Normally, the policy will have a per occurrence limit and an aggregate limit. For example, the company will pay up to $1 million per claim and no more than $3 million in a year. You'll want to make sure that the aggregate amount applies to *each location* being insured. Otherwise, a claim or two from the landlord's other properties will exhaust the fund, leaving nothing available should there be a claim arising from your place of business.

Even if the aggregate limit applies to each property, consider whether the limits are high enough in view of the number and type of tenants in each property. For example, a property full of low-risk tenants (such as office-bound consultants) may be able to live with a level of coverage that would be inadequate for the same number of retail tenants, where the presence of the public raises the risk of accidents.

c. Use a Highly Rated Company

No matter who purchases the policy, you'll want to make sure that a reliable company with adequate financial reserves writes it. The A.M. Best Company rates insurance companies, from A++ to F. The lease should call for use of a company with no less than an A rating, and hopefully higher. Since 80% of rated companies are A or better, there's little reason to choose a lesser-rated company.

You can read more about Best's rating system on its website at www.ambest.com, but you'll have to pay to get a company's rating. It's reasonable to ask your broker for that information.

8. Understand "Occurrence" and "Claims-Made" Policies

Insurance companies are infamous for devising ways to limit their duty to represent you and pay claims. Writing narrow policies, full of exclusions, is one way. Another method is to reject claims that aren't made while the policy is in effect. Here's how it works: Although the event that caused the claim may have happened during the life of the policy, if the claim isn't made while the policy is current, the policy won't cover it.

A policy that restricts claims in this way is known as a "claims-made" policy. It can be bad news. Suppose that you're sued months, even years, after you've moved on by someone who claims to have been injured inside your space. The policy that you purchased is probably no longer in effect (perhaps now you've taken out a different policy for your new place of business). This means that the old policy won't cover you, even though the lawsuit concerns an event that allegedly happened while the policy was alive. And even if a judge ultimately throws out the lawsuit because it violates the statute of limitations (a legal rule that prohibits stale lawsuits), you'll still have to respond to the case and defend yourself.

Some insurance companies will write a policy that *will* cover you even if someone files a claim after the policy ends. These policies are known as "occurrence" policies. They require only that the event that triggers the claim occurred while the policy was in effect. It doesn't matter when the claim is presented to the insurance company.

As you can see, both you and the landlord will want to obtain an occurrence policy—if you can. But be aware that it will cost more than a claims-made policy.

9. Adding the Landlord to Your Policy (and Vice Versa)

After you and the landlord have figured out who will insure the building and carry liability insurance, make sure that whoever takes out the policy agrees to add the other to it as an "additional insured." This will give the added person the right to make a claim or share in the proceeds of any payout.

The Lender's Stake in Insurance

If the landlord has pledged the building as security for a loan, the lender will typically require the landlord to maintain specified levels of fire and casualty insurance.

All well and good, unless the lender has insisted on some control over the proceeds of any insurance payout. This could have dire consequences for you. Suppose a fire severely damages the building, making it impossible for you to run your business. When the insurance money comes through, the lender grabs the entire amount and applies it to the loan. This leaves the landlord with no money to rebuild—and you can't reopen. Especially if you've invested considerable money in sprucing up your space, you lose big and must begin looking for new space. Not nice and, in some states, it's not legal for lenders to wield this amount of power. If you see a lease provision giving the lender complete control over insurance proceeds (the lender may be identified as the sole "loss payee," which means that the lender alone will get the proceeds), call it to the attention of your lawyer.

10. Be Sure to Get Proof of Insurance

The insurance clauses in your lease don't just require you (or the landlord) to take out various forms of insurance. They make you prove that you've done so. Careful landlords and tenants will demand that the insurance company itself send written proof that there's insurance in place as called for in the lease. If either of you has negotiated to be added as an additional insured, that person will want proof of that, too.

A written statement from an insurance company that assures you (or the landlord) that the policy is in force is called a Certificate of Insurance. A private, nonprofit organization, the Association for Cooperative Operations Research and Development (known as ACORD) has written forms that most insurance companies use when asked to supply a Certificate of Insurance. If you're responsible for securing property insurance, your landlord's lease may require you to supply the landlord with an ACORD form, and it may specify the form number. And you, too, will want the landlord to give you an ACORD form if the landlord is the one who has taken out the policy and added you as an additional insured.

Understand that all ACORD forms are not alike. Those that were used before the early 1990s are very dangerous, because they're not binding on the insurance company (the form describes itself as an "information only" notice). Newer forms will obligate the insurer to come through with the representations on the form, including the policy limits and the rights of additional insureds. Here's the scoop on the forms:

- **Avoid ACORD Forms 24 and 25.** These are nonbinding certificates that *may*

be evidence of property and liability insurance, respectively.

- **Insist on ACORD Form 27.** This is the new form, one that you can count on. The carrier will have to come through with every statement on the form. It is designed for property insurance, but can be modified to include liability insurance also.

During your lease negotiations, insist on the use of the ACORD Form 27. No reputable insurance company will refuse to supply one. If you want to be extra careful in assuring yourself that the policy called for in the lease really exists, demand the right to see the policy itself.

D. Operating and Common Area Maintenance Costs As Additional Rent

In addition to taxes and insurance, there is a third ingredient in a net lease—operating costs. This is your share of the cost to maintain the building's upkeep, including common areas such as lobbies, hallways, garages, and elevators. You may also be asked to contribute a proportionate share for the building-wide air and heating costs (called HVAC, for heat, ventilation, and air-conditioning). If you lease space in an office building, there may be an added management fee, which will cover the cost of the building's superintendent or the monthly amount the landlord pays a management company to run the building. All of these costs are part of the landlord's ongoing operating expenses.

➡️ If you lease an entire building, you're probably going to have to pay for all maintenance yourself, and you can skip this section and the one following.

1. Pass-Throughs and Exclusions

One of the biggest issues between landlords and tenants concerns what, exactly, should be included in the operating costs. Landlords will bargain for a clause that makes the tenant pay for as much as possible. In fact, the list of charges that are "passed through" to you is often modified with those slippery words "Tenant will be responsible for the following costs, *without limitation* ...." The effect of "without limitation" is to make it possible for the landlord to tack on extra charges. Tenants, in turn, will press for enumerated exclusions. Your negotiations over operating costs will pit the "pass throughs" against the "exclusions."

Listing excluded items in the lease is just one approach to dealing with this issue. Even better is to agree to a specific list of items that the landlord *can* include—and to state that anything not mentioned is the landlord's sole responsibility.

Pass-Throughs Versus Exclusions

Here's a list of some items that a landlord may consider to be a part of operating expenses that can be passed through to you. You may want to negotiate to exclude some of these items, such as advertising expenses and legal fees.

- Accounting fees
- Travel expenses for landlord and employees
- Legal fees
- Office rental for landlord's office
- Security services
- Major improvements to building (capital expenditures)
- Real estate commissions
- Janitorial expenses
- Association membership fees
- Management fees
- Parking lot repaving
- Light bulb replacement
- Salaries for landlord's employees
- Advertising expenses
- Inspection fees
- Maintenance supplies
- Landscaping
- Broker fees
- Deductible amounts for insurance claims.

2. Allocating Operating and CAM Costs Between Landlord and Tenant

One sensible way to separate costs that should belong to the landlord from those that rightly belong to you is to ask whether the expense is for a capital improvement— a replacement of a structural element of the building, or an improvement that adds lasting value—or is associated with the day-to-day running of the property. Unfortunately, there is no clear and widely accepted understanding of the difference between a capital expense and a noncapital expense. Tenants argue that the costs of maintaining the structure or roof and bringing the building up to code are capital and should be entirely the landlord's responsibility. The costs of servicing the heating and air-conditioning and maintaining the building's electrical equipment are maintenance items that reasonably can be passed on to tenants.

Some landlords attempt to charge tenants for fairly outrageous items, including leasing commissions, other tenants' improvement allowances (these are explained in Chapter 11), and legal fees occasioned by other tenants' misdeeds.

Landlords have very creative ways to bulk up their list of maintenance expenses. For example, capital improvements that have the effect of lowering your operating costs may be shoved your way.

EXAMPLE: The tenants in Ron's small office building were delighted to learn of his plans to replace the age-old furnace with a modern forced-air heater. They knew they'd be warmer and pay lower electricity bills. However, they were shocked to learn that Ron expected them to bear a portion of the cost of the new system, which he justified on the grounds that they'd be saving money. Fortunately for the tenants, their leases included a definitive list of operating costs that couldn't be expanded.

Many capital improvements will also benefit the landlord (and future tenants) long after you have moved out. And if your lease expires soon after you've paid the bill, the benefit you will have received from these improvements will be small indeed. To guard against last-minute pass-throughs that you won't be around to enjoy, press for the right to amortize, or spread, the cost of the expense over the useful life of the item. The landlord is likely to counter with, "amortized over the useful life, or five years, or over the length of the remainder of the lease, whichever is shorter." If the landlord puts in building-wide sprinklers during the last year (or security features such as locks, better doors, or windows), you'll get socked with this pass-through.

On the other hand, when the cost of the item is spread over a few years, the tenants will face a smaller expense each year.

EXAMPLE: Iona replaced the lighting in her second office building. Tenants in that building had successfully negotiated a clause in their leases requiring Iona to amortize the cost of capital improvements before passing on the cost as part of operating obligations.

The lighting system cost $40,000 to install. Amortized over five years, the cost for each year was $8,000. Iona passed this cost on to her four tenants, who paid $2,000 each year. One tenant paid her portion for one year, then moved out when her lease expired. If the cost had not been amortized, this tenant would have paid one-quarter of the entire cost, or $10,000, even though she would have enjoyed the benefits of the new lights for only one year.

Specify that GAAP accounting principles will apply. If your operating costs clause makes you pay for amortized capital expenditures, be sure that the amortization methods follow the principles established in GAAP ("Generally Accepted Accounting Principles," the accountants' bible). If you see that owner-friendly accounting principles "as generally recognized in the real estate industry" will control, bargain to replace them with GAAP.

A smart landlord will lease an item— rather than purchase it—in order to pass through the cost of the payments. Since payments on a leased item, such as a car, are clearly considered operating expenses, this is one way to get tenants to pay for the item's cost. Ask the landlord whether her operating expenses include leased items—then bargain for them to be explicitly excluded from the pass-throughs.

Deductible Amounts As Pass-Throughs

Your landlord's deductible amount is a favorite inclusion in the list of pass-throughs (this is the amount not covered in the event of a claim on the landlord's insurance policy). To keep premiums low, deductible amounts can be quite high. For earthquake and terrorism insurance, for example, they may be 5% to 10% of the replacement costs.

Protect yourself by bargaining for the amortization of these costs. For support, point to the fact that, under general accounting principles, you're entitled to amortize the cost (passed on to you) of repairs. Since paying for the deductible is not much different than paying directly for repairs, it too should be amortized.

3. Allocating Operating Costs Among Tenants

Operating costs, like taxes and insurance costs, are sometimes easy to allocate fairly. By now, having read about the fair allocation of taxes and insurance, you probably know the issue: If all tenants in the building exert an equal "draw" on these services, it makes sense to charge them according to the portion of the building they lease. For example, in a retail building with four shops, each business probably uses the common areas, parking lots, heat, and electricity in roughly the same way. Sharing these costs according to the size of the tenant's space would be fair. The situation is different, however, if there's a mix of tenants, some of whom use more of the common areas than others.

If you're leasing space in a multiuse or multiimpact building, raise your concerns during negotiations. But if there are tenants in place already, you're likely to hear the same objection you'll encounter when pressing for equitable insurance allocations, explained above in Section C6: Even a sympathetic landlord can't shift operating costs to utility-devouring tenants if their leases already specify that costs will be shared based on their portion of the rentable space. And the landlord won't be eager to absorb the difference. You may have to make a note of this inequity and use it to press for another concession from the landlord, such as reduced rent or an extra parking space.

4. "Grossing Up" Provisions in a Net Lease

Unless you rent an entire building, you're likely to encounter this odd term during your discussions of operating expense allocations. The term describes how landlords allocate a tenant's share of operating expenses when the building isn't fully leased. Done right, the method ensures that tenants pay their fair share of operating expenses. Here's how it works.

Suppose you rent one floor in a ten-story building, where all floors are the same size. You have 10% of the rentable space, and the other nine floors are empty. Now suppose you use $100,000 worth of electricity during the first year, while the rest of the building remained empty. If you were to pay for the cost of electricity based on your percent of the rentable space, you'd pay only $10,000, and the landlord would be left to pay the rest (which neither he, nor anyone else but you, used).

To remedy this inequity, when calculating your share, landlords will assume that the building is fully rented ("grossed up"), and that everyone uses the same amount of electricity that you do. In that event, the electricity bill would be $1,000,000, (ten floors of ten tenants each using $100,000 worth of electricity per year), and your ten-percent would mean that you'd pay $100,000—exactly the amount you in fact used.

Grossing up is appropriate only for variable expenses (expenses that rise or fall with the level of occupancy), such as the cost of cleaning, utilities, some repairs, and maintenance. Fixed costs that don't vary with the level of occupancy, such as the landlord's insurance premiums or the cost of a nighttime security guard, should not be grossed up. For instance, if your lease obligates you to pay 10% of the landlord's property taxes, that's all you should pay, regardless of whether the property is fully leased.

Creative Pass-Throughs

Be on the lookout for these pass-throughs, outlandish as they may seem:

- Charge-backs for move-in costs, such as a fee for disposing of your flattened moving boxes.
- Charges for securing a nondisturbance agreement, presumably on the grounds that the landlord had to hire an attorney to do so. (Your reply: "Fine, but you'll of course pay my lawyer every time I need to consult her, right?") (Nondisturbance agreements, which are promises that new owners following the property's sale or foreclosure won't displace you, are explained in Chapter 17, Section A.)
- The cost of gifts and meals lavished on other tenants—and even those given to you!

E. Audit Rights

In a net lease, a large chunk of your monthly rent is going to be made up of charges such as building maintenance costs, tax bills, and insurance premiums that you're expected to pay on faith. In truth, it's very difficult for a landlord to be completely accurate in recording and allocating operating expenses. Depending on the size of the property and the number of tenants, there may be literally thousands of entries per year, on everything from the janitor's monthly waxing of the lobby floor to the plumber who comes now and then to deal with the drains.

Large landlords in particular are apt to do a sloppy job of allocating operating expenses. The task is often given to low-level employees who do not check the leases of every tenant (even if they were to check the leases, they'd probably not find much enlightenment amid the dense, 8-point-type clauses). How, then, are these employees supposed to know, let alone apply, the exclusions that tenants have painstakingly hammered out? And don't forget the temptation factor—when it's not clear whether an expense should be passed-on, many landlords or their employees can't resist giving the benefit to the landlord.

Unless you absolutely trust the landlord, there's no way you can know whether the operating expense numbers are accurate unless you have the right to check. To do this, you need a clause in your lease giving you the right to hire a professional auditor to look at the landlord's books. The auditor looks for mistakes, either deliberate or inadvertent, including any failure to remove an expense that the landlord has been reimbursed for (such as collecting on an equipment warranty). This is called an audit right. Having such a right in your lease can potentially save you hundreds—maybe even thousands—of dollars.

EXAMPLE: PlanetCo's lease with Arbor Plaza Office Suites requires PlanetCo to pay a portion of Arbor's operating expenses for the entire building. But, as a result of PlanetCo's careful negotiations, the lease excludes from operating expenses real estate commissions, attorney fees, and accounting fees. The lease also gives PlanetCo the right to audit the bills it receives for Arbor's operating expenses.

One day, PlanetCo gets a huge bill from Arbor for its share of operating expenses. PlanetCo asks to see the records that the bill is based on. Sure enough, Arbor has made a huge mistake by charging PlanetCo $1,500 for commissions and $500 for legal and accounting fees. Arbor apologizes and promptly deletes the improper items.

Don't be surprised if the landlord objects to your request for an audit right. Many will not take kindly to your request to peruse their books. If you're desperate for this rental or the market is wholly against you, you may have to cave here and move on.

But if you have any clout, consider using it now.

If you pay percentage rent, your land-lord probably has the right to check your books. Percentage rent (whereby you pay a portion of your gross receipts as rent, in addition to a minimum set amount) depends on trust too—and you can be sure that your landlord has secured an audit right on you. Turnabout is only fair—but as you know, ultimately it's power, not fairness, that will sway the negotiation. (Percentage rent is explained in Chapter 4, Section C.)

To counter a landlord's resistance to giving you audit rights, you might point out that if you have reasonable grounds to suspect significant overcharging, in the absence of an audit right you'll protest the charge, refuse to pay it, and start a lawsuit (or invoke the mediation or arbitration clause in your lease, if there is one). If the dispute boils over into arbitration or litigation, you'll have the right, under the discovery rules of every state and most arbitration groups, to examine the landlord's books. True, the two of you would probably settle the dispute, but not before spending much time and money on mediators, arbitrators, or lawyers. Now, if your lease gives you the right to see the landlord's books before you turn to stronger measures, chances are that you and the landlord will resolve any dispute early on.

If you're able to press for an audit right, keep the following points in mind.

1. When Should You Look at the Landlord's Books?

After your tenancy gets under way you'll want to think about whether you should perform an audit. If you reasonably suspect overcharging—for example, the CAM costs come in one-third over your best estimates —the answer will be simple. But even in the absence of suspicions, if you can bear the cost of an audit you might want to check things over anyway. This will send a message to the landlord that you are serious about your rights.

Performing an audit at the end of the first year may result in your landlord being especially careful in the future. There's another, very practical reason to audit the first year. As the "base year," it will be the standard against which all subsequent costs are measured. If you reasonably suspect an error in, say, the seventh year of your ten-year lease and call for an audit of that year, you'll want to know for sure that the first year's figures were correct and, most importantly, available. Don't rely on your landlord's filing cabinet to have safely organized and secured those old records.

2. Who Performs the Audit?

Some auditors work on a contingency fee basis—the size of their pay depends on the size of the irregularities they discover (who pays the auditor is covered below). These professionals are usually former property managers or other real estate pros who know exactly what to look for. The landlord may want to avoid using a contingency fee auditor, for obvious reasons. You can allay the landlord's concerns by suggesting that the lease specify that the auditor must be someone whom you both agree to use. You can even offer to designate the auditor right in the lease. You can also press for the use of contingency fee auditors, but suggest that you'll pay them on a non-contingency basis. Don't be surprised if the landlord still balks—the fact is, these contingency fee auditors are very good at their job.

3. How Quickly Must You Challenge an Overcharge?

If you suspect that you've been overcharged and bring in an auditor who confirms this, you'll want to challenge the expense. Your landlord will likely insist that any challenge to the expense be done very soon, even as quickly as 30 days after your audit, and that the audit itself be done within 90 to 180 days after you receive the landlord's statement of charges. The landlord's position is that allowing you to bring up a challenge many months after you've gone over the books will insert too much uncertainty in the landlord's accounting and may delay the closing of the books.

Fine, you'll say—as long as the landlord, in turn, agrees not to *add* any items to the ledger after the negotiated time period. But the landlord is liable to balk at this proposal, since many items (especially taxes) are submitted to the landlord at irregular times and must be inserted into previously calculated expense sheets. Again, the impasse can be bridged by a gentle reminder that the law (the statute of limitations, which governs how long you have to file a lawsuit) in most states will allow you *four years* from the discovery of an allocation error to the date you must file your legal complaint concerning it. In view of this generous window, it's reasonable for you to insist on a two- or three-year complaint period.

4. Must You Be Squeaky Clean to Exercise Your Audit Right?

Many landlords are afraid that a tenant who's behind in paying rent will use an audit as a fishing expedition, hoping to find something that can be used as an offset to the unpaid rent. (Offsets are explained in Chapter 16, Section C.) Of course, it is entirely possible for you to be behind in your rent *and* for the landlord to have overcharged you, too. One way to allay the landlord's concerns is to agree that you'll pay your rent "under protest" and place the money in escrow, pending the outcome of the audit.

5. Who Pays for the Audit?

Since you've asked for the audit right, it's customary for you, the tenant, to pay. However, there's nothing stopping you from negotiating an understanding that if the audit reveals an overcharge higher than a certain percentage (say, 3% to 5%), the landlord pays for the audit.

6. Dealing With an Overcharge

If you find that you've been overcharged for something like insurance costs or insurance premiums and you've already paid the bill, you'll want reimbursement with interest. The landlord will want to make sure that an error won't give you the right to terminate the lease, which is a reasonable restriction. In the unlikely event that you and the auditor conclude that the "error" was really fraud, you'll normally be able to terminate the lease.

7. You Can Ask, But You Can't Tell

Most landlords will insist that the results of a successful audit be kept in confidence—in particular, you won't be allowed to share the information with other tenants in the building. The reason for this is simple: When the auditor finds an overcharge, the landlord will either pay it, dispute and refuse to pay the overcharge, or dispute it but agree to a settlement. If the landlord pays you anything, the landlord won't want to tip off other tenants by letting them know what this kind of error is worth in settlement. If you can live with the principle that it's every tenant for herself, there's nothing wrong with a provision that you keep the audit settlement confidential.

■

Chapter 10

Security Deposits

Your landlord may ask for a security deposit to assure that cash will be available if you fail to pay the rent or don't make other payments required under the lease. Unlike residential landlords, who in many states may not ask for more than two or three months' rent as a deposit, commercial landlords may demand whatever amount they think they need as a cushion to cover rent and other tenant financial obligations. Unless the lease provides otherwise, the landlord may not increase the deposit during the term of the lease.

If you are facing a hefty deposit, think about whether this makes sense in your case: If you're an established businessperson with an impeccable credit and business history, you have a strong argument that a deposit is unnecessary and will simply tie up capital that you could otherwise use, invest, or plow into your business. And if you're just starting out or have recently experienced some setbacks, tying up a large chunk of your capital in a deposit makes it even harder for you to get your operation off the ground. Ironically, the landlord who insists on a large deposit that depletes his tenant's resources may precipitate the very downturn and failure that the landlord wants to avoid.

So why do many landlords demand a deposit? The dirty little secret is that landlords often simply use deposits as a source of funding, especially when their own investment in a new or remodeled property is high. Deposits that are commingled with the landlord's own money can be used for other tenants' improvements and brokers' fees, for example. And unless you have successfully negotiated for the interest earned on the deposit, the landlord stands to earn a nice rate of return on your money.

It's important to keep these realities in mind if you see a security deposit clause in your landlord's lease. Of course, you'll be primarily concerned about the amount of the deposit. In addition, be sure that you understand and are satisfied with:

- where the deposit will be held and who gets the interest (and at what rate)
- how the landlord can use the deposit, such as for unpaid rent or operating charges, including how much time you have to replenish the deposit
- the rules for when the landlord can tap into the deposit (can the landlord decide unilaterally that you are behind on a financial lease obligation?), and
- how quickly the landlord must return the deposit at the end of the tenancy.

You might also consider alternatives to a cash deposit, such as a letter of credit.

A. Where the Landlord Will Keep the Deposit

Be sure you understand where the landlord will keep your cash deposit. No law requires the landlord to put it into the bank or decrees that the interest will be yours.

As you approach this issue, keep in mind that the deposit money is yours, held by the landlord in case it's needed to pay a sum that you legally owe. It's entirely fitting, therefore, that you should have a say in how the landlord manages the deposit. You obviously want to insist that the money be deposited in a federally insured bank. Likewise, press for language that prohibits the landlord from commingling the money (the landlord won't be able to use it for the landlord's own purposes).

Interest earned by the deposit should in fairness belong to you, but no law says so. If possible, you might negotiate for a higher rate than the bank pays. Think of it this way—if that money were still in your pocket, you could conceivably use (or invest) it in ways that would yield a higher return than the bank's rate of interest. For example, if you could invest the deposit money in your own business, your added earnings might far exceed the bank's interest rate. At the very least, demand an interest rate that's no lower than the default rate provided in the lease—that is, the rate that the landlord will charge *you* if you fail to pay your rent and other monetary obligations on time.

After you establish yourself as a responsible tenant, get the deposit back. As time goes by and you consistently pay your bills, it will become evident that the landlord won't need the cushion provided by the deposit. Bargain for the right to get it back—known as a "burn down"—if you've steadily

met your rent obligations over a certain period of time. Or, establish a set of financial mileposts (such as a minimum level of debt) that will trigger a gradual reduction and return of the deposit.

B. How the Landlord Will Use the Deposit

Landlords often deduct from the deposit at the end of the tenancy—to cover damage that you haven't fixed or outstanding rent. However, landlords may also use this money during the tenancy. A typical deposit clause will state that the landlord may use the deposit if you fail to pay money you owe under the lease. Another way of saying this is that a monetary default on your part will open the door to the landlord's use of the deposit. When the landlord dips into the deposit to cover unpaid rent or another default, you will typically have a set amount of time to replenish the deposit.

Breaking an important term or condition of your lease—a default—also constitutes grounds for *termination* of the lease. Can the landlord use the deposit *and* terminate? It would be cruel indeed for the landlord to both cure the default and declare that the default will cause you to lose the lease. But unless the deposit clause clearly states that the landlord can't do both, that's what might happen. In fact, you'll want to go further and require the landlord to first look to the deposit to make up for any monetary default on your part—in other words, you don't want the landlord to have a choice of curing the default or terminating the lease. If the deposit can cover the money you owe, you'll want a provision in the lease that there will be no termination. If you get a landlord to go along with this, he'll probably insist that this cure right will be extinguished if your defaults are large and/or frequent. Chapter 16, Section A, explains defaults in more detail.

Give yourself adequate time to re-plenish the deposit. If the landlord uses the deposit to cover unpaid rent or cure another default, you're not out of the woods yet. Since the deposit has been depleted, you're in "secondary default" (failure to main-tain the agreed-upon deposit). The landlord may expect you to immediately replenish the deposit—but of course, if you had the money to top the deposit off, you wouldn't be in default in the first place! Press for an extended period in which to bring the deposit back to its original level.

Don't assume you can use the deposit to cover the last month's rent. Many residential tenants are accustomed to asking the landlord to apply the deposit to the last month's rent. Residential landlords don't like this ploy—it means that there will be less money available to cover damage. Commercial landlords like it even less. If you force the landlord to use the deposit for the last rent payment, you will be in default—something that this landlord will surely mention, to your detriment, to your next prospective landlord.

C. When the Landlord May Use the Deposit

You won't want the landlord to be able to dip into the deposit, perhaps without even telling you, every time you owe a payment or are late with rent. At the very least, bargain for a notice and cure right—a promise that the landlord will alert you before using the deposit and give you a few days to come up with the money. For example, if you're going to be slightly late with the rent because a large account will be late paying *you,* you'd want the landlord to notify you before taking the rent out of the deposit—so that you can redouble your efforts to col-lect on that overdue account.

Landlords sometimes take money from a security deposit not only when the debt is clear and undisputed, but even when the very existence of the debt is in question. For example, suppose the two of you are engaged in a dispute regarding the proper calculation of common area maintenance (CAM) costs. If the rent clause doesn't require that these disputes be mediated or arbitrated, the landlord might simply satisfy the claimed debt from the deposit. (You should make sure that CAM disputes are handled by mediation and arbitration, as explained in Chapter 16, Section D.) To guard against this end run, negotiate for a clause that allows the landlord to use the deposit only when you've failed to pay an undisputed debt (one you don't contest) or an adjudicated debt (one that was the subject of court proceedings and was reduced to a judgment against you). A landlord who requires a deposit to serve as a source of security for your debts should be willing to hold off until the debt is clearly established.

D. The Fate of the Deposit at the End of the Lease

When your lease comes to an end, either by its own terms or by early termination, you'll be entitled to the return of the deposit, less any sums that the landlord has properly withheld. It's important to address how and when the landlord will return the money to you. Many leases do not clearly spell out the procedures—no surprise, since most landlords would prefer to return the money when and how they choose. Here are some issues to consider.

1. Tenant Obligations for the Return of the Deposit

Before returning the deposit, your landlord will probably require you to remove your personal property and move out. The leased space may also have to pass the landlord's inspection if the lease requires you to return the property in its original condition (prior to any improvements or alterations you made). In addition, the landlord may insist that all rent and other monies owed be calculated and paid. These conditions are reasonable and, in turn, enable you to raise some of your own—specifically, the timely return of your deposit.

2. Timetable for Returning Deposits

You'll almost never see a landlord's lease clause that imposes a time requirement for the return of the deposit. Usually, there's no mention of the issue, which means that legally the landlord is free to return it in a "reasonable" manner, whatever that is.

This is an opportunity for you to press for the prompt return of your deposit. Surely a few weeks should be sufficient, after all inspections and accounting are done, for the landlord to write that check. Especially if you have successfully negotiated a ban on the commingling of your deposit and the landlord's funds, it should be no great stretch for the landlord to quickly return your money.

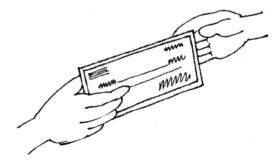

Protect your deposit if the landlord sells or transfers the building. Since any new owner will be bound by the terms and conditions of your lease, make sure the lease states that any successor is deemed to have received your deposit and will bear the burden of returning it to you at the end of your tenancy.

E. Letter of Credit: An Alternative to a Cash Deposit

Cash is by far the most common type of security—and it's what most landlords prefer. But it's not the only way to satisfy the landlord's requirement that you provide a cushion. The most common alternative is a letter of credit, which banks refer to as a "standby letter of credit."

In a letter of credit, a bank promises that it will pay the landlord a certain amount of money by a certain time, as long as specified conditions are met. Landlords want these conditions—what they must do to get their hands on the money—to be as loose as possible. Landlords would like to be able to draw on a letter after simply demanding payment from the bank (not surprisingly, tenants call these demand letters "suicide" letters). As a savvy tenant, you should bargain for a requirement that a landlord show the bank more extensive proof of your failure to pay a certain expense—

perhaps by providing a sworn statement that you haven't paid the rent.

1. Cost of a Letter of Credit

A letter of credit isn't free. For starters, there's always a bank fee, which is tied to the amount of the credit. And the bank usually won't extend what essentially amounts to a loan unless you can post some collateral, such as a mortgage on your home. Also, since there's a limit to the amount of credit you can expect to get from a bank or series of banks, this letter of credit will cut into your potential borrowing power. Collateral that is pledged for a letter of credit won't be available to secure another, business-necessary loan.

2. Attraction of a Letter of Credit

In view of its expense and its potential to curtail your future borrowing potential, why consider using a letter of credit? You may decide that using the cash that would go toward a deposit to grow your own business instead (rather than have it sit in the landlord's bank account) is worth the cost to take out the letter. For example, if you could use the deposit amount to buy needed equipment, your business may prosper significantly, which would more than compensate you for the cost of the letter of credit.

3. Negotiating a Letter of Credit As Your Deposit

If you're considering a letter of credit, be sure to carefully negotiate the conditions that the landlord must meet before making a draw. You'd want the landlord (or a highly placed person in the landlord's organization) to certify that the monies are due and owing, and you'd want advance notice of the landlord's intent to demand a draw (including, ideally, a period in which to cure your default). And in case you might like to substitute the letter with a cash deposit in the future, negotiate for the right to replace the letter with cash. ■

Improvements and Alterations

Your new space may have to be customized to fit your needs. If so, a big chunk of your lease will address this issue. You and the landlord will have to reach an agreement about who does the design, who does the work, when it gets done, and who pays for it. And if you're going to occupy space in a building not yet completed, you'll want to be sure that you pay for as little of the finish-up work as possible.

The lease clause that addresses these issues will be titled "Improvements and Alterations." (Both terms refer to the work that's done at the start of your tenancy; "alterations" may be used to refer to work that you may want to do during your tenancy.) This chapter helps you understand how the clause will address:

- improvements to your leased space, both at the beginning of your tenancy and during its life
- who pays for improvements, and
- who bears the risks of construction overruns and delays.

A. Improvements Versus Trade Fixtures

You may decide to modify your rented space by adding fans, signs, windows, partitions, lights, carpeting, ducts, or other equipment. And you may want to bring in additional items of your own that will help you in your business, such as kitchen equipment for a restaurant, control panels for your computer equipment, or machinery for your production processes. The bulk of this chapter will help you understand how to negotiate a fair deal when it comes to making changes to your new space.

But before getting into these details, you need to clearly understand the difference between "improvements" and "trade fixtures." Broadly speaking, the landlord keeps the former; you take away the latter.

1. What's Yours—and What's the Landlord's

Start by understanding that everything attached to the building or grounds is considered an improvement that becomes the property of the landlord, unless you and the landlord decide otherwise. Items that are built, screwed, nailed, or bolted into the premises or painted onto the walls become the landlord's, no matter who paid for it. Even a rose bush in the courtyard or a towel bar in the bathroom must remain when you leave unless you and the landlord agree to the contrary.

If the definition of "improvements" sounds pretty harsh, take heart. There's an exception to the general rule that's known as the "Trade Fixtures" exception. It's designed to let you remove business items attached to the property, such as decorations, tools, signs, and portable equipment, provided specific criteria are met. Trade fixtures include items that:

- you have paid for
- have not become an integral part of the structure, and
- can be removed without causing undue damage to the property.

Let's look at these criteria more closely.

a. Trade Fixtures Must Be Paid for by the Tenant

The essence of a trade fixture is that it belongs to you—you paid for it. The item must be something that isn't the subject of give and take during lease negotiations. It's equipment that you plan to buy (or have bought) without any financial help from the landlord, either directly or indirectly (through a financial concession from the landlord on another point, for example).

b. Trade Fixtures Must Not Become an Integral Part of the Structure

There is no specific list of what improvements are considered integral parts of the building or structure. Some items are pretty clear-cut (such as a deck, which a tenant clearly couldn't remove and wouldn't want to), while others are less obvious (such as window awnings, which could be removed).

One way to differentiate between integral and nonintegral additions is to ask whether it would take a lot of expensive work to return the structure to its original condition if the item were removed. For example, if you add equipment that requires a redesign of a load-bearing wall, it will be difficult to

return the wall to its original condition if you remove the equipment. If it comes down to a legal fight over who owns the equipment, most judges and arbitrators will not saddle a landlord with a reconstruction job of this magnitude. Instead, a judge will direct that the equipment remain where it is.

c. Removing Trade Fixtures Must Not Cause Undue Damage to the Property

Even if your fixture hasn't become a part of the structure, you may not be able to remove it if doing so will cause undue (read "expensive") damage. For instance, if your system of heavy-duty shelving is bolted to the wall, removal may be simple enough—you just have to use a wrench. But doing so may leave many unsightly holes. Do these holes constitute "undue damage?" If you and the landlord disagree and can't resolve your differences, a judge or arbitrator will make the call.

2. Protecting Your Trade Fixtures

You can avoid any uncertainty regarding the fate of your fixtures by raising the issue when you negotiate the lease. You may want to include a separate clause entitled "Trade Fixtures," which lists those items you intend to bring in, including how you plan to affix them to the property. Then, come to an understanding as to what will happen to them when the term ends. You may decide to leave them behind, but negotiate for compensation from the landlord. Or, you may want the right to take them away, but will agree to pay the landlord for the cost of returning the property to its original condition. The important thing is to plan ahead so that the two of you aren't thrown into a dispute that will be resolved by someone else.

You may not know what trade fixtures you'll need until you start remodeling. Or, you may not be able to purchase the fixtures you want until you've reached a certain profit level. And, some trade fixtures that you may want may not even be available yet—who's to know what as-yet-undesigned

equipment will help your business in years to come? To cover these situations, you'll want your lease clause to provide that you and the landlord will evaluate new equipment during the life of your lease in the same manner that you approach the issue now.

EXAMPLE: Jules and Loren rented office space from Northgate Properties for their orthodontics practice. When they moved in, the space was completely bare. Jules and Loren installed state-of-the-art patient chairs and a small laboratory.

At the end of their 15-year lease, Jules and Loren decided to move to a different part of the city, in an affordable neighborhood where there were likely to be young families with children who needed orthodontic braces. In keeping with the terms of their lease, Jules and Loren:

- Removed the examination chairs, which they intended to use in their new quarters. Knowing that these chairs would be outmoded by the time the lease was up (and that a new tenant would probably not want them), the landlord had insisted in the lease that they be removed.
- Left the laboratory equipment in place. Figuring that basic lab equipment does not change much, Northgate, Jules, and Loren decided it would be foolish to rip it out. However, Northgate paid the orthodontists for the value of the

used equipment, as they agreed in the lease.

💡 **To minimize the money you'll spend to remove your trade fixtures, use equipment that is easy to install and remove, involving little intrusion into walls or floors.** It may cost more to install easy-to-remove shelves, cabinets, light fixtures, and air-conditioning units, but in the long run it will be well worth it.

B. Renting Space in a Building Under Construction

If your rented space is still under construction, you'll want to avoid paying for costs that fairly belong to the landlord. These are "base building" or "core and shell" expenses that the landlord would have to incur simply to finish the building and have it ready for any tenant. These costs include floors, elevators, electrical systems, windows, and HVAC systems—basically, every permanent, necessary-to-all feature of the property.

As you negotiate the Improvements and Alterations clause of the lease, be sure to make these items the responsibility of the landlord. And it's to your advantage to define the "base building" as liberally as possible—the more that you include, the less you'll have to spend, if you pay for improvements. For example, it will cost you a lot less to ready your space if the landlord's base building responsibilities include drywalled and taped walls, draperied win-

dows, complete electricity, and a ready-to-go HVAC system.

Be aware, however, that sometimes the line is hard to draw. For example, if you would like to partition a large space with interior walls, the number of code-required electrical outlets, sprinklers, and vents may increase. It's not fair to ask you to pay for the entire installation of these items, but you could agree to pay for the added expense triggered by your plans.

Some leases call for the landlord to erect a shell building. Then you, as tenant, finish off your own space. Obviously, you want to avoid having to install improvements in a partially constructed building that may not be completed for many months. A good solution is to negotiate for a lease clause saying you don't have to start work on your space until the building is enclosed and the common areas (such as hallways and rest rooms) are done. The lease could also require the landlord to have the local building and safety department make a preliminary inspection of your space before you start making improvements. The inspectors will make sure the landlord has correctly installed the electrical and plumbing lines, and heating, ventilating, and air-conditioning facilities within your leased space. You don't want to risk the possibility that you'll have to rip out and redo your interior work because the landlord's contractor made a mistake.

C. Improvements to Your Space

Most businesses are not fortunate enough to rent a recently remodeled space designed exactly for a business like theirs. Most often, any space you rent will need to be fixed up or modified before it's suitable for your use. At the inexpensive end of the spectrum, you may only need to slap a few coats of paint on the walls or perhaps install new window coverings. At the big-bucks end, you may need thousands of dollars' worth of improvements before you can open that elegant new restaurant (up-to-date kitchen equipment and an appealing décor can cost a bundle) or a small manufacturing facility. In between these two extremes, your business might need more lighting and electrical outlets, air-conditioning, or perhaps a new bathroom for your offices or partitioning for your work areas. How these things get done is all negotiable, and the details of your agreement should be nailed down in your lease. Here, we guide you through questions as to:

- who designs your improvements
- who does the actual construction
- who pays for the improvements, and
- who decides that the work is finished and acceptable, triggering your duty to pay rent.

Work Letters

If the improvements to your space will be minor and inexpensive, you and the landlord may be able to cover all the important points—who designs, who constructs, and who approves the work—in the lease itself. However, if the plans get complex, and especially if a large amount of money is at stake, you may need a separate agreement that you'll attach to the lease. In the commercial real estate world, these construction agreements between landlords and tenants are called "work letters."

A work letter simply gives you more room to capture the details of your project. Legally speaking, it's a contract that spells out who does what and when—and who bears the consequences if something doesn't go right. If your negotiations with your landlord over improvements begin to take on a life of their own, you may want to consider using a work letter. If you find yourself at this level of complexity, you'll probably benefit from the advice of an experienced real estate lawyer.

---

1. Who Designs Your Improvements?

If your business will require special space configurations and specific equipment—such as a kitchen and seating areas for a restaurant, or work stations for a light industrial operation—you may have already engaged a space planner to evaluate the suitability of the property. (Chapter 3, Section B, discusses space planners.) You may even have hired an architect to formalize your design.

On the other hand, if your needs are simple you may not have bothered much with the details. Perhaps a "plain vanilla" job will do, such as basic electrical and phone outlets or new paint and floor coverings. And whether your requirements are complicated or straightforward, designing your space may not be something that you even want to do. In sum, if you haven't yet spent time designing the space, you'll need to decide whether you or the landlord will take on this task.

In most small business leasing situations, it pays for you to have the landlord design the space. The landlord is apt to be more familiar with the process than you—after all, he's in the business of managing and maintaining his property. And if you're renting space in a multitenant property, your landlord may insist on using his own architect to preserve a uniform look to the building. If the landlord will do the designing, be sure that the lease gives you the right to view and approve the plans before any work begins. This will help ensure that the landlord's designs square with your expectations.

If your needs are complicated or sophisticated, you may want to do the design work yourself (or hire someone to do it), assuming the landlord allows this. If you do the designing, expect that the landlord will

need to approve your plans before you begin. The landlord will want to make sure that you're not going to adversely affect the building's structure or its systems or other tenants in the building.

Regardless of who does the design plans and who reviews them, your improvements clause should address what will happen if you (or the landlord) doesn't approve the design plans of the other. You certainly don't want to be stuck leasing space where the landlord refuses to approve your plans; nor does the landlord want to have a tenant who refuses to okay his plans, thus delaying the date that the tenant will open up (and begin paying rent). To protect both of you, the improvements clause should require that the approving party use reason when evaluating the plans (this will prevent whimsical disapprovals). And it should refer disagreements to the mediation and dispute clause and the termination clause, which should have a provision allowing each of you to cancel the lease if you reach an impasse over design plans. (Mediation of disputes is discussed in Chapter 16, Section D; the termination clause is explained in Chapter 14, Section G.)

⚠️ **Beware of "as is" space.** To minimize the obligation to present usable space, a landlord may ask you to take the space "as is," which means that you may be walking into space that contains unworkable systems. For example, the HVAC system may be antiquated and the electrical capacities inadequate. Worse, the space may not conform to current building code and ADA (Americans With Disabilities Act) requirements. If you have to spend your own money or a good portion of your improvement allowance (money the landlord gives you to make alterations) just to bring these aspects of the space up to par, you'll have very little left over for your unique improvements.

Assuming you and the landlord have reached an agreement as to the design, the next step is to agree on who will do the work itself. As with everything in your lease, the answer depends on your personal wishes, your sophistication as a negotiator, and the amount of bargaining power you each bring to the table.

2. The Landlord Does the Work

In most situations, the landlord will prefer to perform the actual construction, even if you're the one handling the design. You'll hear one of two explanations:

- If the building is unfinished, the landlord will have a crew and contractors already on the scene. He won't want to introduce a whole new batch of workers, who might collide with those already there.
- If the property is finished, the landlord is likely to point out that since his own contractors are already familiar with the structure and the building's systems, it's sensible for them to do any additional work.

Each of these arguments boils down to a claim that since the landlord knows his property better than any tenant, he is in a stronger position to oversee the work than you are. And frankly, if you don't know the difference between a joist and a lintel or will be busy with other projects while the space is being readied, you may not want to take on this job anyway.

3. The Tenant Does the Work

You may decide that you want to coordinate the construction of your improvements, which will give you an element of control (over work schedules, workers, and materials) that you won't have if the landlord handles the job. But you'll need to be very sure that you have the time and expertise to oversee the work. If the job is minor, you may want to take it on; but if you are contemplating significant additions or changes to the space, you may find yourself in over your head.

It will be important for you to begin your work on space that's as "finished" as possible. As explained above in Section B, if the "base building" is quite raw, you'll end up paying for basic elements that are arguably the landlord's responsibilities. For example, if the walls aren't drywalled and taped, your painters will spend your time and money on prep work before they can apply paint or wallpaper. As you negotiate the improvements clause, press for a definition of the base building that includes as much as possible.

Before deciding that you want to run the improvements work yourself, be sure you understand that you'll be embarking on a fairly complicated project. A careful landlord will require you to carry insurance, post a bond, and promise to protect him against "mechanics' liens." (See Subsection c, below, for an explanation of mechanics' liens.) These measures will protect the landlord in case your plans go awry. You will need to decide if these legal entanglements are worth the benefits of controlling the improvements projects. It may be wiser to turn the job over to the landlord.

a. Insurance

If someone is hurt on the job, that person will expect compensation for injuries and lost income. Expect that the landlord will require you to carry workers' compensation, liability, and other types of insurance as a condition to your taking on the improvements project. Without such protection, the two of you are likely targets for lawsuits.

b. Bonds

If the job you're proposing is an expensive one, what happens if you mismanage it or simply run out of money? The landlord may be left with an unfinished or botched job that's expensive to fix or complete. To guard against this, the landlord may require you to post a bond, which will cover completion costs in case you mess up. Posting a bond can be very expensive for you, and it will tie up cash that you may need to use for the project itself.

c. Mechanics' Liens

If you don't pay your workers or suppliers, even if you have a completely legitimate beef with them, they may place a lien against the landlord's property. A lien is a notice to anyone who's interested in the property (such as buyers or future lenders who want the property as collateral) that the lienholder claims to be owed money for work done on the property. The notice is part of the property's official record, and is recorded at the local property recorder's office. If the owner doesn't pay, the lienholder can force a sale of the property and get paid from the sale.

Naturally, the landlord wants no part of this, since a lien (appropriately called a "cloud on the title") will scare off any potential buyer or lender. You'll be required to promise the landlord that you won't allow any liens to be placed against the property. In practical terms, this means that even if you have a legitimate dispute with a contractor or supplier, you'll have to pay up and argue about it afterwards. If you refuse to pay them, the contractor or supplier may file a lien, which will put you in violation of your lease.

D. Paying for the Improvements

Regardless of who actually does the work, such as flooring, signage, systems upgrades, equipment, and decorations, you and the landlord must decide how to pay for it. Hopefully, you've raised this issue already and have reached a broad understanding before the two of you sat down with the lease—possibly putting your plan in a letter of intent—as suggested in Chapter 5, Section D. Now it's time to finalize that agreement. Basically, who pays depends on the type of improvement—and whether it's considered a capital or noncapital improvement.

1. Capital Versus Noncapital Improvements

Improvements will fall into one of two categories:

- capital improvements, which are permanent and will enhance the value of the property for years to come, such as new plate glass windows or a modern heating system, or
- noncapital improvements, which will be used only by you or are unnecessary but for your request, such as a reinforced floor to support your wood-burning stove (giving your space that rustic look) or repainting a freshly painted surface to satisfy your tastes.

Once you understand how tenant improvements are categorized, you and the landlord should acknowledge two basic principles of leasing life:

Principle 1: Improvements that permanently increase the value of the property are capital improvements that the landlord benefits from and thus should pay for. Many capital improvements that you suggest probably need to be done anyway. Once complete, they will enhance the value of the property. For example, when the tired-looking linoleum is replaced with a sleek hardwood floor, that's a lasting improvement that will allow the landlord to demand a higher rent from the next tenant. The landlord will recoup his installation costs via that rent. Making you pay for the new floor out-of-pocket allows the landlord to enjoy the benefits of an enhanced building without paying for it.

Principle 2: Improvements that are useful only to you, especially those that may have to be removed after you leave, should be paid for by you. This is simply the flip side of the first principle. If your improvement will only temporarily or quixotically enhance the building, it's of no lasting use to the landlord and she cannot use it to support a higher rent from the next occupant. For example, if your aerobics studio requires a special, cushy subflooring, chances are that the next tenant will not need this feature (and will balk at a rent that's set to compensate the landlord for the floor's cost). Or, if you need blackout draperies in your photo lab, fine, but realize that most subsequent tenants will demand that they be removed. Making the landlord pay for items like this turns your landlord into someone who is underwriting your business.

Even though it's hard to dispute these two principles, don't assume that the landlord will always agree. As we've said repeatedly in this book, it's power, not fairness, that dictates how the lease will ultimately read. If the balance of power is even, you may find that your landlord and you will follow these commonsense approaches. But if one of you has superior bargaining strength, you'll see one of two variations on the principles take shape in the final lease:

The landlord has the power. If the landlord has the upper hand, he may turn Principle 1 on its head and candidly demand that you foot the bill for capital improvements ("Gee, you don't like our quaint 1940s water heater? Replace it yourself!"). Or, he may agree to pay for capital improvements but indirectly charge you by simply upping the rent. And he'll probably resist any variation on Principle 2—don't expect an offer to help you pay for that special wallpaper that will cover the landlord's perfectly adequate, painted walls.

The tenant has the power. A tenant with superior bargaining power will absolutely balk at any attempt to vary Principle 1 ("What! Me pay for sprucing-up your 1950s exterior? Never!"). Or, if the tenant does agree to foot the bill for capital improvements, she may recoup her costs by negotiating a lower rent or extracting another valuable concession or perk. As for Principle 2, she may even get the landlord to foot the bill for her specialized improve-ments, such as fancy lights, that add little or no lasting value to the property.

We realize that it's not always easy to draw a clear line between capital and noncapital improvements. What may look like a neces-sary, standard upgrade to you (a capital improvement) may seem to the landlord to be a mere stylistic request (noncapital). For example, few people would argue that businesses today need electrical wiring and conduit systems that will support computers and Internet access. But what level of engineering is sufficient? Are your demands overkill or simply a shrewd anticipation of what the norm will be in a short time? The more you can convince the landlord that the improvements put in at your request will add necessary and standard upgrades to the property, the easier it will be to convince the owner to pay for them.

⚠ **When negotiating who pays for improvements, consider whether you have to remove them.** If the landlord will insist on your returning the space to its original condition, you may incur a big expense. Factor that cost into your negotiations now. Section A, above, covers in detail the issues involved in returning your space.

2. Construction Overruns

Let's assume now that you have a pretty good idea of whether your improvement plans call for capital or noncapital additions to the landlord's property. If you are a valued tenant whom the landlord wants to please, or if the leasing market is awash with vacancies, you may be able to avoid paying for capital improvements (and perhaps you'll even get some dough for your special, noncapital needs). But if you're not such a great catch or are one of many tenants desperately seeking space, you may have to put up with paying for lasting improvements as well as noncapital ones.

Now it's time to actually hammer out the mechanics of how the improvements will be paid for. You might wonder what's left to negotiate—didn't you just categorize the improvements and allocate the burden according to the muscle-power of the landlord and you? Yes, but there's one additional factor to consider. If the improvements bill ends up higher than the estimate you've based your negotiations on, who will pay for the added expense? (Negotiations over the cost of improvements are covered below in Section E.)

If you've ever added a room to your house or remodeled your kitchen, you know full well that construction costs often exceed their estimates. If that happens with the improvements to your commercial space, all your careful analysis of capital versus noncapital expenses goes out the window. Suddenly you and the landlord are looking at a bigger improvement cost than expected—and it's too late to redo the lease. For example, suppose you and the landlord agree that replacing the bathroom fixtures is a reasonable request for a capital improvement that the landlord will pay for.

Your landlord's willingness to concede this point surely has something to do with the cost—she figures she can upgrade the property and pay for it from her capital reserves or the rent she expects from you, and possibly get a tax deduction, too. But what if the fixtures end up costing twice as much because of a labor dispute experienced by the manufacturer? The landlord isn't necessarily the one who will pay the extra. It depends on who has agreed to take on the risk that the cost will be higher.

There are four basic ways to decide who will assume the risk of cost overruns. The first one puts the risk of overruns on you; the other three put the risk on the landlord (and are thus preferable from a tenant's point of view).

1. The landlord pays a certain portion of the project's cost and you pay the rest, which puts the entire risk of overruns on you. Not surprisingly, this is the arrangement you're most likely to see in your landlord's lease. The amount the landlord "gives" you is known as the "tenant improvement allowance," explained in more detail in Section E, below.

2. The landlord offers you a specified package of improvements and you pay for anything fancier or additional, which puts the risk of overruns on the landlord unless you change the agreed upon improvements. This is called the Building Standard Allowance, or "Build-Out," and is discussed in Section F, below.

3. You pay a fixed amount for improvements and the landlord pays the rest, which puts the entire risk on the landlord (explained in Section G, below).

4. The landlord pays for everything, which also puts the risk of overruns on the landlord (discussed in Section H, below).

After you agree with the landlord on how improvements will be paid for, make sure the lease reflects the understanding. Attach drawings and specifications so that later there can be no doubt about who promised what. If extensive improvements will be made, insist on drawings and specs, prepared by an architect or construction specialist. Include all the details: partitions, special lighting, soundproofing, special floor coverings, painting, wall coverings, woodwork, cabinetry, and so on. You may want to use a work letter, as explained above.

E. The Tenant Improvement Allowance (TIA)

The most common way for landlords and tenants to allocate the expense of improving commercial space is for the landlord to give you what's known as a tenant improvement allowance, or "TIA" or "T/A" for short. The TIA represents the amount of money that the landlord is willing to spend on your improvements. It's stated either as a per foot amount or a total dollar sum. Generally, if the improvements cost more, you pay the

extra. Actually, you usually don't receive the TIA directly. Instead, the landlord pays the contractors and suppliers up to the TIA limit—after that, you pay. Or, the landlord may decide to give you a month or two of "free" rent, which means that you must accomplish all that you want to do with the money you've "saved" by not having to pay the rent.

Avoid having the IRS tax you on your TIA. If the landlord gives you the TIA allowance and you pay the bills, you run the risk that the IRS will consider that income, and tax you accordingly. When the landlord physically keeps the money and pays the bills, you avoid this outcome.

You'll be in a good position to bargain for an adequate TIA if you already know what your improvements are likely to cost. You'll need to rely on your space planners or designers for their advice. If the landlord is not willing to give you a TIA that will meet the budget, you may still decide that it's worth your while to fork over some of your own money in order to get the look and configuration you want.

Since you will be responsible for any expenses above the TIA, you will assume the risk (and expense) of construction overruns. The risk will increase if the landlord, rather than you and your contractor, does the construction. After all, the landlord has little incentive to keep costs within the TIA amount, since the landlord won't pay for any excess. For this reason, of the four options for assigning risk for cost overruns, a TIA may be the least attractive from a tenant's point of view.

1. Protecting Your TIA

One way to control the eventual cost of your improvements is to insist in the lease clause that if the landlord will do the work, the landlord will put the job out to competitive bid, requesting sealed bids that will be opened in your presence. That way, the chances that the landlord will choose a needlessly expensive contractor—or one with whom he has a cozy relationship—are lessened.

Besides controlling construction overruns, you'll want to be on the lookout for fees that come out of your TIA. Landlords typically charge overhead and "administrative" fees for tenant improvement work, even if the landlord does not take charge of the work. These fees (which may also be charged by the landlord's contractor, if he is involved) will come out of your TIA, which the landlord is simply using as a profit source. The more your TIA is depleted by fees, the less you have to spend on the actual work. During lease negotiations, make sure you find out what these fees are going to be and whether they are in keeping with the leasing practice in your area. Check with your broker or other knowledgeable business tenants.

2. Using Your TIA

Don't let your landlord tell you that your TIA is a concession or a gift. As explained earlier, the work may be capital improvements that by rights the landlord ought to pay for. Even if the work is truly tenant-specific, in response to your tastes or unusual business requirements, and the landlord has nevertheless ponied up some cash, don't be fooled—you can be sure that landlords peg their rent demands high enough to compensate them at least in part for the TIA they're paying you.

Once you understand that the TIA is rightfully yours (you've paid for it, one way or the other), you'll want to have some leeway when it comes to spending it. Consider bargaining for the following two agreements in the improvements clause:

You may use the TIA for a wide range of expenses. Especially if the landlord has secured the right to keep any unused TIA, be sure that you have broad discretion as to how you will spend it. For example, you should be able to apply your TIA to architects and attorney fees, permit charges, moving costs, and even your own time spent securing zoning variances or permits.

If you don't use the entire TIA, you will get a set-off against rent. In the unlikely event that the final costs are less than the TIA, the balance should be credited against your rent. Returning it to the landlord in essence deprives you of the benefit of all your hard bargaining over who pays for improvements.

F. The Building Standard Allowance, or "Build-Out"

Instead of agreeing to pay for a portion of your improvements in the form of a tenant improvement allowance, as explained above, your landlord may offer you a set of improvements that are available to every tenant. You are likely to encounter this approach in new buildings especially, where the landlord has a construction crew and materials already on site. The deal offered to you—the "building standard"—may include a certain grade of carpeting or vinyl floor covering, a particular type of drop-ceiling, a set number of fluorescent lights per square feet of floor space, and a specified number of feet of drywall partitions with two coats of paint. Basically, it's like a fixed-price meal in a restaurant—if you want anything fancier, you pay the difference or arrange for your own contractors to come in and do the job.

If the landlord's offer suits you, this could be the simplest and most economic way to go. Its big advantage is that the landlord, not you, pays for any cost overruns (unless you've ordered extra items). And if the work is not done on time, there can be no question as to who is responsible (as long as you've not gotten in the way).

If you don't happen to need the entire package the landlord is offering, you can also negotiate for a credit for those items you don't use. Your landlord may refuse, however, having already purchased the materials.

EXAMPLE: Rachael began looking for new quarters for her tax preparation business when her business grew too large for its current location. She found office space in Marilyn's brand new building, which was just about finished. Rachael negotiated for the standard build-out, which included enough partitions for seven private offices.

The new building would not be ready for four months. Unfortunately for Rachael, during that time her business declined following a major overhaul of the tax code, which made it easier for individuals to prepare their own tax returns. Instead of needing seven private offices, Rachael now needed only five.

Rachael met again with Marilyn, told her that she needed only enough partitions to create five offices, and asked for a credit towards her first rent bill. Marilyn refused, arguing that she did not want to pay for redesigning the space and had already purchased the materials. However, Marilyn wisely realized that it would be against her own interests (let alone Rachael's) to refuse to help her out. Marilyn agreed to substitute a lesser grade of carpeting and to credit Rachael for the difference.

G. Paying a Fixed Amount for Improvements

The advantage of accepting a "building standard" improvements offer, explained just above, is that any risk of cost overruns is carried by the landlord, not you. Another way to get your improvements in and shift the risk of construction overruns to the landlord is to agree, in the lease, that you will pay a specified amount and the landlord will pay the balance. This arrangement is the opposite of the TIA, where the landlord paid a fixed sum and you paid the balance.

Your landlord is not likely to be interested in this method unless you have plans that are clear, firm, and not subject to unexpected cost increases. That way, the landlord can realistically assess what the improvements will cost him and the likelihood of cost overruns. For example, suppose your plans call for the installation of countertops made of Italian marble. If the stone is in stock locally, great; but if it must be ordered from the source, your job may get held up. In the meanwhile, the cost of marble or the price of installation may increase. A savvy landlord may well hesitate to commit to an improvement plan with such contingencies.

H. The Landlord Pays for All Improvements

You may be able to convince the landlord to pay for the entire cost of your improvements, no matter what they end up costing. In leasing lingo, an improvements arrangement like this is known as a "turnkey" job —all the tenant has to do is "turn the key" and open for business. Naturally, you'll need to show your landlord completed, specific plans and estimates. A careful landlord may draft the improvements clause so that you will pay for any changes or additions that you are responsible for after the lease is signed. The advantage of this method is that the risk of cost overruns is entirely on the landlord.

Don't immediately decide that this arrangement is the one for you. Unless you secure approval rights, you may end up with improvements that were hastily or cheaply done. And pay some attention to how much the job will cost. You should understand by now that a landlord who "pays for everything" is getting it back one way or another, usually by setting a high rent. You'll want to ask yourself whether the rent being charged actually *overcompensates* the landlord for the money that's going into the property at your request. If you suspect that the rent's being unfairly jacked up, raise the point and press for a reduction.

I. When Do You Start Paying Rent?

Your lease became enforceable on the date you signed it—after that, neither you nor the landlord could back out without legal repercussions. But chances are you didn't begin paying rent the same day you signed the lease. Most landlords and tenants agree that rent won't be charged until you actually use the space. If you or the landlord have made improvements to the space, the date you start paying rent will be the date the work is finished and approved and you've moved in. This is known as the rent commencement date.

When you're making improvements to your rented space, you usually can't know for sure when you'll be ready to move in and then open up. Construction timetables, like cost estimates, are notoriously inexact. The job is done when it's done, and usually no amount of cajoling, threatening, or meticulous planning can alter that fact of life.

Consequently, you and the landlord need to devise a system for determining when the improvements are deemed finished—one that depends on the realities of the situation, not an arbitrary calendar date. The method you're apt to see in your landlord's lease will depend on who (you or the landlord) has hired the contractor and done the work.

1. When the Landlord Does the Improvements Work

Most landlords will want to do the improvements themselves. They'll assure you that they, not you, are in the real estate business and know their building better than you; and that consequently they can do the work better and faster. They'll tell you that if the improvements end up costing more than your tenant improvement allowance, the landlord will bill you for the difference.

In reality, improvements are often a profit center for landlords—the contractors hired to do the work are often relatives, friends, or even affiliates. Even if the owner and the contractor aren't cozy, there's no real price protection for the tenant—the landlord has no incentive to keep costs down. To protect yourself, insist that the landlord open the job to at least three bids (it's smart to prequalify the bidding contractors, to avoid getting bids from three associates). Rarely will the building's base contractor end up being the low bidder, for the simple reason that contractors who specialize in new construction are normally not as adroit at modification work as those who do nothing but.

If the landlord is in charge of marshalling contractors and workers to ready your space, he'll want to begin collecting rent as soon as the job is done. Normally, he'll promise in the lease to send you a notice of completion, which is a formal statement that he considers his part of the job finished. If a local building inspector needs to approve the job and issue a certificate of occupancy, the notice of completion should follow that certificate. If you need time to install trade fixtures or transport equipment from your previous rental, you may want to bargain for an additional period, say a weekend or a week, before the commencement date will kick in. If you don't need move-in time, at least make the commencement date the first business day of the week following your receipt of the landlord's notice that the improvements work is finished.

It will be important for you to reserve some inspection rights before you begin paying rent. Insisting on a temporary certificate of occupancy will help assure you that the landlord's contractor has done a job that will pass muster with the inspectors (the last thing you want is a major disruption to remedy defects soon after you move in). It may be easy to remedy small inaccuracies after you've opened up, but work on a big fix could significantly disrupt your business. It may be better to delay your move-in—which will, in turn, delay the rent commencement date. If your landlord fears that you will be unnecessarily picky, suggest that any dispute will be handled per your dispute resolution clause, explained in Chapter 16, Section D.

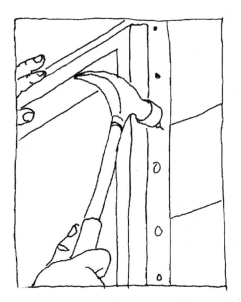

Don't cavalierly cause construction delays. Careful landlords anticipate the possibility that a tenant might delay the course of improvements—and the arrival of the rent commencement date—by making last-minute changes, taking too much time to approve plans, not cooperating with a permit process, or just getting in the way (for example, by installing trade fixtures while the landlord's contractors are attempting to finish their work). Heed lease language that allows the landlord to set the commencement date as of the date you accept the job *or* the date that improvements would have been completed had you not caused a delay.

⚠ **Watch out for "coordination fees."** In keeping with their opinion that the improvements stage is an opportunity to make money, some landlords will charge you a "coordination fee," a percentage of your tenant improvement allowance, to cover the landlord's services to oversee improvements work (up to 5% is common). Don't fall for it—especially if, later in the lease, you see a "hold harmless" clause that absolves the landlord in advance for any mistakes he might make while supervising the work.

2. Protect Yourself If the Landlord's Work Is Late

Tenants sometimes schedule their moves with very little room for error. Often, the landlord's contractors and workers won't have the space ready when promised. If you leave your current location and expect to move right into new quarters, make sure that you'll be compensated if the space isn't ready. Ask the landlord to agree in the lease to pay you a predetermined sum, called *liquidated damages,* if the space isn't handed over on time. The advantage of such an arrangement is that you don't have to prove that you actually lost that sum, should there be a delay. On the other hand, if the sum doesn't adequately cover your losses, you're stuck and normally can't argue for more.

Another way to handle the not-ready problem is to bargain for the right to cancel the lease if the landlord misses the deadline for delivering the space. Of course, such a drastic move would not be undertaken lightly, since this will mean that you'll have to start your space search anew.

If the landlord is late, you'll also want your rent commencement date pushed back for every day that you cannot begin operations. This will put extra pressure on the landlord to finish on time, and will discourage the landlord from attending to other, more important tenants while you wait. For example, suppose an anchor tenant demands improvements or repairs that result in work being halted on your space for a while. The landlord might decide that this important tenant has to be accommodated, and that the liquidated damages he'll have to pay you as a result are simply the "cost of doing business." If the landlord also understands that your rent payment will not come in as expected, the cost of delaying your work goes way up and may result in the landlord honoring your timetable (by hiring extra workers, for example).

💡 **If you don't have a liquidated damages clause, you can still demand to be compensated for your actual losses.** You may decide to forego a liquidated damages agreement, which will limit you to the amount you can collect, if you aren't sure how much you might lose per day or per week if the space isn't ready. In the event that there's a delay, you can demand to be compensated for your actual losses, which you'll have to prove to a judge if the matter ends up in court.

3. When You Do the Improvements

If you are the one hiring and supervising the contractors working on your improvements, you'll have some control over when work starts and its timetable. Your landlord may ask for written notice that the work is complete, and will undoubtedly reserve the right to inspect the final job and declare it acceptable. Assuming you have negotiated for a move-in period, your rent commencement date will be soon afterwards. For example, you and the landlord might agree that he will inspect within five days after receiving notice that the work is done, and you might agree that you'll have an additional four days to set up and move in before the rent commencement date arrives.

Your landlord will want to make sure that you don't handle the job inefficiently, and he won't want the commencement date to be put off due to any unnecessary delays. To maintain some control over how you handle the job, a careful landlord will insist on lease language that gives you a set amount of time in which to complete your improvements. For example, based on your plans and the extent of the work to be done, the landlord may give you 60 days to complete the job, beginning on the date that you've been given access to the property. If you're not ready to move in at the end of the 60 days, the rent commencement date kicks in anyway. This means that if your work isn't finished on time, you could end up paying rent before you even move into the space.

4. Protect Yourself If You Do the Work

The possibility that you may have to pay rent before opening for business might be enough to discourage you from doing the construction yourself. If you aren't dissuaded, however, you'll want to protect yourself by providing that the time in which to complete the job doesn't begin too soon. A careful tenant won't allow time to begin "running" until it's as certain as possible that the deal will go through, you know what you have to work with, and you're in the space. In sum, all of the following events should have occurred:

- You've both signed the lease.
- The landlord has agreed to a nondisturbance agreement (see Chapter 17, Section A, for an explanation of this critical clause, which protects you in case the property is foreclosed).
- You and the landlord have a written description of the "base building" (this will make it clear what the landlord has to supply when turning the space over to you—for example, whether the interior walls must be constructed).
- You have actually "received delivery" of the space—in other words, you have the right to get in and you're in.

You'll also want the right to extend the construction period for delays that aren't your fault, such as:

- holdups caused by labor problems or materials shortage
- the effect of forces beyond your control, including the weather or acts of the government, such as a stop-work order due to a neighborhood gas leak (the lawyerly term for these events is "force majeure"), and
- delays caused by the landlord (by not promptly inspecting the space, for example).

In the Improvements and Alterations clause, negotiate for language that provides that the rent commencement date will not begin if any of the contingencies above occur. Be sure to specify that any disagreements will be handled per the dispute resolution clause (see Chapter 16, Section D).

5. Protect Yourself With Reasonable Approval Criteria

Your landlord's suspicions that you aren't equipped to handle the construction of your improvements won't necessarily disappear when you receive permission to undertake them. Most landlords will insist on final approval rights of your work before allowing you to begin operations. While it's in their best interests to have you up and running (and paying rent) as soon as possible after you finish work, they will not want to let shoddy work into their buildings, or introduce changes that interfere with other tenants' lease rights.

You can accommodate your landlord's legitimate interests while still protecting your own. The key is to limit the landlord's reasons for rejection to reasonable business concerns. Specify in your improvements clause that the landlord must approve the improvement work unless:

- the work violates laws or building codes
- the changes you've introduced adversely affect building systems, such as the air-conditioning, or affect the building's structural integrity
- the construction affects the outside appearance of the building, or
- your improvements adversely affect other tenants' rights (such as covering their signage or impeding their access).

Negotiate who will pay for electricity, parking, water, heating, air-conditioning, and ventilation during the improvements stage. These are not inconsequential costs.

J. Making Alterations During Your Tenancy

In spite of your best attempts to anticipate your space configuration and decoration needs at the time you negotiate the lease, you may find that you'll want to make some changes during your tenancy. Some of these changes may involve expanding or contracting your space—these eventualities are covered in Chapter 14. Other changes will involve the space you already have. In your Improvements and Alterations clause, you and the landlord should address how you will handle alterations should they come up.

Many leases will simply state that you may not make alterations without the landlord's consent. A thoughtful landlord, however, will realize that restricting you so severely and saddling himself with this amount of oversight is often unnecessary. Does he really want to be bothered when you decide to repaint your office? On the other hand, if you propose to cut a second stairwell from the first to the second floor, you can be sure that the landlord will want to be consulted. And in fairness, you ought to consult him, since a modification of this magnitude will affect the value and leasing potential of his property long after you have moved on.

As you and the landlord negotiate the alterations clause, you'll want to come up with a system that identifies the kinds of alterations that will require the landlord's approval and those that shouldn't. A sensible method is to divide alterations into minor (no permission needed) and all the others (permission required), as explained below.

Your landlord's position on alterations will probably be consistent with his approach to tenant improvements. If the landlord insisted on designing and constructing your improvements, or if he offered you a "building standard allowance" build-out and nothing else, don't be surprised if he demands

similar control when it comes to alterations during the life of the lease. On the other hand, if he happily turned the whole project over to you, and particularly if you paid for it, you can expect a more liberal attitude.

1. Minor Alterations

One way to separate minor from major alterations is to provide, in the Alterations clause, that any project that satisfies the following criteria is minor and does not need landlord preapproval. All others can be considered major (or potentially major). Here are the tests for minor work:

- **No significant impact on other tenants.** If your alteration will affect other tenants in the building, the landlord will be held responsible. For example, if you want to install an exhaust system for your light industrial processes, the landlord will want to be consulted in case it produces noise or fumes that may disturb other tenants.

- **Does not decrease the value of the property.** If you propose removing an asset—for example, ripping out expensive track lighting—the landlord may not be able to rent the space for as much as he could have were it in place.

- **No permits or variances required.** The permit and variance process invariably involves the property owner. Since going to City Hall for a variance is often an expensive and time-consuming headache, the owner ought to be consulted first.

- **No impact on the structural integrity of the building.** If your proposal would weaken the structure or adversely affect the building's systems (including plumbing and electricity), the landlord needs to be consulted.
- **Temporary.** An alteration that can be undone poses no lasting problem, and ought to be of little concern to the landlord.

If your lease clause defines minor alterations as suggested above, you should be able to perform them without the landlord's consent. These alterations will almost always be cosmetic changes, involving paint, floor coverings, plastering, and window coverings.

2. All Other Alterations

Your lease should address the possibility that you may want more than simple cosmetic work sometime during your tenancy. In a sense, at this point you're back where you were when you negotiated the improvements clause. The only difference now is that you're already moved in.

Typical lease language will require you to receive permission for all but minor changes.

It is reasonable that the landlord would want to reserve the right to view and approve your plans before work would begin—whether your improvements occur before or after you move in. But you should bargain for a provision that the landlord will use reason when evaluating your requests for non-minor alterations during your tenancy. Requiring the landlord's reasonable consent will mean that she can't use a subjective standard. Instead, the landlord will have to use criteria that any businessperson in her shoes would employ—and this excludes personal tastes. For example, it would be reasonable to block your plan to remove a load-bearing wall, because doing so has implications that any property owner would hesitate over. But it would be unreasonable to object to your installing shutters just because the landlord doesn't like the look.

Many landlords will simply not accept the notion that they must be bound by an objective, reasonable standard when evaluating your requests concerning nonminor alterations. Your landlord may candidly remind you that it's his property, and if he doesn't like the look of your shutters, he won't allow them, period. He may insist on having the "sole discretion" to evaluate your alteration plan. This will mean that he can say no for any or no reason. If the market is tight and the landlord has the upper hand, you may have no choice. ■

Maintenance, Utilities, and Code Compliance

The landlord's lease will undoubtedly contain a maintenance clause that concerns your duties to care for your own rented space (or for the entire building, if you are the sole tenant). If you're a tenant in a multitenant building, you and the landlord will also have to settle on how the utilities should be billed and paid for, so you'll often see a Utilities clause near the Maintenance clause in the lease. Finally, the landlord may expect you to keep the building "up to code"—whatever that means (it often isn't clear), in a lease clause sometimes titled "Compliance" or "Compliance With Laws."

As with all other lease clauses, it's important to understand what the maintenance, utilities, and code compliance clauses mean, and where you should press for variations in your favor. This chapter will help you by explaining how you and the landlord will:

- divide up the maintenance and repair chores for your rented space
- allocate the costs of utilities, and
- pay for bringing the building "up to code," if this becomes an issue during your tenancy, including compliance with the Americans With Disabilities Act and environmental contamination laws.

⚠️ **Don't confuse your own maintenance duties with the landlord's operating costs.** Remember, operating costs (discussed in Chapter 9, Section D) are expenses that are associated with shared physical space, such as hallways and lobbies that all tenants share in

a multitenant building. Maintenance expenses, by contrast, refer to your own space.

A. Maintenance, Repairs, and Janitorial Services

Your landlord's Maintenance and Repair clause probably requires (at a minimum) that you keep the property neat and in good order, and repair nonstructural problems in your rented space that you've caused—for example, replacing the interior door that was ruined when your employees bashed it while moving an oversized desk. It's not unusual, however, for the clause to be completely silent when it comes to the landlord's responsibilities for maintenance and repairs.

Don't accept a lease clause that is silent on the landlord's obligations or overly broad about yours. To make sure that you understand your maintenance responsibilities, insist on specifics in the lease clause as to what you are—and *aren't*—required to do. And you'll want a paragraph detailing the landlord's duties. The way the responsibilities are shared depends on common sense and, as ever, negotiating power.

⚠️ **Don't confuse *doing* the work with *paying* for it.** The maintenance and repairs clause concerns who will do the work necessary to keep up the property and building. The fact that the landlord will take responsibility for doing the work doesn't mean that he won't try to get you to pay for it. Also, even if the landlord pays for maintenance and repairs, you may end up bearing the cost in the form of higher rent.

1. Tenant Maintenance and Repair Responsibilities

It makes perfect sense to require you to take reasonably good care of the property you've rented. This duty has two parts: What you cannot do, and what you must do.

a. What You Can't Do to Rental Property

You may not intentionally destroy the landlord's property or act in an extremely careless way. For example, you can't rip out walls or fixtures without permission, and you can't allow garbage to pile up. Doing so constitutes committing "waste" or perpetrating a "nuisance," antique legal terms still used in leases.

Another age-old legal principle common in leases is "quiet enjoyment." This requires you to refrain from acting in a way that makes it impossible or overly difficult for your neighbors in the building to enjoy the benefit of their leases. This rule boils down to the business form of the cliché that your right to swing your arm stops just short of your neighbor's face. For example, a restaurant whose exhaust fan spewed odorous smoke directly towards a set of adjacent office suites would doubtless hear from the office workers, who in turn would have a legitimate complaint with the landlord. It's ultimately up to the landlord to make sure that his tenants' activities don't collide unreasonably.

Even if your lease doesn't mention waste, nuisance, or quiet enjoyment, the law in all states will apply these prohibitions to you. You and the landlord are free to include them in the lease—by specifying what types of activities, for example, will constitute waste—but it's not necessary. What is important, however, is for you and the landlord to have a good general idea of your respective limits and responsibilities.

b. What You Must Do to Rental Property

Your obligation to use the property reasonably has a positive side. Unless you and the landlord decide otherwise, you will be expected to keep nonstructural elements of your rented space in good shape. This means that cleaning and repairs to carpets, lighting, wall coverings, bathroom and kitchen fixtures, and so on will be your responsibility. Hopefully, your landlord's lease clause has enumerated these items and stopped there.

On the other hand, you won't normally be expected to work on structural aspects of the building or major building systems, such as the building shell, foundation, roof, electrical, heating, and ventilation systems. The reason is pretty clear—most property owners don't want tenants, even experienced ones, making decisions involving the building's walls, roof, and major systems.

⚠️ **Who maintains tenant improvements?** If your rented space was improved at your request, consider who will maintain these improvements. (Improvements are explained in Chapter 11.) For example, if you've asked for additional ductwork to supply your space with needed ventilation, who will clean the ducts? Normally, tenant improvements become the tenant's responsibility, but not necessarily. Raise the issue and reach an understanding before you move on to another clause.

2. Landlord Maintenance and Repair Responsibilities

Having read through the list of common tenant duties, you can probably figure out what's left to the landlord—simply put, all the housekeeping and repair chores that don't concern your use of your rented space, including maintenance on major structural aspects of the building and building systems.

There's nothing to stop the landlord from agreeing to maintain your rented space, too. For example, if you rent space in a multi-tenant office building, the landlord may employ janitors (or hire a service) who clean each tenant's space. Unless you're wedded to your vacuum cleaner, it makes sense to take advantage of this service. And if the landlord is picky and concerned that any job you might do won't measure up, the land-

lord may even insist that you sign on to use the building's maintenance workers.

Be sure you know what type of cleaning the janitors will do, how often, and other details. In particular, build in a mechanism for responding to a cleaning job that you feel is below par. After all, you'll be paying for the service and won't want to spend good money on shoddy work. Bargain for a rent set-off right for skipped or poorly done work. (Rent set-offs are explained in Chapter 16, Section C.)

3. Maintenance Issues to Watch For

You and the landlord are free to allocate the maintenance and repair responsibilities as you wish—if the landlord wants to put you in charge of the building's electrical switches and you agree, there's no law against it. Similarly, if you bargain for the landlord to provide you with janitorial and handyman services, you may have no obligation to maintain even your own quarters. But keep in mind that there are sometimes hidden costs and risks that may result from taking on additional maintenance responsibilities or turning over the upkeep of your space to the landlord. In particular, watch out for the following problems.

a. Avoid Getting in Over Your Head

If you agree to take on repair and maintenance jobs that are normally handled by the landlord, you will probably get something in return—usually, a lower rent. But don't let the prospect of saving money cloud your judgment of your own abilities. It's a mistake to agree to maintenance responsibilities that you don't have the experience, time, or skills to manage. For example, unless you understand the ins and outs of furnace behavior (or are prepared to learn), you wouldn't want to agree to maintain the heating system.

b. Limit Your Responsibilities for Compliance With Laws and Building Codes

In Section C, below, we caution you on the expense of being saddled with building, fire, and safety code compliance responsibilities. If you've insisted on a narrowly drawn compliance clause, which clearly limits your compliance responsibilities to your unique use of your rented space, you've minimized the chance that a significant job, such as building-wide asbestos removal, will be laid at your door. Now, you need to make sure that the maintenance responsibilities you've carefully delineated don't also include code

compliance duties. In other words, you may happily agree to maintain a certain aspect of the building, but you won't want to thereby agree to bring it into compliance every time the building code changes.

Here's how the problem may arise. Let's suppose that you agree to maintain an element of the building that becomes the subject of a compliance order. For example, if you rent an entire structure, you may agree to maintain the fire prevention equipment, including the ceiling sprinklers (hopefully in exchange for lower rent or some other landlord concession). You can expect to pay for regular servicing and replacing worn equipment—but who pays when the fire code changes, requiring that any new sprinklers be a different (and more expensive) design? Even a carefully worded compliance clause might not save you from having to pay for the more expensive model. You can't rest easy unless you have specifically excluded code compliance duties from the maintenance clause, too. If it's ambiguous, a judge or arbitrator may conclude that this added expense is part of your maintenance job.

c. Maintain It, Insure It

Your landlord's property is covered by a property insurance policy. If flood or fire or the landlord's negligent maintenance of the building damages the structure or the contents that belong to the landlord, the policy will step in and pay for repairs. For instance, if the landlord neglects to maintain the electrical wiring and a short causes a fire, the policy will cover any damage or losses.

Most landlords also carry liability insurance, which will cover them in a lawsuit with persons who claim to be injured due to a defect in the property. For example, if a visitor slips and falls on a freshly waxed lobby floor and files a lawsuit, the insurance company will defend the landlord and pay any settlement or judgment.

Now then, what's there to worry about if you agree to maintain some aspect of the building, such as cleaning the lobby or hallways, since the landlord has insurance to cover any mishaps? If *you,* for instance, were the one who forgot to post "Wet Floor" signs and use "Caution" tape, can't you look to the landlord's insurance company for representation and coverage if you're sued by the injured visitor? And if you agree to maintain the furnace but do so poorly, causing a fire, won't the landlord's policy step up to cover the damage to the structure?

Unfortunately, you can't count on coverage from your landlord's carrier. For all sorts of reasons that would take too long to explore, the landlord's insurance company might balk, arguing that it issued the policy to protect the landlord from *his* mistakes, not you from yours. If the tenant wants to take on maintenance responsibilities, reasons the insurance company, let him get his own policy (as do janitorial and repair companies).

The lesson here is that you should not agree to maintenance responsibilities involving the landlord's parts of the building unless you have at least raised the question of insurance, during negotiations and with your broker. (See the discussion of insurance in Chapter 9, Section C.) If the landlord's policy doesn't cover you, your landlord may be able to add you to it (as an "additional insured"). Or, you may have to arrange for coverage of your own.

B. Utilities

In order to run your business, you'll need adequate supplies of water, gas, and/or electricity, as well as sufficient telephone and sewer systems. You may also need in-place computer wiring for a network and high-speed Internet access. The utilities clause in your lease should describe the type and amount available to your rented space. It should also explain how the landlord will allocate utility costs and what happens if service is interrupted.

Landlords typically agree to provide utility service up to the tenant's rented space—that is, to your front door or to the exterior wall of your suite. After that, the tenant has the responsibility of delivering it throughout the rented space as needed, and of maintaining it.

⚠ **Tenants with net leases may pay for HVAC and utility costs.** If you're renting in a multitenant building and have a net lease, you're paying for a portion of the building-wide HVAC (heating, ventilation, and air conditioning). In addition, in a separate lease clause, you'll be assessed electrical, sewage, and water costs.

1. What Utilities Do You Need?

Before you can analyze your landlord's utilities clause and plan a negotiation strategy, you need to think about your utility needs. They may be very simple—perhaps you'll need only the standard amounts of water and electricity, for example, to operate your jewelry repair shop, roommate-finding service, or consulting firm. But your utility needs may be more complex or unusual. For instance, if you run an Internet start-up, you'll want the newest, fastest online connection, and you may need larger amounts of electricity than a normal office. Your machine shop might require high water pressure, or your restaurant may need gas as well as electricity.

Knowing what utilities you need and how much, take a look at what the landlord is offering. If the utility—say, a gas connection or a high-speed Internet connection—is not available, it will need to be brought to the

building. You and the landlord will have to negotiate who pays for the installation. Approach the negotiation as you did when negotiating who pays for improvements, which we explained in Chapter 11. The more you can convince the landlord that the new or enhanced utility will be a valuable addition to the building, allowing him to charge future tenants an increased rent, the more he should—theoretically—pay for it, since it becomes a capital improvement. But if the utility (or the increased capacity) is likely to benefit only you, the landlord may expect you to pay. Of course, if you are a desirable tenant with superior bargaining power, the rules of logic disappear and power wins the day.

2. Who's Paying for Gas, Electricity, and Water?

Whether you pay your gas, electricity, and water directly to the utility company or instead pay your landlord for these services will depend on the type of property you lease and the way the utilities are metered. Here are the possibilities.

a. You Rent the Whole Property

This is a simple situation. Either you pay for the utilities directly or you pay the landlord, who has the accounts in his name. Either way, it's easy to keep track of your usage. If the landlord handles the payments, expect to be charged an administrative fee for the landlord's time and trouble to act as the middleman. The size of the fee is, of course, subject to negotiation (in extreme cases, the landlord will demand an exorbitant amount, which is nothing more than a blatant source of income).

b. You Rent Space in a Multitenant Building With Submeters

Your landlord's rental property may have a set number of units that can't be enlarged or diminished. Since the layout won't change, the landlord may have installed submeters for each space. If you rent one of these spaces, the payment options are the same as those described above in Subsection a.

c. You Rent Space in a Multitenant Building Without Submeters

Rental space in office buildings and some retail buildings usually won't be submetered. That's because the boundaries of each rental often change, depending on how much space the current tenant has leased. For example, the third floor may belong to one tenant during one rental term, but then be leased out to two or three smaller tenants after the first one has moved out. The landlord will not want to reposition utility meters every time he reconfigures space to suit tenants' needs.

Paying for your fair share of water, gas, and electricity in this situation is a bit trickier than when you have submeters covering your own space. Landlords commonly establish a "building usage standard," which is their calculation of the cost of each utility per square foot. Tenants are then charged according to the amount of space they rent. But this method has an obvious drawback: Tenants don't use utilities at the same rate. For example, a computer business that's small in square footage but crammed with electricity-guzzling equipment will devour much more than its neighbor whose cavernous quarters are used to display artwork. If utility costs are allocated according to square feet rented, the art gallery will end up paying more than its fair share.

Be on the lookout for possible disparities of use among the tenants in your building. If everyone is in the same line of work (a building full of dentists, for example), it's more likely that the usage will be uniform than if there is a wide mix of tenants. If you do suspect that another tenant's utility use will be disproportionately high (or that yours will be disproportionately low), press for an adjustment in the allocation of utility charges to reflect reality.

3. Utility Interruptions

Utility interruptions can spell big trouble for tenants. For example, a power outage or water main break may seriously disrupt your ability to do business and make it necessary for you to close up shop. Worse, you may lose valuable inventory or computer files. Landlords don't want you to turn around and sue them for any losses you incur because of an interruption.

Landlords' leases typically include a clause absolving them from any losses you may suffer as the result of utility interruptions. Check to be sure that the don't-blame-me language is limited to interruptions that the landlord could not control, such as those due to the weather, a fire, a flood, or an accident at the source (for instance, a blown transformer). But you will want to preserve your right to sue (or invoke your offset rights, explained in Chapter 16, Section C) if the landlord or landlord's contractor must turn off utilities while working on the building, or if one of them botches a construction job, requiring a shut-off until the problem is fixed.

C. Compliance With Building Codes and Other Laws

The landlord's lease may include an innocuous-sounding clause entitled "Compliance with Laws." A quick reading may lead you to conclude that you're simply being asked to be a law-abiding business-person. Well, that's not a problem is it? Not so fast. Hidden within that clause are potential headaches and expenses that may have nothing to do with your business ethics. In this section, we'll explain:

- which laws and regulations are covered by a "compliance with laws" clause
- why you should be concerned about what this clause means, and
- how you can protect yourself with appropriate lease language.

1. The Meaning of "Code Compliance"

Space that is recently constructed, brand new, or about to be completed is hopefully "up to code," which means that it satisfies the state and local requirements for commercial construction. The space should also comply with the federal Americans With Disabilities Act (ADA), which sets standards for access to buildings by disabled persons. (The ADA is covered separately in Section D, below.) And hopefully your new space is free of environmental hazards, such as lead paint dust, asbestos, and chemical contaminants, as explained in Chapter 3, Section C.

So much for theory. Unfortunately, you shouldn't assume that *any* property will comply with building codes, ADA access requirements, or environmental standards. No matter the age, prestige, or expense of your rented space, it may not be up to par because:

- it was never in compliance and no one's noticed
- the laws have become more strict since the property was built, there's no "grandfather" provision exempting existing structures, and no one's paid any attention to the new standards
- the prior tenant's activities brought the building out of compliance and the landlord doesn't realize it or doesn't care, or
- activities of neighboring buildings have affected the property and no one has dealt with it or perhaps even knows about it (for example, gasoline from the service station next door has seeped into the ground and migrated to the landlord's property).

As a careful businessperson, you must assume that your leased space is out of compliance for one or more of the reasons above. It may have insufficient sprinklers in the ceilings, bathrooms that aren't wheelchair-accessible, or ancient, crumbling asbestos in ceiling tiles. Why should these issues concern you? We'll explain below and suggest how you can protect yourself with an appropriate lease clause.

2. Exposing Noncompliance

Rented space that doesn't measure up to building codes or other legal requirements won't carry a sign announcing this fact.

You and the landlord may go for years without realizing that the building isn't up to par. But circumstances may change, handing you a rude, expensive surprise. Consider the following common scenarios:

- Local building inspectors, stung by a recent expose of their failure to enforce the codes, get busy and inspect your building. It fails when they discover inadequate sprinklers.
- The landlord applies for a loan or a mortgage and the lender inspects the building as part of the application process. It fails because it's riddled with deteriorating asbestos.
- A fire or other disaster damages the building and the insurance money can't cover the entire cost of rebuilding up to code.
- Disabled persons who cannot gain access to the building sue you and/or the owner. They win a big judgment and the judge orders the building into compliance by a certain date.
- Employees complain of feeling sick due to fumes they suspect are in the building. The government inspects, discovers high levels of formaldehyde, and orders the owner to remedy the situation.
- While designing your improvement plans, your designer or architect informs you that your planned renovations will disturb lead paint. To remove it, you will need to follow expensive federal procedures, which

will significantly increase the cost of the job.

- Your own improvements to your rented space require an inspection by local building inspectors. They discover widespread code violations, such as old and inadequate wiring, that you aren't responsible for.

In view of the fact that you may be in this rented space for five or ten years, there's a chance that one of the events mentioned here will befall you.

3. Negotiating a Good Compliance Clause

The financial consequences of any of the scenarios mentioned above could be significant. For that reason, a sophisticated and powerful landlord will attempt to shift the risk that they will happen over to you, the tenant. Here are the approaches that the landlord's lease might take, and how you might respond.

a. No Compliance Clause?

First, understand that the landlord's lease may not even have a "compliance with laws" clause. If so, you're in pretty good shape. If any compliance orders, settlements, judgments, or cleanup costs come down the line and you and the landlord can't resolve who should pay for them, the law (a judge or your arbitrator, if you use a dispute resolution mechanism) will allocate them in

a generally fair way. Here are the rules that judges use unless you and the landlord, in a compliance clause, have decided to play by other guidelines.

The landlord pays. Most of the time, if the noncompliance concerns the structure as a whole or is a result of action (or inaction) by the owner, the landlord will pay. For example, replacing a roof that doesn't pass fire safety standards will be laid at the landlord's door. Removing building-wide asbestos is usually the landlord's responsibility, as is the cost of replacing the locks with new, more secure hardware mandated by local codes.

The tenant pays. You will be responsible for noncompliance that results from your use of the property or your alterations or improvements (sometimes known as your "unique use" of the property). For example, if you open a restaurant, the health codes may require an exhaust fan—the duty to comply and the expense are yours. If your renovations disturb otherwise intact, non-harmful asbestos, you will be the one to deal with the expensive removal process. And if your alterations are extensive, you may have to comply with the ADA access requirements.

⚠ **Environmental cleanups are an exception.** The general rules explained above, which kick in when the landlord and tenant haven't included a compliance clause, won't necessarily apply if the noncompliance involves contamination. As explained in Chapter 3, Section C, government agencies can often pick and choose to whom they send the bill.

b. Landlord-Friendly Compliance Clause

Most leases prepared by landlord lawyers include a compliance clause. If you're lucky, the clause will simply repeat the general rules explained above in Subsection a. Many times, however, you'll see a variation on the general rules, because your landlord sees the compliance clause as an opportunity to shift some or all of what should rightly be the owner's compliance responsibilities to you, the tenant. Not fair, but it's legal.

The most one-sided compliance clause will make you responsible for "compliance with all laws," period. Unbelievable as it may seem, a judge could interpret such a phrase as meaning that preexisting or building-wide compliance duties are now yours. If so, you might have to pay to replace a leaking roof, widen the lobby doorways, or remove building-wide

deteriorating asbestos—even though these noncompliance problems have nothing to do with how you've used your rented space.

Sometimes a landlord-friendly clause will take a different approach—instead of making you responsible for "all compliance," which conceivably includes every task involved in bring the building up to code, the clause may go into detail concerning your compliance duties, including many jobs that ordinarily would be considered the owner's responsibilities. For example, you may be asked to make sure all sprinkler systems, smoke detector appliances, and fire escape equipment are in place and up to code. When landlords write the clause this way, they consider and list all the compliance jobs that they would like to send your way—any not on the list won't be yours. But be aware that there's still a way for landlords to add compliance duties that they didn't think of when they negotiated the lease: If your compliance duties are preceded by the telltale phrase "including but not limited to," the landlord has reserved the right to add to the list.

c. A Compliance Clause You Can Live With

If your landlord's lease includes an onerous compliance clause—one that makes you responsible for all compliance, or includes a lengthy or potentially infinite list of duties —do your best to bargain for one that approaches the general rules explained in

Subsection a. Your compliance responsibilities should:

- exclude preexisting noncompliance, and
- be limited to what you do in your rented space.

A tenant-friendly compliance clause should include the following:

Require the landlord to promise, or "warrant," that the building is in compliance as of the time you take possession. If the landlord will sign off on this one, you'll go a long way towards avoiding responsibility for any noncompliance that existed before you moved in.

If you are moving into a space previously occupied by a business like yours, require the landlord to warrant that your own space is code-compliant for your intended business activities. This promise will insure that you won't have to engage in remedial compliance work as part of your renovations, which could eat up a big chunk of your tenant improvement allowance (or your own bank account, if you're paying for improvements). The landlord should not object if the previous tenant did the necessary compliance work.

If you do take on additional compliance responsibilities, insist that they be specified in the lease. Do not accept a lease clause that includes the open-ended description "including but not limited to."

D. Compliance With the Americans With Disabilities Act (ADA)

If your business serves members of the pubic or you have 15 or more employees, the federal Americans With Disabilities Act (ADA) (42 U.S.C. §§ 1201 and following) makes both you and your landlord responsible for assuring that the premises are accessible to disabled persons. You can work out the details in the compliance clause of your lease. Here are some suggestions for negotiation points:

- Ask the landlord to state (lawyers say "warrant") that the building complies with the ADA, based on a survey or audit performed by an engineer or architect.
- If the landlord will be making improvements, see if the landlord will agree to pay for fully complying with the ADA.
- Make sure that the costs of bringing common areas into compliance aren't passed along to you as part of the operating charges.

Even if the landlord agrees to handle the changes needed to make the building accessible to people with disabilities, you're not fully off the hook. The ADA requires you to make the layout and interior design of your business space free of barriers that may limit access to disabled customers and employees. For example, you must make sure that aisles in your store or office are wide enough for someone using a wheel-chair, walker, or electric scooter, and that counters are low enough for use by some-one who's disabled. Similarly, tables in eating areas need to be tall enough to accommodate someone using a wheelchair. For an excellent introduction to the subject, get the *ADA Guide for Small Businesses,* available from the U.S. Department of Justice by calling 800-514-0301. (You can also visit visit the DOJ website at www.usdoj.gov. Choose "Publications and Documents," then "Legal Documents." Scroll down to the Civil Rights section, choose "ADA Regulations and Technical Assistance Materials," and scroll down until you see the title of the booklet. You can download it for free.)

Insist that the building comply with all laws that apply to new construction, excluding any grandfathered rights or vari-ances. If your improvement plans include renovations, you'll probably lose the benefit of any grandfathered rights or variances, since these apply only to the building as it existed when they were granted. For example, your landlord may not have had to bring washrooms up to compliance with the ADA because the building has not been extensively renovated since the ADA was legislated. Your renova-tion, however, may trigger ADA compliance, which may mean that you'll spend a good portion of your renovation money on bringing the building up to code for new construction.

Getting a Better Deal

If you are moving into a space that was previously occupied by a business whose equipment and setup were very different from yours, you may be looking at signifi-cant code compliance costs when you renovate. As explained, unless you and the landlord decide otherwise, these costs will be borne by you. But it doesn't have to be that way. If you have some bargaining clout, you may want to negotiate for an understanding that the landlord will pay for the costs of bringing your space into compliance.

If the improvements clause puts some of the renovation costs on the landlord, make sure that the code compliance costs are listed as separate, additional responsibilities, or see to it that the money the landlord promises to shell out for improvements is sufficient to cover code work.

Chapter 13

Parking, Signs, Landlord's Entry, & Security

You're likely to find several clauses in the lease that concern practical understandings you have with your landlord, such as parking and business signs. As you negotiate these clauses, you and the landlord will be trying to smoothly integrate your needs to run your businesses wisely. Although these clauses may not pack the punch of a rent or maintenance clause, they can be very important to a successful and convenient tenancy. Spend some time understanding the explanations here and planning your negotiation strategy as necessary.

A. Parking

In many communities, parking is a scarce commodity in business areas. If that's so in your city, the fact that convenient parking comes with the rental may be an attractive incentive to locate your business in the landlord's building, particularly if you rely heavily on customers who drive to your business or employees who want parking.

Location of parking. If parking is available, be sure the details are carefully spelled out in the lease, such as where parking is located inside the building—underground parking, for example—or in an adjacent or nearby lot or parking structure. The lease should also specify whether you have designated spaces for your exclusive use, or simply have the general right to park in the parking area. If you have the exclusive right to use certain spaces or the right to

use a certain number of spaces in a larger area, spell out the location of these spaces —perhaps in an attached drawing—and state whether you or the landlord will be responsible for installing signs labeling your parking space.

⚠ **Watch out for a provision giving the landlord the right to reassign spaces.** With such a provision, the landlord could relocate your spaces to a remote or undesirable portion of the parking area.

Additional cost. If there's a charge for your parking rights over and above the rent you pay for your business space, the lease should specify the charge and if and how it can be increased in future years.

Protections against overuse of parking. If you have a first-come, first-served arrangement where individual spaces aren't reserved for your business, the parking area can fill up because of overuse. To protect yourself, see if the landlord will agree to maintain a lot or structure with a minimum number of parking spaces and limit parking to businesses in your building. To further protect against overuse of the parking area, you might get the landlord to agree that the number of parking spaces won't drop below a certain number of spaces for every 1,000 square feet of rental space in the building.

Consider covering other parking details in the lease, such as whether the spaces will be covered and whether they'll be lighted at night (security issues are explained below in Section E).

B. Hours of Operation

A landlord in a multitenant, retail building —especially in a shopping center—may want to have some control over your hours of operation. For example, the landlord's lease may require you to be open for business during specified hours on specified days, and prohibit you from doing business any other time. The landlord may even reserve the right to change the days and times, or to tie the times to the operating hours of an anchor tenant. But if you're leasing space in an office building or if you have a whole building to yourself, you probably won't be asked to conform to specified operating hours.

The idea behind standard hours is that they'll encourage customer traffic by assuring the public that every store on the premises will be open at the same time. Also, if a shopping center tenant pays percentage rent (a base rent plus a percentage of the store's gross receipts), staying open a minimum number of hours (and generating profit during those hours) will translate indirectly to more rent for the landlord. (Percentage rent is explained in Chapter 4, Section C.)

1. Requirement to Operate During Set Days and Hours

Before agreeing to a lease with a clause requiring minimum operating hours, think long and hard about the implications for your business. Will you be able to adequately staff your store or restaurant during the required hours? Will you lose needed revenue because you can't stay open as late as you'd like? Is it acceptable to you that the landlord has the right to change the hours of operation without your consent? Many businesses are able to operate in lock step with other tenants with no real problem; others, however, find these restrictions and requirements to be a big nuisance.

Negotiate for an operating covenant that excuses you from compliance unless the named major tenant and a minimum percentage of other tenants are open as well. The last thing you want is to be tied to long operating hours when neighboring tenants, and perhaps the anchor store itself, have cut back theirs. Specify that the stores must be actually open, not just "required to be open." That's because if the anchor is required to open but closes anyway, the landlord will have met her obligation to you—which means that you'll have to continue to operate.

2. Permission to Be Open Longer Hours

The flip side of a requirement to be open during certain days and time is the issue of your right to operate during additional times. If you have a restaurant, for example, you may want to stay open longer than normal retail hours. But don't be surprised if the landlord asks you (and other tenants keeping your hours) to pay your share of the maintenance and operation costs generated by the extra hours.

If you succeed in securing longer business days, think about how you'll get access if the building or property is otherwise closed. If you enter through a door, lobby, entryway, or elevator that other tenants also use, make sure you'll have access to your space at all times that you need it. For example, if you like to come in at 6 a.m. or work until midnight, make sure you can do it. If this might be a problem, ask to add language to your lease specifying how and when you can get in when you need to, with specific reference to days and hours.

Be sure all systems are available the hours you work. Make sure you can control the lights, heating and cooling, and any other essential systems when the building is normally closed. For example, if your office is on an upper floor, you'll want to be able to use the elevator.

C. Signs

The landlord's lease may limit the number, size, and overall appearance of signs you can display on the property (either inside or outside) to identify your business. Or, the lease may specify that only the landlord may put up signs, or that any signs must be approved in advance by the landlord. Landlords impose such restrictions to assure a uniform appearance for the building. What-

ever the motivation, the landlord's policy on signs may be too restrictive.

Try to remove any lease clause that requires the landlord's preapproval of your signs. If this doesn't work, see if you can have your sign maker prepare a precise drawing of your sign before you wrap up the lease. The drawing should give the dimensions and materials of the sign and show where you'd like to install it. Then, seek the landlord's approval during lease negotiations and capture that approval in the lease itself. You can attach the drawing and specifications so there can be no question about your agreement on signs.

Similarly, if the landlord is going to be in charge of signs for all businesses in the building, you'll want to make sure that the lease describes the signs that will identify

your business—again, with an attached drawing, if possible.

⚡ **It's a good idea to check with local building and planning officials to see if there are ordinances and regulations that may affect your signs.** You may find restrictions on the size, number, and location of signs—or even what they say.

D. Landlord's Right to Enter Your Rental Space

When your landlord hands over the key, you'll doubtless be relieved to know that now, finally, the space is really yours. If you're handling the improvements, you can start work or, if the space is ready, you can move in and start operations. However, you'll continue to interact with the landlord, who may be a hands-on type whom you'll often see in the building, or one who stays totally in the background, relying on a manager to handle the daily details. Whatever the landlord's style, you'll need to know what to expect when it comes to the owner's need or wish to enter your rented space.

Your landlord can always enter to respond to an emergency, such as a fire, gas leak, burglary, or other mishap. But what about nonemergencies? Most landlords will want the right to enter the premises during your tenancy for the following reasons:

- to make sure that you're taking proper care of the property (tenants' duties

to maintain the rented space are explained in Chapter 12, Section A)
- to inspect periodically to assess the need for repairs to the structure or major building systems (the landlord's duty to maintain the property is explained in Chapter 12, Section A)
- to allow potential new tenants, buyers, or lenders to examine the property
- to make sure that you're using any hazardous substances safely and in keeping with any restrictions in your lease on your use of dangerous materials (explained in Chapter 3, Section C), and
- to make sure that you are abiding by the terms of your use clause, if you have one (use clauses are explained in Chapter 7, Section D).

Some leases give the landlord the right to enter your premises at any time to make inspections or repairs. An entry right as broad as this is an unnecessary invasion of your privacy. Most landlords will settle for some guidelines like the ones above. In your lease negotiations, try to reach an understanding on how much notice you'll receive and when the entry will take place. Then, put that understanding into a lease clause.

1. Adequate Notice

There's little reason why nonemergency visits by your landlord can't be scheduled in advance. How much in advance is the question. The amount of notice you'll bargain for will depend on the nature of your business and the reason for the landlord's visit.

a.   How Sensitive Is Your Business?

For some tenants, an inspection by the landlord, the landlord's contractors, or prospective buyers or tenants won't be a big deal. For retail establishments especially, where the public traipses in and out constantly, a few more folks nosing about won't disrupt business significantly. However, you may still want to know a day or two in advance in order to prepare—for example, by scheduling additional employees so that you can be available to accompany the visitors if you wish.

Other businesses will be significantly affected if the landlord or others appear on the scene. For example, professionals such as doctors, dentists, therapists, and lawyers, all of whom require uninterrupted, private time with their patients and clients, won't be able to work with strangers around. If you're a professional or have other privacy needs, you'll want to know about planned visits several days in advance, so you can reschedule your appointments if necessary.

b.   What Does the Visit Involve?

The amount of lead time you'll want will also depend on what the landlord intends to do inside your rented space. If the purpose of the visit is a quick inspection of the heating vents, for example, you might be able to work around it (or take a short break) while the landlord checks things out. But if the visit will be prolonged—particularly if there's maintenance work or construction to be done—the impact on your business activities will be greater. Since you may need to rearrange your work in response to lengthy, serious intrusions, you'll want more notice of them than for short visits.

2.   Entry Days and Times

The entry clause should address the days and times that the landlord may come in. Ideally, you'd like to restrict the landlord to nonbusiness hours and days. But starting from this position is somewhat unrealistic—contractors, workers, real estate brokers, and financial types all expect to work during normal business hours. You can't expect a loan officer to inspect the landlord's property at 9 p.m. And chances are that even you didn't do your space hunting on Sunday mornings.

Depending on your bargaining power, you may, however, be able to press for some restrictions. If your business has a dependable slack period, try for an understanding that the landlord will make an effort to schedule visits during that time. For example, if your restaurant serves dinner only, you'd ask that any visits be planned for the morning or early afternoon.

E. Building Security

Business tenants and their landlords are paying increasing attention to the issue of building and property security. Crimes against employees, customers, and others in and around commercial establishments have risen in many areas, and it is sadly true that no property, even the most upscale, is immune. And it is equally true to say that a lawsuit, directed at you or the landlord or both, will almost always follow any criminal incident in which someone is injured.

Because of the need to protect your customers and employees—and even the public at large—and in view of the threat of a crippling lawsuit if you are successfully sued, you and the landlord need to assess the need for security and apportion the job and the cost.

1. Assess the Security Situation

The more dangerous the area, the stronger your safety measures need be—especially if you or the landlord are aware of criminal incidents on or around the property. Strong security measures will not only diminish the chances for a criminal problem, but will also diminish your legal liability should an assault or other incident occur. Appropriate protective steps range from the basics, such as sturdy locks and adequate lights, to enhanced features such as alarm systems and a security service.

The local police or merchants' association should be able to give you guidance on appropriate security measures. Also, the landlord's insurance company (or yours) may know how vulnerable the building or neighborhood is to crime. Finally, don't underestimate the value of your own good sense and the experiences of your neighbors and fellow tenants. If you've carefully checked out the neighborhood, as suggested in Chapter 1, Section I, you should have a pretty good idea of how safe it is.

2. Apportion the Responsibility for Security

Next, in the lease itself, you and the landlord need to decide who will provide the requisite security—and who will pay for it. This discussion can be very simple or very complicated, depending on the need for security, how much is in place already, and the number of tenants involved. Here are the possible scenarios:

- **You rent the entire building and it already has adequate locks, security systems, lights, and so on.** Maintaining these features will fall to whomever undertakes maintenance of these elements—in short, you'll take care of this issue at the same time that you negotiate the maintenance clause (see Chapter 12).

- **The building has adequate security measures and it's a multitenant situation.** Maintaining the security features will be factored into the CAM (common area maintenance) costs—you'll pay your share, in the same way that you pay for your share of janitorial work in the lobby (see Chapter 9, Section D).

- **You rent an entire structure and the basic security measures are either missing or need to be enhanced.** You and the landlord need to negotiate who does the work and who pays for it.
- **Enhanced security measures are needed in a multitenant situation.** You'll need to negotiate the extent of the additional measures and who will pay for them.

As you can see, you'll be able to take care of who handles the simple maintenance of existing security features when you negotiate the maintenance and CAM clauses. If that describes your situation, you can skip the rest of this section. But if you and the landlord conclude that more needs to be done, you'll need a stand-alone security clause that does the job. The next section gives you some pointers on how to proceed.

3. Negotiating a Sensible Security Clause

You and the landlord may decide that it makes sense for you to undertake the needed security measures, handling them in much the same way as you've done your improvements. And since you'll be on the scene on a daily basis, you may be in a better position to evaluate their effective-

ness. If you do agree to hire a security service, install an alarm system, or improve existing locks, lights, and entrances, be aware of the consequences of taking on these responsibilities.

a. If You Promise to Provide Security, You Must Follow Through

Once you sign a lease in which you've agreed to provide appropriate security, you must follow through. If you don't, your landlord may, of course, claim that you are breaching the lease and may take steps to force you to live up to your duties. As a last resort, the landlord may claim that your failure is grounds for terminating the lease. (Breaches are covered in Chapter 16.)

Dealing with your landlord may not be the end of the matter. If, in the worst case scenario, someone is injured during a criminal incident and can prove to a judge or jury that your security lapse was a contributing factor, the chances that you will be found liable go way up. You can see why—having agreed in the lease that security was necessary, you've practically admitted that its absence might be critical, too. The lesson here is that you never want to agree to undertake security improvements unless you are really, really sure that you are up to it and will follow through.

EXAMPLE: The ABC partnership leased an entire building to the Westside Café. In the lease, Westside agreed to employ a security service, to keep an eye on the safety of patrons as they entered and left the café. After the security service went out of business, Westside did not replace it. A customer was assaulted as he left the café by a rowdy group of teenagers who were loitering nearby. The customer sued and was able to convince a jury that, had there been a guard on duty, the guard would have been able to help or, at least, call the police. The jury returned a six-figure verdict against Westside.

b. Make Sure Your Insurance Will Cover Security-Related Lawsuits

Never agree to provide security unless you have discussed the matter with your insurance broker. You must be sure that your insurance will cover you if someone sues you in spite of your reasonable precautions. Insuring your business is covered in more detail in Chapter 9, Section C, which explains the type of coverage ("third-party liability") that you will need. ■

Chapter 14

Option to Renew or Sublet and Other Flexibility Clauses

Flexibility may not be the first thing that comes to mind when you contemplate a lease chock-full of binding obligations. In fact, you're probably more concerned with nailing down certain issues such as rent that you do *not* want to change. Yet flexibility is, above all, the key to a profitable business. No matter how thoroughly you anticipate and plan for the future, forces beyond your control will likely intercede.

This chapter explains how to anticipate future business needs while negotiating your lease. Some professionals call these considerations your "Exit Strategy," but they also include your "Stay-Put Strategy." Taken together, they give you a "Flexibility Strategy." Specifically, this chapter covers lease clauses that give you maximum flexibility with minimal risk and expense, including:

- an Option to Renew clause, which allows you to stay after the lease expires
- an Expansion Rights clause, which allows you to get more space if you need it
- a right of first offer and right of first refusal, which give you preference for additional space the landlord may put on the market during your lease
- a Contraction clause, which allows you to shrink the amount of space you're renting in case you don't need it all
- an Assignment and Subletting clause, which allows you to turn all or part of the space over to another tenant without breaking your lease

- a Termination clause, which spells out how you can shorten or end the lease early if you have to, and
- an Option to Purchase clause, which allows you to buy the building.

A. Restrictions on Your Flexibility

Before plunging you into the thicket of leaving, staying, expanding, and contracting, we need to sound a word of caution: Landlords generally view these rights as a concession to you and your future business needs. Accordingly, they come with a price. In particular, for each of the flexibility rights you may ask for, you may encounter an up-front fee, a restriction on transferring the right, and a requirement that you must be living up to the terms and conditions of the lease before you may exercise the right.

1. Up-Front Fee

Your landlord may simply extract a fee in exchange for a particular right. For example, you may be asked to pay now for the right to buy the building if the landlord decides to sell. Or, you may agree that you will pay a fee when you actually exercise the option. Clearly, the latter arrangement is preferable, since under the former, you generally won't get your money back in the event that you never use the option.

2. Restrictions on Transferring

Since landlords generally dislike granting flexibility rights, it's no surprise that they won't want to give the rights to anyone who takes over your space during your lease term, such as a sublessee or an assignee. (Subletting and assigning are covered in Section F.) From the landlord's point of view, a flexibility option is a concession given to you personally, because you're worth the concession. The landlord will not give these rights to an unknown quantity who might turn out to be an unsatisfactory tenant.

To counter this objection, point out that you'll need to get the landlord's consent before assigning or subletting to anyone. If the newcomer will have a flexibility right, and if the landlord can reasonably conclude that it might be risky to have this particular tenant exercise that right, these fears may justify rejecting the proposed sublet or assignment. But if the new tenant's future looks rosy, there will be no reason why the landlord wouldn't want to have the replacement tenant enjoy all of the flexibility options that are in your lease. It will certainly be easier for you to find a tenant willing to sublet or take over if the space comes with these rights. It must also be said that if your proposed new tenant will have your option to stay longer or take up more space, the landlord may be more choosy, knowing that the relationship could be a long or complicated one.

3. Requirement That You Not Be in Default

It's not unusual for landlords to demand that tenants not be in default concerning any important term or condition of the lease, such as paying the rent or abiding by use restrictions, in order to exercise a flexibility right. You can understand why—if you are seriously violating major lease conditions, for example, the landlord may be anxiously awaiting the end of your term—and the last thing he wants is to have to deal with requests to lease more or less space, or to have you stay longer by exercising your option to renew.

So what's to argue about here? You've probably figured it out already—what kind of lease violation is "important" enough to bar your exercise of the flexibility right? At the very least, you'll want to make sure that only "material" violations of the lease will stand in your way. That way, for example, your one-time failure to pay your portion of, say, common area maintenance costs should not stand in the way of renewing the lease. But keep in mind that repeated violations of even relatively minor infractions might add up to a bar.

If a flexibility clause states that you can't exercise it if you're in default, you'll want to bargain for the understanding that you'll have the benefit of the lease's notice and cure provision before you're judged "in default." That way, you'll have time to fix the problem and still be able to exercise the right. (Notice and cure provisions are explained in Chapter 16, Section A.)

B. Option to Renew the Lease

Your efforts to build flexibility into your lease should include the ability to renew your lease under the same or similar rental terms. If you like the setup and the location is convenient, and especially if your business depends on local patronage or you end up investing a lot of your own money in improving the space, you may want to avoid the expense and work of relocating. On the other hand, you may want to move when the lease ends, either because your business needs have changed (you need more space), the location is no longer what it used to be (or never developed as you thought it would), or because dealing with the landlord is a headache. And if your business isn't location-sensitive, you may want to look for a place with cheaper rent.

Of course, when you're just starting out you can't know for sure how you'll feel when the lease term ends. An option to renew your lease is the best way to hedge your bets. From a landlord's point of view, however, option to renew clauses are not desirable, because the landlord won't know your intentions until well into the future. The space can't be rented to anyone else, or even put on the market, until you've declared that you do not want to renew.

If you can get a landlord to offer an option to renew, you may be asked to pay for it now—perhaps by increasing the current rent above the rate if there were no option. In addition to the remaining standard restrictions mentioned above (you'll have to be squeaky clean when you exercise it, and you won't be able to assign the option to anyone else), you may need to accept an early deadline for letting the landlord know whether you want to renew. Most importantly, in exchange for agreeing to renew your lease if you decide to stay on, the landlord will likely expect a rent increase for the new term. Let's look at how you can negotiate the new rent now.

1. Rent for the New Term

There are three ways that landlords and tenants can provide for the new rent after you exercise an option clause. You can:

- agree now on a fixed rate rent for the future
- decide to use an objective measurement of growth, such as the Consumer Price Index, or
- agree that the rent will be the fair market value of the space at the time of the renewal.

a. Fixed Increases

The lease may say the rent will go up by a certain percentage of the old rent or will be a stated amount. For example, you might agree that the new rent will be 120% of the rent charged under the old lease, or that it will simply be a certain dollar figure. This method gives you and the landlord a firm figure on which to make other business decisions. The drawback to committing yourselves now to a fixed number is that, when the option is exercised, this rent may bear little relation to the real value of the space if the market has taken a wild jump or dip. The second and third methods, described below, attempt to take market changes into account.

b.   Cost of Doing Business Adjustment

The lease can tie the new rent to an objective standard that measures growth, such as the Consumer Price Index (the CPI) or the Wholesale Price Index (the WPI). This system has two drawbacks because it assumes that your particular space will keep pace with the local fluctuations, and that your business will mirror them, too. These assumptions don't always pan out. For more on this topic, see Chapter 9, Section A.

c.   Fair Market Value

The lease can provide that the new rent will be the fair market value of the space at the time you exercise the option. The fair market value is what a new tenant could expect to pay at that time. Landlords prefer this method because it means, at least theoretically, that they'll be able to command a rent from you comparable to shopping the space on the open market.

It's one thing to say that the new rent will be the fair market value—it's another to decide how the fair market value will be ascertained. Tackle this issue now, while negotiating the lease. If you leave the valuation method up in the air, you run the risk that the landlord will unilaterally demand an unrealistic amount. If that happens, you and the landlord may end up in court arguing over how to determine the amount of the new rent. Meanwhile, your original lease will have long since expired and your wallet will be considerably thinner by the time a judge decides what the space is worth.

There are ways, however, that you can structure your option clause so that the fair market valuation is both equitable and speedy.

Value the property in the context of the option. If you decide to exercise your option to renew, remind the landlord that he won't have many of the expenses that normally accompany a completely new tenancy, such as broker fees, advertising costs, and build-out, or improvement, expenses. These areas of cost savings make it less necessary for the landlord to cover expenses and profit margins by setting a high rent. It's much cheaper, from the landlord's point of view as well as yours, to renew rather than start over with a new tenant (or in a new location).

Provide for speedy arbitration. If the two of you can't agree on the fair market value, you'll want to turn to a neutral third party for resolution instead of a lawsuit. An experienced real estate appraiser or a broker may be the answer. Or, you may want to invoke the lease's Mediation and Arbitration clause first (this clause is explained in Chapter 16, Section D), and then proceed to arbitration. The bottom line is that your lease clause should provide a method to deal with difficulties that may arise later.

Specify that arbitration or mediation will be *expedited*. This means you'll have a figure for "fair market rent" quickly. A lengthy process will mean you'll waste precious time—time that you'll wish you had for conducting business.

2. Exercising Your Option to Renew

As your lease term nears its end, your landlord will naturally want to know whether you intend to renew or move on. With more notice of your intentions, the landlord has more time to find another tenant. Consequently, the landlord will bargain for a provision that requires you to make up your mind in ample time before the lease ends. You may be given a "window" in which to decide—one that will open when the landlord thinks it's reasonable to expect you to know what you want to do, but will close soon enough to allow the landlord to advertise for another occupant.

It's not necessarily a drawback to be obliged to fish or cut bait a few months before the end of your lease. After all, you,

too, need to make plans, and making decisions at the last minute may not work for your business either.

Think about requiring the landlord to notify you of your option right at some point near the notice period. You won't have to make up your mind about the option for several years after you've signed the lease, and it's quite possible that you'll let the date slip. Negotiate for a provision stating that your right to exercise the option won't lapse unless the landlord has notified you that the time period is about to expire.

Pay attention to the method for giving notice. The lease may require you to notify the landlord in a particular way of your intent to renew—for example, by certified mail. When you exercise the option, you'll have to do exactly what the lease requires. For example, if you use first-class mail when the lease says you must use certified mail, the landlord may decide that your notice was defective—that you failed to exercise the option. If you sue to force the landlord to honor your notice, a judge may not cut you any slack.

3. Restrictions on Exercising Option Rights

All of the three common restrictions on flexibility rights discussed in Section A, above, apply to your exercise of an option to renew your lease. In particular, your landlord is likely to prohibit you from transferring the renewal right to an assignee or sublessee.

You can counter the landlord's objections by pointing to the landlord's veto power over the assignment or the sublease itself. But before you do, consider this: Unless you and the landlord agree otherwise, you'll have to cover the rent if the subtenant or assignee fails to pay. To get out from under this extended risk, you may be just as happy to make the option nontransferable to a subtenant or assignee, in spite of the fact that the space will be less attractive to a potential transferee without this plum option right.

> ⚠️ **Be sure the option clause doesn't permit infinite renewals.** If the option clause can be transferred to a subtenant or assignee, be sure the lease limits the renewal right to "one time only," or two or three times, whatever you and the landlord agree upon. Otherwise, it is theoretically possible that the option provision will carry on to the renewed lease, which itself may be renewed, and so on *ad infinitum*. This will mean that unless you specifically provide otherwise, you'll remain in the background as a guarantor for as long as succeeding tenants renew the lease.

C. Option to Expand Clause

Whether your business is just starting out or you have hopeful plans to expand existing operations, you may need more space before your lease ends. Ideally, you should plan now to take more space if you need it. That's the function of an option to expand clause, also known as a "pure" option. It reserves other space owned by your landlord for your business, either in the same building or elsewhere. If you end up deciding that you don't want the space, you're not obligated to take it.

Unless the commercial real estate market is awash with vacancies, you won't see an expansion option in your landlord's lease. That's because the clause ties up rental space. The landlord will have to make sure that whatever space is described by your option right is open and available at the time(s) that you may exercise your option. To do so, the landlord will have to either leave the space vacant or lease it to a tenant who will accept a lease term that ends when you might pick up the space, which will make it difficult to rent and not as lucrative as a long-term lease.

Economics aside, sheer logistics may hamper your ability to press for an option to expand clause. If the landlord has a multitenant building, granting expansion options to more than a few tenants will create an impossible confusion of off-limits space. Finally, if the space you want is already leased out, the landlord will simply not be able to offer you an option on it.

In spite of these difficulties, however, you may be able to negotiate some expansion rights—perhaps to take over the space contiguous to your own if it becomes vacant. You'll need to focus on:

- an accurate description of the space you may want to take over
- the new rent for the added space, and
- when you may exercise the option.

We'll explain these issues below.

1. Describing the Space

An Option to Expand clause should clearly identify the space that you have in mind. It can be in the same building or property, or in another property held by the same land-lord.

> **EXAMPLE:** Rose located good retail space for her bicycle sales and repair business in a building owned by Ace Properties. Ace also owned several warehouses, one of which was next door, but there was no space available. Rose negotiated an expansion clause that gave her first crack at any 1,000 square feet on the ground floor of the warehouse, which she identified by its street address.

If the option space is in the same building, you'll want to negotiate for contiguous space, for obvious reasons. In addition, consider what it will cost to integrate the space, contiguous or not, into your operation. Will you need to construct stairways or knock out walls? If so, your option clause should settle the issue of who will pay for this construction. As with the build-out for your initial rental, "designer" improvements, which aren't likely to increase the rental value of the property, fall on your plate. Structural improvements that will benefit future tenants or those that will support a high rent after you leave can reasonably be shifted to the landlord. (Negotiating who pays for tenant improvements is covered in Chapter 11.)

2. Setting the Rent

What will the rent be should you decide to take the optioned space? An expansion clause should answer this important point, or at least give a formula for setting the rent. If your rent is based on a simple per-foot figure (as is true in a gross lease), a common solution is to make the new rent either the prevailing market rate or the rent you're paying at the time you exercise the option, whichever is lower. Section B1, above, gives tips on how to approach the issue of determining the fair market value.

Many tenants, however, pay rent under a net lease, not a gross lease. The simple formula of "prevailing rent" won't solve the new-rent problem for tenants who pay a part of the landlord's operating costs—insurance, taxes, and common area maintenance. How can you determine now what the operating costs will be in five or ten years?

In an attempt to estimate future operating costs, landlords often identify a "base year" for purposes of establishing a baseline figure for these expenses. The base year is usually the first year of the lease. Tenants then pay a percentage of any increase to that figure. Assuming that the landlord's operating costs will rise, it will be to your advantage to establish the base year as late as possible into your lease. Tenants with superior bargaining power may even be able to make the first year of the expansion count as the base year.

> **EXAMPLE:** Charles rented half of the second floor under a ten-year net lease. He secured an Option to Expand clause that covered the rest of the second floor. The clause specified that if Charles exercised the option, the "base year" would be the year that he did so. Charles agreed that in the future he would pay additional operating costs that equaled 10% of any increases to the base year rent.
>
> The new space opened up in the third year. Charles exercised the option and paid for the square feet based on the space's current market value. He also paid for current insurance, taxes and other operating costs.
>
> In the fifth year, the landlord's operating costs went up. Charles continued to pay for the square footage based on the fair market value figure that he and the landlord agreed upon when he exercised the option. As for operating costs, however, he paid what they were at the three-year mark plus 10% of the increase beyond that level.

3. Exercising Your Option

The option clause should also address when you can exercise your right to take more space. Ideally, you'll want a fairly large "window"—for example, any time during the third year in a five-year lease. You have maximum flexibility to choose the right time. You'll be even better off if you can exercise the option in stages, which will give you the opportunity to expand gradually. For instance, the option mentioned above could be structured to give you two chances within the third year to take half or all of the available space. You could conceivably take half at the start of the third year and the rest at the end.

Naturally, the landlord will want to narrow your exercise rights as much as possible, since "flexibility" to you spells "tied-up space" to the landlord. Your attractiveness as a tenant and your negotiating power, coupled with the state of the market, will determine how far you can open the window.

EXAMPLE: Mel and Marlene are negotiating a lease for a tanning salon in a neighborhood shopping plaza. They're signing up for 1,500 square feet (Suite A), but would like to be able to occupy the contiguous 1,500 square feet (Suite B). The landlord agrees that Mel and Marlene can pick up Suite B at the same monthly rate as Suite A at the end of the second year of their lease.

⚠️ **Limit the exercise of the expansion right to you, excluding any sublessee or assignees.** If you sublet or assign the space and the new tenant exercises the expansion option, it's possible that the new tenant won't be able to meet its rent obligations. If that happens, you'll be on the hook as a guarantor (unless you've set up the assignment or sublet differently). To avoid potential liability, make sure that the option to expand can't be used by anyone but you. (Subletting and assignment clauses are explained in Section F, below.)

D. Rights of First Refusal and First Offer

The expansion option described in Section C is often known as a "pure" option. The landlord has agreed to hold open designated space for your use should you decide to take it. For the reasons given above, landlords are reluctant to sideline their space so completely.

If you hit a brick wall when asking for a pure option right, consider suggesting one of the two alternatives described below. A "right of first refusal" or a "right of first offer" is more attractive to a landlord because they don't require landlords to put specific space aside until you want it. Instead, the landlord must simply come to you first with the space *when it becomes available.*

1. Right of First Refusal

A right of first refusal is the next best thing to a pure option. If you have a first refusal right, your landlord is free to market the space that's specified in your lease clause to any prospective tenant. But before signing a lease, the landlord must present the specifics of that deal (including rent, tenant improvement allowance, and so on) to you. If you can match the terms, you get the benefit of the deal negotiated by the unfortunate would-be tenant who has done all the work. The advantage to you is that you can always say no—either because you simply don't want the space or because you can't match the deal.

Landlords hate to offer first refusal rights, because they must inform prospective tenants that you're in the background, ready to swoop down and take advantage of any deal that the other guy has hammered out. This information will shrink the pool of interested tenants—many will not be interested in investing time and money in a deal that may ultimately benefit someone else.

a. Limitations on Your Right of First Refusal

If your landlord is willing to consider a first refusal clause, however, be prepared for some restrictions, such as the following:

- **One time only.** To prevent you from scaring off prospective tenants every time the landlord puts the specified space on the market, the landlord will insist that you have a one-time-only right. This means that once you've declined an offer, you have lost the first refusal right as to future offers.

- **Bare-bones information.** A prospective tenant won't want to spend time and money on space planning and full-blown lease negotiations after learning that you may snatch the deal. That tenant will want to know early whether you're going to exercise your option. To accommodate a prospective tenant's hesitation to commit time and money in the face of your lurking option, the option clause may specify that you'll see only an outline of the key lease terms, such as rent and length, but perhaps no more than a letter of intent. (Letters of intent are explained in Chapter 5, Section D.)

- **Short response time.** To placate the nervous prospective tenant who has negotiated the deal you're asked to match, the landlord may also require you to exercise the right quickly, usually within ten to 30 days.

b. Negotiating a Good Clause

If you press for a right of first refusal, consider how you'll deal with the offer of a would-be tenant who proposes to take the space for a term of years that extends beyond the expiration of your lease term. To match this offer, you'll have to extend your lease to end when the term for the new space ends. But extending your lease, time-wise, may not be something you're prepared to do. You'll be better off if the option clause specifies that the term end date for the extra space must coincide with your current space, regardless of the term length that the prospective new tenant has in mind.

Take steps to prevent a bidding war. You don't want the prospective tenant to undercut you once you've matched the terms he's negotiated. Make sure the option clause provides that you'll get the space once you've matched the terms as stated in the deal when it was brought to you.

2. Right of First Offer

A right of first offer is a relatively weak option right—though it's certainly better than nothing if you're in a tight market and really want the space. Here, the landlord must offer space to you as it becomes available but *before* taking it to the open market. The offer must include rental terms that are commercially reasonable, which means that the rent, length of the lease, and other key terms must be within an acceptable range for most tenants who would be interested in this space at this time. If you don't take it, the landlord is free to lower the terms when shopping the space.

There is a way that you can beef up a right of first offer, converting it from a fairly useless "I'll tell you first and I'll be reasonable" promise to something more valuable. If you have a right of first offer, try to structure it so that if you make a counter-offer that the landlord doesn't accept, this counteroffer will become the "floor." This means that the landlord cannot lease the space to any third party for terms that are inferior to your offer. This arrangement gives you the assurance that at least no one else is going to get a better deal—and the landlord may end up coming back to your offer.

E. Option to Lease Less

You may discover that you don't need all the space you've initially leased. You may have overestimated your space needs, or you may find that certain parts of your business are better handled elsewhere or by others ("outsourced"). Perhaps your operations need less space because of innovations in how you work (if computer graphics have replaced your art department, chances are you don't need space for a light table). Businesses that depend heavily on short-term contracts may have space

needs that fluctuate. If you find yourself with empty space, you'll want to get rid of it and save some money.

One way to unload unneeded space is to sublet it to another tenant, as explained in Section F, below. Here, we explain how you can provide in your lease for the right to give back some space to the landlord, by means of a contraction option.

We must warn you that unless the landlord has an eager tenant eyeing the space you'd like to dump, your landlord is not likely to go for this idea, for the simple reason that if you lease less space, you'll pay less rent. The landlord won't want you to be able to drop space just because you've discovered that you're paying above-market rent, either (you made your deal, you live with it). You can answer these objections by agreeing in the lease clause that:

- only certain business situations will allow you to exercise the contraction right
- you'll give adequate notice so the landlord will have ample time to re-rent the space, and
- you'll turn back only rentable space (that is, an area that's big enough and configured sensibly to appeal to a new tenant).

On the other hand, if the market is hot when you want to dump space—and you're paying below-market rates—the landlord may be delighted at the chance to bring in another tenant who will pay higher rent for your returned space. You may find a landlord who operates on the assumption that the value of property unfailingly rises; if so, that landlord may be willing to offer contraction rights cheaply. Most landlords, however, will not be so optimistic and accommodating. Instead, you'll just have to deal with the issue if and when it arises during your tenancy.

Raise the contraction rights issue carefully during lease negotiations. Your landlord may interpret your interest in contraction rights as an indication that you're worried about being overextended—not a good impression to let lie. Try to tread the fine line between optimism and confidence ("My business is solid and my plans are carefully laid out") and realism ("I'll need to be able to make adjustments if unforeseen circumstances intervene").

The landlord's lender may prohibit contraction options. If the landlord has taken out a loan that's secured by the building, the lender made the loan based on the landlord's expected income from the building—including your rental payments. If your ten-year lease for 10,000 square feet can be reduced midway to 5,000 square feet, the landlord's income will drop until he rerents that space. In the meantime, can your reduced rent support the landlord's loan payments? Lenders are nervous about the ability of the landlord to rerent profitably, and may not make any loans unless the landlord promises not to sign any leases that give tenants contraction rights.

1. Your Reasons for Shrinking Your Space

It would be fine indeed if you could reduce your monthly rent obligation upon learning that you're paying above-market rates. One way to do this would be to pack your business into fewer square feet and return the rest to the landlord. You'd continue on, cramped but able to save some money, while the landlord scurries around for a new tenant who will pay a market rent that's lower than what you pay. It's not hard to see why a landlord wants to avoid this scenario.

Accordingly, no savvy landlord will agree to a contraction clause that you can trigger solely to increase your profits. On the other hand, if the landlord thinks that you'll be driven under if you can't reduce your rental obligations, he won't want that, either, for then he'll have no rent at all! Since it's to the landlord's advantage to keep you financially healthy enough to pay the rent, he'll give you a contraction right only if business necessities make it imperative that you reduce your rent obligation. As you negotiate this clause, think about what dire business changes or downturns are likely to affect your space needs, then propose them to the landlord. The list might include:

- the loss of key clients, contracts, or employees, which will make your business less profitable or more difficult to run
- the inability to obtain a patent, which might destroy your market advantage

- your business's net worth or revenue dropping below a certain point, which would lead any reasonable businessperson to suggest trimming operating costs, and
- a need to outsource specific, crucial portions of your business, making it unnecessary to carry unused space.

Think now about how you'll handle a dispute over whether one of these triggers has been met. For example, a key employee to you may look like just another garden-variety MBA to the landlord. Refer disagreements to the mechanism established in your dispute resolution clause, which is discussed in Chapter 16, Section D.

You'll save more than just square-foot rent when you lease less. If you pay a portion of your landlord's operating costs (which include taxes, insurance, and maintenance of common areas), these costs should go down as your proportionate share of the building's square footage diminishes.

2. Paying for Your Contraction Right

Landlords typically charge a flat fee that you pay when you exercise your contraction option. Some landlords will demand a tidy sum and view it as a cushion—if the new rent on the returned space doesn't match what you were paying, the option fee will make up the difference.

At the time you negotiate the contraction clause itself, you could negotiate this flat fee. But there's a better way to figure the cost of the contraction option besides agreeing to a figure that will placate the landlord. Since the landlord will lose some favorable tax consequences if you return space, you could think of the fee as a way to compensate the landlord for this result. Here's how it works.

Unless you waltzed into unadvertised, ready-made space, you know that the landlord has spent money to lease your space to you. These costs include brokers' fees, improvements, attorney fees, code compliance, and perhaps more. Landlords (or their accountants) will spread this cost over the life of your lease, which is called "amortizing" the cost of the lease. At tax time, the landlord benefits by being able to point to amortized expenses, but the benefits are related to the amount of rent received from you. If your rent drops (which will happen when you shrink your space), the tax benefits drop, too. In short, when landlords end up spending a pile of money to secure a relatively puny amount of rent, they pay more taxes.

With some help from the accountant, you and the landlord may be able to estimate the increased taxes that the landlord will face if you rent less at any point in the life of the lease. This figure could become the cost to you of exercising the option.

3. Giving the Landlord Adequate Notice

Landlords who agree to a lease clause giving you the right to return space will want as much lead-time as possible to begin searching for a tenant for that space. For example, you may be required to wait several months between your decision to shrink your space and the date you actually cut back (when your rent goes down). Although a long notice period gives you less ability to respond quickly to business changes, you may have to compromise on this point.

4. Returning Usable Space

The landlord will insist that you return only space that's usable to another tenant in terms of size and configuration. You may want to describe, in the lease itself, the space you can give up. Presumably, you and your space planner took this contingency into consideration when you first laid out your area. Besides delivering usable space back to the landlord, you want to be left with space for yourself that won't require extensive remodeling. (Working with a space planner is explained in Chapter 3, Section B.)

Who will pay for construction costs if shrinking your space means that new walls or additional entrances are necessary for the next tenant? These may be considerable expenses and ought to be negotiated as part of the contraction clause.

F. The Assignment and Sublet Clause

There are several ways to get rid of all or part of space you don't need. You can:

- simply ask to give up some space (this might be difficult if the issue isn't covered in the lease)
- turn part of the space back to the landlord if your lease has a clause enabling you to contract, or shrink, your space (see Section E, above)
- terminate the lease, as explained below in Section G, or
- rent the space out yourself to someone else, by subleasing or assigning it.

This section explains assignments and sublets. You'll need to understand the difference in order to make sense of your landlord's lease clause. After our brief foray into legal hairsplitting, we'll turn to the issues you and the landlord will want to negotiate in your subleasing/assignment clause, including:

- under what circumstances (if any) the landlord may refuse your request to sublet or assign the lease
- whether you'll keep or share the profits, if any, that are made on the sublease or assignment, and
- whether the subleasing and assignment restrictions apply to changes in the ownership of your business.

1. Subleasing and Assigning: What's the Difference?

For lease negotiation purposes, there's usually little difference between subletting and assigning. For that reason, we often lump the two methods together and refer to them as "transfers," and the subtenants and assignees as "transferees." When the differences do become important, however, we'll let you know—and that's when your understanding of the legal differences between the two will come in handy.

a. Sublease

If you transfer just part of your leased space to another tenant, on a temporary or permanent basis, it's called a sublease. Unless your lease prevents it, you may charge any rent you choose. The person who subleases is called a subtenant.

> **EXAMPLE:** Roberta operated a surf and dive shop. During the first winter of her five-year lease, she found that business

was slow, so she subleased her entire space to a ski rental business that wanted a satellite operation in Roberta's area of town. The ski business moved out in April, when its sublease ended. Roberta moved back in and reopened her shop.

In the second winter, Roberta's business improved and she decided she could remain open year-round. She was unwilling to sublet the entire shop to the ski business. Instead, she sublet only a portion of the front room. The skiers moved out in April.

The next year, the owners of the ski business decided that they would like to operate their satellite location year-round. Roberta agreed that they could sublet a portion of her space on a permanent basis.

In a subleasing arrangement, the subtenant pays rent to you and you continue to pay the landlord under the terms of your lease. If the subtenant fails to pay the rent, you have the power to terminate the sublease, evict the subtenant, and retake the space, just as your landlord can do to you.

b. Assignment

By contrast, an assignment occurs when you transfer all your space to someone else (called an assignee) for the entire remaining term of the lease. (You can instead terminate the lease, which is often preferable, as explained below in Section G.) For example, if you want to move on and never come back, you'll look for someone to completely take over the lease—an assignment. As with a sublet, you are free to set the rent with your assignee unless your lease says otherwise.

> **EXAMPLE:** During the third year of her lease, Roberta concluded that despite her success, the workaday life was not for her. She decided to pack up and move to Southern California for some nonstop surfing. Roberta contacted the ski shop owners, who were interested in taking over the entire space. Roberta assigned the entire lease to the skiers.

In an assignment, the new tenant pays rent directly to the landlord. Importantly, since you've given away all of your interest in the lease, you have no rights to retake the property or to evict the assignee for nonpayment of rent.

c. Your Responsibilities Following a Sublet or Assignment

Don't assume that because you've sublet part or all of your space or assigned the entire lease to another tenant, you're relieved of some or all your responsibilities under the lease. On the contrary, in most states, under either arrangement, you're still responsible for

- paying the rent if the subtenant or assignee fails to pay, and

- making good on other lease obligations, such as paying for damages and keeping insurance policies current. (However, when you assign a lease, you may have less responsibility for guaranteeing nonrent duties than when you sublet.)

You'll be free of these future financial obligations only if the landlord releases you in writing.

> **EXAMPLE:** Roberta moved to Malibu, caught some waves, and gave no thought to her former lease. Meanwhile, the ski shop fell on hard times when the winter turned out to be the warmest in history, resulting in no snow in the mountains. The skiers failed to pay their rent, and the landlord contacted Roberta and demanded that she make the payment. To her dismay, Roberta learned that indeed, she remained responsible for rent on a lease that she thought she'd left far behind.

Assignment Means Never Having to Come Back—But Still Paying Rent

Suppose you sublet your entire space to a subtenant, who then fails to pay you the rent. As you know, you're the subtenant's landlord, and can evict the subtenant for nonpayment. But you're still on the hook for the rent. Since a sublease leaves you with the right to retake the space, you can move back in, start up your business, and generate some income from that space to pay the rent. Or, you can sublet to another tenant who can pay the rent.

Now suppose you've assigned the space instead. The landlord will doubtless have given the nonpaying assignee the boot—but you're still responsible for the rent, unless the landlord has released you from that obligation. Having assigned the space, you've given up the right to come back, which means that you cannot reclaim the space and use it as a means to generate the rent. In short, you'll be obligated to pay the rent, but you won't have the right to use the space for the balance of the rent term.

You should consider this consequence if you find yourself wanting to move out completely. If you can't terminate your lease (the cleanest and least complicated solution), be sure that any assignee is rock-solid solvent, with a rosy future. Or, structure the transfer as a sublet, so that if the subtenant falls short, you can at least retake and use the space.

2. Assignments and the Growth of Your Business

Believe it or not, the assignment clause may affect your ability to merge, acquire another company, create a subsidiary, or even change the legal form of your business. The assignment clause may even become relevant if you die and pass the business on to your heirs. That's because all of these acts result in the creation of a new legal entity as the owner of your business—a new company in the case of a merger, for example; or a corporation where there used to be a sole proprietorship; or a set of owners who are the heirs of the originals. Even though the change may make very little difference in terms of the "new" tenant's day-to-day business operations, in the eyes of the law the new entity is a new tenant. And when there's a new tenant, there's a transfer, no matter how ridiculously technical it may seem.

If your landlord's lease clause provides that assignments "by operation of law" are subject to the landlord's consent, you'll know that the clause is referring to these types of transfers. And to be fair, there is some justification for a landlord's insistence that a merger, sale, or simple change in structure will trigger the assignment clause. Remember, the landlord has negotiated the lease with *you*, a known entity of a certain size and with specific owners; and presumably concessions and allowances were based on *your* track record and prospects. If you sell your company to an unproven start-up, buy a business that resembles a rescue dog (unfortunate history but great potential), or exchange your sole proprietorship for a corporation (which means that your personal assets will no longer be reachable by the landlord), you'll suddenly become a different risk—and that's not what the landlord bargained for. Fortunately, there is a way to satisfy a landlord's concerns while still giving you the ability to grow and change—as explained in Section 8, below.

3. The Landlord's View on Sublets and Assignments

Most landlords do not look kindly on your right to bring in a new tenant. Landlords want to retain control over who does business in their buildings, and they definitely want to make sure that if there is any profit to be made on the space, they're the ones to make it. Let's look at these two issues more closely.

a. It's About Control

Your landlord may have carefully checked your reputation, financial stability, and business style before deciding to rent to you. If you're in a multitenant building, especially if it's a retail setting, you may have been chosen because you fit well within the intended tenant mix. And if a lender is watching the landlord's moves, you may have had to pass the lender's scrutiny, too. All that careful planning will go out the window if you're allowed to sublet or assign at will.

b. Profit Goes to the Landlord

Some landlords are candid enough to admit that the main reason they want to contain your rights to sublet or assign has to do with money. If the value of the space has risen, you stand to make a profit if you charge your subtenant or assignee more rent than you're paying. The landlord thinks that it's his business to make money on the property, not yours, and in the lease negotiations he may try to build in a prohibition against your subletting for more than your current rent.

There is a perfectly good answer to the landlord's worries. If the landlord wants to be able to take advantage of a rising market mid-lease, the lease can provide for rent escalation. Look back to your rent clause and see if it provides for upping the rent when the rental value of the property increases. If it does, there is no logical reason for the landlord to forbid you from charging a subtenant that same market rate. If you do *not* see a rent escalation clause, proceed with caution. You don't want to give the landlord ideas (the landllord may never have heard of rent escalation) in exchange for an assignment right that you may never need.

c. Limiting Your Transfer Rights

There are various ways that landlords attempt to limit their tenants' rights to transfer all or part of their leased space. Your landlord may have chosen one of several possible lease clauses, discussed here.

4. No Assignment or Sublease Clause

The landlord's lease may simply not contain an assignment or sublease clause. What then? In most states (Texas is a notable exception), you're entitled to sublease or assign and need not ask for the landlord's permission. Few landlords will present a lease that lacks an assignment or sublease clause, but it does happen occasionally. If so, consider yourself lucky.

5. Flat Prohibition Against Transfers

The lease may have a short, sweet "No sublets or assignments," period. If that's all there is—no qualifiers such as "without the landlord's consent"—then you can't do it. Of course, if you want to assign or sublet during the life of the lease, you can always approach the landlord and ask to reopen the issue. (Changing a lease is covered in Chapter 6, Section D.)

6. Landlord's Reasonable Consent to a Sublease or Assignment

Many leases prohibit subleases and assignments without the landlord's consent, but provide that the landlord will be reasonable when evaluating your proposed sublease or assignment. You and the landlord will both benefit if this type of clause is in your lease. And the law in many states will force the landlord to be reasonable if the clause simply says, "Consent of Landlord will not be unreasonably withheld." Fine, you say—but what's "reasonable"?

Courts have developed a fairly uniform way of determining whether a landlord has acted reasonably when evaluating a would-be transferee (sublessee or assignee). When you negotiate the assignment and sublease clause, you and the landlord can place the same standards in your clause. Having these standards spelled out in the lease will help you evaluate a proposed transferee before you even present the applicant to the landlord.

Your lease clause should contain three conditions for acceptance of a sublessee or assignee. If any of the three conditions are not met, the landlord can reasonably say no. Conversely, if the transferee passes all three, a rejection will be unreasonable.

1. Is the transferee financially healthy and likely to conduct a profitable business?
2. Will the transferee use the space according to the landlord's rules and

plans—for example, as to how the property is used?

3. Does the transferee have an acceptable business reputation—for example, a positive credit history and clean history (no illegal activities)?

The reasonable consent rule gives both tenants and landlords the flexibility and control each needs. If your lease includes this standard for evaluating transferees, you and the landlord need to give some real meaning to terms like "financially healthy," as we explain below in Section 8.

7.   Sole Discretion of Landlord

There's a third variation on a landlord's position on transfers, besides simple silence or a promise to be reasonable. The lease may say that the landlord retains the "sole discretion" to approve or disallow any proposed transfer. This standard means that the landlord may use completely subjective reasons to turn down your proposed transferee. For example, if you'd like to assign your lease to a retailer who passes the "reasonable" test explained above but whose line of goods doesn't meet with the landlord's peculiar notions of quality, the landlord may safely say no. If the landlord were subject to the "reasonable consent" standard, he would have to permit the assignment. Practically speaking, a "sole discretion" standard is about the same as a flat prohibition.

EXAMPLE: Roberta's lease gave the landlord the right to reject a proposed assignee or sublessee based on the landlord's "sole discretion." The landlord rejected the ski rental business. The rejection would have been proper under even a "reasonableness" standard, since a ski shop could not reasonably be expected to draw beach crowds to the mall, as had Roberta's shop.

Roberta looked around for another beach-related business. She found a small but highly successful general sporting goods store that stocked a good selection of beach-related equipment. The landlord rejected this outfit, too, and there was nothing Roberta could do about it, even though it was clear that the store would draw substantially the same customer base as Roberta's business.

8.   Negotiating a Good Sublease and Assignment Clause

Now that you understand why the landlord will be wary of giving you the right to play landlord, and the methods that are available to limit your right to transfer, let's see what you can do to design a lease clause that fairly meets the landlord's concerns but also gives you the flexibility you need to run your business. If the final version of the sublet and assignment clause still makes you uneasy, remember that nothing prevents you and the landlord from reopening the subject down the road, if and when you actually need to transfer and have a specific transferee at the ready.

a. Ask the Landlord to Be Reasonable

It's one thing to require the landlord to use reason when evaluating a proposed transfer—it's another to know what that means. Try to build objective measurements into your lease clause. Here are some suggestions:

- **Financial health.** Avoid using a specific net worth amount (a business worth $250,000 can be just as stable as one worth twice that amount). Requiring the newcomer to have turned a profit in two of the preceding three years might, however, be more sensible. Or, you could specify a debt-to-income ratio that will reflect the company's stability. You'll need to consult experts in your field to determine a reasonable ratio for a business like that of your proposed trasferee.

- **Use.** You can specify that the replacement tenant may not do anything that would violate your use clause or that will materially increase the burden on the building's services. For example, if you may not open at night and during weekends, you'll agree that any replacement will be similarly restricted; and if your business is a moderate energy and water user, you'll agree not to rent to an operation that's an energy hog.

- **Reputation.** Admittedly, it's hard to objectify a business's reputation. At the very least, avoid requirements such as "first class," and don't let the landlord use personal values to measure the transferee. Instead, specify that the transferee's reputation must be acceptable to a reasonable businessperson in the landlord's position. Although this standard is hard to pin down, it gets you away from allowing the landlord to whimsically reject tenants. An alternative method is to agree that you'll bring in a transferee who is equal in quality to the current group of tenants.

- **Leasing to the government.** It's not uncommon for landlords and tenants alike to want to avoid government agencies as neighbors. Bluntly put, they don't want welfare, probation, or unemployment offices nearby (and landlords hate dealing with government bureaucracies). But think twice before agreeing that you won't propose a government entity as a transferee. If times get tough, the government may be the only tenant in town who can pay the market rate. At the very least, condition any agreement not to transfer to a government entity to whether the landlord has already done so— surely if the landlord has already leased to a public tenant, there's no reason why you should be prohibited from transferring to one, too.

Bargain for a provision that the landlord will release you in writing from your continued obligations as a guarantor if you assign the lease. As explained above in Section 1, you will be on the hook for rent if your assignee fails to pay. You might suggest that if the proposed assignee meets a specified financial standard—say, higher than the one the applicant had to meet for approval as an assignee in the first place—the landlord must release you.

b. Protect Your Ability to Grow and Change

In Section 2, we explained how a landlord can word a sublet and assignment clause to require consent if you change the form of your business—from a partnership to an LLC, for example. You can, however, craft an assignment clause that deals with changes in ownership, satisfies your wish for flexibility, *and* meets the landlord's need for security. The following points of compromise are reasonable:

Exempt certain types of transfers. Businesspersons who plan ahead write wills and trusts, specifying who will inherit the business (or the owner's part of the business) when the owner dies. This new owner is, of course, not the same person the landlord agreed to do business with. Yet your landlord surely doesn't expect to be consulted for approval when you make your will. Negotiate for an exemption from the assignment clause for transfers that occur by reason of death or disability. A landlord who knows Junior and is wary of having him take over your business can factor in that risk when deciding whether to rent to you in the first place.

Agree to keep the name. If you're a well-known and respected business, the landlord may want your name to remain on the building's signs or on the lobby directory. If you merge with or acquire a new company, there's a chance you'll change your name, depriving the landlord of the value that it brings to the property. In the assignment and sublease clause, specify that the landlord's consent will not be necessary if the proposed new entity will retain your name.

Agree to remain connected with the transferee. If your transfer involves the creation of a subsidiary, your landlord may worry that you'll cut the subsidiary loose later on, neatly circumventing the entire assignment process—the landlord ends up with an unapproved new tenant, and you are no longer in the picture as a guarantor of the rent, as you would be if you had done a regular assignment. This end run will be prevented if you specify in the assignment and sublease clause that after a transfer to a subsidiary, you'll remain at least an affiliate of the subsidiary.

Agree upon a net worth test for the transferee. If the new business has less net worth than the old one, your landlord is going to be nervous, and with reason. For example, a partnership's net worth includes its assets and those of the partners. If your partnership can't pay its bills, the landlord can look to the personal assets of each partner to make up the difference. Suppose now that you become a limited liability company—this means that the owners' (members') personal assets are off limits (a good reason to form an LLC). Landlords understandably object to your withdrawing a potential source of payment of your business debts.

You can respond to the landlord's concerns by specifying in the assignment and sublease clause that the creation of a new business entity won't require the landlord's consent if the new entity has a minimum net worth that's equal to or greater than the old entity's worth at the time of the transfer. True, this may hamper you if, in the future, you'd like to acquire a heavily indebted business in hopes of turning it around. At that time, however, you can raise the issue again with the landlord and, if your business successes are impressive enough, you may be able to renegotiate this minimum net worth figure down a bit.

There's another common way to handle the landlord's fears that a new entity that provides limited liability for business debts to its owners won't be as useful to the landlord as a prior entity, whose owners' personal assets could be tapped by creditors (such as the landlord). You could offer to sign personal guarantees for the business' debts. This destroys one of the principal reasons for forming a limited liability entity (an LLC or corporation), but you may decide to take the plunge if you're reasonably sure that the business is solid (bargain

for the guarantee to expire if it's not used during the first year or two of the lease).

Agree that you and your co-owners will retain majority control of the new entity. This alone may be enough to satisfy the landlord. For example, a lease signed by a sole proprietor may say it can be assigned to a corporation formed by the sole proprietor and wholly owned by him or her. A variation would be to permit assignment to a corporation in which the sole proprietor holds a majority interest. Of course, the issue of the sole proprietor's continuing personal liability for the lease needs to be addressed. The landlord would probably expect a sole proprietor to personally guarantee the lease if it's assigned to the proprietor's new corporation.

c. Share the Profits

Smart landlords write leases that allow for rent adjustment throughout the term. (See Chapter 9, Section A, for an explanation of rent escalation). If you have such a lease, you'll be paying market rates just about all the time, and there will be very little, if any, profit to be made by leasing out some or all of your space to a sublessee or an assignee.

You may, however, have a lease that doesn't provide for rent increases. If so, you can be sure that the last thing your landlord wants is for you to make money on his property, by leasing out all or a portion at a higher rent than you pay and pocketing the difference. Fortunately, there's a way you can make money when the value of unneeded space has increased. Here's how to do it:

If you sublet, the tenant pays you and you pay the landlord, which gives you a chance to skim the profit every month. If you assign, however, the assignee will pay the landlord directly. To get your cut, called the "bonus value" of the lease, you figure out what your monthly profit would be, multiply that times the number of months left on the lease, and charge the assignee that sum up front (discounted to present value) when you do the assignment. Either way, unless your lease says otherwise, you keep the profit and there's nothing illegal about it. And your making some profit this way does not give the landlord a "reasonable" basis for disapproving the transfer.

EXAMPLE: Anxious to move to Southern California, Roberta found Wisdom Surf Shop to take over the 15 months remaining on her lease. In the years since Roberta negotiated her lease, the value of the retail space had gone way up. Roberta planned to structure the deal as a sublet, so that she would collect the rent from Wisdom. She would charge Wisdom $1,000 a month more than her own rent, and stood to make $15,000 on the deal. That's a lot of surf wax.

Roberta rethought the whole matter when Wisdom demanded an assignment—Wisdom didn't want the complications of having to pay rent to a post office box in Malibu. No dummy, Roberta figured out a way to get her $15,000. She demanded it up front, but asked for a little less in view of the fact that she was getting it in one lump sum instead of monthly installments.

To prevent you from making money on his property, your landlord's assignment and subleasing clause may specify that if the rent you receive from a transferee is more than the rent you pay the landlord, the landlord will get the difference. Unless you have some bargaining clout, you may have to live with this and content yourself with the knowledge that, if you aren't going to make money as a landlord, at least there will be a way for you to dump unnecessary space so that you won't lose money as a tenant.

A better (and fairer) way to resolve the issue is to agree in your lease that you will equally split the profit you might make on a sublease or assignment, after you have accounted for your costs, such as broker fees and build-out costs. That way, both you and the landlord share in the windfall. In fact, a smart landlord will realize that he may make *more* money if he shares the profits than if he takes them all for himself. He'll understand that if you'll get a cut of the excess rent, you have an incentive to sublease or assign at a high rent. But if all you have to do is cover your own rent, you'll stop when you find a transferee able to pay that amount—and the landlord stands to make no additional money at all.

d. Insist on a Fair Recapture Clause

Many landlords cannot abide the thought of being unable to prevent a tenant from becoming a landlord, right under their noses. So they provide for the best of all worlds, by promising to abide by a reasonable consent standard, but reserving the right to take back, or "recapture," the space instead. This approach has potentially annoying ramifications for you—you could do all the work in lining up a transferee, only to have the landlord exercise the recapture right and take back the space—and rent it directly, of course, to the very transferee whom you found and romanced. (It's a bit like the end-run tenants can play on landlords when tenants have a right of first refusal, as explained in Section D, above.)

There's a fair way to deal with a recapture right in your lease. Provide that the landlord must exercise that right within a certain time after you give notice that you're planning to transfer some space—ideally, soon thereafter, before you begin searching for a likely transferee. That way, you won't find yourself acting essentially as your landlord's broker.

9. How to Provide for Speedy Dispute Resolution

It's essential to have an understanding that any disagreements over a proposed transfer will be resolved quickly and fairly. If your dispute gets into court, it will take forever and the proposed transferee will have long since rented space elsewhere.

Be sure that the assignment and sublease clause provides for mediation and arbitration of any differences between you and the landlord. You may even want to specify that the dispute resolution process will be expedited, or sped up, for this type of dispute. You can agree that if the situation arises, the matter will be immediately submitted to an arbitrator for a decision. (Mediation and arbitration are explained in Chapter 16, Section D.)

Suppose the landlord rejects a transferee whom the arbitrator has judged okay? Consider that possibility now, and provide for a remedy in your lease clause. You can provide that you can move out, without further responsibility for paying rent, or that you can go to court and ask a judge to order the landlord to consent to the transfer. A third option would be to sue the landlord for your damages—the money you've lost—that resulted from your inability to sublet or assign. You may need to consult an attorney if the situation arises.

G. Termination Clause

As discussed above, you may reduce your rental obligations during the term of your lease by returning space to the landlord or by subletting or assigning. But if you want to build in a way to terminate the lease early and move out without the lingering rent obligations that come with subleasing or assigning, you'll need to raise the issue during lease negotiations. The trick will be to convince the landlord that granting you this choice has something in it for the landlord.

You may not be the only one interested in setting up an ultimate escape plan. The landlord may be concerned about your ability to prosper, and may want to be able to get rid of you at the first sign of trouble. For example, a landlord who learns that you've defaulted on a loan may want to end the lease right away, before your business situation goes from bad to worse.

When you negotiate the termination clause, you'll need to cover these important issues:

- Under what circumstances can you invoke your termination right?
- Under what circumstances should your landlord be able to terminate?
- When during the lease term can you or the landlord terminate?
- How much will it cost the one who pulls out?

1. Specific, Objective Reasons for Terminating

A judge will enforce a lease only if both parties are bound to it until the end of the term—unless the escape mechanisms are narrowly and clearly spelled out in the lease. If you can get out of the lease for any or no reason, you really aren't bound at all—and in the eyes of the law, the whole thing is no more than a lengthy memo about a lease, nonbinding on both. The upshot: If you and the landlord end up in court—arguing over any aspect of the lease—a judge may look at the lease as a whole, conclude that it is an illusory contract, and refuse to enforce any of it.

> **EXAMPLE:** Marcus rented a storefront from his brother-in-law Joe. Thinking that he had cleverly given himself much-needed flexibility, Marcus persuaded Joe to include a termination clause allowing Marcus to terminate the five-year lease at any time. Marcus prospered in the location and had no plans to terminate the lease.
>
> Unfortunately, in the third year Marcus and Joe had a serious disagreement

over rent payments. Joe sued Marcus for back rent. In court, Marcus got a rude surprise. The judge dealt with the rent issue according to what he thought was fair, but he also ruled that the contract was "illusory" due to Marcus's ability to terminate it at any time. This meant that Marcus did not have a lease, much less the security of two more years. Joe promptly evicted him.

You can avoid this dire result by making sure that you or the landlord can terminate the lease only for narrow, specific, and objective reasons.

2. Your Reasons for Terminating the Lease

Despite your best efforts to succeed in your new rented space, circumstances beyond your control may intervene and make it unwise to continue. It's a delicate matter to raise these concerns at the negotiation stage—you don't want to frighten the landlord off by presenting a laundry list of reasons why you might need to get out of the lease, however remote you hope these events may be. And, naturally, if you're looking for the right to get out of the lease early, don't expect the landlord to do much to improve the space for you.

Before approaching the negotiation, be advised that no landlord will sign a lease that allows you to terminate if and when the deal becomes unattractive to you.

Although you may want to get out of a long lease because it's at above-market rates, that's exactly why the landlord will want you to stay put.

On the other hand, the landlord isn't interested in having a tenant who's about to fail. Far better to set some benchmarks in the lease, which the two of you will recognize as warning signs that suggest it may be wise to call it a day. That way, the parting can at least be orderly—and if the landlord has his way, a little bit profitable, too, since the landlord will want a termination fee, as explained below.

Here are some benchmarks you can include in your termination clause that will reasonably spell out the circumstances justifying a termination:

The renovation plans aren't right. If you're going to build out the space—in a brand new building for example—your landlord will doubtless insist on the right to approve your plans and design. Or, if the landlord is going to do the work, you'll want to check to make sure the work will measure up. (Improvement clauses are explained in Chapter 11.) Either way, the two of you may disagree as to whether the plans meet the expectations. If you're unable to resolve the impasse, you should each have the ability to get out of the lease.

The plans weren't approved. Your build-out may need the approval of local building authorities, the health department, a community association, or may even require a zoning variance. Without the official okay from these groups, you won't be able to proceed as intended. If you can't adapt your plans, you may want the ability to walk away from the lease.

You haven't made your numbers. You might propose a provision that lets you cancel your lease if your gross income projections haven't reached a stated level by a certain time—say, six months after you take occupancy. Although this would be an unusual clause for a landlord to accept, an owner with vacant space and no other prospective tenants might agree to it.

A key tenant moved away. If you rent space in a mall or multitenant building, and there is one key tenant (known as an anchor tenant) whose presence brings needed traffic to your store, you may want the right to pick up and move out if that tenant moves away. Having a right to move in this situation is known as a "cotenancy" clause.

The property has been partially destroyed. If you rent an entire building, your lease will be terminated if the whole building is destroyed. And in most states, if you rent part of a building you can also terminate the lease if the building is destroyed. But what if it's only heavily damaged—for example, a storm damages the entry and foyer for your office rental? If the landlord doesn't make repairs promptly, you may decide to terminate based on a theory of "constructive eviction." (Your argument is that, by refusing to repair, the landlord has in effect evicted you.) But if the landlord disagrees and takes the case to court, a judge may side with the landlord and hold you to the terms of the lease.

A better approach is to provide in your lease that if you can't run your business in your space for 30 days because of damage you didn't cause, you can cancel the lease. Also, make sure your provision covers:

- **Access.** Get the right to terminate if you and your customers can't get to your space because of damage to another part of the building.
- **Suspended rent.** Bargain for the understanding that if you decide to continue as a tenant, you won't have to pay rent until the damage has been repaired.
- **Reduced rent.** If part of the space is still usable, the rent should be reduced proportionately.

Secure the right to terminate if the landlord doesn't deliver on a crucial promise. For example, you may have chosen the location based on the landlord's representation that air-conditioning would be installed by the summer, or that a contract with a nearby parking facility would be concluded, giving needed spaces for your business. If any such promise is truly critical to the success of your business, it was probably a "deal breaker." Now, make it a "lease breaker." Be aware, however, that the landlord's lender may not approve of a termination right that easily excuses you from the lease.

If your lease does not identify the nonperformance of key promises as grounds for terminating the lease, you could still terminate and hope that the landlord won't sue you to enforce the lease. Even if you're sued, a judge might agree that the issue was so important that the deal was effectively gutted when the landlord didn't follow through. But it's far safer to build this conclusion into the lease.

3. The Landlord's Reasons for Terminating

The landlord, as much as you, may have worries about the future that can be answered by building in a way to cancel the lease. Of course, major failings on your part—such as not paying the rent—will trigger the landlord's right to hold you in default and get you out (lease terminations are covered in detail in Chapter 16). But landlords may be concerned about other, less drastic issues, such as:

Changes in the ownership of your business. In Section F, above, we explained why a change in the legal form of your business—from sole proprietorship, for example, to limited liability company—may be cause for concern for your landlord. If you have enough bargaining strength, hopefully you have persuaded the landlord that such a change, if it meets specified criteria, won't constitute an assignment of your lease, and that you won't need the landlord's permission before making the change.

If you were able to secure this understanding in the assignment and subleasing clause, you shouldn't see a termination clause allowing the landlord to cancel if your business changes form. However, if you didn't prevail, expect to see the issue raised here. A cancellation right is, of course, the harshest way to deal with your ownership changes. The landlord need not even consider the merits of your change (as she would when having to give consent to an assignment)—she can simply terminate. To counter this drastic possibility, bargain for some way to limit the landlord's cancellation rights. For example, you might offer to remain as a guarantor for the new entity.

Violating another agreement. The landlord may consider your financial performance with business partners, franchisors, banks, or mortgage lenders as good indicators of what's in store for her. As a kind of "early warning system," the landlord's clause may require that you disclose any financial defaults involving these entities, which will give the landlord the right to cancel the lease.

It may feel unfair for you to lose your lease due to an unrelated financial problem. If the landlord won't budge on this one, at least press for some protections. For example, you won't want the landlord to be able to terminate based on a mere rumor of your business woes. And you may be entirely justified in defaulting on a business contract if the other side has violated first. To avoid losing your lease because you've been prematurely or unfairly labeled a poor risk, insist that any question as to whether you've breached an agreement with another business be submitted to mediation and arbitration before the landlord has the right to terminate.

⚠️ **If you pay percentage rent, your landlord may want the ability to cancel if your rent doesn't rise above a specified level.** In a percentage rent lease, you begin sharing your profits with the landlord after you have grossed a specified amount (percentage rent is explained in Chapter 4, Section C). If the landlord rented to you with the expectation that you'd earn (for yourself and the landlord) a minimum amount, she'll be disappointed if you don't reach that goal. A termination right on this ground allows the landlord to dump you in favor of a better-earning tenant.

back to the drawing board and save the lease.

When your business is doing poorly. If you have the right to terminate due to unrealized profits or growth, you'll want a relatively short notice period. If sales or profits don't turn around within that time, you'll want to be able to get out without further damage.

You should also build in an understanding as to when you must be physically out of the premises. Obviously, you can't move out in a day and will need time to remove your trade fixtures.

4. The Timing of Your Termination

You and the landlord should think about when you want to give each other "notice" of the terminator's intent to cancel the lease, coupled with a right to cure, or fix, the state of affairs that triggered the intent to terminate. The length of the notice and cure period depends on the reason for the termination.

When plans are disapproved. If you or the landlord decide to terminate because one of you, or a third party such as a planning commission, has disapproved the build-out plans, be sure to give the other side a "cure" period. For example, if the landlord gives your design specs a thumbs-down, specify in the termination clause that the landlord may not invoke termination rights for this reason until a period of time, say 30 days, has elapsed. This gives you a chance to go

5. Termination Fees

Don't be surprised if the landlord proposes that if you exercise your right to cancel the lease, you'll need to pay a cancellation fee —which is a reasonable proposition if the fee isn't too high. You, in turn, can bargain for the right to collect a fee from the landlord if she's the one who cancels the lease.

a. When You Cancel the Lease

If you're the one who invokes the termination right, the landlord will want at a minimum to be reimbursed for the unamortized costs of your lease. These are the brokers' and attorneys' fees, build-out costs, and permit fees that the landlord expended in order to lease to you. In Section E2, above, we explained the concept of unamortized costs in the context of returning space to the landlord; the same principle applies here.

The landlord may also insist on some rent "going forward." This is simply a demand for rent beyond the date that you physically move out. Or you may be asked to pay "liquidated damages," which are the landlord's reasonable estimate of how much your early termination of the lease is going to cost her, in terms of advertising for a new tenant, showing the space, and carrying the landlord's own mortgage, insurance, and tax costs until a replacement takes over.

b. When the Landlord Cancels the Lease

You should bargain for the same reimbursements that the landlord is likely to demand, as explained in Subsection a, above. Whether you'll get them depends entirely on your strength and the state of the market.

H. Option to Purchase

In the back of your mind, you may be thinking, "Would I like to own this building someday?" If so, consider a lease clause giving you an option to purchase. It could give you the right to buy at a specified future time at a specified price—and could state all the other terms of the deal if you decided to exercise your option. Maybe the landlord will also agree that a portion of the rent you've paid will be credited against the purchase price.

An alternative is to have the lease give you a right of first refusal or a right of first offer. These concepts are fully explained above in Section D, in the context of renewing your lease, and apply equally here. ■

Insurance Clauses

Several kinds of insurance are available to cover the risks of leasing commercial space, including property and liability insurance, rental interruption insurance, and leasehold insurance. You'll need to evaluate each type of insurance coverage in the context of your lease and landlord's requirements, your business needs, and the property—and negotiate accordingly. Your insurance broker can help too, especially when it comes to choosing adequate levels of coverage.

This chapter provides an overview of the most common types of insurance and explains how they will cover you for property losses or personal injuries you've accidentally caused. It also explains two insurance-related clauses—"subrogation" and "indemnities"—that usually accompany insurance clauses.

A. Property and Liability Insurance

Commercial tenants who have a net lease (in which they pay a portion of the landlord's taxes, insurance, and building operating costs) are normally asked to pay for some of the landlord's property and liability insurance costs. The property policy covers the cost of repairing or replacing the structure; the liability policy will cover claims from customers or clients who are accidentally injured on or near the property. The cost of these policies is part of your rent. Tenants with gross leases (they pay only for the space) don't pay directly for the cost of insurance, but landlords factor in this expense when they set the per-foot rental rate. (Property and liability insurance are explained in detail in Chapter 9, Section C.)

B. Insuring Your Trade Fixtures and Inventory

Landlords will often require you to purchase separate insurance coverage for your trade fixtures and inventory. These items aren't covered by the property policy for the building. Even if the landlord does not insist on trade fixture and inventory coverage, it's wise for you to purchase it anyway. Here's why: Suppose there is a fire that destroys all or part of the structure—and all of your inventory and equipment. The property policy will cover the cost of rebuilding the structure, but you'll be left with bare shelves, literally, while the building is replaced or repaired around you. You'll hardly be able to stay in business, let alone pay the rent.

Your landlord may require you to carry replacement cost coverage, which means that the insurance company will pay you for the cost of buying the fixture or replacing the inventory, irrespective of the actual value of the item when it was destroyed (see the sidebar, "Will Insurance Fully Compensate Your Losses?" in Chapter 9, Section C). The landlord's motives are pure self-interest: The easier it is for you to replenish your fixtures and inventory, the faster you'll be back in business (and paying the rent).

The landlord's lease may also require you to use the insurance proceeds to replace the lost equipment and inventory. Without this requirement, you could decide to use the money in other ways—to finance your next business venture or your daughter's college education, for example—instead of plowing it back into your business. Although you might be able to continue running your business (and paying the rent) without replenishing the lost inventory or equipment, most landlords won't want to take this risk.

C. Rental Interruption Insurance

Hopefully, you've negotiated a termination clause that allows you to suspend rent payments or terminate the lease if you can't operate due to damage that wasn't your fault. (The termination clause is explained in Chapter 14, Section G.) Or, if your business is curtailed—say there is damage to only a portion of your space—you may have secured the right to "abate," or reduce, the rent according to your restricted use. But if you stop or cut back rent payments due to damaged premises, the landlord's income will suffer. The solution: "rental interruption" insurance that covers any suspended or abated rent that results from an incident that's covered by your policy.

Most careful landlords will insert a clause in the lease requiring rental interruption insurance (their lenders may demand it, too). Typically, the landlord will purchase it and the cost (the premiums) will be passed on to you. If you have a net lease, you may see an enumerated charge for this insurance. If you have a gross lease, the landlord no doubt factored in the cost when setting the rent. If your landlord requires rental interruption insurance, you'll want to consider the following two important points when the clause comes up for discussion.

1. Insure the Right Amount of Rent

If you have a gross lease, this calculation is simple: If you can't come up with a full rent payment, the landlord will want a monthly check from the insurance company equal to your monthly rent bill. But if you have a net lease, the monthly rent is hard to calculate with certainty because, in addition to a base rent, you pay fluctuating amounts of taxes, operating, and other insurance costs.

When you and the landlord negotiate this clause, do your best to choose a level of coverage that accurately includes these additional costs, as well as the base rent. If the policy limits prove to be too low—you discover that your real rent is much higher than the maximum the insurance company will pay—you may be stuck paying the difference. It will be a lot cheaper to pay a little more in premiums than it will be to make up the rent shortfall.

2. Choose an Appropriate Coverage Period

The landlord will want rent insurance for as long as it takes to repair or rebuild. How long is that? It depends on the size and complexity of the structure. A small strip mall can be rebuilt in six months; a multistory office building might take two years. If you choose a coverage period that's too short, the landlord won't be covered; and if it's unnecessarily long (for which you've paid large premiums), you've wasted money. Bargain for a coverage period that makes sense.

D. Business Interruption Insurance

If there's a fire or other disaster, your business will be interrupted until the damage is repaired. The property insurance policy will cover repairs to the building, but it won't compensate for the income you lose during the repair period. To make sure that you have money coming in even though you aren't operating, you can purchase Business Interruption Insurance (also known as Business Income Insurance).

You can think of this insurance as the tenant's version of rental insurance, explained above in Section C. Each policy compensates the holder for the loss of income brought about by a casualty loss that's covered by your policy. And as with rental insurance, you'll need to accurately estimate your income and choose appropriate policy limits. That way, the size of the check you'll get from the insurance company will truly replace the income you would have earned but for the calamity that interrupted your business.

It's not hard to understand why your landlord would want you to carry this policy. Without it, your business may go under—and there goes his rent-paying tenant. A landlord who's invested lots of time and money in the form of lease nego-tiations and space improvements has every reason to want you to be able to survive the period of rebuilding.

Business interruption insurance also covers your valuable papers and computer data. If your business is document-dependent (many are), and especially if it relies heavily on computer data, this coverage is essential. It covers loss to your business as a result of not having the equipment, your loss of income resulting from damage to your com-puter system, software, or other vital equipment.

E. Leasehold Insurance

If the landlord's property is totally or substantially destroyed in a disaster, you will probably terminate your lease (your termination clause ought to give you this option). All of a sudden, you'll be pitched back into the quest for new space. If you're fortunate, you'll find new digs for com-parable rent. But if your original lease was an unusual, great deal or the market has suddenly become very tight, you may end up paying lots more in rent.

To make up the difference between your old rent and a new, higher one, you can purchase "leasehold insurance." Many land-lords will not demand that you carry this insurance, having little interest in what happens to you after you clear out of his ravaged property. But a smart landlord will

understand that, if you owe him money for past rent at the moment disaster strikes, you'll be better able to pay off that debt if your new rental expenses are minimized courtesy of leasehold insurance.

If you have a choice in the matter (or if you want to argue your way out of a demand that you carry this insurance), compare the cost of the premiums against the length of your lease and the trend of the rental market. If you have a relatively short lease and you can count on being able to find replacement space at nearly the same rental rate, this coverage may not be worth it.

F. Waivers of Subrogation Rights

Somewhere in or near the end of the lease, you'll see a clause declaring that you agree to waive, or give up, your insurance company's "subrogation rights" against the landlord. There may be a companion phrase stating that the landlord agrees to waive *his* insurance company's subrogation rights against you. Fear not. We'll translate this stuff into English.

1. What Subrogation Means

"Subrogation" is a legal mouthful that stands for a simple concept. Basically, it describes what happens when you give your right to sue someone to somebody else. Suppose your neighbor's poorly trimmed tree falls on your house. You could, of course, sue the neighbor for the damage and cover the cost of repairs that way. But if you have a homeowner's policy, you'll probably file a claim with your company, which is much simpler. After all, that's why you have insurance. But after paying you, your insurance company might sue the neighbor to get reimbursed. Although the insurance company wasn't directly harmed (you were), it has the right to sue the neighbor because you have subrogated, or given, that right to the company. Your insurance company steps into your shoes and has the same right to sue your neighbor as you did. The fine print in your policy says so, though you probably didn't realize it.

However, if the insurance company agrees to waive its right of subrogation, it gives up the right to go after the person who caused the claim. In our example, the company wouldn't be able to sue the neighbor. Understandably, there are few situations in which insurance companies will give up the ability to recoup the money they spend on claims, but commercial leasing is one of them.

2. Why Insurance Companies Give Up Their Subrogation Rights

Let's change our example a little bit to place it in a commercial landlord-tenant situation. Suppose your landlord suffers a

loss due to your carelessness—your failure to switch off the coffeepot causes a small fire. If the landlord has insured the building, he may file a claim with his insurance company, which will pay the loss. Normally, the insurance company would look around to see if they could recoup the cost by suing the responsible party—in this case, you're the culprit. However, if the company has agreed to let the landlord waive, or give up, its subrogation rights against you, the insurance company is stuck. This means that they must eat the cost of the claim. Why would any insurance company do this?

Bear with us for a moment and consider the flip side of the picture—when you suffer a loss that's caused by your landlord. Again, you'd look to your insurance company, which would pay the claim. But when your insurance company searches for the responsible party, they see that it's the landlord. Again, if the company has agreed to let you waive their subrogation rights against the landlord, the company absorbs the cost of the claim. Are insurance companies really such nice guys?

The answer lies in understanding the big picture. Landlords and tenants know that they might accidentally cause damage or loss to the other. That's why they take out insurance. The idea is for the insurance money to cover the loss, so that neither landlord nor tenant is driven out of business being sued for a huge loss. If their own insurance companies can sue them, they've lost the benefit of having insurance.

And if you or the landlord are mortally wounded in a lawsuit brought by an insurance company out to recoup the cost of a claim, that person may go bankrupt or at least out of business, thereby ending the whole leasing relationship. From the insurance company's point of view, the end of the lease ends the opportunity to continue to collect premiums, too. In the end, the insurance industry decided that it was in their best interests to support the leasing transaction by agreeing not to sue the landlord or tenant for the losses that either might cause the other.

3. Make It Mutual

In order for the principle we've just described to work, waivers of subrogation have to be mutual. If you're going to waive your insurance company's subrogation rights against the landlord (which means that the company won't be able to sue the landlord for losses he causes them), then the landlord should waive his company's subrogation rights against you (so you won't be sued for losses you've caused the landlord's insurance company). It's common, however, for landlord leases to be one-way—you waive your insurance company's rights, but the landlord isn't required to waive his insurance company's rights.

One-way subrogation clauses are a mistake. You should bargain to make them reciprocal. When you do, steer clear of arguments that focus on "fairness" or "what's right." Instead, focus on the realities of business. If the landlord's carrier sues you, your business may be stressed or even bankrupted. This spells trouble for the landlord, who wants you to be healthy and prosper so that you can pay the rent and honor the rest of your lease obligations. When you consider that the landlord's insurance company won't even object to the landlord's waiver of their rights of subrogation, it makes little sense for the landlord to refuse your request. In short, it's in the landlord's own best interests to waive his carrier's subrogation rights against you.

G. Indemnity or Hold Harmless Clause

All landlord leases will have a clause entitled "Indemnity" or "Hold Harmless." Paragraph-long sentences manage to obscure the straightforward idea behind this clause. Here's what it means.

When you agree to indemnify someone else, you agree to be financially responsible for certain expenses that the other person might become obliged to pay from third parties. For example, if you agree to indemnify your business partner against losses he might suffer if the two of you got sued by investors, you'd be on the hook if investors brought a successful suit against your partner.

Don't confuse indemnities with exculpatory clauses. Exculpatory clauses are agreements that release someone in advance from liability for specific mistakes. In a nutshell, they're a free pass to screw up. Naturally, you'll see them written in favor of the landlord, applied to issues such as injuries that result from the landlord's negligence. In residential leasing, they're usually thrown out by judges when courts are asked to enforce them, but in a commercial setting, that outcome is not assured. You'll almost always want to use some bargaining capital to get an exculpatory clause out of your lease.

1. Indemnities Fill In Where Insurance Leaves Off

When you agree to indemnify your landlord, you're promising that you'll reimburse him for any losses he might suffer as a result of specified types of claims by third parties. It's that simple. Suppose, for example, that you and your landlord are sued by a customer who claims to have suffered an injury because you and/or the landlord carelessly maintained the property. The indemnity clause in your lease may require you to pay for the landlord's lawyer and any settlement or verdict that may be reached against the landlord. You're basically promising to act like an insurance company for your landlord.

Once you understand that an indemnity promise is like agreeing to be an insurance company, you're on the right track to understanding one very important truth about the real value of this clause. You and the landlord *already* have insurance, which will cover both of you for any of the losses that the indemnity promise might cover, right? So why does your landlord ask you for an indemnity promise—isn't it unnecessary?

The short answer is yes, in most cases. If you and the landlord have adequate insurance coverage, you'll have no need to look to the indemnity clause if a loss occurs. But the indemnity clause may come into play in a number of situations.

- **There's no insurance policy in place.** Perhaps your lease gives you and customers the right to park in the landlord's parking structure next to the building containing your space. If you or the landlord haven't purchased insurance for accidents within the parking structure, the indemnity clause may require you pick up the tab if a customer is hurt in the structure and sues the landlord.

- **The loss exceeds the policy limits.** Every insurance policy has a limit on the amount the insurance company is required to pay. If an insured suffers a loss that exceeds the limit, the insured pays the difference. For example, suppose a customer slips on your floor, sues you and the landlord, and wins a judgment that exceeds the limit of the policy. Your promise to indemnify the landlord means that you will pay the excess, even if you were only partially responsible for the injury.

- **The insurance has lapsed or been canceled.** It's not uncommon for landlords and tenants to fail to pay their premiums on time. And sometimes carriers will cancel policies or refuse to renew them. If you and the landlord lose your insurance protection, it's a very serious matter. That's why you should insist on being notified any time the landlord's carrier sends nasty reminders to him to pay up. A smart landlord will demand the same of you. But if a policy does, indeed, lapse or get cancelled, you will become the insurer for the landlord as a result of your promise, in the indemnity clause, to cover the landlord if you cause him to experience a monetary loss.

In sum, your indemnity promise will come into play where your insurance protection leaves off. If you have a thorough set of insurance policies that the two of you monitor carefully, the chances that your indemnity promise will be called into play are minimal.

Press for a statement in the indemnity clause that your promise to indemnify the landlord will not relieve him of his obligations under the insurance clause. A clever landlord who is obligated under the insurance clause to insure the property or business might decide to rely on your indemnity promise instead. Of course, this would be foolish (your reserves probably aren't sufficient to cover a big claim), but that might not stop a landlord who's looking to cut operating costs.

2. Make It Mutual

The landlord's lease surely requires you to indemnify him—but rarely will a landlord agree, without pressure, to indemnify a tenant. You can see why: The landlord won't want to reach into his wallet in case he causes you to suffer a loss that is not fully compensated by insurance proceeds.

You should try, nevertheless, for a mutual indemnity clause. If the landlord won't give it, you can still protect yourself by purchasing higher amounts of insurance. For example, if the two of you are sued by an injured visitor and the insurance policy limit is lower than the settlement or judgment, you will end up paying the difference if the fault lies with the landlord but he has refused to give you an indemnity promise. You wouldn't have a problem, however, if you had purchased a Commercial General Liability policy with higher limits. If you're worried about the landlord's refusal to give you an indemnity, the solution is to buy more insurance. ∎

Breaking the Lease, Disputes, and Attorney Fees

Despite everyone's best intentions to live up to the lease, either the landlord or you—or both—may fall short. (In legalese, breaking a lease provision is called a "breach.") The landlord, for example, may not come through with improvements as promised, or may renege on maintenance obligations or fail to provide required parking. You, on the other hand, may be late with the rent or not up to snuff when it comes to honoring other parts of the lease, such as promptly disposing of trash. This chapter discusses the lease clauses that concern:

- what you and the landlord can do about each other's breaches—that is, what remedies you have available
- ways you can iron out the problem—using mediation and arbitration—short of resorting to courts and litigation, and
- who pays for attorneys' fees and court costs if the dispute boils over into litigation.

Be advised, however, that we do not cover how to handle court fights over terminations and disputes. A commercial eviction suit is typically fast and complicated—a situation in which you definitely want to have a lawyer from the start.

A. The Landlord's Remedies If You Fail to Pay Rent or Breach Another Lease Term

If you don't spend time negotiating how you'll respond to each other's shortcomings, be forewarned that you're headed for trouble. The two of you will end up arguing about the response to the shortcoming as well as the underlying problem itself. Far better to set up, in advance, an understanding of what can and can't be done in the face of either landlord or tenant misbehavior. That's what the remedies clause of the lease is supposed to do.

An evenhanded lease clause will set the ground rules for each of you. The remedies clause will define what you can do if the landlord breaches, as well as the landlord's options when you breach. Not surprisingly, the landlord's lease is likely to be pretty thin when it comes to explaining what you can do if the landlord messes up. The owner's list of permitted reactions to your failures, however, will be long, detailed and punitive.

If you fail to pay the rent on time or break any other important lease clause, in most cases the landlord will want to be able to pressure you into compliance, but won't want to terminate the lease. (After all, terminating the lease will hardly be advantageous, since that will end the rent stream for sure.) The remedies will be designed to make your lapses sufficiently painful that you won't want to suffer the consequences, but a smart landlord won't impose such harsh terms that you'll be driven out of business. At some point, however, the land-lord will have the right to consider the mis-behavior grounds for terminating the lease. Let's look at the common remedies, from the least painful (where you're notified of the problem and given a chance to fix it) to the final blow (your lease is terminated).

1. Notice and Cure: Your Second Chance

You might break a lease obligation without even knowing it. For example, suppose your lease makes you responsible for com-plying with the Americans With Disabilities Act (ADA). If you've misunderstood the ADA's requirements, you may be in breach of your lease without realizing it. Since most landlords understand that a tenant breach may be inadvertent, they agree in the lease to notify you of the problem (called "notice") and give you a specified amount of time to rectify (or "cure") the problem before taking sterner measures. And even when it comes to deliberate breaches—such as failing to pay the rent because you can't—landlords typically extend the same second chance. They'd rather get their money late than have to start over with a new tenant.

Typically, the notice and cure period will be rather short for monetary misdeeds (such as failure to pay the rent), but may be longer for problems that take longer to fix, such as widening a doorway so that it meets the ADA's accessibility requirements. When you look at the landlord's lease clause, be sure that it gives you a reasonable notice and cure period for both types of defaults.

Repeated defaults may eliminate your right to a cure period. Landlords don't have endless patience, and may decide that they cannot tolerate certain repeated misdeeds (especially late rent payments). The notice and cure provision in the lease may specify that if the same or a similar breach occurs more than a certain number of times within a certain time period, you will no longer be entitled to a cure period. At that point, the landlord will turn to more drastic measures.

Make sure that starting work will constitute a cure. If resolving your breach will take a bit of time (such as con-forming your space to the code requirements that pertain to your business), you won't be able to fully comply in a matter of days. Ne-gotiate for the understanding that if you begin work during the cure period and diligently and reasonably continue, the landlord will recognize these efforts as constituting a cure. On a similar note, bargain for the right to extend the cure time if circumstances beyond your control, such as a materials delivery delay, frustrate your efforts to comply.

2. Landlord Self-Help: Doing It For You

If you fail to live up to a lease obligation during the notice and cure period, the landlord may decide to fix the problem for you. Known as a landlord's right of "self-help," it means that the landlord can do what you should have been doing, then sue you for the expense (or deduct it from your security deposit, which you will then have to top off). For example, if you're late with the rent, the landlord will take it from the security deposit (and then demand that you bring the deposit back up to its original sum). Or, a tenant who doesn't maintain the property as required in the lease, or who parks in others' spaces, may find the maintenance done and his car towed—and a bill from the landlord for the work and the services of the tow truck.

A landlord who wants the right to act on your behalf must spell this out in the lease. A tough self-help clause will give the landlord the option of using self-help or not (giving the landlord the right to terminate instead), and will entitle you to very little notice. You might be charged interest on the money the landlord has had to spend, and will be given little time to pay the bill. If you value your tenancy, however, these consequences will be preferable to a termination.

Landlords have a particularly harsh method of dealing with tenants who fail to reimburse the landlord for money spent on self-help measures. Careful landlords will specify that any sums they have to spend on self-help will be designated "additional rent"—in other words, it's lumped together with your monthly rent bill. Giving the debt this label makes it easier for the landlord to sue you for the unpaid bill. Here's why: You know what happens when you don't pay the nor-mal rent—the landlord can terminate and evict in a court proceeding that is quickly scheduled and very short. By contrast, a typical civil suit over an unpaid bill takes forever. When the unpaid self-help bill is designated as "rent," it means that the landlord can bypass the slow civil suit and instead sue to evict in order to collect—a powerful incentive for you to pay up.

3. Terminating the Lease

The next weapon in the landlord's arsenal is the right to terminate the lease. If the landlord terminates, you'll have to move out. If you don't, the landlord may file an eviction lawsuit against you. Clearly, neither prospect is a welcome event. Even if you plan never to let matters get to this extreme, it's wise to pay attention to this clause.

a. When Can the Landlord Terminate?

A harsh clause will allow the landlord to terminate for any lease violation, but many leases permit termination only for "material" or "significant" breaches. These are slippery concepts, which should be nailed down in the lease. You wouldn't want the landlord to jump to termination over a breach that looks major to the landlord but minor to you.

> **EXAMPLE:** Brandon's lease permitted the landlord to terminate "upon any breach of the aforesaid clauses." The lease required Brandon to lock and

secure the building when he left in the evenings. Brandon was conscientious about this duty, but forgot one night. The next day, his landlord terminated the lease.

Brandon realized that the real reason the landlord wanted him out was to make way for a new tenant, who could be charged a higher rent than the favorable rent Brandon was paying. But Brandon had no grounds for stopping the eviction—after all, he did break the lease, and the clause did not differentiate between minor and major breaches. If it had, Brandon might have been able to convince a judge that his one lapse was not a major breach, and he might have saved his lease.

One way to limit the ability of the landlord to invoke the termination remedy is to make sure that the landlord does not have the unilateral right to decide what is "material" and what is not. If the two of you disagree as to whether your breach is minor or major, using a dispute resolution mechanism, such as binding arbitration, will give you a reasonable assurance of fairness. You should bargain for the right to invoke the lease's arbitration clause, as explained below in Section D, before the landlord may pronounce that the lease is terminated. In addition, you might press for some guidelines right in the termination clause itself, such as allowing the landlord to use the termination right only if your breach has resulted in the landlord's loss of more than a specified amount of money.

b. After the Fall: Your Continued Obligations

Although your lease clause probably won't address it, be sure you understand what happens *after* the landlord terminates the lease. Contrary to what you might expect, you won't normally just walk away without financial consequences. In fact, depending on market conditions, you might end up paying a considerable amount of money in damages. Here's why.

When you and the landlord signed the lease, you promised to pay a certain amount of rent for a specified number of years. The landlord is legally entitled to that money, regardless of the fact that your misbehavior caused him to terminate the lease. In most states, however, the landlord cannot sit back and sue you for unpaid rent as it becomes due. Usually, the landlord must take reasonable steps to rerent the space. Once the space is rerented, the landlord credits the new rent money against your debt. If the new rent doesn't cover what you owe, you pay the difference. In legal jargon, the landlord's duty to rerent and credit your debt is called "mitigation of damages."

You can see that your continued responsibility for rent will depend on market conditions. If you were paying below-market rates, or if the new tenant was simply unable to negotiate as low a rent as you did, you may end up with no rent liability, since the new tenant's rent will cover (or exceed) what the landlord had been charging you. But if the market is soft and the landlord can't rerent for several months, or the value of the location has gone down, or the income from the new tenant doesn't match yours, you'll pay the difference.

4. Recapturing the Space

You might think that a termination of your lease—and the possibility that a new tenant's rent won't cover your obligation to pay the balance of your rent—would be the worst thing that could happen if you fail to honor your lease and it's terminated. Actually, there's a variation on this move that could be even more devastating. If the landlord's remedies clause has a provision allowing "recapture," you could be in for more grief.

Recapture allows the landlord to take over your space and lease it out to another tenant *without* terminating your lease. Or, to add insult to injury, the clause might also allow the landlord to take over your business and run it. Either way, you remain obligated under the terms of the lease for rent *and everything else,* such as insurance obligations, repair responsibilities, and maintenance. If the new tenant (or the landlord, now running your shop) is successful and honors your obligations—in particular, pays the rent on time—you might not be too put out. But if the new operation falls short with respect to any lease obligation, you will be on the hook to satisfy the lease provision until the lease runs out.

If your lease has a recapture right, you'll hesitate to purposefully sabotage the lease in order to get out from under it. For example, if you are paying above-market rates, or the neighborhood has gone downhill, or a new place across town now strikes your fancy, you might be tempted to scuttle your lease in order to be free to move. Knowing that the landlord may decide to exercise his recapture right and keep you in the background as a guarantor for the new tenant will make you think twice.

5. The Landlord's Choices

The landlord's impressive list of permitted responses to your misdeeds should make you think carefully before dishonoring your lease. You need to understand two additional features of your landlord's response rights.

- **The landlord can choose which remedy to use.** Typically, a lease won't require the landlord to pursue milder remedies before turning to more drastic ones. Aside from a requirement that the landlord notify you of a problem and give you the chance to cure it, the lease will probably allow the landlord to go directly for termination or recapture, at the landlord's option—unless you can negotiate otherwise. If you've been saving your negotiation power for anything, here is a good place use it.

- **The landlord can use more than one remedy.** There's no rule against piling on in commercial leases. The remedies clause will undoubtedly let the landlord use self-help (for example, to repair a damaged door, at your expense, if the lease required you to fix it) *and* terminate the lease—again, unless your powers of negotiation result in a different understanding.

What Happens If You Become Insolvent or Declare Bankruptcy?

You may see a clause in your lease entitled "Tenant's Insolvency" or "Tenant's Bankruptcy." These clauses are intended to allow the landlord to terminate the lease if you file for bankruptcy or become insolvent.

Bankruptcy. Under federal law, your landlord cannot automatically terminate your lease if you file for bankruptcy. However, this doesn't stop many landlords from inserting a clause to this effect into their leases. If your landlord's lease includes such a clause, consider it a warning—this person doesn't know the law or is trying to get around it.

Insolvency. Landlords and their lawyers who understand that bankruptcy alone can't legally trigger a termination have come up with an alternative. They use a clause stating that if you can't pay your debts as they come due—in other words, you're insolvent—the lease can be terminated (even if you're managing to pay the rent). Some courts will enforce this clause.

⚠️ **Don't use bankruptcy as a means to get out from under an unfavorable lease.** When you declare bankruptcy, the bankruptcy trustee will take over your lease and often assign it to someone else. Using Bankruptcy Court to get you out of an above-market lease doesn't sit well with judges, and the landlord may successfully prevent your bankruptcy filing if it can convince the judge that dumping an unfavorable lease is your dominant motive in filing. If the space has become unsuitable or too expensive, deal with it by finding a substitute tenant or renegotiating the lease.

B. The "No Waiver" Clause

It's not unusual for a landlord to insist on a remedies clause full of severe responses to a tenant's misbehavior—and then not use those weapons. For example, the lease may allow your landlord to charge you for repairing maintenance items that you fail to fix—but the landlord may let it slide. Or the landlord may repeatedly accept your late rent without consequences, in spite of his right to charge late fees or to cancel your lease after two or three late payments within a year.

1. When the Landlord Ignores Her Remedies

If your landlord foregoes the responses that the lease allows, you may be tempted to conclude that those remedies are no longer available. For example, if you repeatedly get away with paying rent late, you may conclude that the late fee provision is a thing of the past. You may even begin to count on the landlord's forebearance—for instance, if the lease gives you ten parking spots but you've been using 20 without objection from the landlord, you may decide to expand operations in reliance on those extra spots.

Relying on a landlord's apparent disregard of lease remedies can get complicated. Let's say you're later hit with a late rent charge or a termination notice for violating one of the lease clauses you thought the landlord was ignoring. You may feel you're being treated unfairly. After all, wasn't the lease modified by the landlord's apparent willingness to not strictly enforce it? You may decide to challenge the landlord's sudden decision to reactivate the remedies in the lease. If a court gets involved, the judge may side with you, ruling that by consistently foregoing remedies, the landlord has waived the right to use the lease's enforcement clause.

Most landlords want to make sure that they can have their remedies and ignore them too—that their past leniency won't result in losing the remedy in the future. So you'll see a clause in the lease entitled "nonwaiver," which warns you that a decision to forego a remedy won't mean that the landlord has waived it forever. Fortunately for you, even with a nonwaiver clause in a lease, a judge may rule that it

would be unfair to allow a landlord to resurrect a remedy that's been clearly and consistently ignored. This is especially likely if you've spent money or made other business decisions in reliance on the landlord's practice of ignoring remedy rights.

2. When the Landlord Acts Inconsistently

When landlords ignore their remedies and then try to invoke them, they may find themselves cut off, even if they've inserted a no-waiver clause in the lease. But what if the landlord has utilized a remedy—but then does something that affirms the lease? How does the law handle inconsistent behavior?

Fortunately for you, the law is on your side here. Simply put, the landlord can't say, "It's over" and also act as if it's not. For example, accepting rent after the landlord has sent a notice of termination for late rent will typically cancel the effect of the termination. Similarly, a request for an operating expense payment or a reminder that your part of the tax bill is due will generally nullify the landlord's prior termination notice. A court may throw out a lease clause that attempts to change this rule.

C. Your Remedies If the Landlord Breaches

If the landlord breaches important obligations in the lease, such as the duty to pay property taxes or maintain property insurance, your business operations could be placed in grave jeopardy. Unpaid property taxes can lead to tax liens and a forced sale of the building, courtesy of the government. Unpaid insurance premiums mean that the building may not get repaired if a fire or other disaster causes damage. Yet you'll often see lease clauses that merely obligate landlords to use "diligent efforts" to cure any of their lapsed obligations. You can't live safely with this velvet hammer. If possible, negotiate for some reasonable response rights of your own.

1. Give the Landlord a Reasonable Time to Cure

If the landlord doesn't come through with promised maintenance or a host of other obligations that he's taken on via the lease, you'll want to hold his feet to the fire, but not without giving him a chance to fix the problem. It's almost always to your advantage to use gentle persuasion before resorting to the time-consuming, hostile tactics described in the sections below.

Your landlord has hopefully extended to you a similar notice and cure period for your lease violations. It's fair and reasonable for you to do the same. Your landlord will insist on written notice and a fairly long cure period, which you may negotiate to a shorter time if you have the power. You may want to negotiate for the right to bypass the notice and cure requirement if there is imminent danger to people or property. For example, you won't want to be delayed by a notice and cure requirement if a maintenance problem that is usually the responsibility of the landlord poses a serious risk of harm.

2. Negotiate for the Right to Do It Yourself

Just as the landlord has probably negotiated for the right to cure your defaults and bill you for them (see Section A2, above), you too will want to have the same right. As you might expect, landlords hate to give tenants a self-help right because they don't want you or your contractors messing with their property. Nor do they want to be financially beholden to you, which will happen if you perform a maintenance task or pay an important bill.

Having a self-help option is particularly useful when the landlord has retained repair and maintenance responsibilities that, if left undone, will impair your ability to conduct your business. In addition, if the landlord lets monetary obligations go unpaid, such as the need to make payments on a loan secured by the building, it may be to your advantage to pay the debt yourself and then collect from the landlord.

True, collecting will be no picnic (you're probably looking at a lawsuit), but it may be preferable to the alternative—a foreclosure by the landlord's mortgage holder, which may seriously disrupt your business.

As a practical matter, making the landlord's loan payment yourself may sometimes make sense if you're renting an entire building, but you probably couldn't comfortably make the payment on a multi-tenant building.

3. Rent Offsets

When your landlord doesn't follow through with lease obligations, it would be nice if you could simply do what needs to be done and deduct your expenses from your rent. This remedy, called a "rent offset" or "rent set-off," differs from the self-help remedy described above in that self-help doesn't result in your owing less rent (you have to sue to get reimbursed).

An offset right is similar to the "repair and deduct" remedy in residential lease situations. Unlike residential tenants in many states, however, where the right to make repairs and deduct the cost from your rent check is guaranteed by state law, commercial tenants don't automatically have this remedy. To get this right, you must put it in your lease. If your bargaining power allows, consider raising this in lease negotiations. With a lease clause giving you the right to deduct from your rent any sums

you lay out on the landlord's behalf, you won't be out of pocket for repairs or other costs you spring for. Of course, the landlord won't like receiving less rent, and will probably object to a lease clause giving you a right to deduct.

Keep in mind that if the building secures a loan, the loan terms may not allow the landlord to agree to a lease with an offset right. The lender wants to make sure that your rent, which helps fund the loan payments, will be paid in full each month.

> ⚠️ **Use your offset right carefully and only when you're sure you've acted correctly.** If the landlord challenges your use of the offset right (arguing that he really has kept his end of the bargain when it comes to maintenance, for example, and that you're being unreasonably demanding), the consequences could be serious. Remember, offsetting means paying less rent. A landlord who gets a short rent check has the option to terminate the tenancy and sue to evict. If you lose this battle, you'll lose the lease. Instead, pay the expense and then sue the landlord. If you lose *this* lawsuit, you're out some time and money but you still have your tenancy.

4. When Can You Cancel the Lease?

The most obvious and the most drastic remedy you will want in the lease is the right to terminate the lease when the landlord breaches. The landlord has undoubtedly insisted on his right to do the same if you breach; now it's your turn.

It won't be to anyone's advantage if you terminate the lease for unimportant landlord breaches. The landlord will insist on some guidelines—and you, too, will hopefully have established some for the landlord's termination rights, as explained above in Section A. The suggestions there apply equally to your termination rights. For example, providing for binding arbitration to decide whether the landlord's breach justifies termination is a good idea. And it would be reasonable to agree that you won't terminate unless your profits have been reduced by a specified amount. If the landlord's failure to maintain the building has made some of your space unusable, you might agree that you won't have the right to terminate unless a certain percentage has been affected.

D. Mediation and Arbitration

Many leases include a clause that covers what you and the landlord will do if a dispute arises concerning each other's performance of lease obligations. The clause may be called "Arbitration" or "Dispute Resolution" (often referred to as the ADR clause). It's to your advantage to have an ADR clause in the lease. Without it, the landlord may go running off to court over a dispute that could be handled more quickly and cheaply by a mediator or arbitrator.

In addition, an arbitration clause is an essential check on your landlord's ability to invoke his lease termination rights. As explained in Section A, above, your landlord will probably demand the right to terminate if you do not live up to your lease obligations. To prevent termination over minor misdeeds, you'll want a neutral third party to decide whether termination is merited. A separate lease clause with an arbitration mechanism will fill the bill.

1. Mediation

Your dispute resolution clause may provide that the two of you will seek mediation before turning to arbitration or the courts. Mediation is a process in which two or more people involved in a dispute come together to try to work out a solution to their problem with the help of a neutral third person, called the mediator. The mediator is normally trained in conflict resolution, although the extent of this training can

vary greatly. Unlike a judge or an arbitrator, the mediator does not take sides or make decisions. The mediator's job is to help the disputants evaluate their goals and options in order to find their own solution. If mediation fails, you're free to turn to lawyers and litigation or, if your lease provides for it, to arbitration. Mediation obviously works only when there is a good faith dispute. If one side is out to cheat the other, mediation will simply be a waste of time.

The key to understanding mediation is to realize that it is noncoercive. This means that because the mediator has no authority to impose a decision, nothing will be decided unless both you and the landlord agree to it. However, in the event you do arrive at a mutual agreement, its terms can easily be made legally binding. One way to do this is to write the agreement in the form of an enforceable contract.

You each lose nothing by agreeing to a lease clause in which you promise to try mediation before resorting to stronger measures. If the landlord balks at adding a mediation clause, consider it a red flag. Does the landlord think that there's no room for a good-faith disagreement between businesspeople? Does this person assume that every problem deserves a heavy-handed response? When you ask why the landlord refuses to try mediation, listen carefully to the answer. It may reveal a naivete about the process of doing business or a predisposition to respond unthinkingly and harshly. Both spell difficulties ahead.

For more information on mediation, see _Mediate, Don't Litigate,_ by Peter Lovenheim and Lisa Guerin (Nolo). You'll find information on how to choose a mediator, prepare a case, go through the mediation process, and arrive at a win-win agreement.

2. Arbitration

Most leases prepared by landlords or their counsel will have a clause requiring landlord and tenant to submit their unresolved disagreements to arbitration. Unlike mediation, an arbitrator's decision is enforceable, just like a decision from a judge (arbitration that can be enforced is also known as "binding arbitration"). But compared to a court battle, arbitration is sometimes quicker and cheaper (most of the time, the loser will pay the entire expense). It's almost always a better alternative than going to court, but not necessarily because it might be cheaper or faster. Rather, as explained below in Section 3a, the real advantage of arbitration is that it gives you the ability to bring your case before someone knowledgeable about commercial leasing.

The landlord's lender may insist that all his leases have binding arbitration clauses as a condition of his mortgage or loan. Lenders do so out of concern that juries will be biased against property owners—so they are banking on a fairer shake from professional arbitrators. Lenders also don't want landlords to incur the expenses of litigation, which might cut into the landlord's ability to make loan or mortgage payments.

There are, however, some recognized drawbacks to using arbitration instead of litigation. First, although the entire process may be cheaper in the end, the initial cost to both of you is likely to be high, since arbitrators don't come cheap and begin charging by the hour as soon as they get the case (at the end, the loser will pay the entire bill, but at the start you'll need to split the costs). Second, in a lawsuit you have several tools to ferret out the evidence the other side holds. Known collectively as "discovery," these tools (which include depositions, requests for documents, and demands for physical evidence) are often severely curtailed in an arbitration proceeding. Finally, you have very limited rights to appeal an arbitrator's decision. You may have a right to appeal based on the arbitrator's misconduct or clear misuse of discretion, but that's it. With a lawsuit, the loser can raise numerous arguments to support an argument for a reversal.

3. Negotiating a Good Arbitration Clause

Knowing a little about how arbitration works should help you evaluate the landlord's lease clause. If possible, negotiate along the following lines.

a. Choosing the Arbitrator

The key to successful arbitration is to make sure that you present your case to someone familiar with commercial real estate law and practice. If you end up with an arbitrator who has never looked at a commercial lease, chances are you will know more about the issues than the arbitrator does. By the time the arbitrator gets up to speed on the way commercial leasing works and the relevant law, you will have lost precious time (and you'll be paying by the hour for this education).

To make sure you won't get stuck with someone who has handled nothing but wills and estates, press for language in the clause that specifies the requirements for the arbitrator. You'll want the arbitrator to be an attorney with at least ten years of commercial real estate experience, some of it within the last five years at least. The clause should specify that you and the landlord must agree on the arbitrator. There are three ways that you can provide for the choice of arbitrators:

- name the arbitrator now (and waive any conflicts the arbitrator or her law firm may have, which might arise if the arbitrator's partner represented your landlord at some time in the past)
- specify that each of you will choose one person, and the two arbitrators will agree upon a third, or

- agree that you will submit the dispute to an arbitrator from a dispute resolution service (see below).

The American Arbitration Association (AAA, www.adr.org) supplies arbitrators to people who request them. The AAA screens the arbitrators (most of whom are lawyers and retired judges) and has its own set of arbitration rules. (All states have their own rules, also, which the arbitration organization may modify.) There are other arbitration groups that may do business in your area. Your attorney or the landlord's lawyer is likely to be familiar with them.

If you decide to use the AAA or another resolution service, it's smart to include in the lease clause a list of qualifications that your eventual arbitrator must have. For example, you might provide that any dispute will be arbitrated by a person with at least ten years of commercial real estate practice and so on. When the time comes, you'll supply the arbitration service with your requirements and ask for a list of potential arbitrators and a brief resume for each. After each of you has had time to check them out, you can choose.

Most litigants will tell you that juries and judges tend to be biased against landlords. Smart landlords know it and for this reason will readily agree to submit disputes to nonjudges who are commercial leasing experts.

b. Use Baseball Arbitration: It Forces You to Be Reasonable

If you are serious about resolving disputes informally rather than through litigation, use baseball arbitration, so called because it was first used by major league baseball when dealing with players' disputes over salaries. In baseball arbitration, the arbitrator can choose one side's figure or the other's —but nothing else. This rule encourages each side to be realistic, since the arbitrator will reject an inflated claim if the other side's figure is closer to the arbitrator's view of the real measure of damages. And it fosters compromise, since each side knows that the outcome can only be one of two choices. Often, the disputants will decide that it's better to settle than risk having the other side win completely.

c. Get Some Discovery

The single most awful, expensive, petty, and nasty aspect of civil litigation is a discovery fight—an argument among lawyers over whether one side must answer a question or turn over a piece of paper. And even when discovery doesn't turn vicious, it often takes forever, as one after another witness and expert is questioned under oath ("deposed") and asked to answer endless written questions. When you choose arbitration over litigation, you're largely doing so to avoid these lengthy dramas.

However, it's foolish to leave yourself without any means of looking into the landlord's file cabinets and ledgers or requiring him or his experts to answer tough questions under oath. If you cut off your ability to demand key evidence, your session before the arbitrator may degenerate into a swearing match between you and the landlord, devoid of any hard facts. So make sure that the lease clause you sign permits a reasonable amount of discovery. To cut down on the chances of abuse, you might press for a provision that places a timetable on the discovery process, requiring you and the landlord to finish all questioning and requests within 30 days after you've chosen an arbitrator.

E. Attorney Fees

Most commercial leases will have an "Attorney Fees and Costs" clause at the end. This clause usually provides that if you and the landlord end up in a legal battle over the lease, the loser will have to pay the winning (or "prevailing") party's attorney fees, plus the costs of preparing the case, including service of process, depositions, court filings, and expert witness fees. The clause will apply to disputes that have gone to arbitration, too, since one or both of you may hire lawyers to help you prepare for your case (normally, the clause will not apply to lawyers you might hire to help you prepare for mediations).

An attorney fees clause has the laudable effect of making both of you think twice before initiating arbitration or bringing a lawsuit that you aren't quite sure you can win, since the consequences of losing can be quite expensive. But this clause may not be entirely straightforward. You should consider the issues in the following sections when reading the clause presented to you by your landlord. You may want to negotiate for some changes, as suggested.

Who Pays When There's No Attorney Fees Clause?

Unless you and the landlord have an attorney fees clause in your lease, most of the time each side will end up paying their own attorney and court costs, regardless of who wins or prevails. Now and then, a judge orders the losing side to pay the winner's expenses. This happens only rarely, and only when:

- the conduct of the loser was particularly outrageous—for example, filing a totally frivolous lawsuit, or
- the legal theory that the winner has used specifies that the winner gets fees and costs—for example, many antidiscrimination laws provide that the losing defendant must pay the winning plaintiff's costs.

⚠ **Avoid clauses that make the losing tenant pay the landlord's costs—but if the landlord loses, the landlord doesn't have to pay your fees and costs.** This is a pretty shifty arrangement, and it hasn't gone down well. By law in California, New York, and a number of other states, any attorney fees clause in a lease must work both ways, even if it's not written that way. This means that even if the lease states that only your landlord is entitled to attorney fees for winning a lawsuit, you will be entitled to collect your attorney fees from your landlord if you prevail. Your landlord would be ordered to pay whatever amount the judge decides is reasonable.

1. What Kinds of Disputes Are Covered?

An attorney fees clause covers only those disputes that concern the meaning or implementation of your lease, such as a dispute about rent, operating charges, or the meaning of an option. For example, in a multi-tenant building, the lease probably governs your portion of operating charges. If you and the landlord disagree about how the costs are accounted for and divvied up, the next step will be mediation or a request for arbitration (if there's a mediation or arbitration clause in your lease), or a lawsuit to compel you to pay (if there's no ADR clause in the lease).

It's important to understand that the attorney fees clause won't come into play if you and the landlord are involved in a legal hassle that doesn't involve the meaning or implementation of an obligation in the lease, such as a personal injury lawsuit or a discrimination claim. For example, suppose you suspect that the landlord is giving you less favorable terms because you are a woman or a member of another legally protected minority group. You decide to sue, basing your case on a state statute forbidding discrimination in business dealings. If you win, you can't look to the attorney fees clause to support a claim for fees and costs, since the landlord's actions weren't lease violations. But if you're lucky, the anti-discrimination law in your state will itself provide that if you win, the landlord must pay your fees and costs.

2. How Expensive Can Legal Costs Get?

The attorney fees clause will usually specify that the winner is entitled to "reasonable" fees. This means that if the landlord hires the most expensive lawyer in town and the lawyer runs up an enormous bill, you won't necessarily pay the full amount if you lose. A judge may decide that the fees weren't "reasonable," given the facts of your case, and may reduce them to an appropriate amount.

If the "reasonable" modifier isn't in your clause, suggest that it be added. In most situations, a judge can reduce an exorbitant fee demand even without it, but it's a good idea to have that standard in the clause anyway.

3. What Happens If You Settle or the Case Is Dismissed?

If you and the landlord proceed all the way through trial (or arbitration) and end up with a decision by a judge, jury, or arbitrator, in some cases one of you will emerge a clear winner. Then it will be obvious who has to pay whose fees and costs.

But often the outcome isn't so cut and dried. You and the landlord may settle the dispute before you get to a hearing or trial —and there may not be a clear winner or loser. For example, suppose the landlord claims that you owe a specified amount of money for property taxes. Preferring to get the incident over with, you offer to pay a lesser amount and the landlord accepts your offer rather than gamble on losing completely in court. Who won? The same murkiness can attend an arbitrator's or jury's award, too—we've all heard of juries that "find" for one side but award only nominal damages (sometimes only one dollar). Who wins then?

A carefully written attorney fees clause will specify that the "prevailing party" will be the one entitled to collect from the other. But the question remains: Who was the prevailing party? In some states and in some situations, that decision will be made for you by state law or by the judge hearing the case. If a lawsuit is voluntarily dismissed before trial in a settlement, there may be no prevailing party, and each of you will pay your own expenses. Other states allow the disputing parties to work out the matter of fees and costs as part of their settlement discussions. If the case goes to trial or to an arbitration hearing, you can ask the judge or arbitrator to declare who the prevailing party is. For now, understand that your attorney fees clause can be much more complicated in practice than it appears.

4. Should You Have an Attorney Fees Clause?

Is it a good idea to include an attorney fees clause in your lease? It depends. The presence of an attorney fees clause will make it far easier for you to find a willing lawyer to take a case that does not have the potential for a hefty money judgment. For example, if you're hit with a hefty operating cost overcharge and can't resolve the dispute through mediation, you may end up in litigation. If your lease has a clause providing that the loser pays the winner, the landlord will pay your attorney—if you win. Knowing this, a lawyer will be more likely to take your case. Similarly, if your case has the potential for only a small monetary award but will involve a lot of work, a lawyer will be more willing to take it knowing that the fees will come from the landlord and not from your modest winnings.

On the other hand, you may prefer not to have an attorney fees clause. You might reason that your landlord will be more apt to compromise any dispute if he can't sue you and feel confident that he can also recover his attorney fees.

EXAMPLE: Jake rented space for his plumbing store from Toni, his landlady. His lease obligated him to pay a portion of the operating costs. It also had an attorney fees clause that required the losing side to pay the winner's fees and costs.

A year into the five-year term, Toni remodeled the building and gave Jake a separate entrance and his own bathroom facilities. However, she continued to charge him for common area maintenance.

Jake protested the CAM charge, arguing that he shouldn't have to pay it since he no longer shared any common areas with other tenants. Their attempts at mediation failed, and Jake and Toni headed for court, accompanied by their lawyers. The case settled on the eve of trial. Predictably enough, the settlement involved a compromise on both sides. Because there was no clear winner, Jake and Toni each paid their lawyers and court costs themselves. ■

Chapter 17

Foreclosures, Condemnations, Guarantors, and Other Clauses

Most commercial leases include a cluster of clauses at the end that serve to tidy things up. These clauses cover topics such as:

- your right to stay on as a tenant in a foreclosure situation—which might happen if the landlord doesn't make payments on a loan secured by the building
- how you and the landlord will settle matters if the property is partially or wholly condemned by a government entity
- how you should leave the property when you move out
- whether the lease is the sole and complete document describing your leasing deal
- whether someone will stand behind your financial obligations if you can't pay, and
- what will happen to the lease if a portion of it is ruled unenforceable by a judge.

A. Subordination and Attornment

Somewhere near the end of the landlord's lease, you may see a clause entitled "Subordination." Perhaps it will be joined with equally bizarre words, "Nondisturbance and Attornment." This clause, which is also known as the "SNDA" clause, wins the prize for packing the most legal jargon into one paragraph (or maybe three). You may be tempted to pass over it (who can read this stuff?), but that would be a mistake. This clause can determine your right to stay on as a tenant if the landlord doesn't make payments on a loan secured by the building. The landlord's lender—generally a bank—may foreclose and, depending on the law in your state and the wording of this clause, may be able to boot you out before the end of your lease.

An SNDA clause can be the most one-sided provision in the entire lease. If you have the bargaining clout, you'll want to use it here to negotiate some fairness. This section explains what this clause means and how to make sure that your needs (to stay in business and keep your lease) are given the same protection as your landlord's (to be able to use the property as collateral for any loans, past or future).

⚠ **Leases are not wiped out if the landlord sells the building in a nonforeclosure situation.** If your landlord voluntarily sells the property during the lifetime of your lease, the new owner takes over subject to your lease. In other words, you stay and simply deal with the new owner.

1. The Lease Doesn't Address the Consequences of a Foreclosure

If your lease has no clause concerning the consequences of a foreclosure, settled principles of law will supply the answers. Your fate after a foreclosure sale will depend on whether you began your tenancy before or after the landlord took out the loan, and perhaps on the law in the state in which the building is located. Here are the legal rules that will apply by default unless you and the landlord decide otherwise in your lease:

- **Rule 1. Your lease survives if it pre-dates the loan.** If your lease began before the landlord pledged the building as security for a loan, in all states the owner who buys at a foreclosure sale (or the bank, if it decides to keep the building) must honor your lease. Simply put, since you were first, your lease lives on.
- **Rule 2. Your lease usually won't survive if it began *after* the lender made the loan.** If the property was already mortgaged when your lease began, in some states (including California, Georgia, Ohio, Virginia, Washington, and Washington, D.C.) the foreclosure sale will automatically terminate your lease. This means that your lease is over and you'll stay on only if the new owner decides to renew it. In other states (including New York, New Jersey, and Florida), the foreclosing lender may choose whether to terminate your lease or keep it alive. In a nutshell, since the bank was first, your lease does not automatically survive.

EXAMPLES:

Rule 1. Alice rented space for her graphic design firm in an old, estab-lished building downtown. A year after her lease began, the building was sold and Mary, the new owner, took out a mortgage to finance the purchase. Un-fortunately, Mary didn't make her pay-ments, and the bank foreclosed. Will bought the building at the foreclosure sale and became Alice's new landlord. Alice's lease survived the foreclosure sale because it predated Mary's mort-gage.

Rule 2. Brian leased space from Will in the same building. Will wasn't any luckier than Mary—he too was unable to keep up with his mortgage payments. The bank foreclosed, which resulted in the automatic termination of Brian's lease, since Brian's lease began *after* Will's mortgage was made. However, since Alice's lease predated Will's mort-gage, her lease survived the foreclosure, as it had when Mary defaulted.

These legal rules can cause significant problems for both you and the landlord if there is a foreclosure. Section 2 describes how you or the landlord may want to change the lease to get around these rules.

2. Subordination and Nondisturbance

Let's suppose that the landlord would like to take out a loan, secured by the commer-cial property you're renting, after you begin your lease. The bank asks the landlord about any current tenants, and learns that you have a long lease. Per Rule 1, above, the bank understands that if it has to foreclose, the new owner will have to honor your lease.

Now, in order to get its money out after the foreclosure, the bank will want to sell the property for as much as possible. The value of the property will be affected by your worth as a tenant, since you come with the property. When the time comes, is your presence likely to be viewed as an asset, adding value to the property and thus supporting a high price? Or will you be seen as a burden (perhaps you're a lucky tenant with a long lease at below-market rates), thus lowering the potential selling price? If the bank thinks your lease will diminish the value of the building in the eyes of a foreclosure-sale buyer, it may decline to make the loan, and the landlord will come away empty-handed. On the other hand, if the lender thinks you'll prosper and regularly pay rent, your presence won't be an impediment to making the loan.

a. Subordination

Although landlords can't look into the future and predict the value of their property nor how solvent and attractive you'll be when and if there's a foreclosure sale, most landlords feel that it's better to approach a lender with a building in which tenants may be easily evicted if there's a foreclosure. That's why landlords dislike the effect of Rule 1, which will preserve the leases of tenants who predate the loan. Accordingly, many landlords change Rule 1 dramatically, by presenting you with a "subordination" clause, in which you agree that even though you began your lease before the landlord took out the loan, the bank or someone who buys the building at a foreclosure sale *can* evict you. In short, if you go along, a subordination clause will turn Rule 1 on its head and will mean that a sale will extinguish your lease.

b. Nondisturbance

Understandably, you won't be very happy about losing the protection that Rule 1 gives you. The landlord, on the other hand, wants to make sure that it will be easy to use the building as collateral for a loan. Is there a way to accommodate both of you? Yes, there is, by adding a tenant-friendly clause called "Nondisturbance." Here's how it works.

With a nondisturbance clause, you and the landlord agree that, *as long as you continue to pay your rent and abide by the other lease terms,* you'll have the benefit of Rule 1's protection and the subordination clause won't kick in—you can keep your lease, even after a foreclosure sale. However, if you're behind in the rent or otherwise in violation of an important part of the lease, the subordination clause will take over and out you go. In the real world, this type of nondisturbance language in your lease shouldn't prevent the landlord from borrowing money against the building. When you think about it for a moment, you can see why—if you're abiding by the terms of the lease and paid up in rent when the foreclosure happens, you'll be a valuable asset and will support a high asking price. And if you're not following the lease terms (most commonly, not paid up in your rent, although the landlord hasn't evicted you), the landlord can invoke the terms of the subordination clause and get you out. It's fair to all.

EXAMPLES:

Subordination only. Dan was a tenant in Zeke's building. After Dan began his tenancy, Zeke bought a vacation home and secured the loan by putting up his building as collateral. Dan's lease included a subordination clause, in which he agreed that his lease would terminate if any lender foreclosed. When Zeke defaulted on his vacation home loan, the bank foreclosed, terminated Dan's lease, and evicted him. Without the subordination clause, Dan's lease would have survived the sale, since his lease predated the mortgage.

Subordination with nondisturbance. Dan got some expert advice (from Nolo and his lawyer!) before renting again. This time, he insisted that nondisturbance protection accompany the landlord's subordination clause. Once again, the landlord put up the building as collateral, then fell behind on payments, causing

a foreclosure sale. But this time, Dan's lease included a nondisturbance clause, which specified that as long as he was current on the rent and in compliance with other important lease terms, the subordination clause would not kick in. At the time of sale, Dan met these requirements and avoided the consequences of the harsh subordination clause.

3. Attornment Clause

Suppose now that the landlord used the property to secure a loan *before* you began your lease. This situation is quite common —mortgages and loans often last many years, longer than some commercial leases. As you know from Rule 2, if the property is sold at a foreclosure sale, depending on the state in which the building is located, your lease will be automatically wiped out or may be wiped out. (Incidentally, this is one good reason to check out the landlord before you sign the lease.)

Losing your lease could be a genuine disaster for you, especially if you're evicted soon after starting a long-term lease, or if you have gone to considerable expense to build-out your space and establish yourself in the new location. On the other hand, if you happen to be ready to move anyway, or are paying above-market rents, you might be delighted to have your lease canceled. Of course, when you negotiate the lease, you can't know for sure how you'll react.

Landlords and lenders, too, feel equivocal about the effect of Rule 2. If you're paying below-market rents, they will be delighted to be able to get rid of you and put a building on the market that's more attractive to potential buyers, who will hope to fill it with new tenants paying higher, market rents. On the other hand, if you're paying *above-market* rents, losing you will diminish the value of the property; and renting to a new tenant will be time-consuming and expensive. But again, when you negotiate the lease neither the landlord nor the lender can know whether the sudden cancellation of your lease will be a welcome event or not. Is there a way to compromise—to apportion the risk of a rising or falling market equally between you?

For most tenants, it's more important to have the assurance that a buyer who purchases at a foreclosure sale will honor your lease, even though, as explained above, unforeseen circumstances might make the "wipe out" a welcome gift. To protect yourself, you can turn again to the nondisturbance clause, in which the lender promises that as *long as you are not in violation of the lease,* a foreclosure by a preexisting lender will not have the effect of wiping out your lease.

In exchange for getting this assurance, you will often be asked to give up something: the opportunity to skip out happily. Suppose you're not in violation of your lease but you're paying above-market rates —perhaps you'd love to get out of that lease. Too bad—most landlords will insist that you gamble along with them: In exchange for promising to leave you in place (with the nondisturbance clause), they'll expect you to promise to actually stay there even if it's a bad deal for you. In other words, you must give up the windfall that a pure application of Rule 2, plus a falling market, would give you. In legalese, you must promise to "attorn" to the new owner, which simply means that you'll recognize the new owner as your new landlord and won't take advantage of the opportunity to pack up and split.

EXAMPLE:

Nondisturbance. Katie became a tenant in Paul's building, which was mortgaged to the Western Bank. Western foreclosed when Paul fell behind in his payments. Fortunately for Katie, she and her lawyer had successfully negotiated for a nondisturbance clause in the lease, which provided that a foreclosure of a preexisting loan would not terminate Katie's lease as long as she was a tenant in good standing—that is, paid up and not in violation of any important lease clause. Since Katie was in fact a model tenant, her lease survived the foreclosure.

EXAMPLE:

Attornment. Eastern Bank financed Peter's building. Several years later, Peter rented space to Michael. When the lease was negotiated, Peter's building was hot property because it was located in a popular, prosperous area of town. As a result, Michael's rent was high. Unfortunately, zoning decisions and a general business downturn gradually diminished the desirability of renting in Peter's building. And soon thereafter, Peter defaulted on his loan and Eastern foreclosed.

Michael would have loved to get out of his lease, since his rent was higher than the current market rate for Peter's building. He thought he might be able to do so because the loan predated his lease. But then he checked his lease and saw that he had promised to attorn to any new owner who bought at a foreclosure sale. This meant that he had to stay put and recognize the new owner as his landlord.

Sometimes, a landlord's lease doesn't address the foreclosure issue at all, which means that Rules 1 and 2 will apply if there is a foreclosure. But if your landlord is working with an attorney or broker, it's likely that you'll see some variations of these rules that will be to his advantage. The following sections give some tips on how to negotiate in either situation.

4.   When the Landlord's Lease Does Not Include an SNDA Clause

If the lease handed to you by the landlord says nothing about what will happen if there is a foreclosure, both of you will be governed by Rules 1 and 2. Rule 1 protects you, and you'd like it left alone, so there's

no problem there. But Rule 2, which results in the loss of your lease if a preexisting lender forecloses, is harsh and you'd like to insert a lease clause that will change it. You know now what you need: a nondisturbance clause that simply says that *any* buyer at a foreclosure sale must honor your lease.

You're unlikely to get a "pure" nondisturbance promise from most landlords. As explained above, they'll require that you be paidup and in good standing before the bank or new owner will honor the nondisturbance promise. In fact, they will probably tell you that the terms of their loan require them to insert this language—to grant nondisturbance without this proviso will put them in violation of their mortgage or loan. So you ought to be ready to compromise here.

The landlord may go further and demand that you promise to attorn to a new owner. As you now know, this means that you must stay in a lease that otherwise would have been wiped out—you give up your chance to get out happily if the wipeout is actually a welcome event. Again, you may have to make this promise in order to get the important protection of nondisturbance.

There are a few practical issues to keep in mind when you propose a nondisturbance clause.

a.   Finding Out About a Preexisting Loan or Mortgage

There's no simple way to learn if the building in which you're leasing space is subject to a mortgage or deed of trust and, if so, who the lender is. The landlord may not have voluntarily divulged this information, for the self-interested reason that he doesn't want to begin negotiating over a nondisturbance clause. Or, he may not have the latest information on who holds the note, since the bank may have assigned the loan to another lender. Your best bet is to order this information from a local title insurance company. Ask your lawyer for help in doing this.

b. Getting the Promise From the Lender

Since it's the lender who has the right to kick you out if it forecloses on a preexisting loan, it's the lender who must agree not to do so, at the time you negotiate the lease. Make sure that you and your lawyer have proof that the landlord has secured the lender's promise. You'll want to see the nondisturbance agreement signed by the lender (it will be a separate document from your lease). Be forewarned that some lenders may be unwilling to give up their right to kick you out if there's a foreclosure.

5. When the Landlord's Lease Includes an SNDA Clause

Not surprisingly, most landlord-drafted leases include a subordination clause without nondisturbance language. And truly onerous leases include subordination and attornment clauses, giving the landlord the best of both worlds: You lose your lease when a come-lately lender forecloses, *and* you must stay if a preexisting lender forecloses but you'd like to leave because you are paying above-market rents.

If you see a one-sided foreclosure clause like this, it's imperative that you negotiate for nondisturbance, which will give you the protection of Rule 1 (you stay when a preexisting lender forecloses). Be prepared to live with the proviso, "as long as you abide by the terms of the lease." And you may have to live with the attornment clause, too (you promise to stay when a preexisting lender forecloses, even though you'd like to leave).

6. The Ideal Clause

We readily agree that the system of rules and variations described in this section is tricky and hard to keep straight. Lawyer-drafted leases often do a magnificent job of confusing things further. But it doesn't have to be this way. Actually, the nondisturbance promise you want can be worded fairly simply. It need only say: "No default of the Landlord under a mortgage or deed of trust to which this lease is subordinate will affect Tenant's quiet enjoyment of the premises, so long as Tenant performs all of its obligations as stated in this lease."

If the landlord asks you to agree to an attornment clause, it too can be stated clearly and succinctly: "In the event of a foreclosure sale, Tenant will attorn to the purchaser, transferor, or lessor and recognize that party as Landlord under this lease."

B. Estoppel Certificates

You may see a clause in the landlord's lease entitled "Estoppel Letters" or "Estoppel Certificates." You could read the clause over and over without having a clue as to what it's all about. And, depending on what happens during your lease, you might never encounter this clause. In practice, it usually comes up only if your landlord sells or intends to refinance the building.

Suppose your landlord wants to sell the property. A buyer will get the building along with its tenants and their leases. The buyer will want an assurance that the tenants are living up to the terms of their leases and are not owed any money from the landlord (such as a tenant improvement allowance, explained in Chapter 11, which a new owner would be obligated to pay). Or, suppose the landlord needs a loan. A lender will be more inclined to make the loan if it knows that the rent money (which the landlord will use to repay the loan) isn't subject to any set-offs (set-offs are explained in Chapter 16, Section C). Of course, a buyer or lender can get answers to these questions by looking at the lease and talking to the

landlord. But careful buyers and lenders will double check with you, the tenant, to make sure that you are following the lease and that you are not seriously wandering from its terms and conditions.

To assure themselves that all is well with the lease and the tenants, nervous buyers and lenders will ask the landlord for an "estoppel letter" or "estoppel certificate" from each tenant. The letter is simply a statement signed by you certifying that you and the landlord are following the lease and are current with your financial obligations, as far as you know.

Tenants sometimes need an estoppel letter, too. If you want to sell your business, take out a loan, merge, sublease, or assign, you too will need proof that you have a good leasing situation, without hidden or incipient problems. For instance, your lender will want to know that the building is in fact insured and maintained (which your landlord may have promised to do in your lease), since that will help guarantee that you, the borrower, will be able to continue to operate profitably (and repay the loan).

1. How Estoppel Letters Work

Normally, whoever needs an estoppel letter will write it and ask the other to sign it.

Most lease clauses give you a short amount of time, typically five to ten days, to sign and return an estoppel letter. If your landlord's lease clause is particularly aggressive, it may specify that if you fail to sign and return the letter on time, the landlord may sign it for you. Whoever has requested the letter will use it to reassure any intended lender, buyer, or partner that neither party to the lease is in serious default.

2. Accuracy Is Important

If you receive an estoppel letter prepared by the landlord, be sure to read it carefully and compare it with the terms of your lease. It shouldn't vary. For example, the landlord may write an estoppel letter stating that you have no renewal right when you do indeed have one in your lease. Obviously, the landlord was devious or careless in preparing the letter. To avoid future problems, fix the letter to reflect the true state of affairs before you sign it. Similarly, if you're entitled to a set-off because you paid the bill for the quarterly window-washing service that the landlord was supposed to cover, don't sign a statement that "tenant is currently entitled to no set-offs." (Rent set-offs are explained in Chapter 16, Section C.)

The consequences of signing an estoppel that you know is inaccurate could be significant. You certainly don't want to get yourself involved in a fight between your landlord and a lender or buyer over what's going on at the property. More importantly,

your own rights under the lease could be compromised if you sign a letter that diminishes them. For example, suppose you have an option to renew for two successive three-year terms. (Renewal options are explained in Chapter 14, Section B.) If you sign an estoppel letter that simply states that you have an option to renew and doesn't mention the number of terms, you might lose the benefit of the second renewal chance. An arbitrator or judge might rule that the estoppel letter was a legal amendment of the lease—removing the second option period from the option clause.

If you receive an estoppel letter that's clearly (or potentially) inaccurate, bring the matter to your landlord's attention. If you don't know whether an assertion is true, tell the landlord that you don't have the information necessary to sign off on that part. Conversely, never intentionally scuttle the landlord's deal by refusing to sign a correct estoppel. You might end up being sued for interfering with the landlord's business opportunities.

3. Negotiating an Estoppel Letter

There's nothing wrong with a clause requiring you to provide an estoppel letter. In fact, since you'd rather deal with a financially healthy landlord than one strapped for cash or unable to expand, you have every interest in helping the landlord obtain a needed loan or conduct an advantageous business move. As you read over the landlord's estoppel letter clause, keep the following points in mind.

a. Make It Mutual

To be fair, the landlord should agree to furnish an estoppel letter for you, upon request. If the landlord refuses to agree to a two-way clause, understand that your ability to easily get a loan, merge, or sell your business may be impaired.

b. Check the Consequences

The estoppel letter clause probably specifies what will happen to you if you refuse or fail to sign a letter prepared by the landlord. The landlord's right to sign the letter on your behalf, if he's given himself that right in the lease, won't necessarily be the end of the matter.

Oddly, some clauses state that if you refuse to sign an estoppel, you will be in default under the lease, which would give the landlord the right to terminate the lease. This consequence is odd because, of all the things the landlord wants to avoid when wooing a prospective lender or buyer, a lease default by an existing tenant is at the top of the list. The point of asking you to sign an estoppel letter is precisely to reassure the lender or buyer that you're *not* in default!

It makes sense for both of you to craft a more rational consequence. First, make sure that your good-faith refusal to sign an inaccurate estoppel won't trigger any negative consequences. Second, suggest that the proper response should be money damages, which will allow the landlord to continue to pursue the deal, albeit without the certificate. If you have negotiated for the right to demand an estoppel letter from the landlord, this consequence makes sense for the landlord, too.

C. The Condemnation Clause

Condemnation is the process by which a government authority takes over the ownership of private land (the government is exercising its power of "eminent domain"). Federal, state, or local government will swoop in when they need a particular piece of land for an important task or project—such as building a new freeway, razing a block of blighted buildings, or cutting into private property in order to widen a street. The government can decide to take all or part of an owner's land. Usually, there's very little that landowners can do about a government condemnation decision.

1. What Happens to the Lease?

If the government has taken the entire property or all of the space that you have rented, your lease and obligation to pay the rent terminate. Partial takings, however, are a different story. Unless you and the landlord have provided otherwise in your lease, in most states a partial taking (of your space or of other parts of the property that you use, such as common areas and parking areas) will *not* automatically terminate the lease. As a consequence, you might end up with rent obligations but no way to feasibly run your business. For example, if you can't get deliveries to your business because the parking lot and loading dock have been condemned, your ability to continue will be seriously jeopardized. To avoid this unpleasant state of affairs, you can attempt to negotiate a condemnation clause that will give you a way around the consequences of partial but devastating condemnations.

Consider the likelihood of a government taking before spending too much time and energy negotiating this clause. If you're renting in a new building in an up-and-coming area of town, the chances of a government takeover are slight. On the other hand, cheap space in an iffy location or near a redevelopment project whose boundaries may swell should give you pause. It's most important to know the risks by thoroughly investigating the property before choosing it, as we advise in Chapter 3, Section B.

2. Compensating the Landlord and Tenant

Before you can make sense of how to negotiate a practical condemnation clause, you need to understand how the government compensates you and the landlord.

When the government takes private land for public use, either wholly or partially, the government pays the owner the fair market value of the land that the owner has lost. This figure will include the value to the landlord of having you as a tenant—in other words, it will take into account your rent payments and the improvements you've made to the property. For example, if a wing of the landlord's building is condemned in order to make room for a municipal parking structure next door, the condemning authority will pay for the value of the land and the building, plus the rental income that the landlord can no longer collect from that space.

Tenants who lose their leases as a result of a total condemnation may also have a claim on the condemning agency. If you have a great lease and are paying below-market rent, your claim will be the difference between the present value of the space you're leasing minus the actual cost of your lease. For instance, if you're seven years into a ten-year lease and have watched rents in and around the building go sky-high as the neighborhood becomes gentrified, you have a very valuable lease. If the building is taken, your claim would be the fair market value of renting that space today minus the rent you actually pay.

Unfortunately, in some situations the condemning agency will not compensate the tenant directly for its loss. The government will instead make one compensation payment to the owner, and it's up to the landlord and tenant to apportion the award as they see fit. It's impossible for you to know in advance whether you'll be able to deal directly with the government agency or will have to argue about your share with the landlord. For this reason alone, it's very important to have a sharing system in place in the lease, as explained below.

⚠️ **Your casualty insurance won't cover the loss that results from a condemnation.** Landlords and tenants often think that their insurance will compensate them, since the result of a condemnation—loss of use of the property—seems very similar to what happens following accidental damage. Casualty coverage specifically excludes condemnation.

3. Negotiating a Fair Condemnation Clause

You may decide that it's a good idea to spend some attention and bargaining chips on the condemnation clause. For example, if the city has been eyeing your neighborhood for a new civic center or the state has plans to construct a new interstate in your vicinity, condemnation may become a reality during your tenancy. There are three main issues to consider when negotiating the condemnation clause:

- **Rent.** If there's a partial condemnation that affects your operations but leaves you with usable space, will you be required to continue to pay full rent? As noted above, in most states you'll

be required to continue to pay full rent unless you and the landlord decide otherwise in your lease.

- **Termination rights.** Do you want the ability to terminate the lease if you decide that the partial taking has seriously affected your ability to do business?
- **Use of the condemnation award.** How, if at all, will you and the landlord share the award if the condemning agency makes only one award? Should the landlord agree to use it to remedy, as much as possible, the property or services that were lost as a result of the taking?

The sections below give you some tips on how to approach these issues.

a. Reducing the Rent

A partial condemnation of your landlord's building may have a big effect on your business. If your own space is curtailed, your ability to function at your expected levels will be impaired; and if common areas are lost, the convenience and attractiveness of the rental will diminish. Either way, less of a rental ought to mean less rent.

Your condemnation clause can provide that your rent will be reduced (lawyers say "abated") according to a formula. Be wary of agreeing to a method that calculates the abatement in proportion to the number of square feet that have been taken, from either the common areas or from your rented space. The problem with this approach is that it fails to consider the impact of the taking—it's concerned only with the size of the reduction. This system can be unfair to both you and the landlord:

- If the amount of lost space is small but the loss is critical, your rent reduction won't fairly reflect the true loss to you. For example, the loading dock may be small in area but essential to your deliveries. If the rent reduction is proportionate to the area that's taken, it won't begin to compensate you for the loss.

- If the taking is large but it's relatively unimportant space, the rent reduction will be too high. For instance, if the city takes a large part of the lawn in front of the building, the value of your lease and your ability to run your business won't be greatly diminished. But if the rent is reduced according to the size of the taking, your landlord will end up with an unfairly reduced rent.

As you can see, reducing the rent according to the size of the condemned space is potentially unfair to both landlord and tenant. Once you point this out to your landlord, it shouldn't be too hard to get everyone to consider a more realistic method. Here it is: Suggest that the rent reduction be commensurate with the reduced usefulness and value of the remaining premises. In short, you and the landlord can agree that the effect of the government taking, not simply its size, will determine the extent of the rent reduction.

Admittedly, it might be difficult to apply these measuring sticks when the time comes. What feels essential to you—the loss of your view, for instance—may seem piddling to your landlord. If the two of you can't agree, you can always refer to your dispute resolution clause.

b. Terminating the Lease

If a partial condemnation has a significant impact on your business, you may be unsatisfied with a rent reduction. You'll want to be able to choose whether to terminate your lease or continue on. For example, if the city takes the parking lot, you may want to terminate if you think that without parking, your business will suffer irreparably.

Most landlords will not readily give you this choice, because if they lose you, they'll have to start over with another tenant, and incur new leasing costs such as tenant improvements. On the other hand, you won't lightly leave a prosperous location and a good customer base.

A fair compromise would give you the termination right only if your ability to continue in this location has been substantially or materially impaired. Again, the precise meaning of these standards will have to be hammered out when and if the situation arises. As always, refer any unresolved disagreements to your ADR (alternative dispute resolution) clause. An experienced mediator or arbitrator should be able to cut through the arguments and make an impartial decision as to the real effect of the condemnation.

c. Allocating the Award

Depending on the practice of the condemning agency, the landlord alone or each of you can put in a claim for compensation.

If there is only one award, you can be sure that the landlord will ask for the value of the land and building, plus the rents that will be lost. Your landlord will ask for the present market-rate rental value of the property—but suppose you're paying below-market rent? Unless the landlord gives you the difference, known as the "bonus value" of your lease, the landlord will make money on the condemnation. You, meanwhile, will have to go out and rent a comparable space, which will be more expensive than your current rent because you'll have lost the benefit of your below-market deal.

> **EXAMPLE:** Quickie Printers signed a ten-year lease in a building that was on the edge of a redevelopment area. By the fifth year, the area had improved and rents were up. Quickie was paying $2,000 a month for space that would rent on the open market for $3,000.
>
> Unfortunately, the city decided to build a ballpark in the neighborhood and they condemned Quickie's building. The landlord received a sizable compensation.

Quickie's lease specified that the bonus value of their lease would belong to them in the event of a condemnation. This meant that Quickie was entitled to receive from the landlord $1,000 times the number of months remaining on the lease.

You may be able to deal directly with the condemning agency. If so, you'll be asking the agency for the bonus value of your lease. But if there is only one award, it's important to make sure that the lease requires the landlord to give you the bonus value.

d. Using the Award

Sometimes, the consequences of a partial taking can be remedied by some creative thinking, building, or redesigning. For example, if the city takes the building's parking lot, it might be possible to rent parking space in a nearby facility. Or, if an entryway is blocked or removed, perhaps the landlord could create another one that's equally convenient.

Your landlord, however, will be under no obligation to use the compensation award in these ways unless your lease requires it. The landlord can simply pocket the money (and hopefully reduce your rent) and leave you to live out your tenancy with diminished facilities. If it's important to you that the landlord be obliged to try to return the building to the status quo with hammer and saw, you'll need to bargain for a compensation clause that requires the owner to use "best efforts" to restore the remaining portion of the building to its condition or level before the condemnation. Keep in mind that if the restoration is less than thorough, you'll be entitled to pay less rent.

> **EXAMPLE:** Wanda rented retail space in a small strip mall. The city condemned about half the parking lot as part of their street-widening project. Wanda was concerned that, without ample parking, customers would not patronize her store as often.
>
> Fortunately, her lease required the landlord to attempt to restore the property if part of it were taken in a condemnation. Wanda noticed that the mall next door had several vacancies and a large parking lot. She pointed out to the landlord that his obligation to restore meant that he had to try renting additional parking space. He negotiated with the neighboring owner and rented space to compensate his tenants for their loss. Wanda obtained a rent reduction based on the inconvenience of making her customers use the neighboring lot, but it was not as high as it would have been if the landlord had not been able to secure replacement parking.

⚠️ **Watch out for the demands of the landlord's lender.** If your landlord's building secures a loan, the loan contract with the lender may allow the lender to grab the compensation awards to pay down the loan

before the landlord (or you) can use them. Landlords who have loan contracts with provisions like this won't be able to negotiate a contrary understanding with you. In short, you'll get whatever is left over after the loan principal is paid off with the money from the condemnation award.

D. Surrender Clause

Towards the end of the lease, you will often see a clause entitled "Yield Up," "Surrender," or "Condition Upon Vacating." This clause clarifies what you must do to your rented space when you move out—in particular, what you must take with you and leave behind, and how clean it must be in order for you to receive your security deposit back.

1. No Surrender Clause?

Not all leases include a surrender clause. If your landlord's lease doesn't have one, you and the landlord will be bound by the following commonly accepted legal rules.

You must return the property in the same shape as it was when you moved in, minus normal wear and tear. There are no hard and fast guidelines that will help you differentiate normal use from unreasonable use. But at least you'll know that the condition of the property will be judged in the context of the type of business you ran. For example, a retail space with lots of public traffic will deteriorate quicker than a quiet accountant's office. At the end of the term, the retail space may appear more bedraggled than the accountants' suite, but since that's to be expected, the comparison should not result in charging the retail tenant with damaging the premises.

Still, landlords and tenants often argue long and hard over "normal" wear and tear. It's one good reason why thoughtful landlords attempt to clarify their expectations in a surrender clause, as explained below.

If you use your space in ways that the landlord couldn't anticipate when you negotiated the lease, you might have to pay for the added wear and tear. During negotiations, the landlord made concessions and demands based on the type of business you said you'd run. For example, knowing that you intended to use the property as a boutique dress shop, the landlord set his security deposit accordingly. Now, if you decide to run a ceramics studio instead (and assuming you have no use restrictions, as explained in Chapter 7, Section D), chances are that even a well-run operation will result in more wear and tear than you'd see in a shop. Especially if the landlord didn't know about your changed activities, you can expect to pay for the wear and tear that's above what would have resulted from the original, intended use.

You aren't responsible for repairing damage that you didn't cause, unless you've clearly agreed otherwise. For example, damage from a fire that's spread from next door is the landlord's problem. Most of the time, if you

and the landlord have carefully thought about your insurance needs, the damage will be covered anyway.

Unless you and the landlord have agreed otherwise, you don't have to remove or undo improvements that you made with the landlord's consent. As explained in Chapter 11, improvements are changes to the property that you and the landlord intend to remain. If the lease says nothing about what happens when you leave, you can't remove your improvements and the landlord cannot demand that you remove them.

You must remove trade fixtures unless the landlord allows you to leave them in place. As explained in Chapter 11, trade fixtures are equipment that you use in your business and that you intend to keep when you leave. Unless you and the landlord agree otherwise, you must remove trade fixtures when you leave, returning the property to its condition before you installed them.

2. Negotiating a Fair Surrender Clause

Landlords and tenants are free to write their own rules concerning how the rented space must look at the end of the lease term. Most landlords with experience have learned the hard way that it's frustrating, at best, to rely solely on the default rules explained above in Section 1. There's almost always an argument over the meaning of "normal wear and tear."

Many leases require you to return the premises "broom clean." If the landlord goes into detail beyond that, you'll know what's expected (and you can negotiate the point if you wish). But often the lease does not explain the phrase, which makes it little better than "normal wear and tear." We suggest that you ask for some particulars now. That way, when you move out it's less likely that you'll have an argument over whether your cleaning efforts were sufficient.

It's also common to see clauses requiring you to return the premises "in the same condition in which the tenant received it, wear and tear excepted." While this clause does account for wear and tear, it does not account for changes that may have occurred during the lease or, more importantly, for changes in how businesses operate. For example, if you moved into a new building, your space might have been a mere shell—something that will be very difficult to return to. And suppose your office business, like many these days, has dispensed with secretaries. The secretarial areas that you converted into office space when you moved in will be expensive to reestablish when you move out. In sum, you don't want to be required to return the space to a shell, if that's how it looked when you moved in ten years ago; nor does it make sense to return space to an outmoded design.

Videotape the condition of the premises when you move in. Datestamp the tape and, for extra protection, ask a contractor or other neutral but experienced observer to document the appearance of the space and any equipment that comes with it. That way, if there are problems with the space at the outset, the landlord can't easily lay them at your feet when you move out.

During your negotiations, keep in mind that if the space is usable by a wide variety of tenants and likely to be torn apart by the next tenant during improvements, it makes little sense for you to spend time and money shining it up when you leave. On the other hand, if the space is uniquely suited—for instance, a gymnasium that's used by a succession of fitness centers —the landlord has a bigger interest in having you turn it over in a spiffy, attractive condition.

Negotiate for a period of time to move out and clean after the term ends. You won't want to pay rent during the days you move out and clean.

E. The "Entire Agreement" Clause

Neither you nor your landlord want the other to claim that there are more agreements about your rental, either written or oral, besides those recited in or attached to the lease. If either could claim that leasing details were also covered elsewhere, your lease would be much less useful, to say the least.

To make sure that you both understand that the lease is the final and complete word on the whole affair, most landlords will include a clause that simply says so. The lawyers' quaint way of referring to this clause is to call it the "four corners" clause (reflecting the idea that every aspect of the leasing deal is contained within the pages' four corners). There's no reason to suggest any variations on this clause. But be sure that if there are important papers or agreements—a floor plan that accurately describes your rented space, for example—you have attached them to the lease as attachments. And if you later want to amend the lease by changing it or adding clauses, there's nothing to stop you from negotiating the new understandings and adding them to your lease. The way to add pages to a lease is explained in Chapter 6, Section D.

F. The "Severability" or "Survival" Clause

Occasionally, landlords and tenants end up with lease clauses that a judge will not enforce. For example, a use clause that required you to operate your business in violation of fair housing or employment laws would not be upheld. And although it happens rarely, a judge might refuse to enforce a clause if its application would result in extreme unfairness to one of you.

Knowing that this possibility exists, careful landlords and tenants take the precaution of providing that the rest of the lease will survive. This prevents the entire relationship from being derailed over one bad or unjust clause. Again, you have nothing to fear from this clause and no need to argue over it.

EXAMPLE: Paul inherited an office building from his father. For his first leasing deal, he did not use a broker or a lawyer when leasing an office suite to Janice. One clause in the lease provided for liquidated damages in the amount of $2,000 in the event that Janice did not pay her share of the CAM charges.

When Janice refused to pay her share of CAM charges one month (she disputed Paul's allocation of costs), Paul demanded $2,000, which Janice refused to pay on the grounds that it was designed as a penalty and bore no reasonable relation to the amount of money Paul would in fact lose. Paul sued her but lost. The judge ruled that the clause was an unenforceable penalty. But the rest of the lease remained in force since the lease had a severability clause. Paul and Janice resolved their dispute over the CAM charges by referring the matter to a mediator.

G. Lease Guarantors

The reputation of your business and the size of your security deposit may not be enough to assure the landlord that your business will bring in enough money to pay the rent or meet other financial obligations. Even a pledge of your personal assets, which the landlord may require if your business is a corporation or limited liability company, may not provide enough assurance.

A nervous landlord may ask you to provide an outside guarantor—a person or a business who will make good on your lease obligations if you fail to do so. There are two basic ways to give the guarantee: in the lease itself or in a separate agreement that's attached to your lease. If your landlord requires a guarantee, you'll need to understand what it means and how it affects the lease negotiations as a whole.

1. What Is Being Guaranteed?

Your landlord may propose a broad guarantee clause, requiring the guarantor to stand behind every financial obligation under the lease, or a narrower clause, calling for rent guarantees only.

a. Broad Guarantees

A guarantee clause that's wide open, requiring you to furnish a guarantor who will make good on every financial covenant and obligation of the lease, has the potential of making your guarantor responsible for anything that you're obligated to pay for but don't. For example, if your lease requires you to pay for landscaping services but you fail to do so, the landlord can look to the guarantor to fulfill that task. Having a deeply obligated guarantor is like having a silent business partner who does nothing but pay bills when needed. It's hard to find someone who will agree to that wide-open role.

b. Narrow Financial Guarantees

The guarantee clause is more commonly limited to rent matters only, making the guarantor liable for rent, maintenance and CAM expenses, and anything else the landlord has designated as additional rent, such as insurance costs.

2. Who Is the Guarantor?

If your lease includes a guarantee clause, you'll need to supply a guarantor who meets the landlord's approval. Since the guarantor is there to provide needed funds if necessary, your landlord will be primarily interested in that person's financial resources and stability. Sometimes, landlords agree to accept more than one guarantor, as long as the sum of their resources adds up to the requisite level.

⚠ Guarantors usually are jointly and severally liable. This bit of legalese boils down to something rather simple. If you have more than one guarantor—your wife's parents, say, or the three partners in your best friend's business firm—any one of them can be called upon to satisfy the entire debt. For example, if only one of the three partners has any cash, the landlord can demand payment from that partner alone. That partner may be able to sue the other two for reimbursement for their share, but that battle is among the partners and doesn't involve the landlord.

3. Negotiating the Guarantee Clause

As you evaluate the landlord's guarantee clause, remember that you'll have to come up with someone who meets the landlord's requirements. You'll have an easier time finding a willing candidate if you can bargain for some or all of the following points.

- **A rent guarantor only.** In theory, a guarantor who can be called upon to cover all financial obligations would be tapped more frequently than one who stands behind only the rent. It will be much easier to find someone who promises to back you up with respect to the rent only.

- **Priority, notice, and cure.** Some lease guarantees allow the landlord to demand that the guarantor pay a bill before the landlord has even asked you for payment. A potential guarantor may balk at signing on to such a guarantee—and you might not find anyone willing to do so. So bargain for an understanding that, before turning to the guarantor, the landlord will give you written notice of your delinquency. And you'll want a period of time to comply, or cure, before the landlord brings the guarantor into the picture.

- **Surviving your departure.** The landlord may want to keep your guarantor on the hook after you've assigned the lease, reorganized your business, or even after you've gone bankrupt. If any of these things happen to you, your guarantor will be in the position of guaranteeing a totally new tenant, undoubtedly a stranger. Many potential guarantors won't be willing to take this risk.

H. Signatures

At the end of the landlord's lease, there will be a place for you and the landlord to sign the document. Be sure that the person who signs on behalf of the landlord is either the owner or someone authorized to sign on the owner's behalf. If you're not sure whether the person has the power to sign, you can ask to see documentary proof, such as a corporate resolution or a power of attorney.

If you've agreed to personally guarantee a lease you've signed on behalf of your corporation or LLC, you'll have to sign twice—first as a corporate officer or LLC member, and then as an individual guarantor. If your landlord has required that someone else also guarantee the lease, that person must also sign. ■

Index

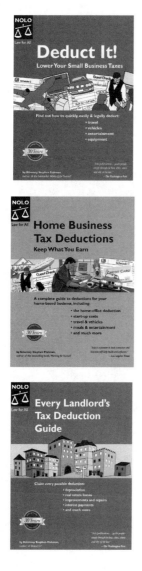

Remember:

Little publishers have big ears.
We really listen to you.

Take 2 Minutes & Give Us Your 2 cents

Your comments make a big difference in the development and revision of Nolo books and software. Please take a few minutes and register your Nolo product—and your comments—with us. Not only will your input make a difference, you'll receive special offers available only to registered owners of Nolo products on our newest books and software. Register now by:

PHONE	**FAX**	**EMAIL**	or **MAIL** us
1-800-728-3555	1-800-645-0895	cs@nolo.com	this registration card

fold here

Registration Card

NAME _____ DATE _____

ADDRESS _____

_____

CITY _____ STATE _____ ZIP _____

PHONE _____ EMAIL _____

WHERE DID YOU HEAR ABOUT THIS PRODUCT? _____

WHERE DID YOU PURCHASE THIS PRODUCT? _____

DID YOU CONSULT A LAWYER? (PLEASE CIRCLE ONE)   YES   NO   NOT APPLICABLE

DID YOU FIND THIS BOOK HELPFUL?   (VERY)   5   4   3   2   1   (NOT AT ALL)

COMMENTS _____

_____

_____

WAS IT EASY TO USE?   (VERY EASY)   5   4   3   2   1   (VERY DIFFICULT)

LESP 2.0

fold here

- -

Place
stamp here

Nolo
950 Parker Street
Berkeley, CA 94710-9867

Attn: LESP 2.0